Accl

The Enemy Within:
Separation Theory and Voice Therapy

Bob Firestone's life and work is a time-honored treasure of humanistic theory, practice, and application. This recent volume--The Enemy Within--is the culmination of a lifetime of insight into the human heart beginning with children's relationships to parents and by implication the wondrous yet trepidating existence around them. Combining both extensive data from his own practice, as well as experience at the forefront of the intentional community movement, Firestone has produced a milestone of incisive, illuminating and practical guidance to the core of therapeutic healing--as well as cultural healing in my view. I found the book to be an invaluable distillation of the best thinking in our field.

> Kirk Schneider, Ph.D., Author of *The Spirituality of Awe: Challenges to the Robotic Revolution, The Polarized Mind*, and *Existential-Humanistic Therapy*

A commanding articulation of Separation Theory and Voice Therapy in the service of fostering "life-affirming death awareness" by one of the most influential theorists and clinicians of our times. An inspired and essential resource for researchers, mental health practitioners, and anyone interested in better understanding themselves and the world around them.

> Sheldon Solomon, PhD Professor of Psychology at Skidmore College
> Co-author of: *In the Wake of 9/11: The Psychology of Terror* and
> *The Worm at the Core: On the Role of Death in Life*

I have followed Dr. Firestone's work for many years as he has developed important theoretical frameworks for understanding the human personality, interactions, and pathologies. In addition he and his colleagues have provided practical approaches for dynamic therapeutic interventions. This latest book presents a compendium of that work, bringing together the origins, formulations, and current conceptualizations. Rich with examples, the work highlights his crucial concepts of the 'inner voice' and 'fantasy bond,' which have enlightened our understanding of dynamic processes of human development, with new implications for understanding current socio-political issues. This volume should be on every therapist's book shelf.

> Donald K. Freedheim, PhD Professor Emeritus of Psychology
> Case Western Reserve University, Editor, History of Psychotherapy

A wonderful book that provides a deep understanding of Firestones life work. It provides fresh insights into the critical inner voice and the fantasy bond. Filled with case examples it illuminates the role of the voice and fantasy bond in such powerful issues as violence and suicide: A must read for clinicians and students who want to learn how to work in depth with the self destructive voice and the fantasy bond.

> Leslie S. Greenberg, PhD Distinguished Research Professor
> Dept. of Psychology, York University

Thank you Robert Firestone for this comprehensive, practical and precious work identifying The Enemy Within and providing clear strategies for addressing resistance in psychotherapy, but more important, our own resistance to a better life. You are an inspiration in your work and your hope for the future.

Pat Love, Ed.D Distinguished professor,
author of *Hot Monogamy*, *The Truth About Love*
and *How to Improve Your Marriage Without Talking About It*

Once again demonstrating the wisdom of integrating psychoanalytic and existential themes, Firestone brings to bear his long and deep experience in understanding and healing the human condition. He introduces important concepts that constitute a kind of psychological matter and anti-matter to unlock some crucial challenges we must face as individual people and as a collective humanity.

James Garbarino, PhD, Maude C. Clarke Chair in Humanistic Psychology
at Loyola University Chicago, Author of *The Lost Boys and Listening to Killers*

Within the pages of this one volume, *The Enemy Within*, Robert Firestone provides the reader with 60 years' worth of clinical wisdom and creative theoretical innovation. Looking back at his life's work and how it developed, he also takes his theoretical body of work further by again formulating, in lucid and compelling prose, his understanding of the human condition. The key theme is this: Faced with the inevitable knowledge of death, we humans can either open up to life or pull away from it in ways destructive of ourselves and others – a message at once timely and timeless."

Tor Wennerberg
Organizational psychologist and author
Stockholm, Sweden

In this book, *The Enemy Within*, Dr. Robert Firestone shares the wisdom he has accumulated from a lifetime of self- reflection and study, alone and in the company of others. His development of Separation Theory to explain often paradoxical self-defeating human behavior and Voice Therapy to ameliorate this behavior make unique contributions to the psychotherapy literature. Both the theory and method of treatment are applicable to many clinical and life issues, as Dr. Firestone illustrates throughout. This book expands the reader's thinking on a variety of individual, family, cultural and societal issues and is absolutely clear in its intention to support mental health and human development. Bravo!

Christine A. Courtois, PhD, ABPP, Licensed Psychologist,
Independent Practice, Washington, DC (now retired)
Consultant/Trainer, Trauma Psychology and Trauma Treatment
Co-Author, *Treating Complex Trauma: A Sequenced, Relationship-based Approach* (with
Julian Ford) Author, *Healing the Incest Wound: Adult Survivors in Therapy*

The Enemy Within

Separation Theory and Voice Therapy

Robert W. Firestone

ZEIG, TUCKER & THEISEN

Phoenix, Arizona

COVER IMAGE:

'Curiosity' by Robert W. Firestone © 2017 Robert W. Firestone

Published by

ZEIG, TUCKER & THEISEN, INC.

2632 East Thomas Rd., Suite 201
Phoenix, AZ 85016

Manufactured in the United States of America

DEDICATION

I am especially appreciative to all of the people in the "friendship circle" for their overall contribution to my work and, more personally, for encouraging me to become an author in the first place. I want to thank them for their honesty and courage in openly sharing their most personal thoughts, feelings and experiences, their insights and their wisdom.

CONTENTS

TABLE OF FIGURES

FOREWORD

"The path is not the path; we create the path by walking."

~ Antonio Machado

When Woody Allen did stand-up comedy, he told a joke about being in the Deep South of the United States. He was invited to a costume party and he put on a white sheet. Outside was a car with three men wearing white sheets. Because he thought they were going to the party, he accepted their invitation. Eventually, at a conclave in the countryside, he was discovered. They pulled the sheet off and put a rope around his neck. His life passes before his eyes: He's back in his childhood in Kansas; swimmin' at the swimmin' hole; he's going down to the general store to buy some gingham for Emmy Lou; and he's "fryin' up a mess o' catfish." Suddenly, he realizes he is about to die and the wrong life is passing before his eyes.

Our fantasies dictate our direction more than we realize. So, how do we clear our vision and intelligently plan a meaningful life path? Most of us desire a purpose-filled, passionate existence. We want to set our sails to the wind and enjoy the adventure. But there can be a compulsion to tilt the rudder into stormy waters. Why do we do this? Is masochism part of our nature? Is the brain hardwired to seek maladaptive states? Do psychological defenses irrevocably blind us? Are there submerged resistances to happiness? Do self-destructive undercurrents determine our destiny?

Fortunately, we have a skipper who can help us chart a better course. Robert Firestone has created in this book a lodestar. *It is also* a *magnum opus* that advances Firestone's explorations into the depths of the human psyche. In it, he advances the theory and practice of Voice Therapy so that therapists can better understand how to help clients reclaim autonomy and find focal points that stimulate into play more adaptive living. We learn about Separation Theory, a de novo amalgamation of existential thought and depth psychology. There is a Fantasy Bond that inadvertently takes the wind out of our sails. When we disavow our anxiety about relationships, love, and death, we lose our compass heading. These processes create stormy "voices" in our minds that send us adrift.

The comic, W.C. Fields, was once on a stage set drinking whiskey and reading the Bible. An inveterate alcoholic, his drinking was well understood, but studying the Bible was not. A stagehand confronted him about his reason for doing this. Fields' reply was "Just looking for loopholes."

But, there are no loopholes in this book. We are trapped on a planet traversing space at incredible speeds, but the reality of momentum escapes us. Our planet faces certain death—as do we. We are challenged to examine our existential situation and meet it with honesty. But, we can only individuate when we throw off the veil of denial. Firestone does not allow a shroud to blind us. He wisely and humanely shows us how we can differentiate ourselves from the imprints of the past.

Considered a giant in the field who has spawned many intellectual heirs, Robert Firestone has had a long and distinguished 60-year career as a therapist. He is a prolific writer and contributor to psychological theory. His devotion to researching, writing, and documenting his psychological ideas has resulted in the publication of 15 books, 26 journal articles and invited chapters, and dozens of documentary films. Firestone is also a visual artist and an avid sailor.

I am honored to write this Foreword, and equally honored to be the publisher of this book. But more importantly, I am delighted to learn from Robert Firestone. He provides missing puzzle pieces in my theoretical thinking, and he offers perspectives on practice that prompt me to be a better clinician.

So, hold onto your sailing caps. You are about to embark on a journey that illuminates aspects of the human spirit that have not been previously examined. You will not only learn how to help others. you will learn how to think theoretically and use theory to advance practice. Moreover, you will better understand yourself, and in doing so you will be better equipped to help others live with integrity, purpose, and passion. As you navigate the following pages, you will chart a course for a more differentiated journey—a more fully liberated life.

Jeffrey K. Zeig, Ph.D.

PREFACE

The Enemy Within elucidates a person's basic struggle to maintain his/her true nature or self against destructive environmental influences, both interpersonal and existential. The tragedy is that negative attitudes from parents and other potential sources of stress tend to be incorporated into the self, forming an alien point of view that not only opposes one's best interests but actively attacks the self. Separation Theory offers an in-depth understanding of the essential split within the personality between the self and the anti-self and its ongoing effect on the life of the individual.

The self system is made up of one's biological temperament, genetic predisposition, synchronistic identification with parents' affirmative qualities, and the ongoing effects of experience and education. In addition, it represents a person's wants, desires and goals in life and his/her individual manner of seeking fulfillment.

The anti-self system is composed of an aggregate of internalized destructive thoughts, attitudes and feelings directed toward the self. When the children are confronted with hurtful experiences in the family, they tend to absolve their parents or other family members from blame and take on attitudes that they themselves are bad, unlovable, or a burden. Gradually, personal trauma and separation anxiety combine to turn children against themselves. The anti-self can be characterized as the "enemy within."

Faced with the primal pain of childhood, individuals have a need to defend themselves. The fantasy bond or primary defense is an illusion of fusion with the parent or caretaker that serves to compensate for rejection, neglect and other abuses experienced during one's developmental years. Later, it acts to partially alleviate death anxiety. While offering some relief from these primal states, the imaginary bond with the mother and/or father is problematic and tends to interfere with optimal functioning. Depending heavily on fantasy and illusion distorts the child's self-image and his/her ability to relate effectively.

In addition to providing a basic understanding of neuroses and self-destructive tendencies, Separation Theory offers a methodology, Voice Therapy, to cope with underlying negative thought processes. In challenging alien and dysfunctional psychological defenses, it supports the client's ability to differentiate and individuate. In summary, this book is a compendium of my life's work as a psychotherapist, theorist and author in the field of psychology. It is essentially a compilation of more than fourteen published books, countless articles in professional journals and a large number of educational videos.

In considering this project, I began to wonder where all of this began, what the roots of my efforts were. I realized that the serious course of my intellectual life started in my teens with the preliminary philosophy that I developed at the time. Early on, I was concerned with people's lack of humanity, their cruelty to themselves and others, their prejudice, tyranny and violence. Many people fleeing from the Holocaust and actual victims of its horrors visited my family as they migrated to the United States. Perhaps this was one of the influences that left me questioning the state of the world and motivated me to search for answers.

I wanted to understand myself and human suffering in general and I was pained about personal as well as existential issues. I was especially concerned about the subject of death and dying. As a young boy, it occurred to me that people were acting as though there was no such thing as mortality; they appeared to me to be living in a constant state of denial. They seemed totally unaware of the impact of death on their lives. Sure, there were endless movies and stories in which crime and violence prevailed: soldiers in battle and cowboys and Indians were dying with regularity, but these portrayals of death were often remote and superficial.

In addition to these concerns, I was curious about the overall meaning of life and in particular wanted to know what made people tick, what motivated them and what caused them to behave the way they did. Within this context, I attempted to develop guidelines for myself as a person. I wanted to face the truth at all costs, even if it were painful. I intended to fully invest myself in love and life despite any rejection or negative consequences. And within these realms I promised myself that I would live my life with integrity.

From that time on, I have been completely devoted to answering the questions noted above. It is not accidental that Separation Theory represents a synthesis of psychoanalytic and existential approaches to psychology. Both aspects are essential to a complete understanding of the individual. I feel that my work has yielded important information about both the highs and lows of human experience, offering unique insight into human suffering and destructiveness to both self and others.

In relation to my continuing search for meaning in life, I have found no hidden answer to my questions. It is my contention that people must imbue life with their own personal meaning, manifested in their investment in creative pursuits or career, their romantic life, their children, etc. It is this type of involvement in life that sustains and nurtures us and makes us truly human. Furthermore, I realize that many of us have been damaged in our upbringing in a manner that seriously limits our development of compassion and the pursuit of meaning in life.

Lastly, I suggest that the core conflict for humankind is whether to invest in life when faced with the certainty of death or to retreat to a defensive posture of self-protection. Most choose to back away from feeling and give up huge parts of their lives. In that sense, they collude with death. These negative tendencies are manifested in the therapeutic encounter where one confronts resistance to both the therapy process and to a better life in general. It is surprising how many people are refractory to accepting being loved or significantly valued and how strongly they hold onto negative views of themselves.

The philosophy underlying my therapeutic work is to challenge one's core defenses, differentiate oneself from one's personal background and prejudices, work toward achieving autonomy and independence, and eventually free oneself to experience life as fully as possible despite the fact of one's eventual demise. This fundamental philosophy can be conceived of as life-affirming death awareness.

ACKNOWLEDGEMENTS

I wish to thank Tamsen Firestone for her intellect and considerable contribution to this work. Her probing and, at times, challenging suggestions helped me better express the ideas that I have spent a lifetime developing. I am also grateful to Mimi Wolfe, Jo Barrington, Susan Short and Sara Bartlett for their editing skills. I want to thank Anne Baker, Maria Vazquez, and Kristina Jansen who compiled and copy-edited the notes and references. I am especially thankful to Joyce Catlett, who has proven invaluable in all of my writing.

I am appreciative to Frank Tobe for assembling and formatting a print-ready manuscript and for founding the Glendon Association. I wish to thank Glendon's staff including Nina, Carolyn and Lena Firestone, Geoff Parr, Jina Carvalho and Maureen Sullivan for their ongoing support of my work. And most importantly, I am grateful to Lisa Firestone, who has not only shared ideas and clinical experience but, over the years, has represented my ideas in the field.

I want to thank Jeffrey Zeig, my publisher, and the architect of the Evolution of Psychotherapy Conference, for recognizing the potential contribution of this book toward fulfilling one of his most valued goals, that of keeping the theories and methodologies of psychotherapy practice alive and vital in today's world.

Lastly, I am grateful to all of my psychotherapy clients for moving me emotionally and inspiring me in my attempt to find answers to basic human questions.

Chapter 1

MY JOURNEY TO
UNDERSTANDING

Early in my life I decided that I wanted to make a contribution to humankind and to be of value to others. For more than 60 years, I have been absorbed in developing my psychological understanding. My principal interest has been the subject of resistance in psychotherapy and of people's resistance to a better life in general. I have studied this subject in various populations ranging from people suffering from psychoses, to neurotic clients in psychotherapy, to a "normal" population of comparatively high-functioning individuals. The theory and methodology that have emerged from this work are at the core of my intellectual legacy.

My theoretical approach, Separation Theory, combines psychoanalytic and existential concepts in psychology, and lends itself to an effective approach to psychotherapy. I have described how the attempt to deny or negate death, along with various other illusions and self-protective adaptations, lead to limitations in living. In the course of these investigations, I have identified the basic defense mechanisms that adversely affect personal relationships and society, as well as issues of morality in everyday life. In the process, I, along with my associates, have contributed to an understanding of how social structures and cultures are formed from the pooling of individual psychological defenses against both interpersonal pain and death anxiety. In this chapter, I will attempt to explain how my early intellectual developments contributed to my knowledge and understanding of individuals, relationships and the human experience.

Early Years

August 14, 1945 was VJ Day; the war was over and there was a jubilant celebration in Times Square. I was 15 years old. People were screaming with delight, soldiers and sailors were kissing girls and the atmosphere was wild. In the midst of these festivities, I met David Unterman. Dave was the most interesting guy I'd ever known because he was both intelligent and intellectual. He talked about provocative subjects like philosophy and psychology. In fact, it was Dave who introduced me to the work of Sigmund Freud.

Initially, I had an aversion to Freud based on the pop-psychoanalytic approach that everyone was applying to literature at the time. I was annoyed at the over-interpretation of symbols stretched to fit the theoretical system. Nevertheless, I soon became completely absorbed by Freud's genius. I was in awe of his brilliance and immensely impressed with the great man's courage. I immersed myself in his work. I learned much from Freud, particularly from his descriptions of the unconscious mind (S. Freud, 1957/1915), the stages of psychosexual development, people's defense mechanisms and his understanding of the dynamics of psychological conflict.

Most importantly, I learned about the concepts of transference and resistance (S. Freud, 1957/1912) (Note 1). Early on, I extended Freud's view of transference beyond the therapy situation and observed how, in many of their relationships, people had transference reactions. In particular, I realized that they were prone to transfer feelings onto authority figures—their bosses, teachers, doctors, etc.

However, I did take issue with Freud's conception of a death instinct, even though it appeared to explain man's inhumanity to man (S. Freud, 1959/1925; 1977/1920). It is true that throughout the world, people commit heinous acts with disastrous effects. However, I see humans as born innocent but corrupted and made hostile by painful experiences in their development. I believe destructiveness is not instinctual, but rather an outcome of the impact of negative events on people's potential to respond with love and compassion.

As I attempted to understand the paradoxical nature of human behavior, I became interested in the conflict between assertion and dependence. I observed that people were torn between their desire for separation and independence and their desire for submission and fusion. They want to be strong and adult, yet commonly revert to a childish regression. My mind raced as I applied Freudian concepts to my own primitive theorizing. Needless to say, these insights have had a profound influence on my life as a therapist and theorist. They have had an enormous impact on my personal life as well.

Ph.D. Candidacy

In the mid-50s, when I was a Ph.D. candidate, I participated in an innovative residential treatment center headed by Dr. John N. Rosen, where the psychologists, psychiatrists and other mental health professionals lived and worked in close proximity to severely regressed schizophrenic patients (Note 2). It was a situation similar to R. D. Laing's program at Kingsley Hall in London, where the "afflicted" and the "healers" cohabitated on a twenty-four-hour basis. Although the treatment modalities were quite different in the two situations, both challenged doctor-patient role-playing and insisted on an authentic interaction on the part of the therapist. It was agonizing for me to experience, at close range, the torment and despair of human beings forced to choose a nightmarish fantasy life over a real existence in this world.

Despite the stressful nature of my involvement, this unique circumstance allowed me to study the full range of mental illness as contrasted with the narrow vantage point of the once or twice weekly, 50-minute office visit. I learned that a therapist could maintain objectivity despite the emotional involvement of living with patients. Even within these close quarters, I found that I could maintain an honest approach, be true to my nature and utilize my real self as a healing agent.

During my time at the treatment center, I developed an understanding of how the reliance on fantasy gratification in schizophrenia essentially involves an imaginary self-parenting process, a severe regression characterized by delusions, hallucinations and impaired thought disturbances. I found that these symptoms indicated a split within the personality. In their minds, schizophrenics were at the same time the highest and the lowest specimens of humanity, the all-powerful, invincible parent and the weak, pathetic, bad child. It was as though they had incorporated the hurtful parent into themselves. Their hallucinated voices attacked them in a parental tone, and all the while, they accepted these attacks as a significant part of their identity. These attitudes prevailed over any realistic sense of self.

After the year at Rosen's, I returned to my Ph.D. program where I revised and adjusted the theory I had formulated during my work with schizophrenic individuals. Schizophrenia is the result of a combination of biological predisposition and emotional trauma during the developmental years. Mental health professionals are polarized in their theories and methodology, emphasizing one or the other aspect as more critical, and there is a legitimate difference of opinion. I was primarily concerned with the environmental component. My theoretical Ph.D. dissertation explained the psychodynamics of schizophrenia based largely on my findings at Rosen's (R. Firestone, 1957).

It was a time rich in discovery for me and, without realizing it, I was being prepared for future events in my life. My mind was captivated as I attempted to unravel the riddle of psychopathology. My major focus was on the means by which those who were hurt or damaged attempted to defend themselves, as well as their resistance to altering their defenses. I became aware that the same theoretical concepts that I was grappling with in my Ph.D. dissertation applied to my understanding of so-called "normal" individuals. I realized that they have the same type of split that I had observed in schizophrenics, but they are not as fragmented. To varying degrees, many "normal" individuals behave in a manner that can be characterized as either parental or childish in contrast to living in the adult mode.

Paradoxically, most of us nurture and punish ourselves throughout our lifetime in a manner similar to the way we were treated in our developmental years. For this reason, we spend the majority of our lives reliving rather than living, thereby restricting our vitality and creative potential.

It became apparent to me that all people have a great deal in common and that all forms of mental problems and their manifestations exist somewhere on the same continuum. As human beings, we all have our conflicts and emotional pain as well as our capacity to use our personal power to develop and change.

Private Practice

My approach to psychotherapy has never involved an attempt to adjust people to a society or social system. If anything, I am interested in adjusting the social process to enhance the individual's development. I am deeply concerned with answering a vital question: Whose life is the client really living? Is he/she truly following his/her own destiny or recapitulating the life of parents or caretakers? Is he/she a programmed robot or a fully vital human being?

When I began my private practice in 1957, I continued my study of people's resistance to change. I was deeply perplexed by a seemingly paradoxical phenomenon: people often avoid or minimize experiences that are warm, successful or constructive. People say that they want success in their work, love in their life and happiness, but their behavior often indicates otherwise. I was searching for an answer to the question of why so many people, in spite of emotional catharsis, understanding and intellectual insight, still hold on to familiar, destructive patterns of the past and refuse to change on a deep character level. I was concerned with the stubborn resistance to changing a conception of self that was self-critical or self-accusatory.

I recognized that just as fantasy gratification played a destructive role in the lives of schizophrenics, the same dynamic was limiting the lives of my clients. I developed the theoretical construct of the *fantasy bond*, a unifying psychological concept that elucidates how human beings seek comfort and security in fantasies of fusion that insulate them from emotional pain. This imagined connection, formed originally with the parent or primary caretaker, arises in response to children's early experiences of rejection, emotional deprivation and separation trauma. The fantasy bond is explained in detail in Chapter 3.

Once the fantasy bond is formed and internalized, idealized parental images, in conjunction with primitive self-nurturing habits, provide the child with an illusion of self-sufficiency or pseudo-independence because they partially gratify basic needs and reduce tension. Rather than conclude that their parents are inadequate or rejecting, a fact that is too threatening for the child to face, children think that they themselves are at fault. In order to maintain the fantasy bond, children must maintain their idealized parental images along with negative views and attitudes toward themselves that they experienced in their family. Choosing this defense allows them to believe that there is hope: that if only they can change or improve themselves then maybe they will be loved.

I observed how the self-parenting aspects of the fantasy bond continued to impair my clients in their adult lives. I understood that the degree to which people rely on fantasy processes is proportional to the amount of pain and rejection they experience in their developmental years.

From my work with schizophrenic patients, it was clear that these seriously disturbed people were involved in a process of idealizing their parents to their own detriment. I found the same pattern in my clients in psychotherapy. As I applied this concept of the idealization of parents and family in a broader perspective, I began to comprehend its central role in psychopathological phenomena.

In my years of private practice, my colleagues and I also observed clinical material that expanded my understanding of human self-destructiveness. I developed an awareness of an underlying critical thought process that supports defenses, including the fantasy bond. I called this critical thought process "the voice." It represents the negative attitudes directed toward the child that were incorporated into the self. This enemy within causes people to feel negative and hostile toward themselves as well as angry, suspicious and fearful of others. The critical inner voice is discussed in Chapters 3 and 4. My associates and I applied our findings to the problem of microsuicidal and suicidal ideology in our clients, and became increasingly involved in the cognitive processes associated with self-destructive behavior (Note 3). I recognized that this internalized negative thought process acts as the core resistance in psychotherapy.

Psychological Community

In the 1970s, after approximately twenty years of working as a practicing psychotherapist, my friends and associates in the field came up with a tantalizing but frightening idea. It all began when I started a psychotherapy group for my clients and organized several extended marathon sessions that were held in a mountain retreat. When I told my associates and friends about the honesty and feeling nature of these experiences and the positive impact on the participants, they were envious and wanted to recreate the same format for themselves. For the next several years, my friends and I held a weekly group during which we spoke openly and felt deeply. We were impressed with what we were learning about ourselves and how warmly we felt toward each other. Finally, one woman said, "If this way of talking and openly sharing our lives is so valuable, why don't we try to live this way all of the time?" Her question set into motion an entire chain of events culminating in the idea of starting a co-op and sharing life on a personal level—in a sense, creating a therapeutic community.

My friends and colleagues asked me to participate in the new situation, to act as a paid consultant. I found the idea compelling. The opportunity to live among friends I respected and admired, to be with people who would talk honestly, to be in the midst of a group of individuals observing their personal behavior and relationships at close hand, sounded like an ideal environment within which to continue to develop my ideas. In essence, it would be a "psychological laboratory."

Despite this initial enthusiasm, I felt ambivalent, even reluctant, to make this happen. But it started me thinking. I was perfectly happy to participate as an equal member of the group, but in no way did I want to become my friends' therapist. I was worried that the ultimate professional responsibility of group leader might fall solely on me. The others tried hard to reassure me that they could and would take full responsibility for their own participation. These were intelligent, effective individuals, who were successful in their professions. Among them were four clinical psychologists, a doctor, an engineer, several lawyers, teachers, and entrepreneurs. They were strong, well-rounded, independent people with a good deal of ego strength. But still I felt mixed.

Lastly, I was worried about my practical life. I would be giving up a large practice that I had worked hard to build. At the same time, there was the possibility, even the likelihood, that the new arrangement would not work out. After months of conversation and contemplation, I agreed to participate and the project was organized.

The community not only grew to more than one hundred individuals but has lasted up to the present day, some forty years later. During this time, we have shared common residences, ongoing personal communication and successful business ventures. Together, we bought a partially finished schooner that we completed building and eventually sailed around the world.

From the beginning, we held seminars and discussions in which we revealed our innermost secrets, shared our pain and grief, and expressed powerful feelings. In exploring these deeper issues, both existential and interpersonal, we became acutely aware of forces within society and the nuclear family that were detrimental to human development and conducive to psychological symptom formation. For example, we were particularly aware of the destructive effect of sarcasm, sadistic tendencies, hostility, vanity, superiority, victimization, paranoia, control, domination and narcissism. As a result, we became strongly motivated to try to minimize these damaging attitudes and behaviors in our personal lives. Without knowing it, we were beginning to formulate the elements of an implicit morality concerned with human rights issues that were based on our mutual insights.

Observations Emerging from the Community

As I continued to study human behavior in this unique population, I developed a number of hypotheses and preliminary conclusions that I believe are generally valid for human behavior in the larger society. My associates and I assembled and documented much information about the emotional damage that people sustained as children and demonstrated how it led to their specific defense formations. We also noted how these adaptations perpetuated people's suffering throughout their lives and cause resistance to a better life. Below are a few of the key observations that emerged from the community:

Many People are Resistant to Love and Intimacy: My associates' and my observations of personal interactions between couples in the group provided data that were as conclusive as they were unpleasant and painful to comprehend. Sadly, the new awareness coincided with my previous observations of couple relationships in therapy. I saw evidence of how the fantasy bond in the family of origin is often extended to new people in one's adult life, and thereafter plays a significant role in couple and family relationships.

This insight came to light on the extended trips my friends and I took, journeys lasting over six weeks at a time, which often involved cruising on our sailboat. Married couples were often separated for parts of the voyage due to their different work schedules, and were reunited later as the trip progressed. The inescapable fact was that nearly all of the individuals fared better when they were "alone." When they were on their own, their faces were vivid; they looked more appealing and alive. They expressed more ideas and indicated a stronger point of view. They missed their partners and looked forward to seeing them again, but when they rejoined their mates, these same people appeared deadened and asexual, and were less interesting to others as well.

The reunited couples would spend time alone, but the privacy intended for intimacy was often used destructively. More often than not, they re-engaged in complicated and tense interactions and, sadly, personal problems and arguments didn't take long to get going. Typically, this pattern was quite clear to everyone except the couple in question. There was usually a great deal of resistance when this information was offered as feedback to the partners. Interestingly, couples fared better when they were in close proximity to others on the boat, as this inhibited arguing and the acting out of hostility. As a result, there was more harmony and accord between them.

I have observed that in a new love relationship, a couple exists for a while in a relatively undefended and vulnerable state, often referred to as the "honeymoon phase." It is unpredictable and exciting, but at the same time it is frightening. The fear of loss or abandonment, the dread of being rejected, together with the poignancy and sadness that the new loving feelings may evoke can, sooner or later, become intolerable, especially for those individuals who have suffered from rejection or lack of love in their early lives. When the feelings of affection and genuine companionship in the new relationship stand in stark contrast with unhappiness and rejection experienced in their family of origin, people unknowingly attempt to erase the difference. At the point that they begin to feel anxious or frightened, they retreat from feeling close and gradually give up the most valued parts of the relationship.

As their relationship matures, symptoms of a fantasy bond appear more frequently. For example, a man and woman who once spent hours talking together may begin to be uninterested in each other. They may avoid direct eye contact and stop noticing what the other person is feeling. They can become less personal and less honest in their communication. After a time, a sense of obligation replaces their desire to be together. They begin to act according to roles; they behave more like a "husband" or "wife," eventually a "mother" or "father," than like real people. One or both members of the couple may begin to hold back their affectionate and sexual responses. Their attraction for each other can diminish and their sex life becomes routine. Despite these negative intrusions on their relationship and the fact that they are acting in ways that contrast with any recognizable definition of love, people's capacity for self-deception enables them to maintain an imagination of closeness and intimacy.

People strongly resist recognizing the negative trends that indicate a fantasy bond in their relationships. They will obliterate themselves as independent, separate individuals in order to hold on to their illusion of union, imagining that they are holding on to real people. Often all that a couple has after years of being together is a fantasy of love which both partners protect by keeping the form of love—the roles, the routines, the accepted behaviors, the observation of birthdays and anniversaries.

R. D. Laing (1971) described this phenomenon: "Desire for confirmation from each is present in both, but each is caught between trust and mistrust, confidence and despair, and both settle for counterfeit acts of confirmation on the basis of pretense"(pp.108-109).

My friends and I were motivated to challenge our fantasy bonds, particularly in our romantic relationships. We sought to treat our partners in a loving and respectful manner. We had a strong desire to further investigate the resistance to intimacy and attempted to change this dynamic. We recognized that there was a strong resistance to combining a long-standing love relationship with a satisfying sexual relationship. Paradoxically, people tend to pull back in one area or the other to avoid the very special combination of love and sexuality that is the most rewarding or ideal.

People Reject Actual Gratification for Fantasy Gratification: I had thought that people would be thrilled and happy in this type of community, where it seems like participants have found much of what they searched for all of their lives. They have close friendships and love relationships, emotional support, an open, caring and understanding environment in which help is always available on virtually every level. Surprisingly, we discovered that people had great difficulty tolerating or accepting the actual satisfaction of their wants.

My friends and I have learned that, to a significant degree, people are not desirous of actualizing or fulfilling their dreams when they have the opportunity. Real success, genuine love and companionship interrupt the inward, self-gratifying fantasy process that people have depended upon since they were young, and this disruption causes many of them anxiety and pain. As Eric Hoffer put it, "We do not really feel grateful toward those who make our dreams come true; they ruin our dreams." Furthermore, the anxiety and sadness that are generated can threaten a person's defensive equilibrium. Therefore, positive achievements, friendships and love relationships are many times diminished or discarded.

It became clear from people's negative reactions to positive circumstances that there is an enormous discrepancy between what people say they want and what they can actually tolerate having. When one's fantasies come true in reality, they are no longer under one's control; they are no longer a safe part of their inward world. Real successes intrude upon and threaten the fantasy gratification that has long acted as an escape or relief from emotional distress.

People React Against Positive Events and Success: I was also surprised to find that the probability of regression in people was highest whenever they achieved personal goals that were especially meaningful to them. In some instances, the symptoms of regression developed suddenly and the negative reactions that followed were dramatic; in others, the deterioration was more gradual but still became harmful over time.

My friends and I were pained and surprised when people who were doing well for a prolonged period would experience a serious decline in their personal lives. It became apparent that while, understandably, negative responses such as criticism, rejection or the painful loss of loved ones could trigger regressive reactions, unusually favorable responses could precipitate a regression as well. In these situations, many people tended to retreat into a more inward and emotionally deadened state. They retreated from, or to varying degrees rejected, those they had felt close to. They appeared to act against their own interests and became confused about many issues in their lives. Indeed, even people's appearances changed; they just didn't look like themselves in their normal state. Some became self-doubting and self-hating where previously they had been confident and insightful. They tended to imagine rejection and anticipate disapproval from people who, in reality, liked and supported them in their personal endeavors. On occasion, serious depressive states were triggered, characterized by a wide range of pathological symptoms, including an increased desire for isolation, self-punishing tendencies and, in some cases, suicidal ideation.

Strange as it may seem, more often than not, positive rather than negative events preceded the onset of these symptoms. The precipitating causes of regression varied from one individual to another. For one man, it was finding friendship and companionship after years of being isolated and alone; for one woman, it was the acknowledgement of her intelligence and intellectual contributions that interrupted her long-standing awkwardness and reserve in social situations. Another man became aloof and distant after his friends gave him a present that held a great deal of personal meaning for him. A woman resumed her pattern of self-destructive drinking after achieving her long-standing goal of being made partner in her company.

My colleagues and I identified two basic circumstances that can lead a person to retreat or regress after an unusual success: (1) if the positive acknowledgment or success conflicts with one's basic identity in the family of origin; (2) if the achievement surpasses the performance of significant family members, particularly the parent of the same sex. We found that the latter was true to a surprising extent; surpassing the parent of the same sex causes guilt and anxiety. This anxiety is related to a fear of aloneness, because in surpassing someone who we previously depended on for survival, we experience a loss of the dependency source.

People Cling to their Defenses and their Negative Identity: My friends, associates and I learned a great deal about resistance as we investigated our own upbringings and observed and discussed our interactions with friends and family members, both in and out of the community. We knew that psychological defenses were formed in childhood to protect against emotional pain and anxiety during the developmental years, but we came to understand how deeply entrenched these defenses are and how resistant they are to change.

We came to realize that virtually every person holds on to a negative concept of self regardless of how unrealistic it was. The critical inner voice supports this negative identity, often leading to self-deprivation, self-punishment and other damaging behaviors. As I explored dynamics of this negative identity and the critical inner voices that support it, I identified a split in the personality between the self system and the anti-self system. This "division of the mind" reflects a primary divide between forces that represent the self and those that oppose or attempt to destroy it. The self system and the anti-self system develop independently; both are dynamic and continually evolve and change over time.

As described in the preface, the self system consists of the unique characteristics of the individual, including his/her biological, temperamental, and genetic traits, the incorporation of parents' affirmative qualities and strivings, and the ongoing effects of experience and education. Parents' lively attitudes, positive values, and active pursuit of life are easily assimilated through the process of identification and imitation and become part of the child's developing personality.

The anti-self system is made up primarily of internalized negative parental attitudes and traits and functions as an alien part of the personality. Children incorporate the angry, hostile aspects of their parents' reactions into themselves because it is too threatening to see the danger as coming from the very person they rely on for survival. Because of their pressing need for love and their utter dependence during their formative years, children must see their parents as adequate, good, and caring, and deny any of their inadequacies, weaknesses, lack of feeling, and concern for their well-being. As they face separation experiences and later death anxiety, these defense mechanisms are strengthened in the personality. The self and anti-self are discussed in more detail in Chapter 6.

Existential Realities Create a Core Conflict for People: In sharing life closely for an extended length of time on such a deep personal level, the participants in the friendship circle have loved and developed lifelong attachments to each other. As a result, existential realities concerning life and death have strongly impacted us. In striving to be less defended and more vulnerable, and in allowing others to be important to us, we feel the full effect of what we stand to lose when any one of us becomes ill or dies. For this reason, I have been able to observe the impact that death has on many people, both positive and negative. Besides, the awareness that we are powerless and will ultimately lose all that we value is a hard reality to live with. The fear that this precipitates is one of the primary reasons that people regress and retreat from caring for others and being invested in their own lives.

There are two opposing reactions that people can have when they are faced with the inevitability of death: choosing to live life in the face of death or retreating from life to protect themselves from death's reality. I consider the choice between these two reactions to be the core conflict. When they choose the latter, their actions can be construed as colluding with death.

People cannot deny existential realities and cut off emotional pain and anxiety without losing real feeling for themselves and others. Most important, they cannot be innocently defended. Their defenses hurt others, in particular those closest to them, their mates and their children. In contrast, facing existential issues with courage and honesty, painful as it is, is potentially liberating and freeing. Living a less defended life allows people to experience all of their emotions and they are better able to tolerate intimacy.

I have observed that in everyday life, we are always faced with live choices as well as dead ones. At every moment, we are making decisions that favor our interest and investment in our lives, or are putting up barriers or resistance to our priorities. People often take solace in giving up and refraining from competing. At times, they even feel relief when faced with circumstances that are antithetical to their goals. As a result, many people lead lifestyles that are self-denying and self-limiting.

There is Therapeutic Value in Friendship: My experiences in this community have confirmed my early understanding that neurosis originates in a social process and, therefore, can potentially be altered in a social milieu. Meaningful exchanges with another person stand in opposition to a fantasy bond. Companionship that is nonintrusive and nonobligatory leads to self-awareness and encourages one to emerge from an inward posture. Personal interaction with a close friend on a daily basis diminishes voice attacks and significantly interferes with the propensity to be self-denying and self-hating. It is also important to have friends who possess the qualities to which one aspires. Emulating the qualities of an admirable person and using him/her as an ally and a role model is an essential step toward developing one's own sense of values and transcendent goals.

Self-disclosure and honest communication have been cited as important elements for maintaining friendship over the long-term. According to Fehr (1996), friends employ a number of strategies to maintain a relationship, including "engaging in self-disclosure [and] providing support and assurance" (p. 172). Yet, in society, it is rare to achieve an adult level of communication between people on personal subjects. A respectful dialogue or mutual self-disclosure about real issues, without coercion, manipulation, or parent-child role playing, is difficult to come by. When people are defended, adult communication uncomplicated by phoniness, dishonesty and efforts to "win points" becomes virtually impossible.

In genuine companionship, people relate to each other as independent individuals with considerable give and take in terms of reciprocal need gratification. Friends refrain from imposing rules and role restrictions on each other; consequently, each person respects the other's point of view and is left alone, in the best sense of the word, to pursue his/her own goals. In contrast to a fantasy bond, friendship between two emotionally mature individuals is characterized by equality and respect for one another's boundaries. Intimacy without bondage, and closeness without illusions of security, enable a person to feel the truth of his/her separateness.

Friendship also alleviates isolation, which is a perfect breeding ground for destructive thought and action. Extended periods of time away from social contact can be conducive to depressive reactions and progressive withdrawal. Self-harm is more likely to be acted out when people withdraw their interest and emotional investment in others. Angry self-attacks and obsessive ruminations further deplete the vitality of people who have denied their wants and desires over a prolonged period of time and, eventually, they may feel they have nothing left to live for.

Lastly, friendship, in addition to being a social process, usually involves acts of generosity. One of the most meaningful advantages of this community has been that it has provided people with countless opportunities to experience generosity, both the giving and receiving of it. We have seen people receive enormous benefits from being thoughtful, kind and offering themselves in a personal way. Behaving in a giving, compassionate manner reinforces each person's sense of worth and is an antidote to the anti-self and the process of self-attack. As such, generosity challenges destructive voices or thoughts, reinforces a positive self-concept and is conducive to better mental health rather than a moral prerogative.

CONCLUDING THOUGHTS

I have learned much since I first became interested in the study of resistance to change and to a better life. I have observed that, for many people, basic changes in identity leave them feeling anxious and disoriented. Their reactions validated my idea about the pervasiveness of the anti-self and its resistance to change. People have difficulty assimilating a new, more affirmative image of themselves and disregard or even reverse behaviors that are particularly valued. Significant positive movement arouses anxiety, especially when it represents a marked difference from the habitual behavior and lifestyles of parents and family members. In this situation both separation anxiety and death anxiety are increased.

However, I have seen that people can challenge their old ways of defending themselves and adjust to a new and more fulfilling life. This appears to be the only viable alternative to an existence of tedium, conformity and alienation from oneself and others. Living a less defended life allows us to experience all of our emotions and we are better able to tolerate intimacy. In general, people who have fewer defenses feel more integrated, and tend to be more humane toward others. Thus, remaining vulnerable and undefended is a positive human value.

Even when confronting painful existential issues, people can choose to embrace life and live with an awareness of death rather than deaden themselves prematurely. Facing the core conflict and choosing life, painful as it may be, is potentially liberating. Sometimes, making the live choice involves relying on some form of outside help or even formal therapy. We almost always experience anxiety when we undergo fundamental changes, yet the result can be worth it—we are more likely to fulfill our unique human destiny. People *can* take control of their lives and in that sense create themselves, but it requires complete honesty, deep self-reflection, courage, persistence and the willingness to take chances. In choosing to live with a minimum of defense, people can move toward a life of adventure characterized by freedom of choice, enthusiasm and optimism.

Notes

1. See also Sigmund Freud's (1955/1905) "Three Essays on the Theory of Sexuality" in *The Standard Edition of the Complete Psychological Works of Sigmund Freud, Volume VII* (1901-1905): A Case of Hysteria, Three Essays on Sexuality and

Other Works, (pp. 123-246); for transference phenomena see "The Dynamics of Transference" in *The Standard Edition of the Complete Psychological Works of Sigmund Freud, Volume XII* (1911-1913): The Case of Schreber, Papers on Technique and Other Works, (pp. 97-108)

2. Also see *Direct Analysis* (selected papers), by John N. Rosen (1953), Grune & Stratton, New York City, NY.

3. "Self-destructive or micro-suicidal behaviors": *Micro-suicide* refers to behaviors, communications, attitudes, or lifestyles that are self-induced and threatening to an individual's physical health, emotional well-being, or personal goals. See R. Firestone & Seiden (1987) "Micro-suicide and Suicidal Threats of Everyday Life," *Psychotherapy, 24*, pp 31-39.

Chapter 2

A BRIEF OVERVIEW OF SEPARATION THEORY

"This approach [Separation Theory] is integrative even beyond the blending of the psychoanalytic and existential views. . . . It views people as being innately innocent rather than destructive or corrupt, and thereby it rejects Id Psychology in favor of an existential view of humankind. Its ties to existentialism and humanism are in its acceptance of the viability of the emerging "self," its observation of the preoccupation of humans with death . . . and its view that there is an inevitable drive of the organism to become a differentiated system."

~ Larry Beutler (1997, p. xiv)

I refer to my theoretical approach as Separation Theory because it conceptualizes life as a series of separation experiences that ends with the finality of death, the ultimate separation. Each successive separation predisposes a state of anxiety and unrest. The resultant fear is compensated for by forming a fantasy or illusion of connection with the mother or father, which I term the *fantasy bond*. The fantasy process soothes the anxiety and pain, but generally predisposes maladaptation as well.

Separation Theory integrates psychoanalytic and existential systems of thought by showing how early interpersonal pain and separation anxiety and, later, death anxiety, lead to the formation of powerful psychological defenses (Bassett, 2007). These defenses attempt to cope with and minimize painful experiences and emotions suffered in one's developmental years; however, as noted, the defensive adaptation tends to become increasingly dysfunctional.

Psychoanalytic theory emphasizes the importance of unconscious motivation, explains how trauma leads to the formation of defenses, identifies conflict and competition within the family system as well as incestuous tendencies, describes levels of psychosexual development and explains how resistance and transference enter into the therapy process. However, psychoanalysis fails to deal effectively with the significant role that death anxiety plays in life and its powerful impact on the ongoing development of the individual.

On the other hand, existential psychology focuses on understanding the importance of death awareness and dying on the personality, as well as other issues of being, such as individuation, autonomy and transcendent goals. However, existential psychology tends to neglect the "down and dirty" psychoanalytic concepts of defense mechanisms, competition and psychosexual development. In my opinion, neither approach by itself is sufficient; both are necessary in order to fully understand human personality development, motivation, and behavior.

Each individual is born with the potential to exhibit a variety of propensities that are essentially human. The basic qualities of our heritage are the ability to love and feel compassion for oneself and others, the capacity for abstract reasoning and creativity, the capability to set goals and develop strategies to accomplish them, an awareness of existential concerns, the desire to search for meaning and social affiliation, and the potential to experience the sacredness and mystery of life. Whenever any of these qualities are damaged, we lose a part of ourselves that is most alive. Yet these basic human potentialities are fractured or limited to varying degrees in the course of growing up in family constellations that are less than ideal. The resultant emotional pain and frustration leads to an inward self-protective attitude and a basic distrust of others.

No child is born bad or sinful; rather, the psychological defenses that children form early in life are appropriate to actual situations that threaten the emerging self. Separation Theory places a strong emphasis on individuation and differentiation from any negative conditioning in the family. The ultimate goal of psychotherapy is to help people overcome their personal limitations and to maintain the healthy balance between feeling and rationality that reflects their basic humanness and supports the development of the true self.

My theory contrasts living with fantasy and illusion with goal-directed lifestyles and points out that people largely relate to themselves as objects, in that they treat themselves the way their parent or primary caretaker treated them. I emphasize that there are conflicted choices in life between defending oneself by cutting off painful emotional experiences and moving toward the fulfillment of one's potentialities. At each moment in time, one is either capitulating to one's internal programming or moving toward individuation.

My philosophy places primary importance on the individual as a unique entity. Efforts toward preserving the life within each person are given priority over supporting any group or system, whether it be the couple, the family, ethnic or political groups, nationality, or religion. Another singular aspect of the theory is endorsing behaviors and ways of living that involve moving toward independence, compassion and the development of transcendent goals. By involving themselves in endeavors that have a deeper meaning than immediate gratifications, people increase their capacity for personal fulfillment and expand their life space.

My emphasis on experience and preserving every aspect of emotional life is central. Feeling one's true sadness frees one to know exhilaration. I agree with Viktor Frankl's (1963) assertion that the pursuit of happiness in itself is doomed to failure. Happiness can only be a by-product of facing the tragic dimensions of life and investing oneself in the pursuit of goals that go beyond the narrow confines of one's self and family.

In contrast to many conceptual frameworks, my theory offers no solace in that it provides no "loopholes." It offers no illusions, no means of escaping existential despair or the inevitable vicissitudes of life; however, it shows that people can choose a life of courage and integrity in which honesty is paramount and adventure and awareness are truly valued.

THE HUMAN CONDITION

> It is all right to say, with Adler, that mental illness is due to "problems in living," but we must remember that life itself is the insurmountable problem.
>
> ~ Ernest Becker (1997, p. 270)

Human beings, unlike other species, are cursed with a conscious awareness of their own mortality. I believe that the tragedy of the human condition is that people's awareness and true self-consciousness concerning this existential issue contributes to an ultimate irony: human beings are both brilliant and aberrant, sensitive and savage, exquisitely caring and painfully indifferent, remarkably creative and incredibly destructive to self and others. The capacity to imagine and conceptualize has negative as well as positive consequences because it predisposes anxiety states that culminate in a defensive form of denial.

The tragedy is that the same defenses that enable us to survive the emotional pain of childhood and existential despair are not only maladaptive and limit our personal potential for living a full life, but they also inevitably lead to negative behaviors toward others, thereby perpetuating the cycle of destructiveness. Similarly, ideologies and religious beliefs that offer spiritual comfort and relief from a sense of aloneness and interpersonal distress also polarize people one against the other. Threatened by those with different customs and belief systems, we mistakenly feel that we must overpower or destroy them (R. Firestone, 1996; Fromm, 1950; Piven, 2004; Solomon, Greenberg & Pyszczynski, 2004).

Feeling and compassion are a significant part of our essential humanness, but when faced with overwhelming primal pain, we develop defenses to minimize our suffering. Cut off from our feelings, we are desensitized to ourselves and are more likely to become self-destructive or to act out aggression toward others. Altering this negative legacy requires a depth of psychological knowledge and compassion, the belief that we can prevail and the fortitude to pursue this endeavor despite the pain it may arouse.

Life Conceptualized as a Series of Progressive Weaning Experiences

Like Otto Rank (1972), I believe that separation is a vital part of the life process (Note 1). Birth, separation from the breast, from the mother, from parents, from other family members, the first day at school, leaving for college, moving away from home, the first sexual experience, moving in with a romantic partner, getting married, buying a home, pregnancy, becoming a parent, becoming a grandparent—all of these are separation experiences. As people go through the stages of individuation, they are cognizant on a deep level that they are moving away emotionally from their security in the family of origin. Each successive event creates new situations that are potentially traumatic because they not only signify a loss of parental support and safety but also remind us that we are a step closer to death.

Stages of Separation During Infancy and Early Childhood

There are a series of stages that infants and young children go through in separating from parents and developing a sense of self. The first occurs at birth, the second during early infancy and the third with the awareness of death.

Birth: The first separation happens with birth and the severing of the umbilical cord, a dramatic event that leads to a realistic, subjective awareness of being separate. Some refer to the baby's first real separation experience as the "birth trauma." Describing how he visualized this traumatic event from the infant's perspective, psychoanalyst Otto Rank (1972), quoting the Talmud, writes:

> Suppose a child in its mother's womb knew that after a lapse of time it will leave the place it occupies. That would seem to it the most grievous thing that could happen. It is so comfortable in the element that surrounds it and protects it against outside influences. However, the time of separation approaches, with terror it sees the protecting envelopes torn asunder and it believes the hour of death has arrived (p. 184).

Early Infancy: From birth, the infant is highly sensitive and vulnerable to sensory inputs from the environment. It is extremely reactive to its surroundings and responds with its whole body when its needs are not immediately met. There is a primitive anxiety that an infant experiences during the inevitable separations that occur in any childhood—for example, when a mother simply leaves the room for a few minutes, or when the infant awakens alone and, lacking any sense of time, feels abandoned forever. The baby is alone, hungry, and desperate, and screams in frustration, fear and protest. An infant's utter helplessness and prolonged dependency on its parents make the formation of defenses imperative. It is absolutely necessary for the infant to protect itself from the wrenching distress it experiences at these times.

The Child's Gradual Awareness of the Reality of Death: Young children, some as early as two years old, become aware of the fact of death—for example, when a pet dies or they learn of the passing of a relative or close family friend. Between three and six years of age, children become consciously aware of the fact that their mother and father are vulnerable to death (Kastenbaum, 2000) (Note 2).

When children realize that their parents will eventually die; at first, they believe themselves to be exempt from this fate. This form of magical thinking is typical of this stage in the child's development. In their desperation to escape a situation that they see as hopeless, children cling more tenaciously to this unconscious solution. Eventually, children realize that they cannot even sustain their own lives. At this point, the world that they originally believed to be permanent is literally turned upside down by their dawning awareness that people, parents, and even they must die.

THE DEFENSE SYSTEM

The Fantasy Bond—The Primary Defense

I consider the fantasy bond to be the primary defense and conceptualize the critical thought process or voice as representing a secondary defense that in part supports the fantasy bond.

The child compensates for emotional trauma, separation experiences and existential angst by forming a fantasy bond or imaginary connection with the mother or parent. This fantasy process relieves stress and can become progressively more addictive. The degree to which children continue to rely on this illusory connection is proportional to the degree of pain, frustration and anxiety that they experienced in growing up, which varies considerably from one family to another and even from one child to another within the same family.

The fantasy bond continues throughout life to relieve pain and frustration because, on a subliminal level, it offers a sense of being protected and cared for. On a subconscious level, it provides a modicum of relief from fears of death and helps maintain an illusion of immortality. The fantasy bond necessarily involves a certain amount of distortion of reality; therefore, the more one relies on fantasy gratification, the more one is limited in coping with the real world. If this defensive fantasy world becomes extreme, a person's ability to function effectively becomes seriously compromised. The fantasy bond is elaborated in Chapter 3.

The Voice—The Secondary Defense

As described in Chapter 1, people possess conflicting points of view and beliefs about themselves and others, their relationships, and events in the world, depending upon which aspect of the personality, self or anti-self, is dominant at any given time. One point of view is rational, objective, and life-affirming. The other is made up of a destructive thought process or voice, an overlay on the personality that is opposed to the ongoing development of the self.

The voice is the language of the defensive process (R. Firestone, 1988). It refers to a well-integrated system of thoughts and attitudes, antithetical toward self and cynical toward others, that is at the core of an individual's maladaptive behavior. The voice supports the fantasy bond and self-parenting, inward behavior patterns. It is a form of intrapsychic communication that ranges from minor self-criticisms to major self-attacks and fosters self-soothing habit patterns, isolation, and a self-destructive lifestyle.

The voice may at times parallel one's value system or moral considerations. However, rather than motivating one to alter behavior in a moral or constructive manner, the voice tends to occur *after* the negative behavior has taken place and is generally harsh and judgmental. The voice is not representative of those thought processes concerned with values or ideals, or thoughts involved in creative thinking, constructive planning, or realistic, compassionate self-appraisal. Voice attacks are directed toward others as well as toward oneself. Both types of voices, those that belittle the self and those that attack other people, predispose alienation.

Voice Therapy is a cognitive/affective/behavioral methodology that brings internalized destructive thought processes to the surface, with accompanying affect, in a dialogue format that allows a client to confront alien components of the personality. The method helps clients develop insight into the sources of their discomfort, and assists them in gradually modifying behavior in the direction of their stated goals. Voice Therapy is discussed in detail in Chapter 3.

THE EFFECTS OF DEFENSES ON RELATIONSHIPS

When individuals develop defenses to protect themselves from anxiety, pain, and sadness—emotions that are inherent in close relationships—they may tend to push away or punish people who care for them the most. Although this damage is minimal with acquaintances, in casual friendships, or with more distant social contacts, it takes a toll on these situations as well.

Basically there is no way to be self-denying or self-destructive without damaging other people. Parents who are defended in one area of their personalities cannot be sensitive to their children in that area: a woman who cannot tolerate an image of herself as a lovable person will punish the one who offers her love; a man who sees himself as cold or unattractive will be suspicious of those who show an interest in him and will be rejecting toward them. If a person cannot tolerate generosity, he will hurt the gift-giver. If she needs to think of herself as bad or inadequate, she will act accordingly, thereby damaging a joint effort to live happily. If he needs to provoke aggression, he will stir up anger and resentment in others, damaging their good feelings toward him.

People often prefer the self-parenting aspects of the fantasy bond to real interactions with real people. The self-soothing behaviors are remnants of the original fantasy connection that partially satisfied primitive drives and emotional needs. They often manifest in addictive behaviors and patterns of self-parenting that come to be preferred over satisfaction in the interpersonal environment.

In an intimate relationship, the sense of vulnerability inherent in loving and being loved arouses fears of loss and death anxiety. Moving toward genuine closeness and mature sexuality is tantamount to separation from the illusory connection with the mother or primary caretaker. As noted, to reduce this anxiety, people unconsciously attempt to merge and form a fantasy bond with the loved one. A person is thereby able to attain a false sense of security and safety by sustaining the illusion of becoming one with his/her partner.

THE EFFECTS OF DEFENSES ON SOCIETY

Each generation has been raised by people whose ancestors were themselves reared by parents who dulled their psychological pain and subsequently lived defensively and retreated from investing in their lives. As a result, most adults remain prisoners of their internal programming and pass this on to succeeding generations. Internalized voices represent the language of both parental and cultural restrictions on one's humanness. The patterns of the voice are the key to the defensive processes that lead to self-denial, negative self-attitudes, moralistic and judgmental views, and conformity.

Moreover, in forming fantasy bonds, people aggrandize their families, their neighborhood and their country. Although families provide comfort and opportunities for social affiliation—an important human need—they also, all too often, transmit attitudes of superiority, intolerance and prejudice toward others from generation to generation. People who live differently or think differently threaten a person's defensive solutions. Paradoxically, the very defenses that offer security and a sense of belonging alienate people from those with other dispositions, customs, and beliefs.

As technology supersedes rationality, mankind is producing increasingly powerful weapons of mass destruction that could eventually destroy life on the planet. This danger is all too real because people have a stronger stake in nationalism than in trying to develop a world view that would support all of humanity. According to Henry Miller (1947), "Wherever there is the jealous urge to exclude, there is the menace of extinction. I see no nation on earth at present, which has an all-inclusive view of things" (p. xxii).

It is imperative for humankind, especially our world leaders, to come to understand how the fear of death impacts individuals and institutions. We need to develop a new perspective on the underlying causes of prejudice, racism, and war, because it offers hope for the future. In contrast, the deterministic assumption that "war is inevitable" may well prove a self-fulfilling prophecy.

PHILOSOPHICAL VIEWS BASED ON SEPARATION THEORY

As I have traveled around the world, I have seen people everywhere walking the streets, driving their cars, sailing their ships, flying around the globe, buying and selling, eating and sleeping, making love and making war. But what kind of animal is man, what moves him, what defines him? Writers, psychologists and philosophers have described man as an animal, different from all other species in that he has the ability to conceptualize, to deal in abstract symbols and is truly self-conscious.

But what is the essence of human experience? What is your experience of life? What is mine? Each of our lives is a variety of perceptions and feelings flowing through us, mixed with our personal motivations and our ways of coping. If any aspect of our feelings are damaged or shut down, we are deprived of a huge amount of what is alive or unique. If we cut off our emotions or actions that are free, spontaneous or non-conforming, actions that differ from either submission or defiance, but are ways of asserting our individuality, we are losing important aspects of ourselves.

Each of us has a basic conflict centering on the choice between contending with or avoiding painful existential realities. We are all presented with an essential paradox and face a no-win situation: If we give up our defenses and fully live our lives, we are immediately struck with the magnitude of the potential loss we face through death; if, on the other hand, we shrink from life and fail to develop our unique potentialities, we are plagued with regret and existential guilt for a life not really lived. Denial leads to more problems than it's worth. As I stated earlier, we cannot deny existential realities and cut off emotional pain and anxiety without losing real feeling for ourselves and others. Most important, we cannot be innocently defended. Our defenses hurt others, especially those closest to us, our mates and our children.

Faced with the tragic elements of human existence—poverty, crime, terrorism, war, illness and eventual dying as well as the interpersonal distress we often experience in our closest relationships, how can we live a constructive life? The answer is that we could choose to stay close to our feelings rather than seek comfort and avoid pain. We could appreciate the mystery of life and death without resorting to illusions and false resolutions, deadening pain-killers and other defense mechanisms. We could pursue goals that transcend the narrow focus of our own lives and relate to others with compassion and empathy because people everywhere face the same destiny. We could lead an honest, *feelingful* existence that would do justice to our real selves and those people close to us.

An awareness of our finite existence makes life all the more precious. My philosophical position is to value every aspect of real experience, however painful or temporal. People who have the courage to face up to issues of death and dying are more capable of experiencing both the pain and joy of living. They are unlikely to infringe on the rights of others because they have a sense that all human beings are fragile, that being alive is an incredible gift, and that we are all in the same boat. Death, the great leveler, also puts our everyday pain in perspective. Differentiating, developing compassion for ourselves and others, and moving away from the defensive denial of death offer a potential for personal freedom and a meaningful existence.

Notes

1. In his paper, "Life Fear and Death Fear," Otto Rank (1972) proposed, "primary fear corresponds to a fear of separation from the whole, therefore a fear of individuation, on account of which I should like to call it fear of life, although it may appear later as fear of the loss of this dearly bought individuality, as fear of death, of being dissolved again into the whole. Between these two fear possibilities, these poles of fear, the individual is thrown back and forth all his life" (p. 123).

2. Some researchers have proposed that children develop an awareness of their personal mortality at some point between ages 3 and 7, or even earlier (Hoffman & Strauss, 1985; Rochlin, 1967; Speece & Brent, 1984). Kastenbaum (2000) noted one example where this more complete understanding appeared to occur in a 16 month-old toddler.

Chapter 3

PRIMARY AND SECONDARY DEFENSES— THE FANTASY BOND AND THE VOICE

No one ever becomes completely emancipated from the state of infantile dependence . . . and there is no one who has completely escaped the necessity of incorporating his early objects.

~ W.R.D. Fairbairn (1952, p. 56)

The fantasy bond, the primary defense, is an attempt to cope with and relieve emotional pain, separation anxiety, and death fears. The capacity of human beings to imagine and symbolize is, at once, a strength and a weakness. The ability to produce an image of oneself merged with another in fantasy, as well as the capacity to partially gratify oneself with such images, is functional as a defense in the face of early environmental deficiencies. However, as with any defense, the continued reliance on fantasy processes as a substitute for reality and as a replacement for seeking gratification in the external environment sets the stage for psychological disturbance.

My use of the word "bond" stands in contrast to the positive emotional bonding that occurs when families are loving, respectful or nurturing. Instead, it describes a form of bondage or connection that offers comfort and a sense of security, but at the same time restricts one's life (R. Firestone, 1984; 1985).

The voice functions as a secondary defense that supports the fantasy bond and the self-parenting, inward behavior patterns that accompany it. It is a form of intrapsychic communication that ranges from minor self-criticisms to major self-attacks, and fosters self-soothing habit patterns, isolation, and a self-destructive lifestyle. The voice represents the introjection of destructive thoughts and attitudes and is also based on identification with the negative attitudes and defenses of one's parents.

THE PRIMARY DEFENSE – THE FANTASY BOND

The concept of the fantasy bond is the basic tenet of my theoretical approach. Faced with emotional trauma, the baby and later the child handle the crisis by relying on fantasy processes to suppress the primal pain. Every child needs protection, love and affection from adults who ideally possess both the desire and ability to provide the satisfaction of the child's basic needs. In instances when a parent is misattuned or emotionally absent, when parental love is missing, the infant suffers heightened anxiety states that can, at times, feel life threatening.

To cope with this overwhelming feeling, babies attempt to deny the reality of their suffering, build fantasies of omnipotence, rely heavily on repression, and imagine that they have a permanent connection to their all-powerful mother and are at one with her.

The original fantasy bond is extended to couple relationships. When romantic relationships deteriorate, its members compensate for the decline in feeling for one another by forming a fantasy of love. In couples therapy, one or another member of a couple at war with each other will run down, criticize and denigrate his/her partner, yet he/she stubbornly maintains the point of view that they love each other. It was hard for me to see the love in those hostile situations.

Later the illusion of merged identity is extended from the parent or family to one's neighborhood, city, nation, a political cause, a philosophy, or a set of religious beliefs. This process supports the "in" group at the expense of the "out" group, pseudo-independent attitudes, superiority feelings towards outsiders and animosity and hatred toward people with different beliefs. At its worst, the fantasy bond, and the polarization that it awakens, play a significant role in prejudice, ethnic strife, genocide and warfare.

Origins of the Fantasy Bond: A Developmental Perspective

As noted, each person experiences varying degrees of emotional pain in his/her earliest relationships. Even in ideal families, there is inevitable frustration, and most family situations are less than ideal (Beavers & Hampson, 1990; Tedeschi & Felson 1994). When they are hurt, children incorporate parental figures into their personalities as internalized objects that serve to comfort them. This imagined fusion is highly effective as a defense because, as noted, a human being's capacity for imagination provides partial gratification of needs and reduces tension (Silverman, Lachmann, & Milich, 1982) (Note 1; Note 2).

In order for a fantasy bond to be formed and to function effectively, four essential elements must be present. First, children idealize the mother or parental object, thereby denying the reality of any emotional abuses that were perpetrated upon them. Second, children internalize negative attitudes that were directed towards them by their parents, basically accepting the fact that they themselves are bad or unlovable. Third, parents' actual emotional mistreatment and abusive characteristics are projected onto the world at large, creating suspicion and fear of other individuals, as well as a general discomfort in life. Lastly, through the process of identification, the child incorporates certain negative traits, personality characteristics and values of the parent as his own.

Once the primary defense is formed and soothing fantasy processes are in place, individuals are reluctant to relinquish the comfort and safety they offer. Once hurt, people are afraid to become vulnerable again. Challenging the fantasy bond predisposes experiencing considerable anxiety. When faced with the choice of relinquishing defenses or hurting another person, there is usually no contest. Maintaining one's defensive posture, whether conscious or unconscious, is almost always the choice.

The paradox is that, as vulnerable children, people need defenses to survive psychologically, yet these same defenses lead to emotional suffering, maladaptive responses, and alienation in their adult lives. It is a destructive legacy that is handed down through generations of family life.

In summary, the primary defense or fantasy bond originates in early childhood to fill a gap where there is environmental deprivation; it "nourishes" the self, but unfortunately, it becomes the motivating force behind subsequent self-limiting, self-destructive behavior. To deal with frustration and pain, all people depend to varying degrees on internal gratification from an imagined connection with the introjected parent.

The Self-Parenting Process

The fantasy bond is essentially a way of parenting oneself internally through fantasies of fusion. The imagined merger with one's parent is reinforced through the use of self-nourishing habit patterns as well as self-punishing attitudes and behaviors. Self-nourishing behaviors begin with thumb-sucking, compulsively fingering or holding onto a blanket, or stroking oneself, and can develop into eating disorders, alcoholism, drug abuse, excessive masturbation, routine or compulsive activities that reduce pain, and/or an impersonal, repetitive style of sexual relating. These behaviors tend to support an illusion of pseudo-independence in the child, a feeling of being able to completely gratify oneself and needing nothing from the outside world. Self-critical thoughts, guilt reactions, attacks on self, and self-limiting, self-destructive actions are examples of the self-punishing component.

The child experiences this false sense of self-sufficiency because he/she has introjected an image of the "good and powerful" parent into the self. At the same time, unfortunately, the child must also incorporate the parent's covertly or overtly rejecting attitudes toward him/her. These incorporated parental attitudes form the basis of the child's negative self-concept. In this way, children develop an illusion of being at once the good, strong parent and the bad, weak child and tend to conceptualize themselves as a complete, self-sufficient system.

Although the self-parenting process allays the anxiety of feeling separate and alone and helps stave off feelings of emotional starvation and emptiness, it creates numerous distortions, e.g., the idealization of the parents at the child's own expense. As noted, children must conceptualize themselves as bad or unlovable to protect themselves against the awareness that their parents are inadequate, rejecting, or destructive. The recognition of real faults in the parents would break the imagined connection and feeling of self-sufficiency, which they have come to depend upon.

As I have mentioned, the extent to which people eventually come to rely on fantasized connections and addictive behaviors is determined by the degree of frustration, pain, and emotional deprivation they experienced early in life. For children who are seriously deprived, the self-parenting process eventually becomes addictive in itself. Children and adults have at their disposal an immediately rewarding method of escaping circumstances that are anxiety provoking. They often come to prefer self-gratifying habit patterns and fantasy over deep feeling and associations with others.

These self-parenting behaviors eventually become part of an addictive process that persists into adult life. For example, parents' efforts to relieve distress in their offspring can deprive children of even the minimal frustration experiences needed for normal development and teach them self-soothing, self-nurturing habit patterns that may limit them as fully functioning adults. Later as adults, they tend to regulate and parent themselves in essentially the same ways that they were by their parents. They may develop rationalizations for avoiding close associations or pursuing goals that would bring them real satisfaction or they may become cynical about other people or relationships in general.

The Mother-Daughter Bond

The mother-daughter bond is the strongest example of a fantasy bond. When there are deficiencies in the mother's ability to adequately provide for her offspring, children attempt to merge with the mother for security. Besides other phenomena, the daughter models herself closely with the mother's personality characteristics. Later, she finds it very difficult to break away from these qualities even when they are negative and dysfunctional. She comes to resent and hate these traits and to even hate her mother; but she still takes them on as her own, and ultimately comes to hate herself.

In our culture, the role of the mother as the primary caretaker during the child's earliest years has important implications. She exerts a powerful influence on the family, especially on the daughter, where the identification is the strongest. When the mother is immature, inadequate or dysfunctional, the fantasy bond that develops between her and her daughter can become the most destructive influence in a woman's adult life. According to Hendrika Freud (2011), "Generally speaking, the bond between mothers and daughters facilitates passing on emotional health as well as pathology to the next generation via the female line" (p. 66). Unfortunately, the negative aspects of the daughter's bond with her mother may outweigh any positive maternal influence and contribute to maladaptation in the daughter's adult life (Fenchel, 1998; Welldon, 1988; 2011).

To the extent that a woman has failed to emancipate herself from the imagined connection with her mother, she will be unable to adequately meet her daughter's needs. The destructive mother-daughter bond that is formed as a compensation for deficient mothering imposes profound limitations on each woman's sense of self, on her sexuality, and on her ability to love and be loved.

In summary, I have described and explained the effect of the fantasy bond on child development in general and the specific effect on the mother-daughter relationship.

The fantasy bond is a maladaptive solution that occurs not only in disturbed individuals but also, to a lesser degree, in "normal" people. The psychodynamics of the fantasy bond in couple relationships is described in Chapter 9.

THE SECONDARY DEFENSE: THE CRITICAL INNER VOICE

Our life is what our thoughts make it.

~ Marcus Aurelius Meditations

The critical inner voice represents a well-integrated pattern of negative thoughts that is the basis of an individual's maladaptive behavior. The voice is not an actual hallucination but rather an identifiable system of thoughts (Note 3).

It is an overlay on the personality that is not natural or harmonious, but learned or imposed from without. Its statements against the self are generally harsh or judgmental. The voice process tends to increase one's self-hatred rather than motivating one to alter behavior in a constructive fashion. Indeed, it excludes those thought processes generally concerned with values or ideals, as well as those involved in creative thinking, constructive planning, and realistic self-appraisal.

In supporting the fantasy bond, the voice functions to tie individuals to their parents in the sense that, even though physically separate or geographically distant from the family, adults still possess an internal parent that directs, criticizes, and punishes them. These voices, albeit unpleasant, serve to maintain the fantasy bond and shield the individual from experiencing his/her aloneness, sense of separation, and death anxiety. People are terrified of losing the internal parent represented by the voice. The irrational fear of disrupting the illusory connection or fantasy bond with the family and the dread of re-experiencing feelings of infantile frustration and a primitive sense of helplessness are at the core of resistance to change in psychotherapy and to a better life in general.

Angry voice attacks in the form of punitive statements toward self are at the core of one's self-concept and are generally reflective of a person's identity within the nuclear family. When these voice attacks are accepted as a part of the individual's identity, they tend to be acted out in a manner that is self-confirming and, therefore, logic tight.

Voices regulate a system of secondary defenses that function to protect the fantasy bond and self-parenting process. For example, voices predict rejection, espouse self-criticism, encourage negative anticipations, and promote cynical views of other people. The critical thought process regulates behavior that causes a person to feel uncomfortable with or outright rejecting of positive experiences.

Investigations of the Self-Destructive Thought Process

A woman on vacation checks into a high-rise hotel, steps onto her balcony to look at the view and, noting the height, thinks to herself: *What if you jump?* Feeling anxious, she steps back from the edge.

While driving along the freeway, Mr. X thinks: *Why don't you just close your eyes for a minute? You could just drive across the center divider! Drive off the side of the road!* He pictures a tragic accident—images that torment him and make him uneasy.

A woman prepares to give a speech and thinks: *You're going to make a fool of yourself. What if you forget everything you were going to say or act stupid?*

A man decides to call an attractive woman for a date and thinks: *Why should she go out with you? Look at you! She probably has lots of better offers.*

During sex, Mr. Y thinks: *You're not going to be able to keep your erection,* and actually begins to feel cut off from his sexual feelings.

In the last moments of life, a suicidal person thinks: *Go ahead, end it all! Just pull the trigger and it'll all be over.*

I was puzzled by this type of thinking and decided to investigate. What were the common threads underlying the attacks on self and self-destructive urges? Why, for example, did the motorist picture himself crashing into the center divider? Were his thoughts and mental images simply part of a self-protective process that was warning him of realistic dangers and potential harm? Were they just meaningless ruminations? Or did these thoughts indicate a human propensity for self-criticism, self-attack and self-hatred?

In studying the manifestations of this kind of thought process, my associates and I have found that this type of thinking is widespread and that a person's actions and general approach to life are regulated or controlled by this manner of thinking. For example, the woman in the hotel did step back from the edge, even though she disregarded the impulse to jump. And Mr. X ignored the urge to drive across the divider, but felt uneasy and depressed after having these thoughts and images. Mr. Y had difficulty sexually after running himself down as a man. We have observed that even when disregarded or contradicted, this type of thought process has negative consequences. We discovered that the pattern of negative thoughts about the self predisposed self-destructive behavior and was at the core of both microsuicidal and suicidal actions.

Psychotherapists have long been aware that people tend to think destructively, that they have many negative conceptions of themselves, and that they have a "shadow" side to their personalities (Note 4). Indeed, biblical prophets, ancient philosophers and modern day psychoanalysts have all made efforts to interpret man's dark side and to discover ways of defeating it. Goldbrunner's (1964) analysis of Carl Jung's works noted that: "Man has to undergo the fateful experience of being conscious of the dark part of the soul. This is the positive quality in neurosis, that it can lead man to knowledge of his nature" (p. 113).

Brief suicidal impulses, distracting and frequently disturbing, are familiar to many people. Internal conflict, ambivalence, contradictions and division are reflected in the symptoms of psychotherapy clients. However, many people underestimate the depth of this division within the personality, as well as the pervasiveness of humankind's tendency for self-destruction.

Discovery of the Critical Inner Voice

In my early work with schizophrenic patients and later in my office practice, I was progressing in my understanding of self-destructive thoughts and behavior, but important aspects were missing. I was excited when my associates and I came upon several new developments in the early 1970s. At that time, I was interested in the emotional pain that people experienced when they were confronted with criticism in group therapy situations. They would have defensive or angry responses to selective information and would feel down, depressed or self-attacking. Initially, I considered the old adage, "It's the truth that hurts," but then I realized that this was not the case. I noticed that when criticism from others supported or validated one's distorted view of one's self, it tended to arouse an obsessive negative thought process. It was not necessarily the truth that hurt; what mattered more was if the feedback coincided with one's own self-attacks.

From these observations, I discovered that most people judged and appraised themselves in ways that tended to be unfavorable and self-punishing. Thus, their reactions to external criticism were usually out of proportion to content, severity or manner of presentation. I thought it would be valuable for people to become aware of the specific issues about which they were the most sensitive, so I began to study this phenomenon with my associates and clients.

In 1973, I formed a therapy group comprised of a number of psychotherapists to investigate this and pool our findings. This group became the focal point for my ongoing study of the specific negative thought patterns associated with neurotic, repetitive behaviors and later with self-destructive actions and lifestyles. Our conclusions corroborated my hypotheses about the existence of a well-integrated pattern of self-attacking thoughts, which I termed the "critical inner voice". I called it the "voice" because it represented a form of internal dialogue, a type of malignant coaching as though someone was speaking to the person. These preliminary explorations led to further investigations into the mechanisms of self-attack.

Those of us in that therapists' group began studying the manifestations of this hostile thought process in our clients as well. As they verbalized their self-critical thoughts out loud, clients learned that it was not so much the adverse circumstances or events in their lives that were causing them discomfort; rather, it was their negative interpretation of those events. In these sessions, I was surprised at the ease with which people not only grasped the idea of an internal self-attacking thought process, but also with how readily they applied this idea to their everyday lives. Once they caught on to the procedure, they were able to identify the countless ways in which they habitually reproached themselves. They were shocked at the degree to which this way of running themselves down undermined their ability to function effectively and limited their satisfaction in personal relationships.

After identifying the content of these destructive thoughts, the participants in the associates' group as well as our clients began to separate these antagonistic attitudes from a more realistic view of themselves. They became more objective and, more importantly, began to understand the source of their self-attacks. This insight alone helped many individuals to become more proactive and effective in their lives.

Development of the Voice Therapy Technique

In these early investigations of self-destructive thinking, participants expressed the content of their self-attacks in a rational, cognitive manner and tone. They articulated them in the first person as "I" statements about themselves, "I am so stupid," "I am ugly," "I am mean," etc. Later, I suggested that they verbalize these same thoughts as statements spoken *to* them in the second person as "you" statements, "You're this or that" rather than "I'm this or that." People adopted this manner of voicing their thoughts after only a minimal amount of instruction.

I was astounded by the malicious tone and ferocity with which both clients and associates attacked themselves. It was surprising to observe even mild-mannered, reasonable individuals being punitive and cruel towards themselves. The dialogue technique brought these forceful emotions to the surface. With this free flow of thoughts and feelings, I became painfully aware of how angry people were at themselves, how divided they were, and how much they sabotaged themselves in their efforts to cope effectively in their daily lives.

In one of our first sessions, a 37-year-old businessman, who complained of anxiety symptoms and panic attacks, attempted to utilize the Voice Therapy technique. He had been feeling increasingly anxious and self-doubting after taking over a supervisory role in his job. His sense of discomfort had escalated to the point where he was thinking about leaving his position and shifting to a more subordinate function. I asked him to tell me what destructive things he was telling himself about his new responsibilities. At first he had difficulty. S.A. began talking in a calm voice, "I'm not the right person for this job. I don't know the first thing about directing other people and I'm afraid I'll really mess up. I just can't do it. I know I can't."

I encouraged him to say his self-attacks in the voice dialogue, as though he were talking to himself. He started off hesitantly: *You should just go back to your old job where you belong,* and then gained momentum*: Don't try to be different. Don't try to be better than you are. You know you can't really do the job. Nobody can stand to be told what to do by someone like you. What makes you think you can direct other people? You can barely manage yourself!*

As S.A. expressed these voice attacks, his tone of voice and speech patterns changed dramatically and they became more and more like a scolding parent. In fact, he sounded much like his own father. This transformation was startling, especially to the associates who knew his father. S.A. continued: *You shouldn't have taken this position. You don't deserve it. You're just a quiet creep. You shouldn't be around people at all, much less try to be boss. You drive people crazy, the way you come across.*

By this time, his body language and expression of the voice revealed a combination of rage and grief as he exploded with a torrent of emotional abuse: *You're second-class. You're worthless. You're disgusting. You're not fit to be around people, and you should really hide. Just be quiet! Shut up! Stay in the background, because when people really get to know you, you are disgusting to be with. Everything about you is disgusting.*

At this point, S.A. broke into deep sobs. When he regained his composure, he said, "I think the basis of my self-attacks are events that happened to me in my family when I was growing up. Sometimes my parents would just light into me, calling me every bad name under the sun." He then reflected, "I really started feeling a lot when I thought about how all of these attacks have affected my life. I can hardly believe that I could be so self-hating. To tell the truth, I can't imagine how I got this far in my life. I know how important it is for me to change this way of thinking for myself."

Before the experience with Voice Therapy, S.A. had had little awareness about why he was having such an adverse reaction at work. Afterward, he had a better understanding of the destructive elements in his personality and how they were affecting his job. He was alert to critical inner voices that punished him for competing. In following sessions, he became aware of critical thoughts that were making him feel guilty about surpassing his father in the business arena. His father had experienced repeated business failures throughout S.A.'s childhood. More importantly, S.A. learned that he had internalized his father's aggression toward him as a child and had come to see himself as worthless and undeserving of any success. In his job, S.A. reported a growing sense of self-confidence and a decrease in anxiety related to assuming the additional responsibilities of his new position.

What I witnessed during that early Voice Therapy session would later be duplicated many times over by others. I felt that the new methodology was a valuable discovery. People's strong destructive propensities toward self could be accessed with the new procedure, and this exposure had profound implications in terms of advancing our knowledge of human behavior (Note 5).

THEORETICAL ORIGINS OF THE VOICE

As I have explained, the origins of the voice can be traced to the overtly or covertly rejecting thoughts and attitudes of parents that have been incorporated by the young child and, thereafter, taken on as his/her own thoughts and attitudes. Many of the participants in our investigations into Voice Therapy identified the criticisms and derogatory attitudes directed toward them by their voices as statements made directly by their mothers and fathers or as attitudes indicated by their behavior. It appeared that these angry parental thoughts and attitudes were internalized at those times when the parent was the most punishing or rejecting, i.e., when the child was under the most stress.

The voice represents (1) the internalization or introjection of destructive attitudes toward a person held by parents and other significant adults in the early environment; (2) a largely unconscious imitation of one or both parents' maladaptive defenses and views about life (i.e. their attitudes concerning relationships, religious beliefs, political ideologies, etc.); and (3) a defensive approach to life based on emotional pain experienced during the formative years. The greater the degree of trauma experienced in childhood, the more intense one's voice attacks become (Note 6).

The role of the voice in perpetuating the cycle of psychological or emotional child abuse through successive generations became apparent to my associates and me over time. To whatever degree individuals have internalized their parents' hostile and punitive attitudes, they continue to hate and punish themselves and eventually their own children in much the same manner. The angry affect associated with the voice provides the impetus behind a person's compulsion to act out destructive feelings on his/her children.

DIMENSIONS OF THE VOICE

Voice attacks are sometimes experienced consciously but, more often than not, they are only partially conscious or may even be totally unconscious. In general, the average person is largely unaware of the extent of his/her self-attacks and how much of his/her behavior is influenced and even controlled by the voice. Indeed, "listening" to the voice predisposes an individual toward self-limiting behavior and negative consequences. In other words, people tend to make their behavior correspond to their self-attacks.

For example, one client, a college student with low self-esteem, was referred to me because of failing grades, procrastination and an inability to concentrate. He first attempted to determine the negative thoughts that lay behind his habitual pattern of procrastinating. In verbalizing the thoughts that occurred to him while he was studying, he discovered that, during the days leading up to each exam, he had been torturing himself with an internal dialogue that went as follows: *You're never going to be able to pass this exam. You should have dropped this course. You'll never catch up. Why bother studying? You're going to fail anyway.* In a later session, with a considerable angry affect, he verbalized a more powerful self-attack: *You don't belong in college anyway. You're stupid! You can't even learn any of this. Your brother is the smart one, not you!*

In my experience with Voice Therapy, as clients become more familiar with verbalizing their self-attacks out loud to a therapist, they are able to make connections between undesirable behavior and negative thought patterns. There was a good deal of commonality of thought content among individuals with a common cultural heritage or similar ages. For example, older clients tended to tell themselves: *You're too old to change. You've always been this way. What makes you think you can change now?*

Young people beginning to pursue a romantic relationship, had thoughts that increased their feelings of self-consciousness and undermined their self-confidence, such as: *You don't know what to do with a guy/girl. You won't be able to think of anything to say. You don't feel comfortable being affectionate.* Negative comparisons with rivals were almost universal. Many reported painful attitudes toward themselves in relation to competitors, such thoughts as: *He's smarter, better-looking, more sophisticated than you.*

During sex, many men reported telling themselves: *You're not going to be able to satisfy her, to make her feel good. You don't know how to touch her. Look at your hands—they're sweating. You're clumsy, inept. Your penis is too small.* Many women reported similar self-attacks: *You're not feeling enough. You're not going to be able to have an orgasm. He isn't attracted to you; your breasts are too small; your hips are too big.*

Both sexes experienced voices about their performance and about their bodies while making love. These increased their anxiety, decreasing their pleasure to a considerable degree. Many forms of sexual dysfunction and inhibited sexual desire appear to be related to the ascendancy of the voice process during lovemaking.

Clients using drugs or alcohol to excess were strongly influenced by voices that urged them to indulge their habit, for example: *What's wrong with taking another drink? You're under a lot of pressure, it will relax you.* When they indulged, they had other voice attacks chastising them: *You're so weak. You have no will power. You might as well give up trying.*

The voice attacks reported by these participants were typically accompanied by agitation, irritability, or depression. Those cited above are merely isolated fragments of a more complete underlying system of critical inner voices that were revealed to me.

The Critical Inner Voice Fosters Vanity

Vanity is a compensation for dormant feelings of worthlessness and self-hatred. Inner voices support this defense by building up a person with aggrandizing views of the self. When there is pressure to perform and a person begins to suffer from self-doubts, his/her vanity is likely to come into play: *You're amazing. You're great at everything you do. You deserve the best treatment.* These flattering, seemingly positive voices set the individual up for subsequent self-recriminations at the first sign of failure. They are as destructive as overtly negative voices, because they are also false and unrealistic. In building a person up, they lead to maladaptive emotional responses and behavior. In addition, vain people are unpleasant and provoking to others, causing them to be rejected or ostracized.

The Critical Inner Voice Encourages Withholding Behavior

Withholding is the mechanism that maintains the primary fantasy of self-sufficiency, the fantasy bond. By reducing the responses of both giving to, and taking from people, the child limits emotional transactions. The underlying feeling is one of not needing anything from others and especially of not wanting to give anything of oneself, out of a deep-seated fear of being drained or depleted. The individual unconsciously rejects real gratification and gives up goal-directed activities in order to hold on to the safety of a fantasy world over which he/she has complete control.

As adults, people often protect themselves against being vulnerable and defend themselves by being withholding, both toward themselves and toward those they love. They deny themselves success and gratification, and they withhold their positive loving traits from their loved ones. They restrict their capabilities and tend to retreat from leading a productive, fulfilling life. These withholding tendencies are regulated by their critical inner voices. These voices influence them to inhibit behaviors or qualities that are an expression of their personal wants, motivation or identity. This interferes with the inherent goal-directed nature of the individual and leaves them prone to failure in their personal or vocational pursuits.

For example, people have revealed self-denying voices: *You don't need to go on a vacation. Stay home tonight, you're fine by yourself.* Some have described voices warning them against being spontaneous and enthusiastic: *Don't get so excited. What's the big deal anyway? Don't make a fool of yourself.* In all of these instances, they recognized their voices as having the same derisive tone that their parents once used toward them.

In relation to their professions, people have described voices urging them to hold back their performance at work, for example with paranoid warnings that their efforts are not being recognized or appreciated by management. They reported voices such as: *Why should you do all the work, while you aren't getting any credit. No one else is working hard, why should you?*

In personal relationships, self-protective voices encourage a posture of pseudo-independence and aloofness: *Don't get too involved. Keep it casual. What do you need him/her for?* Vitality and desire are dampened or totally shut down by withholding that is regulated by these types of voices.

Negative Events that Arouse Critical Inner Voices

Illness, financial setbacks, academic failure, rejection by a loved one, loss through the death of someone close, are all stressful events that can activate critical inner voices and associated feelings of self-hatred.

Failure: Academic and vocational failures are often precipitating factors of self-attacks. People who experienced failures or other setbacks in their professional careers reported voices telling them: *You're a total failure! You'll never get anywhere in life. You always mess up. You might just as well give up.* Over time, this kind of thought process can lead to serious states of depression. It appears that individuals who are perfectionistic and have voices driving them to maintain high levels of performance are exceptionally susceptible to this form of self-attack (Blatt, 1995) (Note 7).

Illness: Poor health tends to activate voice attacks about one's body. Perceived bodily weaknesses and deterioration in physical fitness are often the target of self-deprecating thoughts. Even people in good health, facing their yearly physical checkups, may torment themselves with hypochondrical predictions: *The doctor is going to find something terrible this time. It's going to be bad news. You might have cancer.* Depression and irritability accompany ill health and can be intensified or directly caused by critical inner voices such as: *You're always sick. Nobody wants to be around a sick person like you.* Health concerns can also trigger morbid ruminations about death, thereby increasing one's feelings of despair and futility about life: *This is the beginning of the end for you. Whatever this is, it's probably fatal.*

Rejection: It is difficult to remain objective in one's self-appraisal and maintain a good attitude when one is being rejected. This is partly because rejection arouses memories of early childhood wounds, which left the person feeling fundamentally unlovable and bad. Thus, people tend to interpret rejection as concrete evidence that they are undeserving of love. Their critical inner voices accuse them of being inferior, boring, sexually unattractive, and afflicted by myriad other negative qualities.

Rejection and subsequent feelings of worthlessness turn people against themselves, even when these self-critical thoughts are unrealistic and contradict objective analysis of the situation. But even when critical thoughts have some basis in fact, they still do not justify the demeaning, hostile attitude that is being expressed. Instead, it is appropriate to adopt a compassionate view toward oneself and make appropriate changes when one can.

In addition, personal interactions with someone who is critical or insensitive often catalyze a person's self-attacks. Having contact with people who are judgmental, condescending or evaluative can be damaging psychologically because they tend to support one's own negative, judgmental view of self. Having one's motives misunderstood or actions misconstrued by paranoid individuals also tends to validate one's voice. Thus, these types of people have a toxic effect. It is particularly difficult to maintain an objective, friendly view toward yourself when someone close holds a negative view of you.

Positive Events that Arouse Voice Attacks

Voices Following an Achievement: As I have mentioned, people often feel anxious or nervous when they receive acknowledgment for an unusual success. Many individuals have reported that following such events, they have behaved in ways that undermined their accomplishments. They traced their self-defeating actions to voices that sabotaged their success by undermining their confidence or making them self-conscious or guilty. Following a well-received performance, a singer reported having voices that told her: *You're going to screw up the next one. You're going to be off-key. You're going to forget the lyrics.* A new teacher, who was commended by the principal, spoke of voices warning: *Wait until next year; you won't be able to control your class. You won't earn the respect of your students. You won't be able to hold their interest.*

Voices Following Success in Personal Relationships: Both men and women reported a deterioration in their personal relationships following periods of unusual intimacy and tenderness. These events precipitated a barrage of critical voices, some self-critical and others critical of their partner. One woman reported having voices that told her: *What's so special about him? Are you really satisfied with him?* One man's voices were: *"You're investing too much in her. Be careful.* These attacks usually result in people pulling away from their partner and holding back special traits and behaviors that are valued by the other.

THE DUAL FOCUS OF THE VOICE

The voice not only serves the function of attacking the self; it is also directed toward others. Just as individuals have a split view of themselves, they also possess diametrically opposed views of the people in their lives. Both oppositional viewpoints—toward self and toward others—are symptomatic of the deep division that exists within everyone. At times, people view their loved ones with compassion and affection, while at other times they think of them in cynical or disparaging terms.

Generally, negative views of others tend to correlate with self-depreciating attitudes. In their everyday lives, people typically vacillate between castigating themselves for failures and blaming someone else. Critical, judgmental views of others are inextricably tied to self-attacks. Indeed, a preponderance of angry thoughts about significant relationships indicates the ascendancy of the voice process.

In Voice Therapy sessions, clients often alternated between expressing self-attacks and verbalizing harsh or suspicious attitudes toward others. Examples of these are: *He has no genuine caring feelings for you. He's not interested in making a real commitment. He's losing interest in you. No wonder — you have nothing to offer a man like him. You've never been able to keep a man's interest before; what makes you think this relationship will be any different?*

She said she really loves you? Well, don't believe her. She's erratic, two-faced.

She's a loser. You're in love with her? That's because you're not good enough for anyone better.

In my practice, I observed that voice attacks on the self and on one's partner often predicted rejection at various stages in the relationship. The dual nature of these attacks serves to alienate one from close associations and often leads to the very rejection that the voices are predicting (Note 8).

Sexism and stereotypic attitudes are extensions of this type of hostile thinking and are frequently expressed in voice attacks. For example, some negative attitudes that women have toward men are: *All men want is sex. They don't want love, marriage, or a family. They're uncommunicative. They don't want to be vulnerable to a woman.* Some cynical views that men have about women are: *They're overemotional, impractical, and childish.* These negative, stereotypic attitudes and the voices that support them have a detrimental effect on couple relationships.

In individuals who tend to distort or view other people with suspicion, voice attacks directed toward others are more pronounced than self-attacks. These individuals exhibit a basic paranoid or victimized attitude toward life. On the other hand, self-attacks are more predominant in people who base their behavior primarily on their low opinions of themselves than on their hostile views of others. These individuals more often display symptoms of depression (Note 9). Thus, the voice plays a major role in precipitating and maintaining a wide range of maladaptive behaviors, including self-defeating, self-destructive actions as well as aggressive and violent behavior toward others.

CONCLUSION

In this chapter, I defined and elaborated my understanding of the fantasy bond as a primary defense against emotional trauma. I explained that at the same time it offers comfort, it adversely affects personal relationships. I described how the extension of the fantasy bond to one's identification with one's neighborhood, city, country, religious beliefs etc. leads to a sense of security but also contributes to a destructive form of polarization against outsiders.

To varying degrees, we each depend on fantasy processes and live with a covertly destructive point of view that has a profoundly negative effect on our personality and our overall adjustment in life. Unfortunately, we are largely unaware of being divided or set against ourselves. We are only partially conscious that we possess a hostile, self-denying, and self-attacking aspect of self and therefore continue to be restricted and controlled by its influences.

I developed the techniques of Voice Therapy for the purpose of helping people access and identify the contents of these largely unconscious thought processes. My associates and I discovered that when individuals learned to express their self-critical thoughts in the second person format, powerful emotions were aroused and previously suppressed thoughts, feelings, and memories came to light. The intensity of self-hatred and anger toward self that emerged during these sessions indicated the depth and pervasiveness of this self-destructive process.

Voice Therapy differs from other cognitive-behavioral models in its emphasis on emotion and on the expression of deep feelings. The rationale underlying Voice Therapy is that when clients expose their negative thoughts and accompanying affect, form insight into their sources and gradually modify behavior toward their stated goals in juxtaposition to the dictates of the voice, people are then able to free themselves from its destructive influences. This process involves breaking away from restrictive defenses and maladaptive responses and moving toward self-sufficiency and autonomy.

Notes

1. Regarding illusions of fusion, see Helmuth Kaiser's (1955) concept of a delusion of fusion as the universal symptom in neurosis, which is analogous to my concept of a fantasy bond as the core defense. For other perspectives on Helmuth Kaiser's psychotherapeutic approach, see Hans Welling (2000); see also David Shapiro (2000).

2. "The imagined fusion with the parent is highly effective ...." See research conducted by Keys, Brozek, Henschel, Mickelsen, and Taylor (1950) during World War II demonstrated that fantasy can be rewarding under conditions of physical deprivation. In an experiment, participants whose food intake was restricted to the minimum sustenance level reported that their physical hunger was partly relieved by fantasizing about food.

   Also see continuing research investigating Silverman, Lachmann, and Milich's (1982) experimental studies in where subjects were presented with the subliminal message "Mommy and I are One" on the tachistoscope. Also see Lachmann and Beebe (1989); P. Siegel and Weinberger (1998); Sohlberg, Birgegard, Czartorski, Overfelt and Strombom (2000); and Sohlberg and Jansson (2002).

3. The hallucinated voices experienced by schizophrenic patients have a parental quality that is very similar to the judgmental character of the less disturbed individual's self-critical thoughts. However, the extent to which the process of depersonalization has taken place is far greater in the schizophrenic patient. Psychotic patients, in believing that others hate them and accuse them, also imagine that they hear voices degrading them, ordering them to perform strange or self-destructive acts. Often it may be ascertained from these patients that the voices remind them of parental orders or reprimands.

   Neuroscientists Fletcher & Firth (2009) have attempted to identify regions of the brain that are activated during auditory hallucinations, as in the psychoses, which can be distinguished from those that are activated during internal dialogue. See also Debbane et al., (2016).

4. Several theorists and therapists have described various aspects of an internal negative thought process, including Aaron Beck (1976), Albert Ellis and Robert Harper (1975), and Gershen Kaufman (1993), among others. Beck's descriptions of automatic thoughts closely correspond to our observations of the hostile thought patterns elicited through the procedures of Voice Therapy. For example, Beck (1976) observed that "The patient reacts to his own onslaughts as if they were directed at him by another person: he feels hurt, sad, humiliated" (p. 115). Also see Seymour Epstein (2003).

5. See "A Review of Client Self-Criticism in Psychotherapy" by Kannan and Levitt (2013) in *Journal of Psychotherapy Integration, 23*(2), 166-178, for a descriptive account and evaluation of the concept of the 'voice' and Voice Therapy methodology.

6. Two important psychological processes, identification and introjection, which are critical in terms of the child's development, are also responsible for the inclusion of a systematized "parental" point of view within the self. Neurologists Lewis and Todd (2004) suggested that in punitive, stressful situations, the child may shift his or her attention in a way that facilitates the incorporation of the parents' point of view.

7. Maladaptive perfectionism and its correlation with suicide and depression have been investigated by numerous clinicians and researchers, notably Sidney Blatt (1995).

8. The voice is a dynamic representation of what attachment theorists refer to as "internal working models (IWMs)." Internal working models are based on children's experiences with primary caregivers. They are made up of expectations regarding the availability and reliability of new attachment figures. In describing the development of insecure attachment patterns between parent and infant, Bowlby (1980) explained that, in many of these cases, the associated cognitive working model may become 'defensively excluded' from the infant's awareness. In her work, Bretherton (1996) noted that "insecure individuals develop working models of self and attachment figure in which some schema or schema networks [cognitive processes] may be dissociated from others" (p. 14). These defensively excluded negative working models (critical voices about the self and others) can be triggered by a wide range of circumstances in a new relationship.

Based on findings from brain-imaging studies that examined neural correlates of internal working models, Schore (2000) proposed, "The right brain contains the 'cerebral representation of one's own past' and the substrate of affectively laden autobiographical memory.... These findings suggest that early-forming internal working models of the attachment relationship are processed and stored in implicit-procedural memory systems in the right cortex, the hemisphere dominant for implicit learning" (p. 32). Fonagy and Target (2005) have also suggested, "If the attachment relationship is indeed a major organizer of brain development, it is even more important to understand the processes that underpin the trans-generational transmission of attachment patterns" (p. 333). The voice, as described in this chapter, can be hypothesized to be one of the processes referred to by Fonagy and Target (2005).

9. In *Cognitive therapy for delusions, voices and paranoia*, Chadwick, Birchwood, and Trower (1996) described one form of paranoia and its underlying thoughts or beliefs systems: the "poor-me" as contrasted with the "bad me" orientation. The "poor-me" position is associated with critical inner voices that foster victimized feelings as well as vanity and narcissism.

Sources: *The Fantasy Bond: Structure of Psychological Defenses* (1985); *Voice Therapy: A Psychotherapeutic Approach to Self-Destructive Behavior* (1988), *Combating Destructive Thought Processes: Separation Theory and Voice Therapy* (1997a) and *Conquer Your Critical Inner Voice* (2002)

Chapter 4

THE VOICE AND THE DUAL NATURE OF GUILT REACTIONS

The unconscious force which drives people to deny themselves enjoyment and success, to spoil their chances in life or not to make use of them, may be more accurately defined as the need for punishment. . . .

The origin and the essential features of moral masochism are strange indeed, but anyone can perceive a faint echo in himself if he listens to the melody. We are surprised that the feeling of guilt or the corresponding wish to be punished can remain completely unconscious.

Unconsciously . . . people inflict punishments on themselves to which an inner court has sentenced them. A hidden authority within the ego takes over the judgment originally expected of the parents.

~ Theodore Reik (1941, p. 10-11)

There are two distinguishable forms of guilt that create a basic conflict in each individual, which I refer to as neurotic guilt and existential guilt.

They can be conceptualized as follows: neurotic guilt pertains to feelings of remorse or self-attack for seeking gratification and for moving toward one's goals; existential or ontological guilt is triggered by holding back or withholding one's natural inclinations.

A concept that is frequently confused with guilt is shame. Although both cause people to become self-denying, self-defeating, self-destructive, and, at times, suicidal, there are a number of distinctions to be made between the two. Shame is associated with early phases of development in which the child assimilates a basic feeling of being dirty, bad or unlovable, whereas guilt is associated with learned prohibitions and often follows some form of action on the part of the individual. Many individuals who experience shame feel that there is something basically awful, despicable, or contaminated about their very nature, something that can't be changed or fixed. According to Freud, shame is more connected to the oral and anal phase of development, whereas guilt applies more to the Oedipal stage (S. Freud, 1962/1896; 1957/1914; 1961/1923) (Note 1).

In this chapter, I focus on the two kinds of guilt when describing the conflict between moving away from infantile dependency sources to embrace life versus retreating from personal goal-directed activity into passivity, symbiosis, and fantasy processes. Both forms of guilt refer to a process of self-limitation and self-hatred internalized during early childhood in the form of self-critical thoughts or voices. In a certain sense, each individual is suspended between these polarities of guilt, and they form the boundaries of his/her life experience.

Neurotic guilt is related to emotional deprivation, parental prohibitions, and faulty training procedures in childhood. People come to characterize themselves as selfish for pursuing their independent and personal desires in life. Ernest Becker (1964) defined neurotic guilt as "the action-bind that reaches out of the past to limit new experiences, to block the possibility of broader choices" (p. 186). He attributed the cause of this constriction of life to the "early indoctrination" of the child. Freud (1961/1923) was confounded by the punitive aspects of this unconscious guilt reaction, "How is it that the super-ego manifests itself essentially as a sense of guilt (or criticism) and moreover develops such extraordinary harshness and severity towards the ego?" (p. 53). Both Becker and Freud perceived neurotic guilt as preventing an individual from achieving satisfaction or fulfillment in life, as well as interfering with progress in psychotherapy.

My viewpoint concerning neurotic guilt is similar to their formulations. This type of guilt reaction often arises when a person chooses self-actualization. If we go against our inhibitions and spontaneously embrace life, we have to deal with the fear and guilt aroused by our affirmation of individuality and personal power. We experience anxiety from having separated ourselves from our parents' and family members' attitudes, belief systems and habit patterns and are vulnerable to guilt for being different from or surpassing our parents and peers.

Existential guilt is generally experienced by individuals when they turn their backs on their goals, retreat from life, or seek gratification in fantasy. When we withdraw from life and fail to develop our unique potentialities, we are plagued with regret for a life not truly lived, a fundamental guilt for denying life and foregoing the project of becoming an authentic self. Irvin Yalom (1980) has described existential guilt in terms of responsibility: "Most simply put: one is guilty not only through transgressions against another or against some moral or social code, *but one may be guilty of transgression against oneself*" (p. 277).

Yalom (1980) has also suggested that "existential guilt is a positive constructive force, a guide calling oneself back to oneself" (p. 280). For example, a colleague recently described a powerful "wake-up call" he experienced several years ago, when he was at the point of death from an aggressive form of cancer, which had failed to respond to chemotherapy:

> When I was at the point of really dying, I could sense that where I was was a very profound moment. I was really struggling with "What do I want to do?" Coming back (to life) is going to be painful, is going to be extraordinarily painful. I lost 60 pounds in a month, I was full of drugs, I was in pain all the time, I couldn't think, and they wanted to do more treatments.
>
> I had mostly lost the fear of death itself, and I had the sense that death was really sucking at me, pulling at me. If I wanted to, I could just tell them to turn the switch off and die. But that's not the most important part.
>
> It was at this point that I had this overwhelming sense of regret. And the regret was that I hadn't lived my life. I let other people dictate it. Then I could feel myself! My self came up in a way that brought out

a shrill, angry 'F**k you' to the world. I was saying this for hours, (in my head). "Goddammit, I'm going to live *my* life! Nobody is going to stop me." It was at that point that something changed, that somehow I felt that there was meaning and value in my life.

Yalom (1980) noted that the failure to acknowledge one's existential guilt or regret about not living one's own life inevitably leads to confusion, despair, and alienation such that Joseph K. experienced in Kafka's (1969) novel, *The Trial*. Constricted by neurotic guilt, leading a banal existence, yet stubbornly unaware of his acts of omission, Joseph K. was symbolically imprisoned within the narrow boundaries defined by neurotic guilt and existential guilt (Note 2).

Abraham Maslow (1968) has pointed out the sense of self-loathing one experiences when one moves toward security and stasis rather than toward striving for personal growth or self-actualization:

> If this essential core of the person is denied or suppressed, he gets sick sometimes in obvious ways, sometimes in subtle ways. . . . Every falling away . . . [from our core], every crime against one's own nature . . . *records itself* in our unconscious and makes us despise ourselves (pp. 4-5).

THE RELATIONSHIP OF GUILT TO SEPARATION

Guilt feelings and fear arise when a person moves away from the parents and parental substitutes. Yet there is also guilt if people fail to differentiate themselves from the fantasy bond with their families and fail to maintain a distinct identity. This inevitably leads to regressive behavior that sets up a recurring pattern of guilt reactions.

R.D. Laing (1971) portrayed the dualistic nature of guilt in his descriptive account of couples who collude with each other to maintain a destructive fantasy bond in their relationship:

> The one person does not use the other merely as a hook to hang projections on. He strives to find in the other, or to induce the other to become, the very *embodiment* of projection. The other person's collusion is required to 'complement' the identity self feels impelled to sustain. One can experience a peculiar form of guilt, specific, I think, to this disjunction.

If one refuses collusion, one feels guilt for not being or not becoming the embodiment of the complement demanded by the other for his identity. However if one does succumb, if one is seduced, one becomes estranged from one's self and is guilty thereby of self-betrayal (p. 111).

Laing (1971), in effect, is describing both types of guilt: the guilty feelings aroused when one separates from a fantasy bond and, by contrast, the existential guilt that arises when a person surrenders his individuality for the security connection. Being original, nonconformist, separate, and independent creates anxiety and guilt. This can lead to regressive behavior and increased dependency. On the other hand, submitting to the attachment, remaining fused or linked to the family and later to one's mate for imagined safety also generates feelings of existential guilt and self-castigation.

Otto Rank (1972) was well aware of the contradictory sources of guilt and its dualistic structure. My understanding of the role that neurotic guilt plays in causing a constriction of life-affirming activities is in accord with Rank's thinking. In his essay, "Separation and Guilt," Rank (1972) writes:

The problem of the neurosis itself is a separation problem and as such a blocking of the human life principle, the conscious ability to endure release and separation, first from the biological power represented by parents, and *finally from the lived out parts of the self which this power represents,* [italics added] and which obstruct the development of the individual personality.

It is at this point that the neurotic comes to grief, where, instead of living, of overcoming the past and living in the present, he becomes conscious that he dare not, he cannot, loose himself because he is bound by guilt (pp. 73-74).

This transcendental quality has mutual benefits: The parent "continues on" through the sameness of his/her progeny, and the child remains "protected" by never relinquishing the parents to become an autonomous individual. However, the illusory merger is costly; the person is often too guilty to "loose oneself" from his/her bonds.

When children differentiate and move away from the family, they often experience considerable guilt in relation to the pain and anxiety that they believe they may be causing their parents. To avoid this, they tend to cling to the fantasy bond with their parents by maintaining a sameness with them rather than "living out the parts" of themselves that would cause them to stand out from family patterns and traditions.

In other writings, I have referred to the guilt and anger associated with separation experiences:

Each successive stage of maturity confronts the child and later, the adult, with the basic facts of personal existence—aloneness and separateness, as well as the vulnerability to death. . . . Each phase is also marked by guilt at leaving the mother [parents] behind, and by anger and resentment at having to face the world alone (R. Firestone, 1985; pp. 173-174).

As noted earlier, bonds or fantasies of connection between parents and children are powerful agents of security, often far more significant than the realistic security of the actual relationship. Breaking a bond is analogous to letting the other person die because an individual has difficulty maintaining the illusory connection without the cooperation of the other. Independence and individuation disrupt the fantasy bond with one's parents and arouses one's guilt and anxiety.

Many parents experience distress at their child's growing freedom and independence and openly indicate their displeasure. The child senses the parents' pain or grief over the anticipated loss and responds by feeling guilty. If the parents are immature and dependent, these feelings are even more exaggerated, and the child comes to feel that movement toward adulthood and his/her own goals is mean or destructive. Threats of desertion or rejection as well as subtle or direct threats of parental illness or an emotional breakdown occur in families more often than is commonly thought (Bowlby, 1973).

For example, one mother routinely manipulated her family through a hypochondriacal focus on her chronic ailments. On the evening before her 18-year-old son was to embark on a trip across country that she opposed, she developed chest pains. Her husband prevailed upon his son to cancel his trip for fear of it making her condition worse. Out of a deep sense of guilt, he did cancel his trip. The repeated use of this type of manipulation significantly affected the young man's approach to life. His guilt generalized to other situations, causing him to be fearful and nonassertive. It played a part in the formation of his basic character defenses of self-denial and passivity.

SELF-HATRED AND GUILT

There is a strong relationship between feelings of guilt and one's feeling of self-hatred. Theodore Rubin was well aware of the major importance of guilt in man's propensity for self-destruction. In his book, *Compassion and Self-Hate*, Rubin (1975) writes with an acute sensitivity of the methods that people use to destroy themselves.

> We "murder" ourselves when we invoke self-hating devices and when we annihilate our potential for enjoying life's realistic good offerings. . . . The victim rationalizes . . . guilt as a high sense of responsibility and morality . . . [But guilt has] a depleting, fatiguing, constricting effect and is ultimately destructive to self-esteem and to one's actual person. (pp. 72-73)

In a similar vein, I have described the mechanism of the voice in maintaining guilt reactions in the individual:

> Withholding and self-denial are regulated by destructive thought processes. The effect of chronic patterns of withholding is an ultimate shutting down, a paralysis, of that part of the individual that strives for emotional health and growth—the part that contributes to feelings of self-esteem (R. Firestone, 1985, pp. 153-154).

Clinicians are familiar with the neurotic guilt reactions clients experience when they attempt to overcome inhibitions of the past and actively pursue a more fulfilling life. Therapists understand the relationship of this form of guilt to early parental training and prohibitions. Similarly, they also recognize that many clients feel a sense of guilt when they indulge in self-nourishing habits, e.g. overeating, excessive drinking, masturbating, smoking, or drug abuse.

Less is understood about the existential guilt aroused by surrendering one's independent point of view and submitting to sameness and conformity. It is hard to conceptualize the full extent to which people feel guilty when they retreat from life and act out a self-destructive, self-limiting process. In fact, a person's most stubborn or oppositional behavior centers on this form of guilt. Individuals go to great lengths to cover up or hide their propensity for self-destruction. People in therapy are often the most defensive, disagreeable, and hostile toward the therapist when they are defending or attempting to cover up their self-denial and self-destructiveness. These urges are humiliating and shameful facets of the personality.

THE VOICE AND NEUROTIC GUILT

When parents are unable to sensitively care for and love their children because of their own inadequacies or dependency needs, children come to feel guilty for expressing or even having natural wants and needs. As adults, they rationalize their habit of rationing or limiting themselves in an ever-widening range of situations and, as a result, become increasingly alienated from themselves as vital, feeling human beings.

Guilt About Being Alive

As described earlier, the voice represents an external point of view toward the self initially derived from the parents' overt or covert hostile feelings toward the child. If, for example, a child was unwanted or was born at an inopportune time, he/she might grow up believing that he/she is a burden to his/her parents or might entertain fantasies of having been adopted, of not really belonging to his/her family. Later, such individuals would feel undeserving, believing that they had no rights, or might, on a deeper level, feel guilty for even being alive. In this case, the voice would attack them derisively: *People don't like you.* Or, *You don't belong.* Or, *No one would choose you.*

For example, a very reticent, inward young woman had been raised in a family that she described as having been dominated by her mother's chronic alcoholism and resultant neglect of her children. Consequently, the woman was painfully shy, quiet, and extremely self-conscious. In a Voice Therapy session, she revealed a voice that directed her to be unobtrusive and to remain in the background. Afterward, she identified this voice as representing her mother's rejecting attitudes toward her:

> She felt so badly towards me as I was growing up, and I think as the result of that, that I'm quiet. I constantly act on the feeling that I'm a bother. I even thought that I felt guilty for just being around. I thought it would be interesting to say more of that feeling." *Just don't say anything! Look, leave me alone! I don't care about you. Don't ask me for*

anything! (Angrily) Stay away. I don't want you here. Stay out of my way!
(cries).

The young woman's symptoms had inhibited her natural expression and significantly constricted her life. After verbalizing her voice attacks, she answered back to them from her own point of view.

I just feel like I would say: I hate you! I hate you, you selfish bitch! You don't feel anything for me. You don't care about anyone! Go ahead and drink your life away! You selfish, immature bitch—grow up! Grow up and feel for someone besides yourself for a change! [pauses; her anger has subsided] I feel good to get angry.

Following these sessions where she verbalized her voice attacks, identified their origins, and answered back to them, she experienced a sense of relief from guilt and became more outspoken and assertive. She also reported feeling a stronger sense of identity for the first time in her life.

An associate recalled being told by his parents that he had nearly died during a long childhood illness. The boy's mother had confided to him that at one point his father had said he would kill himself if the boy died. His parents were thrilled when the boy lived; however, the weeks of constant fear had evidently taken their toll. The threat of loss had damaged their emotional attachment to their son and they became more distant from the youngster. His parents' unconscious rejection of him affirmed his sense of being "bad" for having been sick and causing his parents suffering. Later, as an adult, whenever he became ill or sensed weakness in himself, he felt guilty and bad. The feelings of self-recrimination he felt for inadvertently causing his parents grief were also extended and generalized to a guilty feeling for enjoying life. It was difficult for this man to maintain a sense of legitimacy, in spite of unusual achievement and dedication.

Guilt About Being Different from the Family

Guilt about moving in a direction that is different from or more fulfilling than one's family is often expressed by the voice in the following terms: *You always want your own way! You only think of yourself. You're so selfish! You never think about how bad you're making me feel!*

One man verbalized a series of self-attacks representing guilty reactions he had in relation to new friendships he was developing. As he talked, his voice assumed a snide, parental tone, which he identified as sounding like his father's.

What do you need these friends for? All you need is us, your family. You think you're too good for us? You never wanted to be like us. You acted like you were better than us.

The key dynamic in this case concerned the man's guilt about his movement away from his family and its problems. Achieving more financial success, developing friendships, and choosing to live life more fully than the other members of his family gave rise to a considerable amount of anxiety and led to feelings of remorse and self-reproach.

Many people suffer intense feelings of guilt about leaving others behind and succeeding where those close to them have failed, and these successes arouse strong voice attacks. Often, contact with a family member will serve as a reminder that one has stepped out of line or broken the family tradition.

A former client, who had been seriously depressed for most of her life, was, after two years of depth psychotherapy, in the process of forming closer relationships and, in general, feeling cheerful and confident. She was in an optimistic state when her sister called her on the phone. After the client told her sister about her progress and her sense of hopefulness, she asked her sister how she was feeling. Her sister responded bitterly and sarcastically with: "You want to know how I'm feeling? Well, I'll tell you how I'm feeling. I feel like killing myself!"

Tragically, the client, torn by unbearable guilt feelings about her sister's unhappiness, turned against herself and soon afterwards impulsively discontinued her sessions. Follow up indicated that she resumed the unhappy, isolated lifestyle in which she had existed prior to psychotherapy. Although this is a dramatic example of regression following renewed contact with a family member, it is not a singular or isolated phenomenon.

In reviewing the client's case material, several factors became evident. In her sessions, her feelings of deep remorse and culpability had come to light. For instance, early in therapy she had reported feeling guilty about revealing details of her family life to the therapist. In one session, she verbalized her voice as follows:

This man doesn't want to hear what you have to say. You'd better keep your mouth shut if you know what's good for you! You'd better not talk about the family!

Toward the end of therapy, she approached issues that lay at the core of her depression. In one session, she expressed the rage she had internalized early in childhood, which represented her mother's hostility toward her as well as her mother's obvious preference for her sister. The introjection of her mother's critical attitudes contributed to the client's generalized guilt reactions, specifically about being different from her sister:

Why can't you be like your sister? She's beautiful, but look at you! You have the ugliest face. Why don't you just die? Why weren't you one of the ones who died? [Her mother had had several miscarriages.] Just get out of here! Just leave me alone!

It was not long after this that the client received the call from her sister. Guilt about her attempt to separate herself symbolically from her mother's and sister's wretched outlook on life made it impossible for her to tolerate the difference between her own state of happiness and her sister's depression and misery. The woman's brief contact with her sister, through that single phone call, was a key factor in disrupting her adjustment.

Guilt Reactions to Significant Accomplishments

Individuals often experience feelings of guilt when they achieve a greater degree of success than associates, friends, or family members, particularly their parent of the same sex. These reactions usually involve some form of giving up their new success by sabotaging their achievements. One woman, whose parents were high school graduates, attended a university and law school. Upon passing the Bar Exam, she got a job in a prestigious firm and excelled as a lawyer. However, when she was made junior partner, she became less effective and uncharacteristically self-doubting. She identified a voice that she felt reflected her parents' view of her promotion.

So now you think you're a big success? A hotshot attorney! It was one thing to be a lawyer, but this whole partner thing is going to go to your head! You're too good for us now. You think we're beneath you. You've always had this superiority. You are such a snob.

These self-critical, belittling voice attacks left her feeling guilty about achieving the position she had worked so hard to attain. When her performance at work faltered, she then had voices that attacked her for not doing her best. This client was suspended in a state between two types of guilt—guilt about surpassing her father who had failed in business and guilt about regressing to a less mature level of functioning. Voices expressing both forms of guilt tormented her, first deriding her for her success, and later castigating her for her inadequacies.

THE VOICE AND EXISTENTIAL GUILT

A person may feel consciously guilty for not pleasing authorities, while unconsciously he feels guilty for not living up to his own expectations of himself.

~ Erich Fromm (1947, p. 169)

People often experience strong guilt feelings when they act in a manner that goes against their stated goals and real preferences. They regret that they have basically betrayed themselves and their guilt feeds upon itself. In these instances, individuals often have voice attacks telling them that they are no different than their families. For example, a client who was managing his diabetes would attack himself when he violated his diet. Regardless of the fact that he was taking his health seriously and that his deviations were infrequent, he attacked himself savagely whenever he slipped, with attacks like:

You have no self-control. You are going to kill yourself! You watched your father abuse his health and die of this same disease. And now you're just like him! You can't even take care of yourself!

This man's guilt and self-recrimination only served to further demoralize him and prevented him from feeling compassion for himself. Self-critical thoughts reminding people that their negative traits are no different from their parents' are significant factors in their acting against their own interests.

When people regress and act against themselves, they often withdraw and become alienated from those close to them. Their existential guilt is then compounded because they are guilty for inadvertently hurting their loved ones. They then castigate themselves with voices like: *Now look what you've done. You're hurting him/her and making him/her hate you. You're ruining your relationship.*

In a previous work (R. Firestone, 1985), I referred to a client, Joanne, who wrote a letter to friends in her therapy group describing the guilt and self-hatred that revolved around her self-destructive pattern of living. The following excerpts from her letter demonstrate an unusual understanding of the part played by her voice in preserving her isolated, inward life-style and her self-hatred:

> Self-loathing has become so firmly entrenched in my being, it feels like the very core of me—in some crazy way, self-hatred feels like my "life-force." I can't hang on to self-hatred around you any more—even with briefest contact of groups and weekly sessions. *No matter how I "insure" the feeling by acts of self-destructiveness during the week—the eating, picking at myself, calling up my mother's voice to ridicule and denounce myself*—you just have to see me, I mean really see me and address the person that's real in me, to strip away the self-hate, even for just a second or two. . . . In my case, self-hatred was formed very early, to protect myself from the certain total insanity that rejection would have led me into. From there, keeping a layer of fat surrounding me, twisting my face into ugly expressions, kept that basic or primal defense alive in me.

This letter was written over 35 years ago, about the same time that my conceptualization and understanding of the voice process were unfolding. This client, who described herself so honestly, showed insight that was partially ahead of my knowledge at that time. For example, Joanne writes of "calling up her mother's voice" to denounce her during the week for her self-destructive habits. Prior to therapy, this woman had become progressively demoralized by her self-hatred, guilt, and a chronic sense of despair and futility. As she improved, she became more intolerant of her life of self-loathing and guilt and, at the time she wrote the letter, was making concerted efforts to change the behaviors that caused her to despise herself.

GUILT AND DEATH ANXIETY

A form of guilt closely related to separation and death anxiety is "death guilt," or more appropriately named "survival guilt" described by Robert

Lifton and Eric Olson (1976) in their paper, "The Human Meaning of Total Disaster". They define death guilt as "the survivor's sense of painful self-condemnation over having lived while others died" (p. 3). Interviewing survivors from the Buffalo Creek Flood of 1972, Lifton and Olson determined that:

People who have gone through this kind of experience are never quite able to forgive themselves for having survived. Another side of them, however, experiences relief and gratitude that it was they who had the good fortune to survive in contrast to the fate of those [many of whom were close relatives] who died—a universal and all-too-human survivor reaction that in turn intensifies their guilt (p. 5).

Lifton and Olson's (1976) concept of "death guilt" coincides with the descriptions of "survival guilt" revealed by individuals who were incarcerated in concentration camps and survived the trauma. In other writings, they relate survivor guilt indirectly to death anxiety and to people's attempts to cope with the kinds of experiences where this anxiety is aroused. Lifton and Olson contend that when people suppress these painful feelings of guilt, the result is a kind of "psychic numbing—a diminished capacity for feeling of all kinds—in the form of various manifestations of apathy, withdrawal, depression, and overall constriction in living" (p. 5).

William Styron's (1979) novel, *Sophie's Choice*, graphically portrays this form of self-blame and the painful self-accusations associated with survival guilt. After choosing to save her son by sacrificing her daughter in order to avert death for both her children at the hands of the SS guards, Sophie was tormented by guilt for surviving her ordeal. Her torturous choice essentially involved choosing her own life, for which she was never able to forgive herself.

Later, Sophie's lover, Nathan, became a tool she used in her self-destruction. His accusations and questions about the methods she employed that allowed her to survive echoed Sophie's own self-condemnations. In a sense, she projected her voice onto Nathan and used him to punish herself. In her own eyes, the punishment was not severe enough to equal her crime—that of being alive—and Sophie ended her life by submitting to Nathan's plan for them to die together.

To feel one's guilt about surviving, simply living, or valuing one's life is painful. For this reason, it is typically repressed, surfacing at times as feelings of self-consciousness or in apologetic gestures toward others who are less fortunate. People restrict their lives in order to minimize or avoid painful feelings associated with the potential death anxiety that so often follows fully investing in life. Living a rich fulfilling existence leaves people with an awareness of how much they have to lose. For this reason, many individuals are willing to pay the price of living a defended, self-hating existence (as in the case of Joanne) and choose an emotionally deadened, self-limiting lifestyle.

In fact, a common response to survivor guilt and death anxiety is to renounce the very activities and relationships that give one's life the most value. In a previous work (R. Firestone, 1985), I described this form of progressive self-denial as an accommodation to death and a defense against death anxiety:

> We attempt to gain control over death through a process of progressive self-denial; that is, we deny ourselves experiences that would enhance our lives and give them value. . . . In withdrawing feeling or affect from personal pursuits and goal-directed activity, [we attempt to reduce our] vulnerability to hurt, rejection or loss (p. 256).

This process, which is suicidal in nature, diminishes the guilt about choosing life, yet it inevitably leads to the second type of guilt, existential guilt, of which Becker (1997) has written: "Guilt results from unused life, from 'the unlived in us'" (p. 180). This guilt, in turn, is responsible for some people acting out destructive impulses—in effect, to punish themselves for their withdrawal from life.

The verbalization of the thoughts underlying feelings of guilt in Voice Therapy sessions evokes feelings of compassion and support for the self and for one's personal point of view (Note 3). In contrast, when these attacks are not challenged, people increasingly submit to the injunctions of the voice and progressively abandon their real self and unique point of view.

CONCLUSION

Many people feel guilty about pursuing goals directly. They often come to prefer fantasy gratification to fulfilling their wants in reality. Early in life, they learn to moderate, control and restrict their behavior. However, when they choose fantasy, passivity, and self-nourishing lifestyles, they experience existential guilt.

As individuals retreat from pursuing life fully, they feel guilty of self-betrayal and, incidentally, betrayal of their loved ones as well. Indeed, many disputes between couples are triggered by concern about the self-destructive impulses and actions of one or the other partner. Whenever people become withholding and less responsive in their overall functioning, they feel considerable guilt. Furthermore, in their attempt to cover up their withdrawal from a loved one most people try to act as if they are still pursuing satisfying relationships and personal goals, and, as a result, their communications become duplicitous. This lack of integrity further intensifies their guilt.

Guilt reactions can predispose serious consequences and regressions that are detrimental to a person's development. The range of an individual's experience is defined by the boundaries imposed by neurotic guilt on the one hand and existential guilt on the other and by the thought process that mediates both forms of guilt reactions. By utilizing Voice Therapy, people can identify their voices, make them conscious, answer back to them responsibly, and take actions to challenge them. In doing so, they can progress and cope more successfully in relationships and other significant aspects of life.

The techniques of Voice Therapy help people become aware of both neurotic and existential guilt reactions and move on toward personal freedom. This methodology has also proven to be a valuable research tool in developing my understanding of people's conflicting nature. By systematically challenging the voice, clients are strengthened in their pursuit of life, thereby minimizing regressive trends and the complicated feelings of guilt and self-recrimination.

Notes

1. On the notion of shame, Tangney and Dearing (2002) write, "In his early writings, Freud (1953/1896) considered the potential relevance of both shame and guilt to psychological disorders. In 1905, he discussed shame as a reaction formation against sexually exhibitionistic impulses. . . . From Freud's (1961/1923) perspective, a sense of guilt comes about when forbidden wishes or deeds clash with the moral standards of the ever-vigilant superego" (p. 113). Morrison (1989), asserted that "In his movement from narcissism to structural

theory, Freud introduced guilt where shame would more appropriately have been placed, (for example, with respect to inferiority feelings)" (p. 25).

In *Modernity and Self-Identity*, sociologist Anthony Giddens (1991) concluded that "Shame connects to difficulties individuals have in separating out their self-identity from their original 'oneness' with the caretaking agents, and with poorly constrained omnipotence. [pseudo-independence and narcissism] . . . Erikson has observed that 'the patient of today suffers most under the problem of what he should believe in and who he should be—or, indeed, might— be or become; while the patient of early psychoanalysis suffered most under inhibitions which prevented him from being what and who he thought he knew he was" (pp. 68-69). Giddens' ideas regarding identity and self are similar in many respects to my thinking about identity (see Chapter 5, this volume).

2. Israel Orbach (2008) proposed: "Existential guilt results from a perceived disparity between one's obligations and possibilities, and one's fulfillment of them. Thus, existential guilt is directly linked with one's subjective evaluation of their actualization... Existential freedom bestows the responsibility of independently creating life-structure, a task that some individuals may find overwhelming" (pp. 290-291).

3. "Verbalization of thoughts underlying guilt feeling . . . ": see Gershen Kaufmann's (1993) explanation of dynamics and therapy techniques similar to those underlying Voice Therapy. He writes, "Not only do we internalize specific ways of treating ourselves in this process [identification], but we also and inevitably internalize *identification images* principally based on those individuals who are most vital for our survival, namely our parents. . . . Phenomenologically, an identification image eventually comes to be experienced as an *auditory voice* inside that remains distinct from the self's own voice" (p. 43).

"In this way, all experience becomes stored in memory in the form of discrete scenes which also comprise visual, auditory, and kinesthetic features...For a large group of individuals, only the language component of the scene remains available to consciousness. These individuals experience an *inner voice* which is the conscious residue of the scene; this voice is the language component of the scene" (p. 194).

Source: "The Voice: The Dual Nature of Guilt Reactions" (1987) *The American Journal of Psychoanalysis, 47*(3), (pp. 210-229)

Chapter 5

THE SELF UNDER SIEGE

To be nobody but yourself in a world that is doing its best, day and night, to make you everybody else means to fight the hardest battle which any human being can fight; and never stop fighting.

~ e.e. cummings

An individual faces an enormous struggle against overwhelming odds to retain a unique selfhood. In this postmodern era, we exist in a restrictive social structure that largely deprives us of essential human qualities, among them the capacity for maintaining personal feelings, the drive to search for meaning, and the ability to live with harmony and compassion towards others. Demands for uniformity and conformity lead to a life of dishonesty, self-deception, deadening habit patterns, and addictive relationships. Sadly, too many people fall by the wayside in their attempt to numb their pain and anxiety with habit patterns that offer the illusion of security at the price of integrity and individuality.

In our work, my associates and I have been primarily concerned with preserving the fundamental humanity of our clients and ourselves, and in particular the human spirit. My major interest has been in understanding and overcoming people's resistance to finding a freer, more fulfilling life. It was inevitable that my quest would lead me to identify and challenge the primary forces that act as a barrier to self-differentiation.

Differentiation refers to becoming an independent person who functions primarily in the adult mode, lives with integrity, and has an inclusive worldview. It involves being human to the fullest extent. It is crucial at this juncture in our evolution to develop a new and truly humanitarian perspective not only in order to transcend destructive familial and social influences that reinforce the individual's defensive mode of living, but also to preserve the species in relation to climate change, ethnic warfare, terrorism, and other crucial problems.

CONCEPTUALIZATIONS OF THE SELF

Philosophical Views of the Self

Philosophers and psychologists have long debated the nature of the "self." William James (2017) categorized different senses of the self at the end of the 19th century, and since then philosophers have refined and expanded the possible variations of this concept. Many contemporary Eastern thinkers believe that our perception of "having a self" is merely an illusion; whereas Western philosophers tend to conceptualize the "self" as a process that is embedded in and influenced by other people and the larger society. Metzinger (2003) describes the "phenomenal self" as "the subjective experience of being someone. . . . In conscious experience, there is a world, there is a self, and there is a relation between both" (p. 5). George Herbert Mead (1934), the founder of Pragmatism, emphasized the extent to which the self is continually being shaped by the social process:

> The process out of which the self arises is a social process which implies interaction of individuals in the group, implies the pre-existence of the group (p. 188).

With respect to society's profound influence or sway over the self in our postmodern world, Roderick (1993) describes "the human species as plunging headlong into cybernetics and virtual reality. The task of becoming a self has only grown and the dangers have increased in a world where, to quote William Gibson, 'the sky above the port was the color of television tuned to a dead channel'" (from the introduction to the audio cassette).

Psychological Views of the Self

Although Freud did not describe a systematic theory of the self, the concept of the self is implied in his model of the mind as composed of the id, ego, and superego. Most contemporary psychologists and sociologists agree with philosophical thinkers that the "self" can only be understood in the context of society. In their descriptions of the "narrative self," Ochs and Capps (1996) contend that the self can be "understood to be an unfolding reflective awareness of being-in the-world, including a sense of one's past and future" (pp. 20-21).

Regarding the ongoing debate with respect to the nature of the self, Daniel Stern (1985) pronounced, "Even though the nature of self may forever elude the behavioral sciences, the sense of self stands as an important subjective reality, a reliable, evident phenomenon that the sciences cannot dismiss" (p. 6). Contact with another human being is a major prerequisite for the development of self and personal identity (Auerbach & Blatt, 2001) (Note 2).

THE DEVELOPMENT OF SELF AND IDENTITY

Erik Erikson (1963) frequently used the terms "identity" and "self" interchangeably. For Erikson, personal identity represents one's set of goals, values and beliefs. As Schwartz, Zamboanga and Weisskirch (2008) write, for Erikson, "what is most important is the extent to which this set of goals, values and beliefs are internally consistent and, taken together, form a coherent sense of self" (p. 635).

Jeffrey Arnett (2000) proposed a new stage in identity formation— "emerging adulthood," that spans the years between 19 and 29. In this distinctive stage, "It is notable that emerging adults . . . indicate that deciding on their own beliefs and values is an essential criterion for attaining adult status" (p. 474).

Erikson's and Arnett's formulations are congenial with my own way of thinking about self and identity. In my conceptualization, the self system, in contrast to the anti-self system, is composed of the unique wants, desires, goals, and values that hold special meaning for the individual as well as the specific manner and means that he/she utilizes to fulfill these goals.

Today, the self is under siege in almost every aspect of a person's daily life. My goal in this chapter is to provide an uncompromising and illuminating view of myriad forces existing within the family and society that impinge on the self and contribute significantly to psychological distress. These influences include: prenatal factors; negative family dynamics; the detrimental effect of psychological defenses; the impact of death awareness; the potential negative effect of new relationships on one's autonomy, and aversive societal influences (Note 3).

Prenatal Influences

Genetically determined tendencies, temperamental differences, and physiological predispositions combine with prenatal environmental stresses to form the embryonic "self." Interactions between the genes and the environment, as well as epigenetic influences, determine the phenotypic makeup of the infant. In other words, both nature and nurture impact the as yet undeveloped self.

According to Jacobson (2009), "Emerging lines of research from epigenetics suggest that not only can nature alter nurture, but nurture, in turn, has the power to modify nature. . . . Environmental experiences, particularly those related to stress, have the capacity to alter biological and genetic mechanisms associated with increased risk of problem behavior" (p. 2). For example, epigenetic influences from the parents' genetic makeup "can potentially lead to errors in how certain genes are expressed in a newborn's traits and behaviors. In some cases, "the process goes awry, [and] neurological disorders can result" (p. 54) (Note 4).

There are other influences that can potentially impact the rapidly growing infant in utero, as well as trauma that can occur during the birth process itself. For example, fetal alcohol syndrome, now categorized as a "birth trauma," leads to "deficits in intellectual, academic, and adaptive living skills" in the children of women who abuse alcohol. Physical illness, depression, or environmental stressors that take place during a woman's pregnancy can significantly distress her unborn child and compromise its future development. For example, studies found that many of the babies born to 51 women who had experienced the events of 9/11 had lower birth weight and decrements in head circumference; in addition, some of the newborns were assessed with abnormal levels of cortisol, a stress hormone that interferes with the development of the ability to regulate one's emotions and cope with stress (Yehuda, et al., 2005; 2009).

Negative Family Dynamics

There is a wide variety of aversive events or inputs that can impinge on a young child during its earliest years, events such as accidents, illnesses, a traumatic separation, and the actual loss of a parent or sibling. Even in a relatively benign atmosphere, a certain amount of damage occurs because of the infant's heightened reactivity to sensory inputs, e.g., overstimulation and/or under-stimulation. In his work, Daniel Stern (1985) delineated the effects of these two extremes on the infant's emerging self, including:

> ...influences that disrupt the organized perceptions of self: over-stimulation, situations that disrupt the flow of toxic perceptions that maintain the sense of 'self', (being thrown too high in the air with too long a fall); experiences of self/other similarity that confound the self/other boundary cues; maternal under-stimulation that reduces certain toxic and phasic self-experiences (p. 199).

When parents are sensitively attuned to the infant, they adjust the intensity and emotional tone of their responses to accurately match the child's feeling state and needs. Obviously, no one can ever be completely consistent in adjusting his/her responses to these cues; in fact, research has indicated that attuned interactions occur in only one out of three of parent/infant exchanges (Siegel & Hartzell, 2003).

Interactions with well-meaning but emotionally immature parents, who themselves have suffered a good deal of unresolved personal trauma and loss in their own upbringing, will be detrimental in innumerable ways to the healthy growth and development of the child's emerging self (Cassidy & Mohr, 2001). In general, parental deficiencies lead to harmful, insensitive treatment and repeated failures to repair disruptions in attuned interactions between parent and child. These conditions intensify the child's feeling of isolation and fear of abandonment. In such circumstances, children are diverted from what would have been their natural developmental *pathway* and they go on to lead primarily defended lives.

The Impact of Misattunement on the Child

Recent studies in the neurosciences suggest that children as young as one year are able to accurately perceive a parent's purpose or intent from his/her facial expression and tone of voice (Cozolino, 2006; Schore, 2003a,

2003b; Siegel, 2001). During a misattuned or otherwise frightening interaction with a parent, an infant can detect, through specialized cells in its brain (the mirror neuron system), the parent's emotional state and intentions at that moment in time. Iacoboni (2009) was the first to investigate mirror neurons, a region of the brain hypothesized to be essential for imitation and the development of empathy.

According to Badenoch (2008), "With the discovery and exploration of mirror neurons in the last decade, we are becoming aware of how we constantly embed within ourselves the intentional and feeling states of those with whom we are engaged" (p. 37). For example, Daniel Siegel (Personal communication, 2013) speculated about what an infant or young child might experience during a fear-provoking interaction with an angry parent. Taking the role of the infant in this scenario, Siegel said:

> What this looks like from my mirror neuron point of view is you [the parent] come at me, really angry and you're terrifying me with your fury. Now I see your intention. You may not want this intention to be there, but it is. Your intention is to hurt me. Even though it's not your global intention, at that moment, you have it because of your own unresolved trauma. And I look at you and my mirror neuron grouping makes the assessment that the intention of this caregiver is to do me harm.
>
> What is a child supposed to do when his mirror neurons, like sponges, are soaking up the intention to be harmed by the one who's supposed to protect? He fragments. And in that fragmentation is dissociation of the usual continuity of the self.

Numerous studies in the neurosciences indicate how the child's developing mind adapts to a parent's feeling state and intentionality (Cozolino, 2006; Siegel & Hartzell, 2003). The data tend to support my conceptualization of the process of introjection and its role in the transmission of negative parental attitudes, abusive child-rearing practices, and blatant or more subtle forms of neglect from one generation to the next.

The Story of Kevin

Several years ago, I had an interaction with Kevin, a three-year-old boy, which underscored how critical it is for each of us to develop and maintain an independent, authentic, and differentiated sense of ourselves. Kevin's parents, Jenny and Michael, were distraught because their son exhibited violent behavior and impulsivity and would attack other children without provocation. Seemingly out of nowhere, he would hit or try to bite a younger child. He was agitated a good deal of the time, often pretended to be an aggressive animal like a dinosaur or a tiger, and threw a tantrum if interrupted. He manifested certain risk-taking behaviors and appeared unconcerned about things that would frighten most children. There were times when he would hit himself in the face with his fists while saying he was bad. At other times, for no apparent reason, he would suddenly collapse on the floor and scream out.

Amy, a close friend and neighbor of the couple and an associate of mine, suggested that they seek professional help for their child. Amy had spoken to me about her worries about Kevin. She described his demeanor as being unpleasant and said that he appeared to be unlovable. She provided me with valuable insight into the family's dynamics. In her opinion, Jenny was somewhat immature and misattuned to her son, and seemed to have difficulty being nurturing. Amy said that although she knew Jenny felt loving toward Kevin, she would often act strangely with him. She would engage in scary games, jumping out at him and making mean faces. While Jenny thought they were playing and having fun, the child looked terrified to Amy (Note 5).

Later, when Kevin's parents discussed their concerns with me, they spoke of their fear that Kevin's violence, lack of control, and bravado might, in part, be related to genetic factors (Fowles & Kochanska, 2000). Kevin, a nice-looking boy with blond hair, was small for his age. On the day that I met him, he looked like he felt angry and scared. It was obvious to me that this child was highly intelligent. My initial reaction was that I had an uneasy feeling and it was hard to warm up to him. I found him unlikeable, a rare feeling for me to have toward any child. Then I sat down next to him and started to talk with him.

To keep his attention, I encouraged him to look at my eyes. We engaged in some friendly small talk, and then I asked him about the things that scared him. His face looked serious and, in an earnest voice, he began to tell me a story. He said that there were two Kevins, a regular Kevin and a Kevin witch, as well as a Mommy witch. Based on what I knew about the fantasy bond, I conjectured that the Kevin witch was the destructive aspect of

Jenny's mothering that he had assimilated. I intuitively challenged him, saying, "There is only one Kevin." Kevin responded, "No, there are two Kevins." To which I repeated, "There is only one Kevin."

Kevin objected for a while, but I repeated the sentence over and over. Suddenly he caught on and his eyes lit up. He jumped out of his chair and said, "This is what Mommy does." He imitated his mother, raising his arms in a menacing manner and making an angry, distorted face. Then he said, "Let's attack the Mommy monster!" and started pummeling a pillow, hitting it with his fists. I allowed him to fully express his anger. I said that he was killing the monster, but that I would protect him. After the outburst, Kevin felt relaxed and self-possessed; his face had changed and he looked sweet. I had a warm feeling toward him.

Immediately following this conversation, Kevin's family told me that he seemed more vulnerable and relaxed. His outward behavior was friendlier and more affectionate, which was significantly different from his usual demeanor. Whereas in the past he had frequently called himself a "bad boy" or a "monster," his parents reported that he had begun referring to himself more often as a "good boy."

My unusual encounter with this child and its positive outcome surprised and impressed me. I found it unusual that I could verbally communicate with someone so young. I pondered the significance of our conversation and interpreted the exchange as follows: When I said that there was only one Kevin, I was really indicating that the Kevin witch represented the threatening persona of his mother that Kevin had incorporated into himself. In his fantasy of fusion with his mother, he saw himself as the monster. That is the reason he judged himself as bad and acted out elements of the raging, incorporated monster on other children. When he made the separation from the Kevin witch and conceptualized himself as simply Kevin, he was able to mobilize his anger toward his mother and he felt relief.

When children are especially frightened or hurt, they incorporate the aggressor (the person causing them emotional pain) into themselves. This is a psychological survival mechanism that reduces intolerable stress. Because of this incorporation process, Kevin had a split within himself that was part him (the self) and part his scary mother (the anti-self) that was alien to him and aggressively directed outward toward other children. After Kevin made the separation from his internalized parent, he seemed like a different person. He maintained a pleasant disposition with only occasional outbursts of anger. When these fits did occur, they were much more moderate and he was reachable. Following my conversation with Kevin, he and his parents entered into an ongoing treatment program and Kevin continued to make progress. My brief exchange with him was significant and meaningful both to Kevin and to me.

Specific Emotional Abuses that Impact the Developing Self

Physical and sexual abuses experienced by children in the course of a so-called normal upbringing are far more common and the effects are far more damaging to the child's sense of self than most people recognize (Edwards et al., 2003; Steele, 1990) (Note 6). In particular, sexual abuse violates the integrity of the child's body and interferes with the development of a stable self-concept. In addition, there is a wide range of specific forms of emotional maltreatment that also have lasting effects on the developing self and personality of the child. Indeed, no child enters adulthood without suffering a certain amount of damage in basic areas of personality development that disturb psychological functioning yet leaves no visible scars. The child's emotional suffering can exceed the distress caused by physical beatings (Garbarino, Guttman, & Seeley, 1986; Rohner, 1986).

I have defined emotional child abuse as damage to the child's psychological development and emerging personal identity, primarily caused by parents' or primary caretakers' immaturity, defended lifestyle, and conscious or unconscious aggression toward the child. It must be considered abuse when imprinting from early interactions with family members has long-term debilitating effects on a person's conception of self and personal relationships, leads to a condition of general unhappiness, causes pain and anxiety in one's sexual life, and interferes with and stifles development of career and vocational pursuits.

Parental Rejection: Parents' rejecting attitudes toward a child arouse overwhelming feelings of shame, a painful affect that Orbach (1988), Shengold (1989), and J. Gilligan (Parr, 2008) have referred to as "soul deadening." Rejected children tend to assimilate a basic feeling of being dirty, despicable, or contaminated about their very nature. They feel that there is something about them that can't be changed or "fixed" and try to hide the "shameful self" from others.

Shame stems from parents' inhibitions and their rejecting attitudes toward the infant's bodily needs, specifically his/her need for warmth, affectionate contact, and physical care. Shame can also result from parents' disgust with the child's body or productions, particularly related to toilet training. In addition, when parents covertly or overtly reject their child, he/she, in turn, learns not to trust other people and progressively becomes insulated from significant others as an adult. Children who have been consistently rejected become needy, desperate, hostile, unappealing, and difficult to be with, inspiring further rejection by parents and other people as well.

Verbal Abuse: Parental hostility is often communicated to a child through sarcastic, derisive, or condescending commentary. Interactions are considered verbally aggressive when the spoken words are characteristically negative, overly critical, or severe. On-going derogatory statements directed toward children about their appearance, performance, and mannerisms are debilitating. Many parents habitually make unfavorable comparisons with siblings or peers. Children have no way to combat parents who maliciously tease them or humiliate them.

Many parents tend to define or categorize children, which dehumanizes and detracts from being able to maintain an overall view of each child. They may pigeonhole a particular child as "the shy one," "the beautiful one," "the plain one," or "the defiant one," the "trouble-maker." Because of their desperation to hold on to their parents, children take on these labels as their personal identity, as definitions of who they really are.

Harsh Mistreatment: Many parents believe that children must be made to submit to parental authority "for their own good" in order to be properly socialized. They feel justified in angrily punishing the child when he/she refuses to comply immediately with their directives or demands. In direct confrontations or showdowns, parents manifest fierce, punitive attitudes and, at times, violent rage, which stand out from their usual behavior. Explosive outbursts intimidate and terrify children, who perceive the adults as out of control. This type of parental response in regard to discipline is weak and ineffectual, and is threatening to the child's sense of security.

Lack of Respect: Parents who believe that their children "belong" to them, in the proprietary sense, tend to speak *for* their children, take over their child's productions as their own, brag excessively about their child's accomplishments, and, in general, live vicariously through their children. Other parents who are unable to feel for their children offer them flattery and special praise as a substitute for affection and love. This exaggerated buildup leads to irrational feelings of omnipotence and vanity in the child and contributes to performance anxiety.

Many parents overstep the personal boundaries of their offspring by inappropriately touching them, over-directing them, invading their privacy, going through their belongings, or by requiring them to perform for friends and relatives; the latter exacerbates feelings of social anxiety or shyness. An extreme violation of a child's rights is manifested in many parents' insistence that their child reveal his/her innermost thoughts and emotions. Children who are intruded on and utilized for a parent's narcissistic needs grow up feeling as though they don't belong to themselves, but exist only as an object for others.

Threats of Abandonment: Threats of being sent away (to boarding school, hospital, or jail) are far more common than one might think and frighten children unnecessarily. John Bowlby (1973) reported that threats of this sort are widely used by parents as disciplinary measures and frequently lead to serious school phobias, psychosomatic illness, and other symptoms in children. Warnings or threats that a parent might leave or desert the family, run away and abandon the child, or commit suicide are even more terrifying and, in addition, impose an enormous burden of guilt on the child.

Stifling or Punishing a Child's Aliveness: The spontaneous action, liveliness, noise, and lack of shame typical of young children often arouse tension, embarrassment, guilt, and anger in many parents, who then feel compelled to control and restrict their children. Statements such as "What are you getting so excited for?" "Stop asking so many questions!" suppress the child's natural expressions of enthusiasm, curiosity, and freedom of movement. Children are also admonished: "Don't be so full of yourself!" "Don't be conceited." They eventually stop taking pride in their accomplishments and have difficulty acknowledging their self-worth.

Destructive Practices Based on Indifference: Neglect is a passive form of abuse. Some parents fail to take even the minimum precautions for their child's physical health and safety. Emotional neglect is manifested in parents who reject or ignore their children, refuse to speak to them for extended time periods, or are unconcerned with their whereabouts. These children tend to take on a rejected, pathetic appearance. Their unappealing demeanor, combined with clinging, dependent, or negativistic behaviors, provoke rejection by others, thereby diminishing the possibility for corrective experiences.

Lack of Genuine Physical Affection: Parents who have been deprived of love during *their* formative years often lack the emotional resources to offer the love and affection needed to gratify their child. Some parents rationalize their lack of response as an attempt to avoid spoiling the child by giving him/her "too much" affection or attention. As noted above, when there is little or no outward expression of physical warmth, children feel unacceptable or unlovable. On the other hand, the type of intrusive touching and nervous caressing manifested by emotionally hungry parents attempting to fill their own dependency needs through their child tends to drain the emotional resources of the child.

Excessive Permissiveness: Over-permissiveness is a form of neglect because the child fails to develop appropriate inner controls over acting-out behavior. Immature parents are remiss in failing to provide sufficient direction and control for their offspring. If children are not properly socialized, in the best sense of the word (for example, if they fail to learn to control their aggressive impulses), they become anxious as adults because of their inability to manage their emotions. As a result, they tend to act out irresponsibly, develop negative attitudes toward themselves, and manifest a high degree of self-hatred (Shengold, 2000). When children fail to receive sufficient regulation, which is a basic need, they grow up feeling unloved and unlovable.

Isolation: Perhaps one of the more destructive forms of emotional abuse is that of isolating children and adolescents from social contacts, including peers or extra-familial influences who would offer a different point of view from that of the parents. Many parents, assuming that children are easily influenced (adversely) by "outsiders" strictly limit their child's or adolescent's contact with other people. With respect to the overall mental health and psychological development of a child, the importance of an extended family situation or support network cannot be overemphasized (Note 7). Studies have shown that certain resilient children who experienced severe abuse and neglect, yet failed to develop symptoms as adults, usually had a significant other—a relative, family friend, or teacher—who took an interest in them and provided them with support (E.J. Anthony, 1987).

THE DETRIMENTAL EFFECT OF
PSYCHOLOGICAL DEFENSES

The abuses delineated above as well as the attempt to defend oneself from the resultant pain significantly perpetuate self-limitation. In fact, defenses become the core psychological problem for the future development of the individual.

When faced with frustration, deprivation and emotional pain, children make the best adaptation possible in order to preserve a form of rationality, sanity, and equilibrium. The self-protective mechanisms or defenses that the child forms are in fact appropriate to actual situations that threaten his/her emerging self. A particular style or mode of defense will tend to generate specific symptoms, i.e., compulsive-obsessional disorders, addictions, psychosomatic illness, delusions, or other forms of psychopathology. These patterns of defense tend to persist and become habitual, lead to progressive problems in broad areas of functioning, and impede movement toward individuation.

As explained in Chapter 3, the fantasy bond, the imaginary connection with the parent, in some measure heals the fracture brought about by early separation experiences; it also alleviates anxiety and frustration by partially gratifying the infant's emotional and physical hunger. This core defense is composed of the idealization of one's parents, the development of a negative self-concept, and child's projection of parents' weaknesses and negative traits onto other people (Note 8). In treating themselves much as they were treated by their parents, children both nurture themselves with self-aggrandizing thoughts and self-soothing addictive habit patterns, and punish themselves with self-critical thoughts and self-destructive behavior.

Psychological defenses and self-protective behavior patterns are formed very early in life. By the time many children are 2 or 3 years old, they no longer are the naive, innocent, pure creatures they once were. They learn early in life to withhold their capabilities, to act out passive or active aggression, whine, complain, and embarrass and manipulate their parents through "learned helplessness." Contrary to popular opinion, children are not just "going through a phase" when they act out these "bad" or unpleasant behaviors. Unless interrupted, the toxic behaviors and defenses that children develop at an early age will persist and evolve into more sophisticated negative behavior patterns and deep character defenses when they are adults. Many fathers and mothers, observing traits developing in their offspring that they dislike within themselves, find the youngster increasingly unappealing and unpleasant to be with. Parents' efforts to correct bad habits in their children often fail because they do not deal with the underlying causes of these negative manifestations.

Thus, as a result of forming defenses, all individuals experience a split within their personality between destructive tendencies and life-affirming, goal-directed tendencies. Early in their development, they incorporate critical attitudes and self-destructive elements into their personalities. To varying degrees, most people remain undifferentiated from these internalized harmful influences throughout their lives.

THE IMPACT OF DEATH AWARENESS

As noted earlier, when children reach a certain age, they must contend with the anxiety surrounding their evolving awareness of a finite existence. When the child learns about death, his/her psychological defenses become crystallized, and from that point on, death issues impact every aspect of life. Although death anxiety is often unconscious, it reinforces psychological defenses that children formed earlier in life and intensifies the division within the personality between the self and anti-self systems.

Unconsciously, many children deny the reality of their personal death by regressing to a previous stage of development, to a phase before death was a reality to them (Note 9). While they accept the idea of death on an intellectual or conscious level, from a deeper psychological perspective, they attempt to escape from a situation that they recognize as hopeless by holding on tenaciously to the familiar defensive solution. At this point, the fantasy bond and the self-parenting process are strengthened and become more deeply entrenched as core defenses. The impact of death awareness affects an individual throughout his/her lifespan.

The fear of death is the ultimate enemy of differentiation because when people become afraid they tend to retreat from life and desperately rely on defenses that include subordinating themselves to other people, engaging in addictive habit patterns and other self-destructive behaviors, and attempting to re-establish fantasies of fusion with parents or parental substitutes.

THE POTENTIAL NEGATIVE EFFECT OF A ROMANTIC RELATIONSHIP ON ONE'S AUTONOMY

Intimate or romantic relationships also pose a potential threat to the process of differentiation and to each partner's individuality and independence. In a misguided attempt to find and maintain safety and security in a relationship, partners are often diverted from following their own destiny. Consequently, they may suppress their personal interests, goals, and dreams and even at times compromise their ideals and basic values. In order to hold on to the relationship, maintain the status quo, and "keep the peace," people deceive themselves, confuse their partners, and manipulate one another in ways that are destructive to their ongoing state of being.

Relationships can be conceptualized in terms of the differential effects they have on each person's sense of self. In constructive relationships, each person's self-esteem is affirmed and nurtured, as contrasted with destructive relationships in which the negative attitudes and voices of the anti-self system of each partner are reinforced. In our study of couples and families, I discovered that any personal communication or interaction between partners could be evaluated as being either supportive of or interfering with each person's positive sense of self and personal development.

There are a number of collusive patterns of relating that negatively impact individuals' personalities and disrupt the movement toward higher levels of self-differentiation. For example, partners who engage in a parent/child dynamic tend to become progressively more polarized in their functioning over time. The childlike partner gradually becomes incompetent or helpless, which elicits parental response—domination, anger, or even punishment—from the other. The person who has taken on the parental role denies his/her own feelings of helplessness, and behaves in a condescending, controlling, analytical manner (Willi, 1982).

Another manifestation of the parent/child mode of relating is that of dominance and submission. Partners stop being equal companions in sharing their lives to manipulate and control each other through domineering or submissive behavior. The dominating partner controls through bullying, which includes responses that indicate approval and disapproval and provide rewards and punishment. This type of partner may become verbally or physically abusive. Some even use threats of reprisal, warning their partner of potential withdrawal of financial support or actual abandonment.

The submissive partner controls through weakness. A partner's display of helplessness, childishness, victimized complaints, unnecessary incompetency, and passive-aggression are remarkably effective in manipulating the other. People can successfully keep their partner "in line" using these techniques, but they damage themselves and each other in the process. The manipulation of another person through provoking guilt reactions arouses anger and tension within the couple and subverts any genuine feelings that may exist.

Other behavior patterns that are seen as "complimentary" in relationships are: when one partner is more extroverted, outward, and friendly while the other is more introverted, inward, and shy; when one person is outspoken while his/her partner is quiet or reticent; when one is active and adventurous and the other passive or more "laid-back." People involved in collusive relationships of this type often imagine they have found their soul mate and feel that they are finally whole. However, over time, as individuals, each becomes progressively more dysfunctional. For example, the shy person who relies on the talkative partner to interact in social situations becomes more socially awkward while his/her mate becomes more gregarious and longwinded. As a result, the partners rarely relate to each other from an adult ego-state.

Laura Kipnis (2003) has delineated more than a hundred implicit rules that reinforce parent-child modes of interaction. These rules, routines, and rituals are automatically accepted by couples, because they offer protection from potential threats to their fantasy of love or illusion of connection. Her examples include:

> You can't sleep apart, you can't go to bed at different times, you can't fall asleep without getting woken up to go to bed, you can't get out of bed right away after sex. . . . You can't go to parties alone. You can't go out just to go out, because you can't not be considerate of the other person's worries about where you are, or their natural insecurities that you're not where you should be.

> Thus is love obtained: what matters is the form . . . Exchanging obedience for love comes naturally—we were all once children after all, whose survival depended on the caprices of love. And thus you have

the template for future intimacies. If you love me, you'll do what I want or need or demand to make me feel secure and complete and I'll love you back (pp. 84-94).

These rules and routines take a serious toll on the people involved. In the process of playing out these roles and adhering to their unspoken rules, people end up substituting a fantasy of still being in love for the genuine love and affection they once enjoyed with each other. As they enact the everyday routines, customs, rituals, and role-determined behaviors that provide the structure and form of their relationship, they gradually lose a sense of themselves as individuals.

NEGATIVE SOCIETAL INFLUENCES THAT IMPACT THE SELF

The defenses that people formed early in life are compounded by the suffering inherent in the human condition, including illness, accidents, physical and mental deterioration, economic hardship, poverty, and crime, and on a larger scale, by ethnic strife, warfare and terrorism. These latter events of global significance encroach on each person's awareness and sensibility on a daily basis. Just watching the evening news on television is a disturbing reminder of the insanity of today's world, which can lead us to be cynical and despairing, or even worse, indifferent or apathetic.

Aversive forces operating in the larger society have powerful negative effects on individuals throughout their lives. Social mores and distorted, institutionalized attitudes seriously interfere with people's ongoing struggle to differentiate from the defensive adaptations they made to faulty programming within their family.

Conformity, Stereotyping, and Prejudice

Conformity: The socialization process in the family tends to categorize, standardize, and put the stamp of conformity on most children. It imposes a negative structure, a self-regulating system that cuts deeply into the child's feeling reactions and conditions his/her thoughts and behaviors to meet certain accepted standards. Thereafter, the child continues to impose the same structure and programming on him/herself. On a broader scale, all societies and complex social structures tend to be restrictive of individuality and personal expression in the face of existential anxiety. Increased submission to the defensive process of conformity represents a generalized movement toward a suicidal process and destruction of all that is human (Berke, 1988; Lasch, 1979).

Conformity and adjustment to society are seen as moral and healthy by many people; whereas nonconformity to societal expectations is perceived as aberrant and a threat to society. Therefore, an individual must subordinate him/herself to preserve the couple, family, or society's norms; otherwise he/she is considered abnormal. For example, when people do not live up to society's expectations to get conventionally married or to live together in a committed relationship, they may be considered peculiar, immature, or deviant.

Conventional society and institutions also support a myth of exclusive and enduring love in couples. In conforming to the society's standards and expectations based on this myth, married couples vow to "forsake all others." Often, they end up renouncing old friends and systematically exclude new ones (potential rivals) from their small kingdom in order to preserve the illusion that they are forever preferred. When this illusion is destroyed, there can be dire consequences. Many times, this fantasy is interrupted by the discovery of the partner's unfaithfulness, leading to catastrophic anxiety.

Stereotyping: Gender stereotyping, which is widespread in society, creates animosity between men and women and undermines personal relationships. The sexist attitudes and stereotypic views of gender roles disseminated through the media, educational institutions, and other forms of public discourse seriously restrict people's thinking and adversely affect their behavior. Social psychologist Geis (1993) concluded that "Gender stereotypes, operating as implicit expectations, bias perception and treatment of women and men and the results of the discriminatory perceptions and treatment—sex differences in behavior and achievement—then seemingly confirm that the stereotypes were true all along" (p. 37).

In a similar vein, Carol Gilligan has censured sexist and patriarchal attitudes that are circulated through both popular media and professional texts. In a recent interview, she explained, "In patriarchy, you divide human beings into these two incoherent categories, and then you say that's somehow the way men and women are, and it's absolutely false for both" (Parr, 2012b). The resultant distorted perceptions of what constitutes "real" masculinity and "true" femininity contribute to parents' differential treatment of boys and girls (Chu, 2014; C. Gilligan, 1982) (Note 10). Society promulgates certain values and views that limit the psychological development of children by encouraging compliance and conformity to these images and roles.

Stereotypical attitudes that define age-appropriate roles and behaviors in a severely restrictive manner (ageism) tend to reinforce self-destructive tendencies in many older individuals. Despite society's focus on remaining youthful, popular concepts of "maturity" support the gradual retreat from energetic activities as one grows older. Each withdrawal is supported by social mores, institutions, and the media: early retirement, diminished participation in sports and other physical activities, a waning interest in sex and a decline in sexual relating, loss of contact with old friends, and a dwindling social life. At the same time, people tend to engage in more sedentary or self-nourishing activities, and many come to experience their lives as boring and tedious.

Prejudice: Attitudes held in families often encourage prejudice toward other families, groups, and cultures that approach life differently. These distinctions support core beliefs that individuals who do not look "like we do," who do not act "like we do" are inferior, worthless, immoral, or even dangerous. The result of this form of programming and its extension into society has a drastic negative effect on individuals and their relationships, and sets groups of people against one another.

Another basis for prejudice and racism is the defense of disowning one's own negative or despised characteristics by projecting them onto others in an attempt to maintain self-esteem. This is operating on a societal level when people of one ethnic group dispose of their self-hatred by projecting it onto the people of another, perceiving them as subhuman, dirty, impure, and inherently evil (Newman, Duff, & Baumeister, 1997). Therefore, the removal of this imperfection, impurity, and evil is seen as a valid means by which to perfect themselves and "cleanse" the world.

The degree of prejudice and intolerance that individuals express toward those of different ethnicity, religious persuasion, or racial background is influenced by the extent to which they rely on the fantasy bond as a source of security. Attachment theorists Fonagy and Higgitt (2007) explained that malignant prejudice "is associated with disorganization of the attachment system" (p. 71). People who have been significantly damaged in early family interactions are generally more defended or rigid regarding their beliefs than their less damaged counterparts and tend to react with fear and aggression when confronted by racial and cultural differences (Erlich, 1973).

People's defensive attitudes in relation to death are at the core of their prejudicial attitudes and aggression toward others, polarizing one group of people against others who hold different customs and beliefs, and eventually they result in violence. As Becker (1971) emphasized, "It seems clear that comfortable illusion is now a danger to human survival" (pp. 198-199).

Religion

For the most part, religious dogma consists of consensually validated concepts of existential "truth" that contribute to a collective defense against death anxiety. This generally supports a self-destructive process of self-limitation and self-abrogation. However, restricting or suppressing people's natural desires—their sexual and aggressive thoughts and feelings—unwittingly contributes to an increase in the incidence of violence and immoral acting-out behavior (Prescott, 1996; Vergote, 1988).

The majority of Western religions tend to instill a sense of basic shame. Historically, in postulating a soul that could survive, people turned against the body because they knew that the body ceased to exist at death. In this trade-off, they turned their backs on their physical nature and sexuality. Subsequently, everything associated with the body or bodily functions tended to take on a shameful, dirty, or sinful connotation.

Secular attitudes toward sex and the human body derived from traditional religious beliefs could be construed to be a kind of institutionalized sexual abuse because they cause so much damage to people in their sexual lives. In my clinical experience, I have found that many people developed a negative point of view about their bodies, especially about bodily parts associated with sex. In socializing their children, parents are under tremendous pressure from society to teach restrictive values and narrow, distorted views of sexuality. When children internalize these views of sex, their adult sexuality and intimate relationships are subsequently profoundly influenced by them. Negative views held by parents in relation to nudity and the human body cause children to develop a deep sense of shame about their bodies and guilt in relation to sexual feelings (Gunderson & McCary, 1979).

Closely related to distorted views of sexuality are attitudes toward children based on the concept of original sin. Some people believe that children are born sinful or basically evil. Moralistic and restrictive training procedures based on this supposition produce children who perceive themselves as innately bad and behave accordingly. Social mores based on religious dogma have also created strong prohibitions against feelings, especially the so-called negative emotions of anger and sadness. People are taught to feel only in a socially prescribed manner. Children are socialized to suppress their genuine feelings, particularly those that would indicate that they are in pain.

Throughout history, the level of religious fanaticism has resulted in atrocities such as the Inquisition, ethnic cleansing and terrorism. In fact, in some religious factions, individual sacrifice in war is a basic tenet of their doctrine: a heroic death in a religious war guarantees entry into the afterlife. Yet, on some level, most people still remain uncertain and insecure despite their adherence to strong and rigid belief systems. These socially constructed defensive solutions never fully succeed in resolving life's unresolvable problems. If they did, there would be no need for controversy and no reason to go to war over differences in religion, race, or customs (Becker, 1997; Solomon et al., 2004).

Nationalism

Nationalism, totalitarianism and other "isms," such as communism and capitalism, can foster a deep dependency in people who are searching for comfort, security and relief from ontological anxiety. Any cause, whether potentially good or evil, is capable of engendering this reaction. James Gilligan (2007) has defined nationalism as:

A form of prejudice that privileges members of one's own nation and discredits those who belong to others. Once religion—the divine right of kings—lost its credibility as the source of legitimacy, another basis had to be found. With belief in nationalism came the belief that governments, or states, derived their legitimacy from the nation they represented and defended. The concept of nationhood and the nation-state thus replaced the now-defunct concepts of God, religion, and the divine right of kings (p. 39).

The fear of death not only drives people to reinforce the fantasy bond with family, but also to extend it to society in the form of group identification. The primitive feelings that initially characterized the illusion of fusion with one's parents are transferred onto new figures and ideologies. Conformity to the belief system of the culture and adherence to its collective symbols of immortality protect one against the horror of facing the objective loss of self.

According to Falk (2004), nationalism represents a collective illusion, a fusion of one's narcissistic, grandiose image, with the image of greatness embedded in the national group. He proposed that, "Nationalism can be viewed as defensive group narcissism" (p. 99). Falk went on to explain that nationalism, patriotism, and fascism "may result from an unconscious displacement of the personal narcissism of each of the individuals belonging to the group onto the national group, and of an identification with the group as a mirror image of one's own grandiose self" (p. 99).

In the struggle to achieve and maintain autonomy and a strong sense of self, an individual must resist the tendency toward unnecessary conformity and avoid becoming a passive part of a group process. The social pressures described here impose limitations on a person's unique approach to life and sense of freedom and pose a significant threat to his/her individuality. It is a full-time job to cope with alien elements from both interpersonal sources and societal influences.

CONCLUSION

Each individual is unique. Differentiation from distorted attitudes and negative imprinting of one's parents and other significant figures in one's childhood is essential for optimal functioning. Whereas parents' positive traits and attitudes are easily assimilated and identified with, the negative aspects of their point of view function as an alien element of the personality, the anti-self system and negative self-concept. This malevolent portion of the self is both maladaptive and self-destructive and, at its extreme, ends in micro-suicidal and even suicidal thought and action.

Negative aspects of the diverse forms of programming that we encounter as we go through life—whether familial, existential, or societal—have an undermining effect on our ability to maintain a distinct outlook and set of values. It is difficult for most people to survive the process and still remain creative, independent, and inner-directed versus outer-directed. Yet to fulfill one's personal destiny and to make full use of one's life and lifetime, one must make every effort to differentiate. Identity is essentially a flexible and evolving variable rather than a fixed or stable entity. Thus, the project of coming to know oneself, discovering one's likes and dislikes, wants and priorities, dreams and aspirations, becomes a fascinating, life-long enterprise.

Notes

1. These quotes are excerpted from the Introduction to the Guide to *The Self Under Siege: Philosophy in the Twentieth Century,* [tape cassettes, © The Great Courses, Rick Roderick, 1993].

2. See Auerbach and Blatt's (2001) theory of intersubjectivity in which they propose "children become independent subjects only if they are recognized as such – that is, as beings with minds, wills, and feelings of their own – by their caregivers...a child becomes an independent subject only if he/she in turn recognizes the independent subjectivity—in more familiar language, the autonomy and separateness—of his/her caregiver...Thus, intersubjectivity as an interpersonal interaction—in Aron's (1996) phrase, a meeting of minds—and intersubjectivity as a psychological capacity are deeply intertwined concepts, with the former constituting the transactional matrix from which the latter emerges" (p. 429). The ability to recognize both one's own mental state and that of others, has been described by Fonagy (2008) as "mentalization".

3. Regarding societal influences on the emerging self, see Bronfenbrernner and Morris (2006). "In the bioecological model, development is defined as the phenomenon of continuity and change in the biopsychological characteristics of human beings, both as individuals and as groups" (p. 793). Bronfenbrenner's & Morris's model includes what he refers to as the 'microsystem' (for example, heritability or one-to-one interactions), the 'mesosystem' (for example, parents' marital relationship), and the 'exosystem' (for example, the neighborhood or parent's work situation). The relationship between individual, the family and society is a system with continual reciprocal movement among these systems.

4. For a recent review of relevant studies, see "A post-genomic view of behavioral development and adaptation to the environment" by LaFreniere and MacDonald (2013). According to Meaney (2010), "the recent integration of epigenetics into developmental psychobiology illustrates the processes by which environmental conditions in early life structurally alter DNA, providing a physical basis for the influence of perinatal environmental signals on phenotype over the life of the individual" (p. 41).

5. It appears that Kevin's mother was largely unaware of the effect she was having on her son. Her frightening facial expression, aggressiveness, lack of awareness, and failure to repair the resulting misattunments all pointed to the development of a disorganized/disoriented attachment pattern between the mother and son. See Judith Solomon and Carol George's (2011) recent compilation of research and theoretical advances in this area.

6. For a recent meta-review, see "Childhood Interpersonal Trauma and its Repercussions in Adulthood: An Analysis of Psychological and Interpersonal Sequelae" by Dugal, Bigras, Godbout, and Belanger (2016). In a separate study, Edwards et al. (2003), concluded that "Among those reporting any maltreatment, more than one-third had experienced more than one type of maltreatment. A dose-response relation was found between the number of types of maltreatment reported and mental health scores. In addition, an emotionally abusive family environment accentuated the decrements in mental health scores" (p. 1453).

7. There are numerous advantages for children and parents alike in an extended family arrangement. Yet, according to Bruce Perry (2002), "recent inadvertent impacts of technology have spawned declines in extended families, family means, and spontaneous peer interactions. The latter changes have deprived many children of experiences that promote positive growth of the cognitive and caring potentials of their developing brains" (p. 79).

   Also see *Mothers and Others* by Sarah Hrdy (2009). Writing from an evolutionary perspective, Hrdy (2009) proposed that "within the brains of early Homo sapiens, who lived in small tribal groups composed of 25-50 individuals, a 'novel nervous system' probably developed that would in turn have been exposed to selection pressures that favored the survival of any child born with slightly better aptitudes for enlisting, maintaining, and manipulating [several] alloparental [substitute caregiver] ministrations. In this way, natural selection would lead to the evolution of cognitive tendencies that further encouraged infants to monitor and influence the emotions, mental states, and intentions of others" (p. 121).

   In contrast, within the modern nuclear family, the child may have only one of two caregivers with whom to develop these capabilities, to build empathy and to learn how to engage in prosocial, collaborative interactions with others. Hrdy concludes her book with the following prediction:

   "If empathy and understanding develop only under particular rearing conditions, and if an ever-increasing proportion of the species fails to encounter those conditions but nevertheless survives to reproduce, it won't matter how valuable the underpinnings for collaboration were in the past. Compassion and the quest for emotional connection will fade away as surely as sight in cave-dwelling fish" (p. 293).

8. Re: the idealization of parents: Bretherton and Munholland (2016) wrote that "Bowlby stressed that having two distinct types of memory storage could be problematic if a child's episodic memory of a troubling experience such as sexual abuse was disavowed or denied by a parent who did not wish the child to understand its meaning. Incorporating this idea into his theory of defensive processes, Bowlby proposed that to allay anxiety caused by seeing attachment figures in a bad light, a child in such situations was likely to defensively exclude

or repress his/her own episodic memories and retain conscious access only to semantically stored knowledge acquired from parents" (Loc. 3171).

9. For children's regression to utilizing defenses formed earlier in life, see Sylvia Anthony's (1973) research indicating underlying fantasies on the part of many children that a reunion with the mother, in a deep sense, insures immortality: "In all these instances, anxiety is clearly about death as separation from the love-object, and the defense has taken the form of a belief or hope of union in death; indeed, unconsciously of a closer union in death than was possible in life" (p. 151). Anthony's findings tend to coincide with my observations and hypothesis that the unconscious, fantasized connection with the mother is associated with a general sense of immortality in children.

10. Carol Gilligan (1982) and Gilligan, Rogers, & Tolman (1991) observed that in the socialization process, at home and at school, preadolescent girls give up their "voice" that is, their intuition, honest perceptions, and opinions so as *not* to lose relationships: "The relational crisis of boys' early childhood and of girls' adolescence is marked by a struggle to stay in relationship – a healthy resistance to disconnections which are psychologically wounding (from the body, from feelings, from relationships, from reality). . . . As young boys are pressured to take on images of heroes, or superheroes, as the grail which informs their quest to inherit their birthright or their manhood, so girls are pressed at adolescence to take on images of perfection as the model of the pure or perfectly good women: the women whom everyone will promote and value and want to be with" (Gilligan et al., 1991, p. 24).

In her observations of the effects of socialization on young boys, Chu (2104) noted that "boys' socialization towards cultural constructions of masculinity that are defined in opposition to femininity seems mainly to force a split between what boys know (e.g., about themselves, their relationships, and their world) and what boys show. In the process of becoming "boys," these boys essentially were learning to dissociate their outward behaviors from their innermost thoughts, feelings and desires" (Loc. 3970).

Source: *The Self Under Siege: A Therapeutic Model of Differentiation* (2013)

Note on Source: Republished with permission of Routledge from *The Self Under Siege: A Therapeutic Model for Differentiation* Robert W. Firestone, Lisa Firestone, and Joyce Catlett, 2013; permission through Copyright Clearance Center, Inc.

Chapter 6

SELF-DESTRUCTIVE BEHAVIOR AND SUICIDE

[Suicide's] essential nature is *psychological.* That is, each suicidal drama occurs in the *mind* of a unique individual. . . . Every single instance of suicide is an action by the dictator or emperor of your mind. But in every case of suicide, the person is getting bad advice from a part of that mind, the inner chamber of councilors, who are temporarily in a panicked state and in no position to serve the person's best long-term interests.

~ Edwin Shneidman, (1996, p. 165)

Suicide is a tragic ending to life that in most cases can be averted. According to Verrocchio et al. (2016), suicide is a public health problem of considerable magnitude in the United States, occurring at a 67% higher rate than homicide. In 2015, suicide was the second leading cause of death for 15 to 34 year olds (Curtin, Warner, & Hedegaard, 2016). "Approximately 9% of people report having serious thoughts of suicide at some point in their lives, and 3% actually make a suicide attempt" (Borges, et al., 2010, p. 1618).

Understanding this seemingly perverse anti-life phenomenon is of immense concern to practitioners in the mental health field. It is also important to try to comprehend the "contagion" effect that one person committing suicide has on other vulnerable individuals. In *The Enigma of Suicide,*

George Colt (1991) emphasized, "To the survivor [a family member or friend of the suicide victim] there is no statistic more chilling than the research that shows survivors to be at eight times higher risk for suicide than the general population" (p. 450). Because suicide has a very low base rate, prediction and prevention is complex and challenging; however, these are not impossible goals.

My colleagues and I were excited to discover a unique window into this complicated problem. By accessing and identifying the negative thought process (voice) along with the accompanying affect, we developed a theoretical framework and psychotherapeutic methodology that illuminated the psychodynamics of self-destruction.

THE PSYCHODYNAMICS OF SELF-DESTRUCTIVE BEHAVIOR AND SUICIDE

Negative reactions against the self are an integral part of each person's psyche, ranging from critical attitudes and mild self-attacks to severe assaults on the self. The latter includes feelings and attitudes that predispose physical injury to the self and eventually the complete obliteration of the self. No one reaches maturity completely unscathed by their personal experiences during their developmental years and no person is completely exempt from a suicidal process that leaves its mark on every life (Briere, 1992) (Note 1).

Psychopathology can more accurately be conceptualized as a limitation in living imposed on the individual by inadequate, immature or hostile parenting, internalized in the form of voices, and later manifested in self-limiting and/or self-destructive lifestyles. In this sense, the various forms of mental illness could be conceptualized as subclasses of suicide rather than the reverse (R. Firestone & Seiden, 1987) (Note 2).

As described in the previous chapters, all aspects of giving up of self— one's sense of reality, goal-directed activity, and appropriate emotional responses—represent a defensive, self-destructive orientation toward life that leads to neurotic or psychotic symptom formation. The extent of emotional deprivation and destructive parenting will determine the degree of dependence on psychological defenses. Inimical thought patterns and emotional attitudes that are introjected or incorporated into the self system strongly influence or control the relinquishing of one's unique identity and the narrowing of life experiences. As such, suicide represents the ultimate renunciation of self; the final submission to one's self-destructive machinations.

All mental and emotional phenomena are psychosomatic; that is, they involve both physical and psychological components. In other words, all factors must be considered in understanding human behavior. It is clear that suicide, depression, and self-destructive actions are multi-determined. Hereditary predispositions and biological components are significant factors in the etiology of suicidal behavior and are positively correlated with bipolar disorders. However, studies have also shown that behavior patterns manifested by depressed and addicted individuals are imitated by their offspring. The process of identification and imitation may well be a more influential factor than genetic inheritability in the intergenerational transmission of negative parental traits, behaviors, and defenses.

My approach to suicide is of a psychodynamic nature. In the majority of cases that I have examined, the impact of psychological elements on the child's development in all probability exceeds the influence of innate predispositions. More specifically, self-destructive propensities and suicidal actions appear to be overdetermined by interactions in the early interpersonal environment.

THE SELF AND ANTI-SELF IN SELF DESTRUCTIVE BEHAVIOR

I have a good self, that loves skies, hills, ideas, tasty meals, bright colors. My demon would murder this self by demanding that it be a paragon, and saying it should run away if it is anything less.

~ Sylvia Plath (Hughes and McCullough, 1982, p. 177)

People acquire a sense of self in an interpersonal context. Unfortunately, it is this same social milieu in which this delicate sense of self is fractured. This "division of the mind," represented in Figure 6.1, reflects the basic split between forces that represent the self (the self system) and those that oppose or attempt to destroy it (the anti-self system). To varying degrees, all people experience this split in their psyche. They are both friend and intimate enemy to themselves. In the case of suicide, this enmity reaches epic proportions.

Ironically, the child's desperate struggle to preserve intactness and wholeness is what produces this fragmentation. As previously explained, when conditions are painful or terrifying, aspects of an observing, punishing, parental self become dominant and form the anti-self system. In their work, Fonagy and Bateman (2007) have described this part of the personality as the "alien self:"

> We speculate that when a child does not have the opportunity to develop a self-representation through the caregiver's mirroring, he internalizes the non-contingent image of the caregiver as part of his self-representation (Winnicott, 1956), we have called this discontinuity within the self the "alien self" (p. 90).

Figure 6.1 Division of the Mind

Self System

Parental Nurturance/ Genetic Predisposition/Temperament

Attunement, Affection, Control

Other factors: effect of positive experience and education on the maturing self system.

Greater Degree of Differentiation

Unique make-up of the individual –harmonious identification and incorporation of parent's positive attitudes and traits.

Personal Goals/Conscience

Voice Process	Behaviors
Realistic, Positive Attitudes Toward Self Realistic evaluation of talents, abilities, etc., with generally positive/ compassionate attitude towards self and others.	Ethical behavior towards self and others
Goals Needs, wants, search for meaning in life	Goal Directed Behavior

Anti-Self System

Destructive Parental Behavior/Genetic Predisposition/Temperament

Misattunement, lack of affection, reject, neglect, hostility, permissiveness

Other Factors: Accidents, illnesses, traumatic separation

The Fantasy Bond

The Fantasy Bond (core defense) furthers a self-parenting process made up of both the helpless, needy child, and the self-punishing, self-nurturing parent. Either may be acted out in relationship content. The degree of reliance on this defense is proportional to the amount of damage sustained while growing up.

The Self-Parenting Process

Self-Punishing Voices

Voice Process	Behaviors
1. Critical thoughts toward self	Verbal attacks-a generally negative attitude toward self and others pre-disposing alienation
2. Micro-suicidal injunctions	Actions contrary to one's own interest and goals, and one's own emotional/ physical health
3. Suicidal injunctions-suicidal ideation	Actions that jeopardize one's health and safety; physical attacks, physical attacks on the self and actual suicide

Self-Soothing Voices

Voice Process	Behaviors
1. Self-soothing attitudes	Self-limiting or self-protective
2. Micro-suicidal injunctions (to the life-affirmative) self-indulgent thoughts	Addictive Patterns Actions contrary to one's own interest and goals, and one's own emotional/ physical health
3. Aggrandizing thoughts towards self	Narcissism/Vanity, acting superior to others and demeaning others, seeing they/man them as such, and punishing those who don't
4. Suspicions, paranoid thoughts toward others	Alienation toward others and hostile attitudes toward others, aggressive behavior toward others

Because of the power and size differential in relation to their parents, children tend to feel small, vulnerable and powerless. The more they feel victimized, the stronger the fantasy bond they develop with the parental power structure. Children unconsciously identify with their parents and tend to incorporate their negative attitudes—unfortunately, not as the parents are most of the time, but as they are at their worst. In extreme situations of trauma or abuse, parental aggression, murderous rage, and unconscious death wishes are internalized, which later in adolescence or adulthood, may be acted out in self-mutilation or suicide.

THE VOICE IN SELF-DESTRUCTIVE BEHAVIOR AND SUICIDE

A worldwide survey of risk factors for attempted suicide conducted by the World Health Organization began with these words, "Although suicide is a leading cause of death worldwide, clinicians and researchers lack a data-driven method to assess the risk of suicide attempts" (Borges et al., 2010, p. 1618). However, there *are* certain recognizable signs of suicidal intent that can be identified in suicidal ideation.

My point of view regarding the underlying thought process in suicide is threefold: (1) There is clinical evidence that the majority of potentially suicidal individuals are tortured by a subliminal voice process that is degrading and derisive to the self. This pattern of negative thoughts is generally accompanied by depression and lowered self-esteem; (2) under certain conditions, this system of hostile thoughts becomes progressively ascendant until it finally takes precedence over thought processes of rational self-interest; (3) these thoughts can be formulated and brought directly into consciousness by expressing them in terms of an inner voice.

In my work, I have been able to study the impact of critical inner voices and estimate the deleterious effect on the individual's personality and functioning level. I went on to study the voice process in depressed clients, people who had a history of suicidal thoughts, and those who had attempted suicide. These self-destructive thought patterns appeared to influence and control every aspect of their life-threatening behaviors and lifestyles.

When my colleagues and I interviewed depressed and/or suicidal individuals, we discovered that they were able to identify the contents of this harmful way of thinking about themselves. Although many interviewees had no previous knowledge of the concept of the voice, they usually related to it with familiarity and ease. I hypothesized that the thought process that I had observed in "normal" and neurotic individuals was essentially the same mechanism that leads to severe depressive states as well as to self-destructive behavior and suicide. Similarly, in his interviews with 50 survivors of serious suicide attempts, Richard Heckler (1994) noted the prevalence of the voice in the thinking of these individuals prior to their attempt:

> At this point in the [suicidal] trance, the inner pull toward suicide dramatically intensifies. Often it comes in the form of a voice. In fact, mention of a voice is so common that I've learned to inquire directly about this during interviews. This voice grows in volume with the stress of the suicidal ordeal. It demands increasingly to be heard above everything else, and it begins to occupy a greater part of the person's psyche until it smothers more reasonable voices altogether. Often people experience this voice as relentlessly driving them toward self-destruction (p. 74).

THE CONTINUUM OF SELF-DESTRUCTIVE THOUGHTS AND BEHAVIORS

I conceptualize suicide as representing the extreme end of a continuum of destructive mental processes that results in the ultimate annihilation of self. Clients who see suicide as "the best solution" are not basing their perception on rational thinking, but instead on irrational, malevolent cognitive processes. Cautious optimism with respect to prevention also comes from anecdotal accounts from survivors of potentially lethal suicide attempts who later reported feeling ambivalent, up to the last moment, about taking their own lives. The fact that most people who commit suicide are usually ambivalent about ending their lives offers an opportunity for interrupting the suicidal process at some point prior to actual completion. Shneidman (1985) has asserted that "the vast majority (about 80%) of suicides have a recognizable pre-suicidal phase" (p. 39) (Note 3).

My conceptual model suggests an incisive approach to understanding the precursors and warning signs of suicide and provides a basis for intervening in and preventing an ultimate act of self-destruction. I have developed the following hypotheses regarding the relationship between the voice process and self-destructive behavior and suicide:

(1) A conflict exists within each individual between life-affirming propensities to actively pursue goals in the real world, and self-denying, self-protective, self-destructive tendencies that are related to seeking gratification primarily through fantasy processes.

(2) Thoughts antithetical to the self vary along a continuum of intensity from mild self-reproach to strong self-attack and actual suicidal thoughts.

(3) Self-destructive behavior exists on a continuum from self-denial and self-limitation at one end, to isolation, drug abuse, and other self-defeating behaviors, culminating in actual bodily harm.

(4) Both of these processes, cognitive and behavioral, parallel each other, with suicide representing the acting out of the extreme destructive end of the continuum (R. Firestone & Seiden, 1990). [See Figure 6.2]

Figure 6.2 The Continuum of Negative Thoughts
Levels of Increasing Suicidal Intention Content of Voice Statements

Thoughts that Lead to Low Self-Esteem or Inwardness (Self-Defeating Thoughts)

1. Self-depreciating thoughts of everyday life: *You're incompetent, stupid. You're not very attractive.*

2. Thoughts rationalizing self-denial: thoughts discouraging the person from engaging in pleasurable activities: *You're too young (old) and inexperienced to apply for this job. You're too shy to make any new friends. Why go on this trip? It'll be such a hassle.*

3. Cynical attitudes toward others, leading to alienation and distancing: *Why go out with her (him)? She's cold, unreliable; she'll reject you. You can't trust men (women).*

4. Thoughts influencing isolation: rationalizations for time alone, but using time to become more negative toward oneself: *Just be by yourself. You're miserable company anyway; who'd want to be with you? Just stay in the background, out of view.*

5. Self-contempt; vicious self-abusive thoughts and accusations (accompanied by intense angry affect) *You idiot! You bitch! You creep! You stupid shit! You don't deserve anything; you're worthless!*

Thoughts that Lead to the Cycle of Addiction

6. Thoughts urging use of substances or food followed by self-criticisms (weakens inhibitions against self-destructive actions, while increasing guilt and self-recrimination following acting out) *It's okay to do drugs, you'll be more relaxed. Go ahead and have a drink, you deserve it. (Later) You weak-willed jerk! You're nothing but a drugged-out drunken freak.*

Self-Annihilating Thoughts

7. Thoughts contributing to a sense of hopelessness, urging withdrawal or removal of oneself completely from the lives of people closest: *See how bad you make your family (friends) feel. They'd be better off without you. It's the only decent thing to do. Just stay away and stop bothering them.*

8. Thoughts influencing a person to give up priorities and favored activities: *What's the use? Your work doesn't matter any more. Why bother trying? Nothing matters anyway.*

9. Injunctions to inflict self-harm at an action level; intense rage against self: *Why don't you just drive across the center divider? Just shove your hand under that power saw!*

10. Thoughts planning details of suicide (calm, rational, often obsessive, indicating complete loss of feeling for the self) *You have to get hold of some pills, then go to a hotel.*

11. Injunctions to carry out suicide plans; thoughts baiting the person to commit suicide (extreme thought constriction): *You've thought about this long enough. Just get it over with. It's the only way out!*

Any combination of behaviors listed in Figure 6.2 can eventually culminate in suicidal action. Most particularly, thoughts promoting isolation, ideation about removing oneself from people's lives, beliefs that one has a destructive effect on others, voices urging one to give up favorite activities, malevolent, angry self-attacks, and, of course, voices urging self-injury or actual suicide, are all indications of high suicide risk.

Clients may remain stabilized for long periods at lower (subclinical) levels of adjustment, pursuing, for example, an ascetic existence and rationalizing self-denial. However, any movement toward successive levels should be taken very seriously as a potential indicator that the client is embarking on a regressive trend that could eventuate in destructive acting-out behavior. A downward spiraling movement along the continuum of self-destructive behaviors is a sign of suicidal intent. Therein lies the predictive value of eliciting and identifying the content of these individuals' negative voices and evaluating the intensity of their aggression toward self.

MICRO-SUICIDE: DEATH OF THE SPIRIT

All self-destructive behaviors are interrelated; that is, they differ only in quantity, nature and degree. In introducing his term, "partial suicide," in his classic book *Man Against Himself,* Karl Menninger (1938) asserted that, "In the end each man kills himself in his own selected way, fast or slow, soon or late" (p. vii). In this sense, all people have the potential for suicide; it is only the individual style and strength of the movement toward self-destruction that varies from one person to the next.

Suicidal behavior does not always entail such direct and overt means as putting a gun to one's head. It includes an entire range of behaviors not always thought of as suicidal. In my work, I refer to these actions and lifestyles as *micro-suicide.* They include those behaviors, communications, attitudes or lifestyles that are self-induced and threatening to an individual's physical health, emotional well-being or personal goals. While these behaviors may not literally be life-threatening, they progressively diminish the quality of one's life and they are so widely disseminated in the general population that I have termed them the "micro-suicides of everyday life."

Micro-suicidal behaviors encompass the primary components of the syndrome of inwardness or an inward, self-protective lifestyle. The behaviors and ways of living that are manifested by an inward person correspond directly to a number of the precursors of suicide delineated by leading suicidologists, including David Shaffer and Edwin Shneidman (MacNeil-Lerher, 1987). In his descriptions of these "inimical" (unfriendly) patterns of living, Shneidman (1966), highlighted the "multitudinous ways in which an individual can reduce, truncate, demean, narrow, shorten, or destroy his own life" (p. 199).

Inwardness

As people become inward, they tend to neutralize their experiences and lose considerable feeling for themselves and others. When they are in this self-protective state, their gaze is focused inward on themselves rather than outward toward others. Their capacity for giving and accepting love is impaired, and they tend to limit personal transactions of both giving and receiving.

Inwardness needs to be distinguished from self-reflection, introspection, time spent alone for creative work, meditation, or other spiritual and intellectual pursuits. Essentially, inwardness involves an insidious process of regarding oneself more as an object than as a person. Each individual develops idiosyncratic ways of dulling, deadening and disconnecting from emotions and from life experience. To better understand the narrow focus inherent in living an inward lifestyle, the loss of experience, and the propensity for self-destruction, it is necessary to take an incisive look at the characteristics of the inward person.

The major characteristics of the inward person are: (a) a loss of feeling and sense of depersonalization, (b) a reliance on addictive, self-nourishing behaviors, (c) a preference for isolation and fantasy gratification over satisfactions derived from real achievements or in an intimate relationship, (d) cynical, suspicious attitudes toward others and self-critical, self-hating attitudes toward oneself, and (e) a lack of a direction in life that leads to a sense of despair and futility, depression, micro-suicidal ideation and behavior and in some extreme cases, actual suicide. The overall effects of inwardness contribute to a self-limiting, self-denying, and micro-suicidal lifestyle.

The Dynamics of Micro-suicide

Micro-suicidal behaviors derive from feelings of self-hatred and negative attitudes toward the self, which are manifestations of incorporated parental attitudes that have come to have their own functional autonomy within the adult personality. Feelings of worthlessness, self-critical thoughts, and the erratic mood swings that characterize certain types of depressive states are controlled or strongly influenced by the voice. The core of the voice is directed toward unnecessary self-denial and ultimately toward the self-destruction of the individual. The voice is the mechanism that regulates and dictates a person's self-denying, micro-suicidal behavior.

Under certain conditions, the voice can become progressively ascendant and take precedence over thoughts of rational self-interest. When self-accusations and self-critical attitudes are articulated in Voice Therapy in the second person format, they can be effectively evaluated and countered. My colleagues and I also discovered that the unexpected thoughts or brief suicidal impulses which sometimes erupt into the conscious mind of "normal" individuals are indications of the presence of this underlying system of negative thoughts.

Micro-suicide as an Accommodation to Death Anxiety

> The common denominator of all negative ways of dealing with anxiety is a shrinking of the area of awareness and of activity... We are afraid to die, and therefore we are afraid to live, or as Tillich put it, we avoid nonbeing by avoiding being. The avoidance of anxiety then means a kind of death in life.
>
> ~ Joseph C. Rheingold (1967, pp. 204-205)

It is a well-known statistic that suicide rates are very high in inmates awaiting execution on death row (A. Smith, 2007) (Note 4). The prisoner takes his own life in an effort to have some measure of control over death rather than live with the agony of knowing the exact time of execution. The "normal" individual engages in micro-suicidal behaviors for similar reasons. Why invest feelings in a life that one most certainly will lose? Through the process of progressive self-denial and other forms of micro-suicide, the fear of death evolves into a fear of living, of becoming too involved in or attached to life.

When individuals give up their lives through micro-suicidal behavior, they are able to maintain a false sense of omnipotence, as if they have retained some power over life and death. An overall analysis of the destructive thought process indicates that the majority of the voice's injunctions and rationalizations are attempts to limit life by persuading the individual to gradually eliminate exciting and spontaneous pursuits. Physical life is thus maintained, yet psychological suicide is being committed on an everyday basis as people gradually narrow their world and trivialize their experience.

This universal propensity to become self-denying and self-destructive represents a powerful defense against the fear of death. The anticipation of losing one's life and losing all consciousness through death can be so agonizing that giving up provides welcome relief. The idea that suicidal and self-destructive behavior can alleviate fears of death and dying may at first seem paradoxical, yet the phenomenon has been a topic in literature, philosophy, and psychology for centuries. In *Six Tales of the Jazz Age*, F. Scott Fitzgerald (1960) succinctly wrote about self-limiting, self-denying behaviors that serve the function of helping people adapt to existential inevitabilities:

> The years between thirty-five and sixty-five revolve before the passive mind as one unexplained, confusing merry-go-round. For most men and women these thirty years are taken up with a gradual withdrawal from life, a retreat first from a front with many shelters, those myriad amusements and curiosities of youth, to a life with less, when we peel down our ambitions to one ambition, our recreations to one recreation, our friends to a few to whom we are anesthetic; ending up at last in a solitary, desolate strong point that is not strong where, by turns frightened and tired, we sit waiting for death (p. 110).

Neurotic and psychotic symptoms are reflected in the repetitive, self-sabotaging ways of living in which many defended individuals act out micro-suicidal behavior in an effort to alleviate existential dread and terror. Laing (1969), Searles (1961; 1979), and Karon and VandenBos (1981) have hypothesized that the terror of death or of being killed is at the core of severe mental illness, particularly schizoid disorders and schizophrenia. Karon and VandenBos (1981) observed: "In several schizophrenic patients whom we have treated, both acute and chronic, it was clear that an overwhelming conscious fear of death immediately preceded the psychotic break. It is certainly clear that every schizophrenic patient believes that he could not live without his symptoms" (p. 143).

The process of progressively relinquishing one's interests and desires over an extended period of time can lead to a state of emptiness and futility, feelings that Orbach (2008) believes contribute to a sense of meaninglessness, a feeling that "nothing matters." When life is trivialized in this manner, there can be a corresponding decrease in conscious death anxiety because one has much less to lose through death. To avoid the associated anxiety and dread that come with the full realization that their lives are temporary, people often retreat to an inward, self-protective state in which they narrow their life experience by cutting off feeling for themselves and others (Note 5).

In summary, in attempting to elude death, people eventually give up their lives to varying degrees, rationing their aliveness and spontaneity, carefully doling out or restricting pleasant or enriching experiences. They gradually become indifferent to important or relevant events and numb themselves by attending to life's trivialities. Living a full life, with meaningful activity, compassion for oneself, and a poignant awareness that all people share the same fate, appears to be too agonizing for most to endure. The majority are not strong enough to live fully in the face of death, and therefore tend to withdraw to a more defended, inward lifestyle. However, the process of identifying one's defenses and learning to change them can move life in the opposite direction.

THE INNER VOICE IN SUICIDE

Suicides are not always triggered by negative circumstances; they are also sometimes motivated by positive events. The statistics of suicide indicate that the favored segments of the population paradoxically have the highest rates of self-destruction; for example, the suicide rate for whites is several times that for nonwhites.

Our clinical material indicated that a process of self-denial on a behavioral level parallels voice attacks and this self-denial can lead to a cycle of serious pathology. At the extreme end of the continuum, severely depressed individuals become exhausted and listless in struggling against self-destructive urges and self-abusive thoughts. Furthermore, they lack the means of determining an accurate view of self and cannot differentiate an objective assessment from the habitual negative view of themselves that they have accepted since childhood. They have reached a stage where the balance has shifted to such a degree that the alien point of view represented by the voice has become their own point of view.

The severely depressed or suicidal person has adopted the voice and its vicious strictures, commands, and directives, as his/her own and is now more *against* him/herself than *for* him/herself. The person wholeheartedly believes the negative, hostile statements of the voice about him/herself and other people. Consequently, to a great extent, the person no longer has contact with his/her real self and feels hopelessly estranged from others as well.

At this point, the person is at high risk for suicide. By now, his/her way of thinking is severely constricted; the person is almost completely "possessed" by the voice process, and he/she finds the alternatives narrowed down to the two options described by Shneidman (1985), as:

Either having some magical resolution or being dead . . . Such deaths . . . are annihilations of the 'self,' of the personality, of the ego. At the time it happens, the individual is primarily 'self-contained' and responds to the 'voices' (not in the sense of hallucinatory voices) within him (p. 140).

Case Example

Here I describe a case that illustrates the core conflict and the essential ambivalence toward life and death manifested by the suicidal individual.

At 5:00 p.m. on October 10, 1976, Sharon drove her car to a hotel, registered, went to her room, and took a lethal combination of Seconal, Miltown, and Valium. At the last moment before losing consciousness, she managed to pick up the phone and reach an operator at a nearby university, leaving only her first name and hotel before losing consciousness. Paramedics rushed to the scene, raced frantically through the hallways and, with no last name or room number, unlocked or banged loudly on every door until they finally found Sharon, lying unconscious across her bed. Fortunately, there was a hospital located directly across the street and they rushed her to emergency treatment. She remained on the critical list in the intensive care unit for the next 18 hours. Miraculously, she survived. From that time on, with the aid of psychotherapy, she steadily progressed and gradually resumed a normal life. Several years later, I interviewed her about the events leading up to the suicide attempt.

Sharon was 30 years old when she made the decision to end her life. A pretty, petite woman, she was successful in her career. However, she had become increasingly unhappy in a relationship that had been meaningful to her. A slow deterioration in feelings had occurred over a period of two years from the time the couple had first been close. As the story unfolds, Sharon refers to a pattern of negative thoughts that dominated her thinking during that period in her life.

Sharon: Sitting here now, the first thing I thought of was that that wasn't the only time I actually thought of killing myself. Even as a young child, I often thought about suicide when I felt really bad, which I did a lot of the time. I thought that if things really got bad enough, I could just kill myself.

Dr. F.: What was tormenting you in your current situation that you wanted to get out of?

Sharon: I remember feeling depressed, down a lot. I felt like I was bad. Like there was something really bad about me that I couldn't fix. I couldn't stand myself, that's what I couldn't live with. It's hard to talk about this because I don't feel like this now.

Dr. F.: I'm glad that you don't. Do you remember, though, what kind of actual thoughts you had about suicide? And what form they took?

Sharon: That I wanted to kill myself and I tried to get myself to the point that I didn't care enough about anything so that I could do it. Thoughts like: *You don't really like him. He doesn't matter that much to you. There are other people that he likes. You're so ugly. Who would choose you? There are other people important in his life. It doesn't matter. You don't matter that much to him. You don't matter to yourself. You don't matter to anybody. Who would care if you weren't around? People would miss you a little at the beginning but who would really care? You don't care.* It's hard to believe I really thought these things, but I did.

I tried to get alone, because this process occurred when I was alone. The voice was weak when I was around other people, so the voice got me to be alone, saying: *Get alone. Look, don't you need some time for yourself? Get alone so you can think.*

Then once I would get alone, either driving around somewhere or just walking around by myself, then these other voices, the more destructive ones, would start. Like they took the form of: *If you don't matter, what does matter? Nothing matters. What are you waking up for? You know you hate waking up every morning. Why bother? It's so agonizing to wake up in the morning, why bother doing it? Just end it. Just end it. Stop it!*

Dr. F.: Did you hear that voice like a hallucination, like somebody else saying it?

Sharon: No, it wasn't a hallucination at all. It was totally thoughts. It was thoughts in my head. Whenever I was alone, the voice was more vicious and angry: *You'd better do it! It's the only thing you can do. You'd better do it! I hate you! I hate you.*

In therapy, I had a lot of thoughts about my relationship with my mother. I remembered the feelings she directed toward me when we were alone. I remember the hatred. *I hate you. I hate you.* And that was like that voice, my own voice. It turned into my own voice when it was the most vicious, hating myself.

As Sharon made preparations to actually take her life, the voice became progressively dissociated from her own point of view and sounded monotonous, cold and rational.

Sharon: I was so cut off that the voice seemed rational. *Here's the hotel. You gotta pull into the driveway. Be careful, you don't want to call any attention to yourself. Don't act stupid. Don't make this take longer than it has to. Now here is the key. Go to the elevator, go up to the room, and unlock the door.* Which I did. Then I remember that I wanted to eat. I ordered a large room-service meal, which took some time.

At the last moment, when Sharon delayed taking the pills in order to eat the dinner she had ordered (an action that may have saved her life), the voice ridiculed her for procrastinating.

Sharon: Then, after eating the meal: *Okay, okay, you had the meal that you wanted. Now you can die in peace. Okay, go ahead now, you've got these pills. Go ahead, start taking them.* This is something I haven't had a memory of before, of taking the pills. But I sort of remember it now. *Okay, you've had your meal. Now do it! Do it. Coward! Now do it already. You had your pleasure, now do it.*

Dr. F.: And you listened to those voices, and they almost killed you. [In a gentle tone] You took a lethal dosage of pills and you almost died.

Sharon: Yes, I took enough pills to kill myself. But, I also called the information number of the university. I knew their number because I went to school there.

Dr. F.: After you took the pills.

Sharon: After I took the pills, I was lying on the bed.

Dr. F.: Were you getting drowsy?

Sharon: I can't remember, but I do know that it took every effort that I had to make the call.

Dr. F.: Something in you wanted to save yourself, obviously.

Sharon: At some point when I realized what was happening, that it was working, I thought, "My God, this is working! I don't want this to work." That wasn't a voice anymore. That was me.

Dr. F.: You could tell the difference.

Sharon: Yes.

Case Analysis

The most important aspect of this interview is that Sharon chose to live and did save herself at the last moment. Her drive for survival overcame the self-destructive process, even though she came within inches of dying in spite of her call for help. Her ambivalent attitudes toward herself were manifested in actions that played a role in saving her life. She chose to eat a big meal before ingesting the pills and this kept the pills from having a lethal effect. She chose a hotel adjacent to a hospital emergency room. And, finally, at the last minute, she called the university and reached out for help. Later, her desire for life was supported by her close friends and a successful psychotherapy program.

Prior to her suicide attempt, Sharon seemed actually to be possessed by the critical inner voice, to be at the mercy of a point of view hostile to her self-interest. Somewhere in the midst of the suicidal crisis, she found herself and was no longer bound by the destructive dictates of her voice. In the early stages of the "suicidal trance," voices instructed Sharon to isolate herself and cut off feelings for herself and others. She turned inward and resented experiences that intruded on her withdrawn state and resolution to complete the act. Later, angry voices cajoled her to get on with the deed, and, finally, the voices drove her to the point of action.

ASSESSMENT AND TREATMENT OF THE
SUICIDAL INDIVIDUAL

Identification of the Suicidal Individual

In planning interventions with people identified as potentially suicidal, clinicians can focus their attention on (1) exposing and understanding cognitive patterns that dictate micro-suicidal behavior and (2) on helping prevent the client from acting out the commands in a suicide attempt.

First clinicians need to assess the presence of psychological and social risk factors. They should determine if the client has a history of a psychiatric disorder, including major depression, bipolar disorder, alcohol dependence, drug addiction, schizophrenia, organic psychosis, borderline, or compulsive personality disorder, a history of suicide or suicidal behavior in the family, or a history of abuse. They should also ask questions regarding current stressors such as loss of an important relationship, loss of a valued job, lack of a social support system, and physical health problems and how these relate to past losses, such as loss of a parent in childhood. However, as Oquendo, Currier & Mann (2006) observed in prospective studies of suicidal behavior, "Different risk factors may have predictive validity in the long and short term, [and] prediction of suicidal behavior remains an elusive goal" (p. 151).

Suicidal intent can be assessed by inquiring into the client's suicidal ideation, plans, methods under consideration, availability of means, precautions against discovery, and past suicide attempts. In addition, therapists need to focus on specific symptoms of "psychache" in the client which were described by Shneidman (1993), "especially such distressing feelings as guilt, shame, fear, anger, thwarted ambition, unrequited love, hopelessness, helplessness, and loneliness" (p. 152). It is also crucial to look into the client's past suicidal thinking and self-destructive behaviors and the frequency and intensity of current suicidal ideology (Note 6).

Research studies by cognitive therapist Aaron Beck (A. Beck, Steer, J. Beck, & Newman, 1993) and others showing correlations between suicide and suicidal ideation have led to the development of a number of self-report instruments to assess aspects of the suicidal client's belief system and thinking. One instrument in particular, the Beck Hopelessness Scale (Beck,

1978b), showed that hopelessness was more important than depression as a risk factor for suicide.

Development of The Firestone Assessment of Self-Destructive Thoughts [FAST]

Background of the Study: Part of the inspiration for developing a scale to assess suicide potential originated in a suggestion by Dr. C. Everett Koop, who was the U.S. Surgeon General. Frank Tobe, a political consultant and close friend of mine, was on an airplane flying to a conference in Washington, D.C. when he found himself sitting beside Surgeon General Koop. Frank began talking about my ideas in relation to suicide and Dr. Koop responded with interest and emphasized the need for rigorous scientific research on the subject.

When Frank told me about his encounter, I immediately decided to pursue a research methodology based on Voice Therapy theory. I had two motives. First, I felt that developing a scale utilizing voice attacks to determine self-destructive and suicide potential could save lives, and, second, I thought that a scientific study using this type of scale would offer empirical validation of my underlying theory. My assumption was that a scale of voice attacks on the self would parallel destructive acting-out behavior, and that those who scored very high on this scale would be more likely to injure themselves.

My daughter, Lisa Firestone, began to gather items for the new scale from the negative self-attacks of colleagues and clients. After constructing the scale, she administered it to 507 subjects who were currently in treatment (the majority in outpatient psychotherapy). In a second study, inpatients from selected groups representing various diagnostic categories were administered the FAST and six other instruments, including the Beck Hopelessness Scale (Beck, 1978b). Our study included 479 inpatients diagnosed with schizophrenia, depression, and bipolar disorder. The FAST distinguished suicide ideators from non-ideators in each of the diagnostic categories.

Description of the Scale: The FAST was derived from 20 years of clinical research into the voice. Lisa and I believed that it was logical to use these negative thought patterns to predict increasingly aggressive cognition and affect toward the self that are closely related to self-destructive behavior and actual suicide (R. Firestone, 1986; 1988).

The *Firestone Assessment of Self-Destructive Thoughts [FAST]* (R. Firestone & L. Firestone, 2006) is a self-report questionnaire consisting of 84 items drawn from 11 levels of progressively self-destructive thoughts. Clients endorse the items on a 5-point, Likert-type scale from "Never" to "Most of the time." The scale includes items drawn from each level of the "Continuum of Negative Thought Patterns" as shown in Figure 6.2. Items on the FAST are made up of actual "voice" statements reported by subjects in the earlier clinical studies. Results of reliability and validation studies show that the FAST effectively discriminates between suicidal and non-suicidal subjects at a high level of significance.

The FAST is used not only to assess an individual's suicide potential, but also to identify the aspects of self-destructive behavior and psychological functioning in which the person has experienced the greatest degree of difficulty (Note 7). In 1996, the FAST was added to the repertoire of instruments utilized by mental health professionals for assessing suicide, as well as the self-destructive thinking that controls micro-suicidal actions and lifestyles.

TREATMENT OF THE SUICIDAL INDIVIDUAL

Dealing with potentially suicidal individuals who seek treatment has proven difficult for psychologists and psychiatrists. Surveys show that clients in a suicidal crisis are the therapist's worst fear, often paralyzing clinicians emotionally and interfering with their sound judgment. Voice Therapy is especially useful in the treatment of depression and suicidal trends. In developing the methodology over the past 30 years, I have found that in no other mental condition are internalized voices more obvious to the client or the self-attacks more uncritically accepted as real. Two clinical uses for Voice Therapy can be elucidated: (a) in crisis intervention and (b) in long-term treatment for suicidal individuals.

Crisis Intervention

In Crisis Intervention, Voice Therapy methods are valuable in ameliorating perturbation and lethality during the crisis and are conducive to quickly establishing the therapeutic alliance or relationship. The client's agitation and angry affect toward self are directly associated with the voice attacks typical of the "suicidal trance." Thus, the therapist or crisis hot line worker who shows an understanding of voices has tremendous leverage in creating the rapport necessary to continue the dialogue and possibly save the person's life.

Judgmental or parental attitudes on the part of clinicians or caseworkers that arouse either neurotic or existential guilt have a negative effect on the suicidal client. Any response that supports a person's self-attacks or negative voices is detrimental, whereas any communication or behavior on the therapist's part that shows genuine feeling, support, and compassion can act to strengthen the self and support the client's desire to live. It is the sincere and personal expression of caring, without judgment, that is most likely to reach a person at risk.

Long Term Treatment

The Intake Interview: For a comprehensive evaluation of suicide risk, the clinician should conduct a clinical interview to establish rapport and help the client feel at ease, listened to and cared about. A mental status examination should be performed, involving observations of the client's presentation, appearance, mood, expressed affect, intellectual functioning, thought processes, insight, judgment, and presence or absence of hallucinations or delusions.

Direct questions should be asked regarding the client's thoughts about suicide. In particular, the clinician needs to ask the following: Do you currently consider suicide an option? How suicidal do you see yourself as being now? Do you have a plan for committing suicide? Do you have the means to carry out your suicide plan? What is the time frame for your plan? Clients often feel understood by the therapist's inquiries and regard these questions as permission to talk about their painful thoughts and feelings. The clinician should investigate the meaning of the present crisis for the client by asking about precipitating events connected to it. How does the client interpret the crisis? Does he/she perceive his/her situation realistically? Are cognitive distortions affecting his/her perceptions and interfering with his/her ability to cope?

Therapists must pay close attention to their own emotional reactions because suicidal clients tend to provoke feelings of fear, dislike, aggression, and even malice in therapists. Negative feelings that suicidal clients feel toward themselves can also be evoked in the therapist during sessions or interviews. Experiencing these reactions should alert the therapist that the client may be at risk for suicide (Jobes & Berman, 1993; Maltsberger & Buie, 1989).

During my 22 years of practicing psychotherapy, I used the intake interview to assess the suicide potential, ego strength, and type and level of defenses of new clients and to begin to establish the therapeutic relationship. One of my questions was, "How do you feel when you feel the most down?" I followed up with other questions, such as, "What's the lowest you ever felt?" "What are the worst attitudes you ever had toward yourself?" Later, I inquired about previous suicide attempts and self-destructive or suicidal thoughts or fantasies. I also asked clients to estimate how depressed they were when they considered suicide or made the attempt.

As the interview continued, I found it valuable to delve more deeply into their history of depression. I requested information about the content of their thoughts and the intensity of the affect they experienced. My questions were an attempt to discern whether their suicidality was at an action level or occurred only as thoughts. Finally, I asked the clients who reported a history of depression or suicide attempts: Are you currently in that frame of mind?

Through these inquiries, asked in a spirit of genuine interest and consideration, I was generally able to glean most of the information I needed regarding a person's suicide potential. My questions also had the purpose of determining a particular client's ability to withstand the highs and lows of the treatment process. During the course of therapy, regression and negative therapeutic reactions are bound to occur, and I needed to assess how clients would handle the low points. Would they become suicidal during a therapeutic crisis? With borderline clients, how would they handle the underlying depression?

Anti-suicide Contracts: Some clinicians use anti-suicide contracts whereas others (Jobes, 2012) use a collaborative approach (CAMS) to engage suicidal outpatients in keeping track of and managing their suicidality (Note 8). In establishing an anti-suicide agreement, I informed clients that they could call me at any time, day or night, whenever they felt overwhelmed by anxiety states, depressed affect, or suicidal thoughts or impulses. (Incidentally, not one person ever abused this privilege.) My regard for their well-being conveyed to clients my feeling that they should not suffer unnecessarily when help was available. I wanted them to learn that being open about their feelings and communicating with a concerned person could help alleviate their pain. I was particularly sensitive to any nuance or attempt to break this anti-suicide contract.

For example, if a client revealed that she had gone through a particularly hard time between sessions and had not called me, I would take it seriously and respond with something like, "Look, we agreed to keep contact. If you felt terrible, you should have called. Even if you weren't close to actually hurting yourself, you should call before it gets too bad. Don't let the depression sink in. Discuss your voices before they get out of hand. Being outward about your self-destructive thoughts is the way out of this mess." It is critical to establish and adhere to this principle before clients are enveloped in the suicidal trance phase. By the time it reaches those proportions, the destructive voices often preclude any communication.

In general, the compassionate, feeling practitioner who is not afraid of suicidal clients will fare better than those who approach them without a balance of warmth and strength. In dealing with highly lethal clients, this type of therapist will feel more confident about taking certain chances on being spontaneous, straightforward, and even confrontational in his/her responses. On certain occasions, honest anger expressed directly as a concerned response on the part of a sensitive therapist will be experienced by the suicidal individual as supportive and can serve to circumvent a potential suicide. Nevertheless, there are always risks, and it is the therapist's peace of mind that is often at stake.

To illustrate, in an intake interview several years ago, I became alarmed at a client's self-destructive tendencies and allowed myself to angrily challenge his defenses. This behavior was in sharp contrast to my usual therapeutic calm and neutrality. His appointment happened to occur on a Friday afternoon, and because of the man's depressed state, I scheduled our next meeting for the following Monday at 9:00 a.m. The client dispiritedly and reluctantly agreed to my conditions of treatment, including the requirement that he call if things got too horrendous for him over the weekend.

After he departed, I was afraid that my confrontational manner might have provoked a suicidal outcome rather than averting one. I spent the entire weekend with the problem on the edge of my consciousness. On Monday morning as I approached the reception room door, I heard the sound of cheerful whistling and my doubts and fears were immediately allayed. I cursed myself for spoiling my weekend. I realized that I had done the right thing and that I should trust my intuition in the future.

My thoughts were affirmed by the client's opening words: "Gee, Doc, you hit me like a ton of bricks. On Friday when I walked in here, I thought my life was over. When you let me have it, oddly enough I began to see things in perspective. I didn't at first, but by the time I got to my car, I noticed that I felt different. Your anger surprised and shocked me, made me kind of laugh at my stupid mood. Funny thing, when you were pissed off, I felt like you really cared."

I responded by saying: "I'm glad that you could look at it that way, and I'm pleased that you feel better. Now it's important for us to get at the issues, to see how you got into trouble with yourself in the first place."

Voice Therapy and Suicide: In the context of long-term treatment, Voice Therapy methods are highly effective in helping to avert regression to severely depressed states as well as suicide attempts. By identifying the negative cognitions driving suicidal actions, clients gain a measure of control over all aspects of their self-destructive or suicidal behavior. They become aware that the principal cause of their depression, dysphoria or hopelessness is the way they negatively perceive or distort stressful events, not the events themselves. Clients are able to generalize this understanding, which they develop in Voice Therapy sessions, to their everyday lives.

In my clinical experience, I have found that if people simply recognize when they are attacking themselves, this awareness is, in itself, enormously therapeutic. Merely becoming conscious that one is thinking in terms that are opposed to one's self-interest enables one to begin challenging the process of destructive, obsessive ruminations.

Being allowed to express the negative parental introjects in their sessions helps depressed clients to perceive these cognitive distortions as coming from an external source so that they can begin to question and challenge their validity. The therapist who is knowledgeable about the voice process is acutely sensitive to which aspect of self (the self or the anti-self) the client is expressing or manifesting. In general, clients tend to feel understood by therapists who recognize the voice process, and this aids in establishing the rapport necessary for long-term treatment.

In more serious cases, the identification of the specific content of negative thinking and the release of associated affect provide clients with tools to counter injunctions to harm themselves. They learn to deduce from their own behavior or change in mood that, on some level, they must be experiencing an onslaught of self-accusations. Subsequently, they can attempt to identify the specific voices motivating their behavior.

Uncovering elements of negative thinking that have previously existed only on an unconscious level interferes with or can even prevent the acting out of destructive impulses. This type of awareness is crucial for clients who have little or no insight; it provides them with a sense of mastery over behaviors they previously perceived as being beyond their control.

Finally, Voice Therapy methods are fundamental to identifying and supporting the special wants, priorities and interests of clients that give meaning to their lives. These unique predilections keep the client's spirit alive; the therapist's awareness of these factors can help in crisis intervention.

An understanding of the various aspects of the self and anti-self systems helps clinicians focus attention on the specific needs of their clients that were being frustrated and that may have precipitated the suicidal crisis. Shneidman (1985) contends that the "common stressors in both suicide and parasuicide are frustrated psychological needs" (p. 215). When the suicidal crisis is over and clients are on the upgrade, their personal goals become the primary focus of attention in the therapy. In an interview, David Jobes (Parr, 2012a) emphasized in advising therapists who treat suicidal individuals:

> You start with the behaviors, you eliminate the cutting and the verbal threats and those overt actions that they've learned over a lifetime, and those are a series of little battles. But if you're going to win the war with suicide, at the end of the day, you're going to make their life worth living, or be a part of a process that makes their life worth living (Note 9).

CONCLUSION

Each person tends to develop a specific, idiosyncratic method for dulling, deadening, and disconnecting from life's experiences. The tragic fact is that so many people live out their lives largely in the destructive anti-self system or defended posture, ensnared by the repetitive acting out of micro-suicidal behavior.

Patterns of micro-suicidal behavior are not confined to addictions, depressed states, or risk-taking actions; they are representative of the norm in our culture. Deadening routines, self-denial, antagonistic attitudes toward self, and prejudicial biases toward others are not exceptional phenomena; they are all too common. They disrupt personal relationships and cause disharmony and misery on a pervasive scale in everyday life.

The way that defended individuals are damaged and the way they function are closely linked to negative internalized thoughts. The knowledge gained through accessing and identifying the partially unconscious thought processes driving a suicidal person toward death can be used to set potentially lifesaving interventions into motion. Understanding the voice process elucidates the self-destructive machinations of the personality and points the way to a successful resolution.

The case described in this chapter demonstrates that the suicidal individual is ambivalent up to the very last minute. Because ambivalence is always present within persons who are in a suicidal trance, every opportunity must be offered to help them. The clinician who understands the critical inner voice and its impact on human behavior can often be instrumental in averting a suicidal crisis.

In long-term treatment, therapeutic success involves identifying self-destructive voices, releasing the associated affect, and restructuring one's life in the direction of individuation and personal fulfillment. It involves challenging habitual responses and going against internalized negative parental prescriptions. It necessitates the strength to break with the fantasy bond. Voice Therapy helps self-destructive and suicidal individuals pursue their personal goals in the real world as contrasted with relying on fantasy gratification. It is a motivating force in creating a meaningful life in which the self predominates.

Notes

1. According to Briere (1992),"The majority of adults raised in North America, regardless of gender, age, race, or social class, probably experienced some level of maltreatment as children" (p. xvii). Briere also cited empirical findings supporting correlations between child maltreatment and intimacy disturbance, al-

tered sexuality, tendencies toward victimization due to impaired self-reference, and/or aggression in later relationships, adversariality and "manipulation," use of substances, suicidality, tension-reducing behaviors such as self-mutilation, compulsive sexual behavior, binging and purging, co-dependency, and borderline personality disorders.

Also see Perry and Marcellus (1997) who reported that "Each year in the United States alone, there are over three million children that are abused or neglected. These destructive experiences impact the developing child, increasing risk for emotional, behavioral, academic, social and physical problems throughout life" (pp. 1-4).

2. "Mental illness conceptualized as a subclass of suicide": For example, thoughts of suicide may well be indicative of psychopathology: "Subjects with suicidal ideation were twice as likely to have an axis 1 disorder and twelve times more likely to have attempted suicide by age 30, and 15 times more likely to have expressed suicidal thoughts in the past 4 years" (Reinhertz et al., 2006, p. 1226).

3. According to Shneidman (1996), "Suicide is the result of an internal dialogue. The mind scans its options, the topic of suicide comes up, the mind rejects it, scans again; there is suicide, it is rejected again, and then finally the mind accepts suicide as *a* solution" (p. 15).

4. For a discussion of the "Death row phenomenon", see David Lester and Christine Tartaro (2002), *Suicide on Death Row*, reporting death row suicide rates at 113 per 100,000; National Center for Health Statistics, retrieved from: http://www.cdc.gov/nchs/fastats/suicide.htm, (last visited April 2, 2008): reporting a rate of 11 suicides per 100,000 in the general population in 2004; Bureau of Justice Statistics, retrieved from: http://www.ojp.usdoj.gov/bjs/glance/shipj.htm, (last visited April 2, 2008): reporting prison suicide rates in 2003 at 16 per 100,000 and jail suicide rates at 43 per 100,000. See also, Tartaro & Lester (2005), *An Application of Durkheim's Theory of Suicide to Prison Suicide Rates in the United States.*

5. Regarding withdrawal, "inwardness," and the suicidal trance, see Richard Heckler's (1994) book *Waking Up Alive*. He noted that the initial step into the person's descent into the "suicidal trance" is characterized by withdrawal from social contact. This consists of "a tangible, emotional, spiritual and even physical pulling away from contact and connection [with others.] It is an active response to intense unabated suffering" (p. 46).

6. Assessing suicide risk: Bedrosian and Beck (1979) established that suicidal ideation is a precursor to suicidal action. Beck has developed scales that are relevant to suicide: the Beck Depression Inventory (Beck, 1978a), the Beck Suicide Inventory (Beck, 1991), and the Beck Hopelessness Scale (Beck, 1978b). A follow-up study (of 5 to 10 years) by Beck, Steer, Kovacs, and Garrison (1985) of 207 patients hospitalized for suicidal ideation showed that "only the Beck Hopelessness Scale and the pessimism item on the Beck Depression Inventory

predicted the eventual suicides [of 14 patients]" (p. 559). Also see Reasons for Living Inventory (RFL) (Linehan, Goodstein, Nielsen, & Chiles, 1983) which taps into cognitive abilities including the ability to sustain hope for the future and to visualize change.

The Firestone Assessment of Self-Destructive Thoughts (FAST) (R. Firestone & L. Firestone, 2006) has been added to the repertoire of instruments for assessing suicide risk. Studies investigating the reliability and validity of the FAST demonstrated that the scale discriminated suicide attempters from non-attempters more accurately than other scales, including the Beck Hopelessness Scale, currently used in clinical practice.

7. Use of the *Firestone Assessment of Self-Destructvie Thoughts* in treatment. The FAST identifies the level at which the client is experiencing the highest frequency (intensity) of self-destructive thoughts. Using this information, clinicians can direct their interventions toward the area where clients are experiencing psychological pain, thereby potentially averting the acting out of the corresponding self-destructive behavior. In addition, scores on the FAST identify less extreme types of self-destructive thoughts so that they can be addressed by the clinician before they lead to or precipitate a suicidal crisis.

8. Re CAMS, see David Jobes (2012): "The Collaborative Assessment and Management of Suicidality (CAMS) is an evidence-based clinical intervention that has significantly evolved over 25 years of clinical research. CAMS is best understood as a therapeutic framework that emphasizes a unique collaborative assessment and treatment planning process between the suicidal patient and clinician. This process is designed to enhance the therapeutic alliance and increase treatment motivation in the suicidal patient. Central to the CAMS approach is the use of the Suicide Status Form (SSF), which is a multipurpose clinical assessment, treatment planning, tracking, and outcome tool" (p. 640).

9. Jobes' statement is from *Advances in the Treatment of Suicidal Clients,* (Parr, 2012) an interview with Dr. Jobes on his treatment approach.

Source*: Suicide and the Inner Voice: Risk Assessment, Treatment and Case Management* (1997b)

Chapter 7

THE PSYCHODYNAMICS OF VIOLENCE

It is not poverty, racism, sexism, or age-discrimination, as such, that actually cause violence. It is, rather, that each correlates with violence because each increases the statistical probability that individuals exposed to these social forces will be subjected to intolerable and potentially self-destroying intensities of shame, from which they do not perceive themselves as having any means of rescuing themselves except by violence.

~ James Gilligan (2001, p. 66)

Violence is a serious problem in our society. A recent analysis of mortality rates showed that "US homicide rates were 7.0 times higher than in 22 other high-income countries, driven by a gun homicide rate that was 25.2 times higher" (Grinshteyn & Hemenway, 2016, p. 266). During 2014, 15,872 people were victims of homicide (Centers for Disease Control and Prevention, 2015a), and 42,826 took their own lives (Centers for Disease Control and Prevention, 2015b). Other surveys indicate that each year over 10 million women and men experience physical violence by a current or former intimate partner. And violence among young people in this country has grown dramatically since the mid-1980s (Nansel et al., 2001) (Note 1).

The World Health Organization (WHO) defines violence as "The intentional use of physical force or power, threatened or actual, against oneself, another person, or against a group or community, that either results in or has a high likelihood of resulting in injury, death, psychological harm, maldevelopment or deprivation" (2002, summary). However, as Richard Bernstein (2013) rightfully points out, "Our age may well be called the 'Age of Violence' because representations of real or imagined violence (sometimes blurred and fused together) are inescapable. But this surfeit of images and talk dulls and even inhibits thinking. What do we mean by violence? How are we to characterize the different types of violence?" (Loc. 144) (Note 2).

RISK FACTORS IN VIOLENCE

Violence is a highly complex emotional phenomenon driven by diverse motivations. For example, there is a great deal of difference between the emotions motivating interpersonal violence and the physical, emotional, and sexual maltreatment of children, domestic abuse, gang clashes, terrorism, and warfare. In some situations, aggression is culturally acceptable, while in others there are strong social sanctions against it. Within most societies, criminal activity, physical aggression, and mistreatment acted out in personal relationships are considered anti-social.

Suicide and Violence

Violence is closely related to suicide because the underlying voice process attacks both the self and others. Demographic studies have shown that violence, the extreme manifestation of externalized anger, and suicide, the ultimate expression of internalized anger, overlap to a certain extent (van Praag, Plutchik, & Apter, 1990). Imbalances in specific brain chemicals are known to be correlated with impulsivity and problems in regulating emotions, which, in turn, are recognized as risk factors for both suicidal and violent behavior.

Approximately 30% of violent individuals have a history of self-destructive behavior, while about 10-20% of suicidal persons have a history of violent behavior. These people tend to shift between self-harm or suicide attempts and aggressive, violent assaults on others. In a large epidemiological survey, Verona, Patrick and Joiner (2001) found a statistically significant relationship between a history of suicidal behavior and a history of impulsive, deviant behaviors. Based on their results, they recommended that "persons exhibiting antisocial (and/or violent) behaviors should receive rigorous assessment for suicidal ideation and behavior" (p. 444).

Several clinicians, including Norman Farberow (1980), have observed that homicide can sometimes be categorized as "victim precipitated" or self-inflicted in that, on certain occasions, victims may provoke their own deaths. Researchers van Praag and Plutchik (van Praag et al., 1990) have conducted studies in an attempt to better understand why some individuals turn to suicide and others to violence. Part of the answer may lie in identifying the specific voice attacks that are experienced by individuals who are at high risk for suicide and/or violence. My associates and I conjectured that since the use of voices in developing the *Firestone Assessment of Self-Destructive Thoughts* [FAST] (R. Firestone & L. Firestone, 2006) proved valuable in predicting suicide, the same methodology would be effective in predicting violence. We went on to develop an instrument for that purpose, *The Firestone Assessment of Violent Behavior* [FAVT] (R. Firestone & L. Firestone, 2008a; 2008b). Our empirical studies showed that the FAVT proved to be effective in distinguishing violent individuals from nonviolent individuals. The FAVT will be discussed in detail later in this chapter.

Alcohol, Drugs, Firearms, and Violence

Studies have shown that the use of addictive substances is strongly correlated with both violence and suicide. According to Roizen (2002), "in 14 studies of homicide, alcohol was present in between 28 and 86% of the offenders; in eight studies of assaults, it was present in 24 to 72% of the assault offenders. Alcohol also was present in 21 to 50% of the victims or assailants in seven studies of marital violence" (p. 42). Drinking to excess weakens brain mechanisms that usually restrain impulsive behavior, including inappropriate hostility. Habitual use of alcohol also predisposes faulty information processing, causing people to misjudge social cues and overreact aggressively to a perceived threat or danger.

Many drugs, both legal and illegal, are associated with violent responses. Stimulants, in particular, methamphetamines, cocaine, mephedrone (MDPV), Spice (synthetic marijuana), the hallucinogens, LSD and PCP, and a relatively new drug "Flakka" have a strong potential for increasing violent behavior. The fact that research findings show that drug and alcohol abuse exacerbate the acting out of aggressive, self-destructive or suicidal behaviors underscores the destructive consequences of these types of addictions.

Additionally, the easy access of assault weapons to the citizens of the United States has led to a gradual, yet significant, increase in gun-related deaths over the last decade. The combination of alcohol, drugs and guns has facilitated increasingly lethal forms of confrontation and violence, resulting in higher mortality rates and larger numbers of injuries to victims. In 2013, for example, 21,175 people in the US committed suicide by firearms and 11,208 died in gun homicides (brilliantmaps.com, 2015).

TYPES OF AGGRESSION

There are two major types of aggression: reactive and instrumental (predatory). Reactive aggression is a form of violence in which an individual perceives a threat and reacts with aggression, whereas instrumental aggression is a form of violence in which an individual sees the act as a means to obtain a desired goal. The causal factors associated with both types are complex and multidimensional and include physiological, environmental, social, and situational variables. Some researchers believe that neurological deficits that characterize instrumental or psychopathic violence are genetically based, whereas others believe that there is a genetic/environmental interaction that impacts the developing brain. Other studies suggest that violence is learned and therefore can be unlearned.

Research has shown that the tendency to engage in assaultive, violent behavior is mediated by psychosocial factors such as impulse control, poverty, social and economic inequality, joblessness, access to guns, use of drugs and alcohol, and peer influences. Our studies, as well as research conducted by others, (Baglivio, 2015; Fox, Perez, Cass, Baglivio, & Epps, 2015) have found that exposure to childhood abuse and/or neglect is a strong predictor of continued violence and aggression (R. Firestone & L. Firestone, 2008a).

Destructive actions directed against other people occur when feelings of frustration are combined with negative cognitive processes. Since people filter events through the critical voice process, during times of stress even innocuous incidents are imbued with a negative loading and heightened angry responses.

Aggressive Reactions to Perceived Threats to the Fantasy Bond

As noted in Chapter 3, the fantasy bond, an illusion of connection to one's parent or caregiver, arises early in life to counter interpersonal trauma and separation anxiety. To continue to offer a psychological safe haven, it must be defended against any threat. This predisposes antagonism, resentment, and malice toward those who challenge the self-parenting, self-destructive manifestations that persist in adulthood.

In a personal relationship, anything that threatens to disturb the fantasy bond with one's partner arouses considerable fear and initiates hostile, destructive reactions. On a larger scale, people who merge their identity with members of a group, nation, or religious and/or secular cause react to such threats with hatred and angry retaliation. Although issues of economics and territoriality are also stimuli for inter-group hostility, I support the position that religious differences and bigotry constitute the more significant threat at this point in history.

THE ROOTS OF MALADAPTIVE AGGRESSION AND VIOLENCE

Causal Factors

Suppression of Angry Feelings: Anger is an automatic response to frustration and stress and it is proportional to the degree of frustration. Most people have difficulty dealing with angry emotions. When they suppress or repress rage, it is either internalized, that is, directed against oneself or it is externalized and projected on to others. The former results in depression, attacks on self and self-destructive behavior, while the latter leads to aggression toward others and a buildup of rage that can lead to explosive verbal abuse, violent acts, or homicide.

There are a number of reasons why people are reluctant to feel their anger or fail to even recognize this emotion. For one, as children they are taught that anger is unacceptable; many are punished or criticized for simply feeling it. They are encouraged to deny or suppress this feeling by adults who perceive it as unreasonable. People then continue to suppress any anger that they believe to be illogical or too intense. As a result, their anger often takes maladaptive forms.

Externalized Anger: When people project their anger onto others and perceive them as more threatening than they actually are, they tend to act out preemptively against them. This can provoke the very aggression or abusive treatment they fear. The end result is a self-fulfilling prophecy and a spiraling effect that can culminate in an escalation of aggressive behavior or violence.

In general, the tendency to externalize anger is more prominent in males than in females (Geen, 1998). Narcissistic rage aroused by events perceived as threatening to the man's vanity or inflated self-esteem is a primary factor in cases of domestic and criminal violence. Dutton (1995) has found that men who engage in interpersonal or domestic violence often do so as a reaction to abandonment anxiety. Intense fear often comes to the surface when their partner indicates an intention to leave or break up. The disruption of the fantasy bond that existed within the couple incites rage in these men.

A Victimized Orientation Toward Life: "Externalizers" often develop a victimized or paranoid orientation toward life, responding with self-righteous indignation and rage to real or imagined slights, insults or disappointments. Those who are intolerant of their own anger are likely to feel powerless, helpless, and victimized. They blame others for their problems, hold grudges, and have a desire for revenge. With their passive, victimized approach, they suppress their anger and there is a corresponding buildup of rage. In some instances, the increase of hatred and paranoia become serious enough to erupt into violent, explosive behavior that can even lead to homicide.

Men and women who act out violent impulses justify their actions as being rightfully deserved by their victims. A mode of thinking that rationalizes revengeful action is also characteristic of perpetrators of domestic violence: *She had it coming to her. She knew what she was doing. She knew which buttons to push to make me blow up.* Or, *I'll get even with that bastard. He thought he could get away with it. Maybe next time he'll think twice before he fools around.* Extreme negative voices toward and about others are at the core of most forms of explosive, violent behavior.

Societal Suppression of Anger and Sexuality: The suppression of anger is also influenced by social factors. For example, there are a number of religions that promulgate a basic view that angry or other "sinful" thoughts are unacceptable and immoral. This attitude equates thoughts and feelings with behavior in terms of morality. In this context, angry or lustful thoughts are as reprehensible and subject to condemnation as "forbidden" behavior. This view is psychologically damaging to those people who, in attempting to live a good life, try to suppress any thought or feeling they judge as bad.

It also appears that dogmatic religious beliefs that are suppressive of sexuality and pleasure contribute indirectly to the expression of aggression and/or violence. Findings from anthropological research (Prescott, 1975; 1996) have shown that politically or religiously suppressive societies are especially restrictive in relation to anger and sexual behavior. These restrictions in turn lead to increased crime, sexual assault, rape, and deviant forms of sexuality.

Early Environmental Factors

I agree with Freud (1977) that human beings are a dangerous and violent species. However, as I have mentioned, contrary to Freud, who believed that aggressive behavior and violence are instinctive, I believe that these qualities are largely derivative of the emotional pain, fear, rejection or deprivation suffered during the formative years.

The escalation of violence in our culture warrants more emphasis on prevention as opposed to only managing individuals who are already engaged in violent behavior. Therefore, a focus on the child's experiences during the early years, the parent-child relationship, parental traits, and child-rearing practices can provide insight into the manner in which childhood trauma becomes the antecedent of violent behaviors in adolescence and adulthood.

Emotional and Physical Abuse and Neglect: There are many parenting situations that are emotionally abusive in the sense that they arouse unnecessarily aggressive responses in children. Parents who are immature, defensive, who feel burdened, or who are hostile or emotionally rejecting, cause excessive frustration as well as intense anger in their offspring, and these patterns usually persist into adult life.

Ridicule, condescension, and punitive attitudes acted out by parents in relation to their children, particularly in the presence of other people, are degrading and humiliating, creating intensely painful feelings of shame in their offspring. Children who experience this may develop an aggrandized self-image to compensate for feelings of extreme self-hate and shame. However, when this fragile image is challenged, the individual experiences an onslaught of destructive thoughts toward him/herself that creates psychological distress and deep, unbearable shame. Violent behavior is often a desperate attempt to reestablish the aggrandized self-image or to lash out and destroy the perceived source of the shame.

Many children experience deprivation through physical and/or emotional neglect. If a child lacks a stable emotional attachment and physical affection from a parent or primary caregiver, brain development both for caring behavior and cognitive capabilities is damaged. In fact, early neglect can lead to a permanent impairment in empathy. Psychiatrist Alan Schore (2003a) has observed, "There is a link between neglect in childhood and antisocial personality disorders in later life... and to subsequent violent behavior" (p. 268). According to Schore,

> Physically abused infants show high levels of negative affect, while neglected infants demonstrate flattened affect. . . . But the worst case scenario is, not infrequently, found in a child who experiences both abuse and neglect. . . . There is agreement that severe trauma of interpersonal origin may override any genetic, constitutional, social, or psychological resilience factor (pp. 268-269).

Emotional or psychological neglect in particular predisposes impairment in neuronal structures that are responsible for regulating the emotions and for accurately perceiving social cues regarding emotions in others. Research has shown that deficits in these areas often lead to a decreased ability to inhibit impulsivity with respect to the acting out of aggressive, violent behavior (Perry, 2002; Schore, 2001).

Individuals who have experienced extreme emotional and/or physical neglect tend to develop a self-protective, self-parenting stance. Their voices reinforce this detachment, e.g. *You don't need anyone else, you can take care of yourself.* These individuals often appear cold and unemotional, and lack a sense of emotional connection to others, which facilitates instrumental/predatory violent behavior. They are more likely to use aggression to accomplish both psychological and practical goals.

Excessive permissiveness can be considered a form of neglect because the child fails to develop appropriate internal controls over acting-out behavior. Immature parents are usually unable to provide sufficient direction or structure for their children. The result is that these children become adults who are anxious and unable to successfully regulate or manage their emotions, particularly aggression. Consequently, they tend to act out destructively, either toward themselves, or in aggressive or violent behavior toward others.

At the other extreme, parents who tend to be rigid, authoritarian, or harsh, mistreat their children in myriad ways, ranging from mild irritability to sadism and brutality. They believe that to be properly socialized, children must be made to submit to parental authority "for their own good." Parents who attempt to force their child to submit, who issue unreasonable ultimatums, or who take a rigid stance in relation to unnecessary rules are responsible for setting up situations that inevitably lead to destructive power struggles. During a direct confrontation or "battle of wills," parents often express fierce, punitive attitude and even rage, reactions that stand in contrast to their typically more reasonable responses. These outbursts intimidate and terrify children, who perceive their parents as dangerously out of control.

When parents' behavior is terrifying in this way, their children often develop a disorganized attachment. According to Siegel and Hartzell (2003), "Children with disorganized attachment have repeated experiences of communication in which the parents' behavior is overwhelming, frightening, and chaotic" (Loc. 1754). They find themselves in a "double bind" situation, with no solution to the paradox of having to seek comfort from the very source of their terror.

High rates of disorganized attachment are seen in children who are abused by their parents. Parental abuse has actually been shown to damage the areas of the child's growing brain that enable neural integration. For children with disorganized attachment, impaired neural integration may be one mechanism that leads a child to have difficulty with regulating emotions, trouble in social communication, difficulties with academic reasoning tasks, a tendency toward interpersonal violence, and a predisposition to dissociation—a process in which normally integrated cognition becomes fragmented. [Loc. 1768]

Witnessing Violence: Witnessing, or being the victim of physical abuse within the family is one of the most serious forms of trauma that can occur in the life of a young child (Note 3). According to attachment researchers

Davies and Cummings (1995; 1998), observing violence between parents can threaten a child's confidence in the parents' availability. Also see:

> The child's appraisal of marital violence is likely to include fear that harm may come to one or both parents . . . parents living with constant conflict and fear are likely to have reduced capacities to attend to the child. . . . In addition to the obvious threat to the parent's physical accessibility, the child is faced with the fear of violence and the prospect of loss (Kobak, Zajac & Madsen 2016, Loc. 1506).

According to psychiatrists Perry and Szalavotz (2006), "Up to ten million American children are believed to be exposed to domestic violence annually" (LOC 92). In describing the profoundly abusive childhoods of the violent men that he treated in prison settings, James Gilligan (Parr, 2008) commented on this phenomenon:

> The people that I have worked with who have committed serious violence gave a whole new meaning for me to the term 'child abuse.' The most violent of them were survivors of their own attempted murders, often at the hands of their own parents or were survivors of family violence in which they had seen their closest family members killed, often in front of their own eyes and frequently by other family members.

Research shows that children who witness violence in their families or communities are at increased risk of becoming violent later in life (Fonagy, 2004). For example, in a recent interview (personal communication, 2013), Kevin Penn, who today works as a youth counselor, described his experiences growing up. Convicted in his late teens of attempted murder and assault with a deadly weapon, Kevin spent 18 years in prison, during which time he turned his life around.

> Kevin: How did I become a violent person? Well, I was exposed to violence very early in my life. Domestic violence. My father beat my mother, frequently. . . . There came a point in time when one morning, he hit my mother, he hit her in her eye and her eye had swelled up. And she took me in my room and she told me to stay in my room. And shortly thereafter, I heard her come up out of her room and I followed her. And she had a gun in her hand and my father was eating breakfast in the kitchen and she just walked to the front of the kitchen door and she shot him.

She shot him five times . . . then she turned around, she came back, she sat down on the couch and she rocked. She just kept rocking . . . it was like she wasn't there. So, I walked over to her. She had the gun in her hand. I took the gun out of her hand. I put it on the table and I just sat next to her, while she rocked. And, finally, she stopped and hugged me and we just sat there until the police finally came.

By the time I was 11, I was an active gang member. I was breaking in houses, smoking weed. We drank up all my mother's alcohol. I ended up going to the Department of Youth Authority at the age of 13. I did four years there.

The traumatic fear states aroused by such horrific events cause the brain to release toxins that can actually alter its structure and that of the central nervous system, destroying neurons that are responsible for the regulation of emotions and the development of compassion and empathy. Lacking this ability, these children substitute defensive and destructive ways of handling stress and pain that can persist for a lifetime.

When children who are damaged in this way enter adolescence, they find that they are literally controlled by their feelings, much as a toddler is when in the throes of a temper tantrum; their emotions are like a runaway roller-coaster that they can't get off (D. Siegel & Bryson, 2014). Early in life, they learned that anger is always dangerous and later find it difficult to counter this overgeneralization. They react as though the person who provokes or frustrates them is responsible for their angry reactions and feel justified in responding with physical aggression or violence.

Psychodynamics—Intervening Variables

Identification with the Aggressor: Violence can be conceptualized as a reactivation of covert or overt aggression that was once directed at the child. In situations such as those depicted above, the child identifies with the aggressor, the punishing parent. As noted in previous chapters, the child takes on the identity of the all-powerful, angry parent. This defense helps to allay severe anxiety states, but in the process, the child internalizes the parent's anger, which he/she may later unleash in assaultive, violent acts against others. In his research, Herzog (2001) found that toddlers who had suffered physical abuse and had dissociated during the episodes, later tended to repeat the abusive pattern with younger children. His interpretation was that "in such a situation, identification with the aggressor seemed to be the resultant patterning. When faced in the play group situation with a child in distress, they acted the part of aggressor and sought to inflict further distress on the victim" (Loc. 1626).

Imitation: My understanding of how aggression is transmitted through successive generations also takes into account social learning theory (Bandura & Walters, 1963; Bandura, 1986), which proposes that children learn through example (role modeling) to imitate a parent's or other family member's overt aggressive behavior. In this way, parents necessarily pass on to their offspring their own hostile attitudes and their defensive ways of dealing with anger. In doing so, they unintentionally teach their children maladaptive attitudes and behaviors to the extent that they themselves manifest the same traits. When the child grows up, he/she manifests the same aggressive patterns; in particular, those that are characteristic of the parent of the same sex.

Thus, being a victim of maltreatment, abuse, neglect, poor parental supervision, or severely misattuned parents makes a person more likely to engage in violence. However, data also indicate that not all abused and/or neglected children engage in violent behavior. Why some individuals appear more resilient to these early childhood traumas while others are more susceptible to negative outcomes is largely open to question.

Dissociation: Of those children who are exposed to abuse, the ones who have one safe adult to whom they can turn do not have as great a need to dissociate as those who have no stable attachment figure. Studies of adults who were abused as children found that those children who had dissociated went on to abuse their own children, while those who hadn't did not (Schore, 2001). For some children, there is no safe haven, no secure adult to turn to for safety, and inward flight is the only escape from this intolerable situation (D. Siegel & Hartzell, 2003) (Note 4).

James Gilligan (Gilligan, 2001; Gilligan & Lee, 2004) has written extensively about prisoners who experienced a kind of emotional deadness, which characterized the dissociated state they existed in. In a documentary film, he comented:

> One of the most surprising things to me in talking with the most violent men in our society is that they told me that they themselves had died before they started killing anyone themselves. What they meant

by that was that their personality had died, and what they meant by that was they felt dead inside, they felt numb. They were incapable of having feelings, either emotional feelings or physical sensations (Parr, 2008).

Individuals who dissociate are more prone to experience strong voice attacks that distort their perceptions, dominate their thought processes, and direct their behavior. Thus, those who experienced abusive, neglectful or traumatic childhoods and who dissociated during these episodes, tend to experience voice attacks that are more destructive in content, with more frequency and with greater intensity than those who experienced less severely abusive or non-abusive childhoods, and did not have to employ dissociation as a primary defense.

Social and Economic Factors: According to James Gilligan, "The main social and economic causes of violence . . . are those that divide the population into the superior and the inferior, the strong and the weak, the rich and the poor. The more highly unequal a society is, the higher its rates of violence. Every time we divide one group of human beings from another on this scale of superior vs. inferior, we are shaming people at the bottom, who are placed in an inferior position. And also, that's a recipe for violence because people don't like to be treated as inferior" (Parr, 2009) (Note 5). Moreover, people who grow up in disadvantaged or poor communities with high levels of violence develop the belief that, as James Garbarino (2015) put it, "violence is a moral imperative when one is threatened, challenged, or disrespected—and that death is morally preferable to dishonor" (Loc. 1678).

THE ASSESSMENT OF VIOLENCE

The media is an almost constant reminder that our efforts to stem criminal or interpersonal violence have been less than effective. Furthermore, there has been little headway in predicting violent behavior (Note 6). For example, why do some individuals engage in violent behaviors, while others with similar backgrounds and characteristics do not? Clearly, a need exists for a more accurate assessment of the causes of violence.

In his research, Berkowitz (1993) emphasized that an impulsive, knee-jerk reaction to frustration is just an initial stage in an aggressive response.

Beyond this point, he believed that cognitive processes play a major role in the way that anger or aggression is acted upon. Thus, identifying specific cognitions or thought processes that regulate aggressive behavioral responses could be crucial to a more accurate assessment of the violence potential in high-risk individuals.

Development of the FAVT

In my work, I have found it valuable to access and identify destructive thoughts or internalized voices that influence or control maladaptive aggressive and/or violent behavior. In our early investigations, my associates and I found a close connection between negative, cynical, or paranoid thought processes and destructive behavior toward others. *The Firestone Assessment of Violent Thoughts* [FAVT], described earlier, was developed as an instrument to test this hypothesis and provide mental health professionals and criminologists with a scale to determine an individual's violence potential. Results from a pilot study as well as reliability and validity studies indicated that the FAVT significantly discriminated between violent and nonviolent subjects, correctly classifying 74% of the subjects in each study (R. Firestone & L. Firestone, 2008a).

The items on the FAVT were derived from actual statements gathered from inmates, parolees, domestic abusers and inpatients. Five levels or factors were found to be significantly correlated with violent behavior. They were labeled: (1) Social Mistrust, (2) Being Disregarded, (3) Negative Critical Thoughts, (4) Overt Aggression, and (5) Self-Aggrandizing Thoughts. Levels of violence and examples of representative voices are listed in Figure 7.1.

The rationale for Factor 5 is also supported by research conducted by Baumeister, Smart, and Boden (1996) showing that violence is related to vanity, and specifically "threatened egotism."

We found compelling evidence that specific attitudes or voices were predictive of aggression and/or violence: conversely one could deduce from an individual's violent behavior patterns the types of thoughts he/she was experiencing.

Figure 7.1 FAVT: Levels of Violence and Representative Voices

Level 1 <u>Paranoid/suspicious</u> *You can only trust your own kind. Everybody knows something and they're not telling you. Keep those immigrants out—They don't deserve anything. You can never trust a woman (man). Doctors and lawyers are only in it for the money.*

Level 2 <u>Persecuted Misfit</u>: *They don't give one damn about you. They're just doing this to get you upset. Nobody sees how much you contribute. No one appreciates you. So just forget them! He (She) is just taking advantage of you.*

Level 3 <u>Self-depreciating/pseudo-independent</u>: *You're really in trouble now. People act afraid of you. Nobody believes you. You'd better look after yourself. No one else will. You were always a troublemaker. It's always your fault.*

Level 4 <u>Overt Aggressive:</u> *Smash him (her) if he (she) doesn't listen. You'll show him (her) who's boss! Look, you couldn't swallow that crap anymore. Doesn't that gun feel good in your hand? You had to stop him (her).*

Level 5 <u>Self-Aggrandizing Thoughts:</u> *You're a very special person. You can do anything you can put your mind to. You're strong. You really don't need them in your life. You deserve better than this.*

Evaluation using the FAVT is beneficial as a first step in Voice Therapy for violent clients for two reasons. It allows the clinician to gain direct access to voices that are governing their client's destructive acting out behavior, thereby providing a direction for intervention. The FAVT also alerts clients to the presence of specific negative cognitions and brings them more fully into their conscious awareness.

Exploring the Voices Underlying Violence

What does it take to really listen to killers? I believe it all starts with a fundamental refusal to dissociate and disconnect from their humanity. It starts with a profound empathy for their human condition.

~ James Garbarino (2015, Loc. 990)

After completing validity and reliability studies of the FAVT, my daughter, Lisa Firestone, had the rare opportunity to conduct in-depth interviews with a number of inmates at the Grendon Therapeutic Prison in Oxford, England, and at the Restorative Justice Program [RSVP] at the San Francisco Jail. Her goal was two-fold: (1) to record the life stories related by the men in response to her question: "What do you think led you to a point in your life where you became violent, (or committed a violent act)?" and (2) to identify the destructive thoughts or voices driving the violent behavior for which they were incarcerated.

The following excerpts from these interviews reveal some of the destructive voices the men reported experiencing prior to their assaultive act, aspects of their life history, and commentary from forensic psychologists and myself. The voice statements of the men are in italics and were classified according to the level on the FAVT to which they belong, as indicated by a factor analysis. [the material is taken from the documentary film Lisa and I made, "Voices in Violence" Parts I and II, (Parr, 2008; 2009)].

EXAMPLES OF VOICES AT EACH LEVEL OF THE FAVT

LEVEL 1: Paranoid/Suspicious Voices

Neils (Serving life sentence for murder, Grendon Therapeutic Prison, Oxford UK):

I was thinking to myself, *What's he lookin' at? What's he doin'? Does he think he can have one over on me! Does he think he can do this?* So I just started attackin' em all, until the point where I beat a guy to death. Before that happened, I was becoming more and more violent every pub I went into. I was causing fights and threatening people.

I went to me uncle's, he's the uncle who abused me, who had been dead for a few years, and obviously he wasn't there, so when I've come out of his house, I just started attackin' anybody that was there basically.

I think a lot of the time, in my mind's eye, I seen people as big, as adults. So if I seen somebody big, I'd wanna attack them. Because I suppose I had repressed memories of me uncle being over me brother and me, and towering above us. So I could become really aggressive and, and in slightest situation, I could just fly off the handle.

I do understand now that a lot of it was just my thoughts and my fears, and me paranoia. I used to get really paranoid in certain situations. I was really fearful of strange people because it wasn't just me uncle that abused me when I was a kid; it was a multitude of people.

LEVEL 2: Persecuted Misfit

Emarko: (Former inmate, currently in the RSVP Program):

When I was a kid, I was really homophobic, and if one would just touch you, automatically you'd become gay or something like that. At that time when I was physically touched by this dude and I knew I was standing in front of this gay bar, everything from back then was comin' up in my mind, telling me if you get touched by a gay person, you're gay, just flashed in my face, it's like the worst of being ridiculed.

It was like havin' all my friends pointin', laughin' at me and callin' me the worst of the names they can call me, 'punk, faggot, sissy,' all those different things. And in that moment, I'm like, *'No, no, no! That's not what I am. So let me show you that I'm not. Alright! And this'll prove it!'* [makes a fist.] And I beat him up and they told me he was going to die, and that I was going to get a murder beef.

Dr. James Gilligan: (Principal Investigator, Outcome Research at RSVP):

When I would ask violent prisoners why they had assaulted somebody, whether it was in the prison itself or what provoked them to commit the assault that had led to their being imprisoned, I was amazed to discover how regularly they basically gave me the same response. They would say it was because, "He disrespected me," or "She disrespected me," or "He disrespected my visitor, or my mother, or my girlfriend." But they use that term "disrespect" so often they abbreviated it into the slang term "he dissed me." And it struck me that any time a word gets used so often that people feel a need to abbreviate it, it tells you something about how central it is in their moral and emotional vocabulary.

LEVEL 3: Self-depreciation/Pseudo-independence

David: (Serving four years for rape in Grendon Prison):

There's always that small voice in your head that says, *You're a worthless piece of shit and you're never going to make it nowhere!* And that's the voice that keeps you in that violent place.

With my mother, she used to just beat us. She was an alcoholic on drugs. I hated the person what she was. I hated the stuff she done to us. I hated the stuff that she let happen to us. . . . There was just violence there. There weren't no praise, like 'That was good.' You know, coming home from school or nothing like that. I don't know whether that's why I do it to myself now. That's probably feeding into them angry thoughts as well, isn't it? — the self-criticisms and stuff like that, saying to myself, *Well, I'm such a horrible bastard, so you might as well carry on being a horrible bastard 'cause that's what you are!*

This uncle physically raped my brother. He didn't rape me. He molested me and made us do things to him. He used to hurt us physically as well as sexually. He used to kick the fuck out of us really. I raped my wife when she was two months pregnant, after we got married.

Having a conscience and knowing I didn't have no right to do that, didn't come into my head. I just felt that I wanted something and I was going to take it. I was that cold to emotion. I didn't care that she was crying to me, telling me to leave her alone. I wanted to care, but I just couldn't. I didn't know how to care. I tried to care but at the end of the day, I didn't know what care was. Care to me was swearing and shouting and being violent and hitting and abusing.

Dr. Peter Fonagy: (Professor of Psychoanalysis, University College London):

Individuals who are at risk of becoming violent are people who are able to lose the capacity to envision the psychological experience of the person they're being violent to. And the reason that they can lose it is because they had an inadequate experience of having been thought of as a person in the context of an early attachment relationship. If we are deprived of that experience, if we have been neglected, we will always be vulnerable to losing that something we call "mentalization," that capacity to envision mental states in others and in ourselves.

LEVEL 4: Overtly Aggressive Voices

Michael: (Serving 9 years for robbery at Grendon Prison):

I'd been arguing with me girlfriend and I ended up going out drinking with me co-defendant all day and all night, and I was thinking of a way in the pub how I could, I suppose relieve the anger, and so I said to myself, "The first person that I see is getting it," which made me feel better, so I just carried on drinking, drinking. And sure enough, when I walked out the pub, a fella was walking up the side of the street, and I just went up there and attacked him.

History: My mum and dad went out drinking and they were arguing in the bedroom, and me dad ended up trying to strangle her. So, all four brothers went in there and started hittin' him, and then he just lost it and smashed the whole house up. Later on, me mum come up, and I was up against the wardrobe, and me mum was aiming for me dad, but ended up knocking all me front teeth out, and basically well, just demolished me mouth. And that was the only time she ever hit me. I don't obviously blame her, or hold anything against her, its just one of them things, I suppose.

I had this thing for biting people, biting people's ears off, noses. I wouldn't actually punch 'em or kick 'em, or whatever. I used to just go straight for a bite to the face and after I'd done that I'd be all right.

Dr. Robert Firestone:

You tend to do what was done to you; that seems to be the pattern in these cases. The men tend to act out the violence that was directed at them, they identified with the person that was so frightening, so hurtful, so big and menacing. It's so torturous to identify yourself as the child in that situation that you identify with the aggressor to save yourself. In that sense, you feel less fear but you incorporate into yourself a potential for that type of behavior.

LEVEL 5: Self-Aggrandizing Voices

Dave M (Formerly on Probation for Domestic Abuse: Currently Facilitator of RSVP Program):

I worked my way through Cal Berkeley, loading trucks at night and going to school in the daytime. I was even more of a macho thing 'I can do it all. I'm invincible. Not only can I do all the work at the top university in the country, I can drink with the guys.'

I had this expectation of male authority. Because I'm a man, you know, *Women are supposed to take care of the house, take care of the kids, get a job, take care of me.* There were these whole head tapes spinning deep within me saying, *I wouldn't have to do this if you'd get a job. I wouldn't have to do this if you'd hold up your end of the deal. I wouldn't have to do this if whatever. . . . "*

I needed to let her know who is the boss here. *You don't play me like this.* I grabbed her by the arms, spun her around and pushed her into the bedroom and said, 'Come out when you cool down.' Then I thought, *She's no good. She's wrong. She's a tramp. She's this, she's that.* This is when I hit her—my ex-partner.

Every interaction I had with my father was, 'A man does this, a man does that, this is how it has to be, second best is never good enough. You have to be the best at everything all the time.' So I said, 'Women don't talk to me that way. You do what I say. I know how it works here. I'm the head of this house.'

TWO TREATMENT PROGRAMS

The Resolve to Stop the Violence Project, or RSVP Program is based on a cognitive-behavioral, educational approach. The Grendon Therapeutic Prison Program is more psychodynamic and based largely on attachment theory. These programs, however, have several common goals: (1) to maintain a standard of zero tolerance for violence for the men; (2) to provide the men with a safe environment in which to explore their feelings and the dynamics of their behavior; and (3) to treat the men with respect and ensure they feel listened to.

The RSVP Program

The RSVP treatment program at the San Francisco Jail is intense—12 hours a day, 6 days a week—and includes group discussion, academic classes, theatrical enactments and role-play, counseling sessions, and discussions with victims of violent crime.

The first part of the RSVP Program is a cognitively oriented group called "Man-Alive." These groups run for 2-1/2 hours, three times a week. The program is also designed as an out-of-jail alternative to a jail sentence. Many of the men in this latter group are perpetrators of domestic violence.

The participants begin the group discussion by "checking in" regarding their two identities, their "authentic self" and their "hit man" persona, concepts that are analogous to the real self and the anti-self in Separation Theory. They have learned to recognize the basic split between the self and anti-self systems that exists within them. The men have given the self and anti-self concepts their own labels, terms that are meaningful to them with respect to their own unique experiences and backgrounds.

In the Man-Alive group, the men, one at a time, describe recent moments when their "hit man" was triggered and they were tempted to react with violence. Subsequently, they reveal how they actually responded in the situation, how they used their understanding of the "hit man" to avert the acting out of either verbal or physical violence. The following men participated in the San Francisco program.

Devon (Inmate):

My 'hit man' is the justified, vengeful equalizer. So I'm justified in my violence, I always have a reason or a blame for my violence, I always have just cause. The way that I do my violence is vengeful. I get back at people, I have revenge, I even the score, that's the equalizer, that's the role I play. My authentic self is a gentle, loving, giving man. And I stay there most of the time.

Dave M (Currently a facilitator in RSVP group run for men on probation):

A person that stands behind the words that come from their heart, we call that our 'authentic self.' As opposed to the violent guy, which we call our 'hit man.' That's the guy who's trying to maintain an image of superiority, when actually, what I really want to be is soft and gentle. If I can stay in that authentic self, I have a shot at being happy.

Dr. James Gilligan:

One of the Man-Alive groups consisted of the systematic deconstruction and reconstruction of what we called the Male Role Belief System, that is, the whole set of beliefs and assumptions that all of us males in our society are raised with: how you define masculinity, what you have to do to be a man, and what men should be able to expect from women.

The men began to say things like, 'I've been brainwashed. I've been taught to believe this nonsensical set of beliefs about manhood—Boys don't cry, men don't feel pain, if you complain you're a crybaby—I mean, they've been taught this from the time they were infants. And they saw how it had ruined their lives, had destroyed relationships that, in fact, they were grieving the loss of.

What we found in a follow up for the RSVP Program was that when we compared the rate of re-offending—committing new crimes—during the first year after release from the jail, the rate was 83% lower than it was for the prisoners who had been in an ordinary jail for at least 4 months or more.

Dave M:

This program has changed the way I look at myself, I look at my friends, I look at my entire life. I learned that in the moment when somebody challenges me, gets right in my face, I have options. My default was always to step forward and double up my fist. Or yell or holler. Now I can take a step back, not lose any of my male role sensibility about my male role, and figure out what's going on with me.

Robert Firestone:

I think it's interesting that these men (in the RSVP Program) have shown remarkable progress from their violent days. They're building in mechanisms that protect against their acting out that violence.

Having gone through this program, they're aware of their inner voices, their destructive thoughts, and the things that trigger their angry reactions. In a sense, they're more likely to be what they said, this soft gentle humble person, [their authentic self]. So it speaks well for a treatment program of this sort where people learn about themselves and learn to deal with their feelings.

The Grendon Program

Similarly, a follow-up at Grendon Therapeutic Program showed that for those who stay 18 months or longer, there is only a 20% risk of recidivism compared to 50% for the wait list of those who were selected for Grendon, but no space was available at the time (Note 7).

Marvin (Inmate):

It seems like I've come to the right place to finally go through my life and sort out where and what things affected me and what made me the way I've turned out.

David (Inmate):

Instead of starting off with one angry thought over an argument and building it into where I'm wanting to kill the person, now I speak through it here, and I try to work it out why I get to that stage. I've grown a conscience since I've been here.

PERSONAL QUALITIES NEEDED BY THERAPISTS TREATING VIOLENT INDIVIDUALS

In the 2009 documentary *Voices of Violence, Part II, Treatment*, Lisa and I, along with other colleagues and several inmates, discussed the outcomes of the two treatment programs (Note 8). We also described the personal qualities needed by therapists who treat violent individuals.

Dr. Robert Firestone:

You have to be ready to deal with a lot of aggressive feelings directed toward you in the course of treatment. I think a therapist would have to be very tolerant of anger and allowing that type of expression in the sessions. He/she has to be a person of strong character to work with these people, and serve as a transitional object of meaning in the person's life. And it can have a powerful effect. I've had clients who exhibited these violent characteristics and they formed a very intense, close relationship with me that carried through the difficult period, in helping them to control their aggressive impulses. And it's a long-term therapy issue. I also think you have to very actively challenge the victimized orientation, because if you allow a paranoid person to go on and on, even if you're just reflecting, you can encourage the pre-delusional attitudes.

Dr. Peter Fonagy:

When a person starts shouting at you in the session, and you are a well-trained psychotherapist, you say things like, 'I think you're feeling very angry with me,' and the person might say, 'OF COURSE, I'M BLOODY ANGRY WITH YOU!' and then you'd say, 'You must be feeling very, very angry with me.' All the time, you're kind of soothing them. . . .

Now if you behave like that with young men who are violent, their anger very quickly turns into physical assault. What you actually have to be able to do is you have to say things like, 'When you shout at me like that, I can't think. Do you really not want me to think about what you're saying? I don't mind, but if you shout, I can't think.' The point being that you present yourself, your mind, your experience of them close up and force them to see you for what you are, and then they become reflective about it, and they become a lot less dangerous.

I walk through it with them, 'You're doing this made me think this, which kind of makes me think it may be this, but I may be wrong, but I'm really, really interested.' And that combination of being non-threatening, being really genuinely interested in the person's state of mind, makes them feel a little bit more reliably that they are a person whose thoughts and feelings matter. And once they start respecting their own thoughts and feelings, they invariably start respecting those of others as well.

Dr. Lisa Firestone:

If you have ruptures in the psychotherapeutic relationship, that's when you're going to get hurt by these individuals. So you have to stay attuned and you have to repair any ruptures that happen, because they will occur. You will slight them at times and you've got to repair those ruptures by understanding what happened in those moments when you got them angry and upset and be really good at de-escalating anger.

Research shows that most of the violence in our society is perpetrated by a relatively small number of people who keep re-offending. In an appropriate therapeutic setting, the majority of these individuals could be treated and, as we have seen, treated effectively. Not only would this enable them to be returned to useful roles in the community, but it would also spare the suffering of their future victims.

In addressing the critical need for prison reform, James Gilligan (Parr, 2009) asserted, "Instead of regarding prisons as places for punishment, we need to regard them as places for education and healing. We would be far more effective in making our communities safer and reducing the rates of violence in our communities if we got rid of these anachronistic monsters called prisons and replaced them with truly therapeutic communities and educational institutions."

CONCLUSION

There are many forms of violence; spousal and family abuses, other interpersonal abuses, gang warfare, terrorism, war etc. The key to understanding violence lies in exposing and articulating—giving a voice to—the destructive thought process driving the acts of criminal and social violence. The degree to which these voices escalate or become more intense will determine the degree of violent behavior.

The ability to acknowledge and tolerate angry emotions allows for a person's anger to remain under conscious control. Yet, parental and societal influences, as well as religious dogma, teach people that such thoughts are bad. People must learn that any and all hostile feelings are acceptable, no matter how mean or violent, whereas angry or hostile actions must be subjected to critical evaluation in terms of both morality and realistic self-interest.

Angry, even violent clients can be helped to control the acting out of these emotions. In individual psychotherapy or group sessions, clients learn to be alert to the destructive inner voices that control their behavior. Therapists working with violent people must be warm, non-judgmental and emotionally strong to function as successful transitional objects. Violence treatment programs for prison inmates have proven to be effective in diminishing rates of recidivism.

Much of the social violence we are witness to on a global scale originates in people's hostile reactions to a perceived disruption in their fantasy bond with a person, group, nation or cause. Faced with differences in race, religious beliefs, lifestyles, and habit patterns that characterize members of the "out group," people experience anxiety, aggression, revulsion, and ethnic hatred. These "out groups" are the enemy.

But with education and a better understanding of human destructiveness and violence, people could come to know themselves in a manner that could effectively alter the harmful childrearing practices that cause children to feel shame and maladaptive aggression. In order to overcome hostilities associated with racism and ethnic differences, we need to develop a tolerant, and compassionate view of people everywhere. Inclusion, not exclusion, is the key to our survival.

Notes

1. Regarding death rates from homicide in the US, see Grinshteyn & Hemenway (2016), who noted declines in violent crimes have been observed over the last decade, but rates of aggravated assault and self-reports of nonlethal violence remain high. See also "Relationships between bullying and violence among US youth," by Nansel et al. (2001).

2. Re: "types of violence", see Bernstein's (2013) summary of Hannah Arendt's distinction between "terrorists" and "terror." Also see Hannah Arendt (1976), *The origins of totalitarianism.*

3. "Witnessing violence": Fonagy (2004) has observed that "brutalization of affectional bonds can arise without the experience of physical harm, when the individual [child] is forced to witness an attachment figure undergoing battering. The experience of shame and humiliation, followed by rage and a thirst for revenge, appear strikingly similar, regardless of whether the person is the victim of the battering or a witness. The family is not always involved in the brutalization. In about 70 percent of our cases, the prisoners, as children or

adolescents, experienced by a combination of the family or the adolescent's intimate peer group (or gang) (pp 40-41).

4. Dissociation and impaired brain functioning under stressful circumstances, (i.e., witnessing and/or being a victim of violence) predispose aggression and/or violent acting-out behavior: "Siegel & Hartzell (2003) suggest that persons with a history of unresolved trauma and grief are more easily triggered into a state of middle prefrontal cortex (PFC) shut down, more likely to remain in this state longer, and more likely to have trouble recovering from environmental stressors than individuals without a history of unresolved trauma and grief. . . .

    During shutdown, the important functions of the prefrontal cortex (PFC) are 'off-line' or disrupted. Research has demonstrated (Siegel, 2007) that the PFC has 9 important functions. These include: (a) body regulation; (b) attuned communication; (c) emotional balance; (d) response flexibility; (e) empathy; (f) self-knowing awareness; (g) fear extinction; (h) intuition; and (i) morality. This low-road state may be a necessary condition for violent behavior to occur. The link between these functions of the PFC and violence is borne out by research in the field of violence risk assessment." (R. Firestone & L. Firestone, 2008a, p. 13).

5. See *Why Some Politicians Are More Dangerous Than Others* (2011) in which James Gilligan noted that, 'The association between political party and lethal violence was statistically significant. Suicide and homicide increased when Republicans were in the White House and decreased under Democratic administrations, with a magnitude and consistency that could not be attributed to chance alone (Loc. 74) . . . .A severe loss of socio-economic status . . . has been more frequent and prolonged under Republican than under Democratic administrations throughout the twentieth century (Loc. 2057). . . . Socio-economic distress and suffering in the form of unemployment, relative poverty and the sudden loss of social and economic status stimulate feelings of shame and humiliation" (Loc. 2099), which have been shown by many research studies to "motivate and hence increase the rates of both suicide and homicide" (Loc. 3382).

    In a previous work, (R. Firestone, 1997b), I described an important dynamic underlying the phenomenon described by Gilligan: "In a society characterized by an unjust power structure and the presence of a disenfranchised group or groups, minority individuals incorporate the aggression that is directed toward them. When this internalized rage is activated (as it was following the judgment in the Rodney King case), they turn their rage against themselves. People living in an oppressive, inequitable society tend to direct their aggression against themselves rather than against the power structure for two reasons: (a) Their fear of the majority group and its retaliatory powers prevents them from attacking the aggressor, and (b), even more important, people have a strong propensity to identify with the more powerful, punishing figure" (pp. 76-77).

With respect to interpersonal violence, see "The Coherence between Shame and Violence" (Groen & Lawick, 2009). They assert, "Psychoanalytic studies point out that shame is hurtful because it questions somebody's identity...In the counseling sessions, which Lewis (1971) has coded, shame appears to play a more significant par than other feelings such as pride, love, anger, sadness, or fear. A striking discovery in Lewis' study is the fact that shame which goes unrecognized and unacknowledged, and which lies within the realms of the subconscious, will often leads to aggression and subsequent feelings of guilt about this aggression. The shame is denied and repressed in order to avoid feeling the pain" (p. 158).

6. "Predicting violent behavior in a specific individual": With the exception of the Psychopathy-Checklist PCL-R (Hare, 1991) and the Hare Psychopathy Checklist-Revised HCR-20 (Hare, 1998; Webster, 1997), the assessment of violence potential has largely relied on actuarial estimates of the probability of an individual committing future criminal acts, notably the Violence Risk Appraisal Guide (VRAG) (Quinsey, Harris, Rice, & Cormier, 1998). The VRAG includes a report of childhood history, adult adjustment, offense characteristics, and other assessment information, such as IQ scores and in some cases, scores on the PCL-R and HCR-20.

7. Regarding outcomes of these two programs, see "Resolve to Stop the Violence" (RSVP) by J. Gilligan & Lee, (2004). The Grendon program, based on attachment theory and psychodynamic principles, has been in existence as a therapeutic community at Grendon Prison near Oxford, England since 1962: "Reconviction rates were lower for prisoners who stayed for at least 18 months" (R. Taylor, 2000, p. 1).

    Also see "Finding a Secure Base: Attachment in Grendon Prison" by Michael Parker and Mark Morris (2004), and "Concluding Comments: A Humane Approach to Working with Dangerous People" by David Jones and Richard Shuker (2004). Skeem, Monahan, and Mulvey (2002) suggest, based on findings from one study, that "psychopathic patients appear as likely as nonpsychopathic patients to benefit from adequate doses of treatment in terms of violence reduction" (p. 577).

Sources: "Assessing Violent Thoughts: The Relationship between Thought Processes and Violent Behavior" (Doucette-Gates, R. Firestone & L. Firestone, 1999) in *Psychologies Belgica* and Chapter 4 "Mastering Anger" in *The Ethics of Interpersonal Relationships* (R. Firestone & Catlett, 2009) Karnac.

Documentary Films: Voices of Violence: Part I, The Roots of Violence and Part II, Effective Treatment for Violent Individuals (2008, 2009) distributed by www.psychotherapy.net

Note on Sources: Portions of this chapter were originally published in *The Ethics of Interpersonal Relationships* by Robert W. Firestone and Joyce Catlett (Published by Karnac Books in 2009), and are reprinted with the kind permission of Karnac Books.

Chapter 8

DEATH ANXIETY

There is now compelling evidence that, as William James suggested a century ago, death is indeed the worm at the core of the human condition. The awareness that we humans will die has a profound and pervasive effect on our thoughts, feelings and behaviors in almost every domain of human life—whether we are conscious of it or not.

~ Sheldon Solomon, Jeff Greenberg, and Tom Pyszczynski
(2015, Loc. 110)

My purpose in this chapter is to describe specific defenses against death anxiety in the context of the cultural framework that supports them. I integrate psychoanalytic and existential thought in explaining how early trauma leads to defense formation and how these defenses are reinforced as the developing child gradually becomes aware of his/her mortality. Thereafter, people adapt to death anxiety through a process of self-denial and withdrawal of interest in life-affirming activities. The denial of death through progressive self-denial leads to premature physical or psychological death; reinforces an anti-feeling, anti-sexual existence, supports the choice of addictive attachment over genuine involvement, love and concern; and predisposes alienation from others and from personal goals.

By moving out of the familiar safety of this defended adaptation and expanding their lives, people begin to experience their aloneness, separateness and existential anxiety; the more invested they are in life, the more they have to lose. Generally, they respond to this anxiety on a preconscious or unconscious level by forming defenses without being aware of them (Note 1). Paradoxically, as clients progress in psychotherapy, they place greater value on their lives yet are more aware of death. Without recognition of this underlying pressure, some degree of regression may follow significant improvement. On the basis of extensive clinical data, I have concluded that there is a correlation between the degree of individuation, self-actualization and life satisfaction of an individual and his/her facing painful feelings of deep sadness and concern about the finitude of life.

TRENDS IN EXISTENTIAL THOUGHT

Existential philosophers and psychotherapists have written extensively of people's attempts to transcend their dualistic nature and the fact of mortality. However, until recently, fear of death (the complete transformation or termination of one's existence as one knows it) has been almost completely excluded from psychoanalytic theory or has been equated in a reductionistic way with castration and other fears. Regarding this omission, M. M. Stern (1972) wrote,

> It is surprising that psychoanalytic psychology, despite its characteristic tendency to uncover the hidden truth behind all denials and repressions, nevertheless, in its studies up to this day has rather neglected the fear of death, our steady companion (p.901).

With few exceptions, most classical psychoanalytic themes of the human response to death have been derived from Freud's (1957/1915) well-known dictum: "Our unconscious . . . does not know its own death" (p. 296).

In contrast, Becker (1997) and M. Stern (1972) contended that reactions to the realistic fear of death have profound consequences in relation to the development and continuation of neurosis. Meyer emphasized that the part played by death and dying in neurosis had "until now barely been considered" (p. xi). M. Stern argued that working through the fear of death is an indispensable part of every treatment and the failure of adaptation to this fear, a significant cause of neurosis.

Frankl (1963) asserted that individuals have the capacity to transcend tragic aspects of the human condition. He stated,

I speak of a tragic optimism, that is, an optimism in the face of tragedy and in view of the human potential which at its best always allows for: (1) turning suffering into a human achievement and accomplishment; (2) deriving from guilt the opportunity to change oneself for the better; and (3) *deriving from life's transitoriness an incentive to take responsible action* (p. 162, emphasis added).

Human beings are very frightened animals because they are privy to the conscious awareness of their own mortality. This "curse of consciousness" gives rise to a fear of serious proportions. Indeed, the manner in which an individual, as an evolving being, handles death anxiety is one of the primary determinants of the course of his/her psychological life.

Most of us would say that we don't think about death that often. Nevertheless, on an unconscious level, knowledge of our eventual demise arouses death anxiety and influences significant aspects of our lives and motivates many of our actions.

People attempt to defend themselves against death anxiety in a variety of ways. Although defenses do help to avert anxiety states, they are costly in that they tend to cause damage to the individual, the couple, the family and, ultimately, society. Blocking out or distorting experience in an attempt to avoid pain leads to a constriction of feeling and progressive maladaptation. Moreover, most people are threatened when their defensive resolution to death is challenged by nonbelievers. At these times, they become hostile and aggressive toward others with different beliefs, attitudes and customs. Much of the destruction caused by warfare and ethnic cleansing is due to these defensive machinations.

DEFINITION OF DEATH ANXIETY

Death anxiety is a complex phenomenon that represents the blend of many different thought processes and emotions: the dread of death and the total annihilation of self, the horror of losing consciousness forever, the fear of physical and mental deterioration, the anguish of personal losses, the terror of being alone (the ultimate experience of separation anxiety), and the rage and despair regarding circumstances over which we have no control (Note 2). In some ways, death anxiety reflects a basic paranoid attitude toward life because, from the beginning, human beings are at the mercy of physical and social forces that render them helpless, forces that jeopardize their very existence. It is tragic when this core paranoia distorts our perception of our interpersonal world.

Although death anxiety includes the broader spectrum of painful emotions noted above, my definition refers to both the conscious and unconscious reactions to the fact that our lives are terminal and we face eternal separation from our loved ones. Most of us do not necessarily experience or react to this stark awareness of death from an adult perspective or mind set. Instead, what we re-experience is the terror and unconscious existential angst that we successfully repressed as young children when we first faced the realization of death.

When children learn that their parents will die and later that they will die, they suffer extreme anxiety and their world is turned upside down. Children cannot tolerate the thought and therefore find it necessary to repress it. These repressions surface when adults contemplate the fear of death, exaggerating their fear. Clinical studies (Anthony, 1973; Nagy, 1959; Rochlin, 1967) have shown that a child's denial of the knowledge of death may be almost immediate or may develop gradually. Rochlin (1967), on the basis of play therapy sessions with children ages 3-5, came to the following conclusion:

> Very young children seem to learn that life ends. They apply this information to themselves. . . . The clinical facts show that the child's views of dying and death are inseparable from the psychological defenses against the reality of death. They form a hard matrix of beliefs which is shaped early and deep in emotional life. It appears not to alter throughout life (p. 63).

In contemplating his existence years ago, a client wrote: "The concept that my life is terminable is too awful. How could it be that life ends when it feels so permanent? I know it can't really end; there must be a way out. How can death stalk me on such a sunny day? Death should be reserved for the nighttime or at the very least for a cloudy or rainy day. Is there no respite? It's like the story of Orpheus and Eurydice and their desperate struggle to escape the dark shadow that followed her. He fought valiantly for her, but he could not save her, or himself."

Another woman conceived of death as a punishment: "What have I done to deserve this predicament? Is it some sort of punishment? I have searched my memory for clues to unimaginable crimes I might have committed and then banned from my consciousness. The verdict is already in; my crime will remain unspecified forever. It might provide some solace if I could fathom the charges. Then perhaps there would be the possibility of atonement."

Death anxiety must be distinguished from the poignant feelings of sadness that emerge when we contemplate the inescapable end of our existence. We can never overcome the sadness associated with the obliteration of the self as we know it and experience it in our everyday lives. In a sense, we must mourn this anticipated loss to retain our capacity for genuine feeling. Sadness is therefore an essential part of a feeling existence.

EFFECTS OF DEATH ANXIETY ON EVERYDAY LIFE

> The irony of man's condition is that the deepest need is to be free of the anxiety of death and annihilation; but it is life itself which awakens it, and so we must shrink from being fully alive.
>
> ~ Ernest Becker (1997, p.66)

People's defensive reactions to death anxiety impact their lives at three distinct levels: (1) on an individual level, their reactions predispose withdrawal into a more inward, self-nurturing, and self-protective lifestyle; (2) on the level of interpersonal relationships, their responses can trigger a retreat from love or loving relationships and/or a generalized rejection or avoidance of intimacy and sexuality; and (3) at the societal level, their fear reactions intensify the need for people to subordinate themselves to a leader or authority figure and the need to conform to the beliefs and mores of a particular group, institution, or nation.

My hypotheses about the impact of death anxiety at each level of experience have been validated by empirical data accumulated over the past 35 years by researchers in Terror Management Theory (TMT). Numerous studies by Solomon, Pyszczynski and Greenberg (2004; 2015) have repeatedly demonstrated people's increased reliance on defense mechanisms as a result of experimentally manipulating their death salience. They describe the effect that these defenses have on human behavior individually, socially, and politically.

Effects of Death Anxiety on the Individual

When their death anxiety is aroused, people tend to become increasingly defensive in ways that are harmful to themselves and often to others as well. Even though they may initially respond positively by embracing life more fully, over time, people usually retreat to a defended posture. As they deny death to protect themselves, they live as though they will never die and can afford to squander their most valuable experiences.

These defensive reactions to death have a demoralizing effect on the individual. Tragically, many people end up losing their spirit and excitement in life. They gradually become rigid and controlling, diminishing their range of experiences to such a degree that it could be said they are no longer invested in living. They become cynical and hateful toward self and others, give up interests that once excited them, engage in behaviors that are harmful to their physical and mental health, and become increasingly depressed and futile about life.

On a deeper, more unconscious level, most of us believe that death happens only to other people, but not to us. In this magical thinking, we are special and excluded from the fate that awaits the masses. Others find a different solution: they believe that someone will ultimately save them—a relationship partner, a guru, or celebrity—or, at the very least, they believe that they will live on through their children.

This regression to a state of denial takes on many forms: some people increase their drinking or turn to drugs to numb themselves to existential realities; others adopt compulsive work habits or routines to distract themselves from the passage of time. Some embrace a religious dogma to maintain the hope or promise of an afterlife. Still others preoccupy themselves with trivial matters and obsess over pseudo-problems to divert themselves from realistic concerns about life and death. Many people over-intellectualize the subject of death, taking a more philosophical position to keep themselves one step removed from experiencing any feeling about their own mortality.

In summary, in attempting to elude death, people eventually give up their lives to varying degrees, rationing their aliveness and spontaneity, carefully doling out or restricting pleasant or enriching experiences. They gradually become indifferent to important or relevant events and numb themselves by attending to life's trivialities. Indeed, living a full life, with meaningful activity, compassion for oneself, and a poignant awareness that all people share the same fate appears to be too agonizing for many to endure. It takes courage to live fully in the face of death, and there is always the temptation to retreat to a self-protective, inward lifestyle. However, the process of identifying one's defenses and learning to change them can strengthen the part of us that desires to choose life.

Denial is the major defense against death anxiety. It manifests in two forms: in literal immortality and symbolic immortality. Literal immortality is sought in religion or religiosity and is the key defense that negates the obvious scientific conclusion that human beings die like other species and that there is no proof of an afterlife. Monotheistic religious beliefs as well as some pantheistic or monistic spiritual traditions also offer the believer various forms of literal immortality. Symbolic immortality is sought in living on through one's creative productions, investment in causes, and one's children. There is the fantasy of leaving a legacy or imprint that lives on after one dies.

Literal Immortality: All religions and belief systems seek to answer the primary existential questions that torture human beings: where do we come from and where do we go? Each offers its own creation myth and version of life after death to relieve the death anxiety that is caused by the unknowable. Human beings have projected an all-powerful male parent on to God and imbued Him with very human qualities, even negative attributes, in a defensive effort to achieve a modicum of comfort. They believe that He is waiting for them in Heaven.

Reincarnation is another widespread religious explanation that relates to a literal negation of ending and death. These belief systems take many forms, but all fall short of offering the full comfort people desire. For even if one believes that one will be reborn, how can one take full comfort in the thought of losing all one loves in this life, including loved ones, treasured experiences, and the wisdom one has have spent a lifetime developing? Nonetheless, religious dogma and ritual continue to function to reduce death anxiety. When there is an increase in fear, there is a concomitant increase in ritual and other defensive behaviors (Arndt, Greenberg, Pyszczynski, & Solomon, 1997).

Over many millennia, conventional religious ideologies from both Western and Eastern societies have contributed to the denial or negation of death. While they relieve death anxiety by assuring an afterlife, they also reinforce the tendencies to denigrate and move away from bodily concerns and pleasures or to obliterate all desire and ego. Typically, Western religious belief systems offer the hope of immortality, but it is achieved at the cost of forsaking a real life in the present, a trade-off of the body that must die for the surviving soul.

Yet such is the power of magical thinking: even if one is not religious or is a nonbeliever, and consciously knows that one will ultimately die, one may still unconsciously harbor a sense of immortality. This is manifested through elaborate fantasies of connection to persons, places, groups, organizations, institutions and ideologies.

Using a spiritual teaching to procure absolute, unqualified security in the face of a realistically uncertain future often destroys the inherent value and meaning of that teaching. Paradoxically, religious dogmatism supports self-limitation and self-abrogation, leading to the restriction or suppression of people's natural desires and feelings, which in turn contributes to an increase in violence and immorality (Prescott, 1975; Vergote, 1988). Moreover, religious philosophies that equate thought with action are in essence a form of thought control. These judgmental values lead to guilt and suppression which play a prominent role in psychological maladies.

Symbolic Immortality: Symbolic immortality is a way to imagine extending one's life and meaning through believing that one can live on through one's works, through one's children, through vanity (imagining one's life being spared because of one's specialness), and through the accumulation of power and wealth.

Living On Through One's Works: A number of theorists, including Robert J. Lifton, conceptualize creativity as a mode of symbolic immortality. Lifton (1979) has emphasized the continuity of artistic creation through time. He goes on to say, "Similarly, each scientific investigator becomes part of an enterprise larger than himself, limitless in its past and future continuity. Whatever his additional motivations—the need to know and the quest for personal glory and reward—he operates within a framework of larger connectedness" (p. 21).

Personal contributions as a mode of symbolic immortality may be manifested in dedication to a life of service and helping others. Physicians, psychotherapists, and social workers can derive satisfaction in knowing that they are having a healing or positive effect on people. According to Lifton (1979), caregivers often feel that their therapeutic efforts exert beneficial influences which "carry forward indefinitely in the lives of patients and clients and *their* children or posterity. Consequently, any sense on the part of caregivers that those efforts are ineffective can set off in them deep anxieties about ultimate personal questions" (p. 22).

Other theorists, including Becker (1997), Rank (1972) and Yalom (1980), acknowledge the obvious limitations to this mode of symbolic immortality, as when people are driven by the desperate need to utilize their talents, their work, and their dedication to others as a way of ensuring their eternal life. The illusion that one can truly live on through one's creative works, whether in art, literature or science, is doomed to failure.

I agree with Lifton in the sense that there *is* a thread or an interconnectedness in people's life stories and contributions, which survives after they are gone. The vision of an unending chain of beautiful statues, sculptures, art works, and literature from the past that still exist to inspire people the world over does offer a certain degree of satisfaction and sense of continuity. However, the notion of symbolically living on through a tangible or material piece of work fails to allay people's core anxieties when contemplating the finality of death, the separation from their imaginative powers, and the cessation of their conscious awareness as they know it. In reality, there is no living on through our creative endeavors or service to humanity. In fact, the work that is the closest to us during our lives is separated from us in death.

Nevertheless, the use of creative works and humanitarian efforts as a defense against death anxiety does not exclude the fact that the desire to make such a contribution can be an integral part of the search for meaning in life. However, it is necessary to distinguish one from the other. Because human beings are capable of deep feeling, logic, and symbolism, they need to seek authentic personal meaning in their lives through their relationships, children, work, and creativity. There are many diverse endeavors that lend significance and purpose to one's life: artists, writers, poets, and musicians find meaning in self-expression; others through serving people; and still others by contributing to a humanitarian cause or to policies that will improve the lives of future generations. These causes are usually personally gratifying and beneficial to others. Their function as a defense against death anxiety is limited, but their true value to humankind is limitless. The sense of purpose and transcendent goals has considerable value.

Living On Through One's Children: Gene survival, or as Lifton (1979) describes it, "the biological mode of immortality, is epitomized by family continuity, living on through—psychologically speaking, *in*—one's sons and daughters and their sons and daughters, with imagery of an endless chain of biological attachment. This has been the most fundamental and universal of all modes" (p. 18).

In my observations of the psychological community, I found that the birth of a child affects parents in conflicting ways: On the one hand, children are an existential threat to parents because they are vulnerable and completely dependent on them for their very survival. Also, becoming a parent, especially a first-time parent, is a step into adulthood that represents another turn of the wheel of time, a turn that brings one closer to old age and death.

On the other hand, parents can utilize their offspring to establish a sense of connection to the future. In this sense, children represent a symbolic victory over death by perpetuating one's identity into the future, a concept referred to as *gene survival.* Both parents and children imagine that this belonging or merger somehow imbues them with immortality. In this sense, the family symbolizes immortality; it is the link in an unending chain of persons passing on unique traits from one generation to the next. To the extent that children resemble their parents in appearance, characteristics, and behavior, they are the parents' legacy to be left in the world after the parents' death as evidence that their lives were meaningful and made a difference.

Parents' proprietary attitudes (i.e., the notion that children belong to their biological parents) are driven by the need to shape the child into the right kind of legacy. Society supports parents' assumption that their children belong to them. Evidence of the connection between this supposition and death anxiety can be found in Terror Management research where reminders of death led to increased scores on a measure of the importance of the biological mode of symbolic immortality (Mikulincer & Florian, 2000).

This defense against death anxiety has disadvantages for both the parent and the child. Children are only able to relieve or buffer parents' death anxiety if they adopt the cultural worldview or religious beliefs of their parents. When children are too dissimilar from their parents, they become an added source of existential concern. The child who chooses not to carry on the family business or who embraces a different religious, political, or sexual orientation negates the possibility of the biological mode of symbolic immortality, and also poses a threat to the validity of the parents' cultural worldview. Parents often become critical, even angry or hostile, with their children when their offspring adopt different careers, beliefs or values.

In his brilliant synthesis of Rank's work, Becker (1997) writes of children's identification with their parents as being a "special case of the urge for immortality."

> The child merges himself with the representatives of the cosmic process. . . . When one merges with the self-transcending parents . . . he is, in some real sense, trying to live in some larger expansiveness of meaning (p. 152).

The more a child is differentiated from a parent in looks, character traits, behavior, or significant career choices, the more guilt he/she feels about breaking the chain symbolically linking the generations. By disrupting this continuity, children become acutely aware of their own vulnerability to death and of the fact that their movement toward individuality and independence challenges their parents' sense of immortality. To avoid these reactions, children tend to cling to the fantasy bond with their parents by maintaining a sameness with them and rejecting the parts of themselves that would cause them to stand apart from family patterns and traditions.

Vanity—Specialness and Magical Thinking: Vanity is an exaggerated positive view of the self that an individual uses to compensate for feelings of inadequacy and inferiority. It represents remnants of the child's imagined invincibility and omnipotence that live on in the psyche. The sense of unlimited power and supremacy that is experienced by individuals who have inflated self-images can be traced to early childhood and to primary narcissism (Note 3).

To varying degrees, people retain elements of primary narcissism which involve "the creation of fantasies which hallucinate a sense of self-importance, grandiosity, security, invincibility, or love" (Piven, 2004a, p 98). They include illusions of being exceptional and special, and of having the capability to perform at unreasonably high levels. When their performance falls short of perfection, severe self-castigation and demoralization result. Vanity helps people to deny their mortality through the construction of various fictions that negate the fact of death. It expresses itself in the magical thinking that "death will spare me because I am special or different." People are willing to endure blows to their vanity and the tension associated with maintaining it in a desperate attempt to avoid feeling ordinary and, therefore, subject to death as ordinary people are.

The Accumulation of Power and Wealth: In business, politics, and organizational life in general, the drive to accumulate power and wealth is often motivated by a misguided belief that equates power and wealth with invincibility. Although conscious fears of death may be temporarily alleviated, these same fears still exist on an unconscious level and often increase in intensity as an individual amasses greater power. For this reason, the accumulation of power has addictive properties; leaders must increase their power base in order to compensate for feelings of inferiority, insignificance, and vulnerability.

Like a narcotic, power offers a feeling of exhilaration. The power-struck individual becomes progressively more addicted to the "high" of being powerful. When one's power is threatened, either internally or externally, one requires greater power to quell the ensuing anxiety and dread. As Yalom (1980) rightly observed: "Absolute power, as we have always known, corrupts absolutely; it corrupts because it does not do the trick for the individual. Reality always creeps in—the reality of our helplessness and our mortality; the reality that, despite our reach for the stars, a creaturely fate awaits us" (p. 127).

The Effects of Death Anxiety on Relationships

People's fear reactions to the awareness of death can create a need to regulate all aspects of their interpersonal world. They try to maintain control and regulate their vulnerability by placing limits on what they are willing to give and accept in their intimate relationships. To varying degrees, they unconsciously ration the amount of affection, tenderness and sexuality they will accept as well as how much they will give.

In relation to fantasies of fusion with other persons to combat death fears, Hart and Goldenberg (2008) observed that, "As Becker suggested, the modern era seems to have ushered in a spirituality of romantic love, an explicitly human-attachment-related solution to merge with others. Modern psychodynamic research shows that people can use romantic relations to protect themselves from the fear of death" (pp. 107-108). Yet when there is real love between two distinct individuals, as contrasted with a fantasy bond, conscious death awareness is often aroused. When this happens, people tend to distance themselves from their partners.

In the psychological community, my associates and I had the opportunity to investigate the function of the fantasy bond in relation to death anxiety. In couples' discussion groups, people talked about how their defensive behaviors were often motivated by threats to their fantasy bond. They realized that they often had negative reactions and hostile communications after feeling exceptionally close to their partner.

In exploring their deeper motivations, many people found that there was a correlation between their increased death concerns and their cutting off of feelings, retreating from emotional intimacy, and denying themselves satisfying sexual experiences. They reported having voices that warned them about death. *Why care, when life is so futile? Why want anything? If you don't want anything, you won't have anything to lose.*

Some couples spoke of times, when feeling particularly loving or compassionate, they could not bear the thought of losing their partner or themselves. They also talked of being painfully aware that, when they distanced themselves to protect against these fears of loss, they gradually gave up the real substance of their life together while preserving only the form, a fantasy of love and connection.

The Effects of Death Anxiety at the Societal Level

> Everything that man does in his symbolic world is an attempt to deny and overcome his grotesque fate. He literally drives himself into a blind obliviousness with social games, psychological tricks, personal preoccupations so far removed from the reality of his situations that they are forms of madness—agreed madness, shared madness, disguised and dignified madness, but madness all the same.
>
> ~ Earnest Becker (1997, p. 27)

If the single word "death" introduced subliminally in an experiment can produce notable changes in subjects' attitudes and actions, one can only imagine the impact of countless events in the real world that remind people of their finite existence (Note 4).

Faced with death, people develop individual lifestyles based on psychological defenses and these combine to affect society. Most people choose reliving over living, bondage over freedom, the old over the new, the past over the now (R. Firestone, 1984). They try to recreate a parent or parents in other people or institutions and search for a personal savior on earth or in the heavens. Their solution is the abrogation of real power in exchange for a form of childish dependency. They are willing to relinquish genuine friendship, free choice, and love in favor of familiarity and false safety. The pooling of these defensive lifestyles forms a social pressure that then acts back upon the individual, creating a perpetual cycle.

Religion and Spirituality: As mentioned earlier in this chapter, religious ideology and secular belief systems represent serious efforts to cope with and allay death anxiety.

Despite religion's palliative effect, the anticipation of an altered state of consciousness is frightening; any transition in life arouses separation anxiety, and death clearly represents a transition of major proportions (Note 5). Both Western and Eastern religious doctrines sacrifice the body, the ego or the self system for the higher good, but neither salves the break in continuity. They offer a modicum of comfort and security, but they fail to completely reassure us about the subject of our own death. The thought of the cessation of all consciousness and feeling for oneself as well as the loss of loved ones, remains an experience of agonizing proportions.

Furthermore, few people are completely satisfied by the idea that living a pious life will lead to the hard-won victory of an afterlife in heaven. It is difficult to conceptualize the form this eternal life will take; the concept of an infinite life is in itself disquieting. Nor does the postulation of one's salvation through reincarnation or becoming at one with the universe offer total relief. The only appropriate response is despair. According to Kierkegaard (1954/1849), despair is endemic to the human condition and the inability to experience despair is an even greater torture.

Group Identification, the Ultimate Rescuer, and Cultural Worldviews: Empirical studies by Terror Management Theorists (TMT)

Sheldon Solomon, Tom Pyszczynski, and Jeff Greenberg (2004; 2015) have added a great deal to our understanding of Ernest Becker's (1997) assertion that an awareness of death impels people to first construct and then immerse themselves in cultural worldviews and institutions that deny existential realities, i.e., the temporal nature of their lives and their basic insignificance in the universe. For example, TMT findings indicate that after subjects were subliminally presented with the word "death" in an experimental setting, they more strongly endorsed the worldview of their own ethnic group or nation; at the same time, they denigrated members of other groups whose worldviews differed from their own. Other studies showed that people tend to be more moralistic toward those whose behavior conflicts with society's social or moral codes.

The acute awareness of death and the accompanying anxiety generate forceful needs in people to become securely embedded in a collective social order (McCoy, Pyszczynski, Solomon, & Greenberg, 2000). The sense of being alone, on one's own, and standing out from the crowd evokes existential fears.

In their work, Ernest Becker (1997) and Erich Fromm (1941) have pointed out that most individuals seek an ultimate rescuer or idolized hero, whether within a personal relationship, in the entertainment, sports or music world, or in the business or political sphere. People who are more submissive or conforming in their orientation transfer the desperation and dependency needs that originally characterized their relationship with their parents onto new figures and ideologies and thus obtain relief from existential fears. They are especially susceptible to the influence of appealing, authoritarian leaders who promise them certainty and safety. In fact, in two post 9/11 studies, Terror Management researchers found that subjects in the high death awareness group favored a candidate whom they perceived as charismatic and who insisted on an aggressive agenda toward their enemies (Cohen, Ogilvie, Solomon, Greenberg, & Pyszczynski, 2005).

The fear of death can drive individuals to support destructive, toxic leaders and embrace patriotic, nationalistic movements in a search for security and immortality. Dependence on a particular group, idolization of a leader, and mindless allegiance to a cause function as forceful defenses against existential anxiety. By subordinating their views to those propagated by an idolized leader and by conforming to the group consensus, frightened individuals merge their identities with that of the group. This illusory fusion imbues them with a feeling of immortality and invulnerability. They imagine that, although they may not survive as separate individual entities, they will live on as part of something larger that *will* continue to exist after they are gone (Note 6).

As noted earlier, people have a stake in their particular mode of defense and are threatened by those with different outlooks, customs, and worldviews. They are afraid of alternative philosophies and ideologies because they perceive them as threats to their own defensive solution. This can lead to anxiety, aggression, and hostility. One must either convert those who are "misguided and mistaken," or take the necessary action to eradicate them, for they disturb one's frame of mind. They are the enemy.

These defensive reactions are also evident at the behavioral level: In experiments when death salience was aroused, subjects administered larger amounts of an aversive substance to people of a religious denomination and ethnic background different than their own. According to Solomon et al. (2015), "Our first line of psychological defense against those whose conceptions of reality are different from our own is to derogate or belittle them, diminishing the threat their beliefs pose to our own" (Loc. 2242).

On a societal level, such defensive thinking is at the core of nationalism, patriotism, and other "isms." This accounts for the pervasiveness of ethnic strife in the world today. People around the globe continue to fight about age-old religious differences without the slightest conception of why they hate and why they must destroy each other. Yet these negative reactions to ethnic and cultural differences threaten to annihilate life on the planet (R. Firestone, 1996).

FACING DEATH WITH EQUANIMITY AND APPROPRIATE FEELING

Perhaps, once we fully recognize the central role that mortal terror plays in persistent strife, human ingenuity can also find ways of counteracting the destructive potential our fears can, and do unleash.

~ Solomon et al. (2015, Loc. 2556)

There are two separate aspects of death anxiety to contend with: latent or unconscious death anxiety and conscious existential fears. Obviously, people cannot cope directly with latent death anxiety because they are unaware of their fear. However, they *can* become aware of and challenge key psychological defenses that are reactions to their fear and dread and in this way expand their lives.

Sadness

In contrast to the feelings of anger and despair about death and dying, there is a poignant sadness that often arises when one contemplates the potential loss of self and loved ones. Expressing deep feelings of sadness and sorrow regarding these existential realities appears to have an ameliorative, rather than a disturbing, effect on individuals who are open to the experience. The process of feeling one's sadness, sorrow and grief helps dispel self-hating thoughts and other defensive reactions to death anxiety.

The concept of anticipatory grief described by Ivancovich and Wong (2008) is similar in some respects to my emphasis on the value of mourning one's future death in the present-day. Theorists and researchers have shown that this form of anticipatory grief or mourning often lends new meaning to one's life and enhances one's ability to deal with personal distress and existential concerns. As Ivancovich and Wong put it: "Anticipatory grief of our own death as well as the death of a loved one may trigger the quest for meaning and spirituality" (p. 209).

I have found that when people are able to fully express their sadness and grief related to existential concerns, they tend to feel closer to themselves and their loved ones. This form of sadness appears to be more fundamental than other emotional responses—anger, rage, or fear—to the realization of death. In "Awareness of Death: A Controllable Process or A Traumatic Experience?" Moor (2002) noted that "In the actualization process the fact of one's mortality brings forth fear, anger, sense of guilt, sadness" (p. 108).

Methods for Coping with Death Anxiety

Because there is no ultimate solution to the death problem, the only appropriate reaction is to maintain awareness and feel one's way through the painful emotions. When death fears surface, people can face the reality of mortality, identify and express the accompanying emotions of fear, sadness, and rage, and find a way to communicate their thoughts and feelings with others.

It is vital to find a healthy outlet for expressing the underlying emotions concerning death and dying. Although a person could release these deep feelings in private, it is more valuable to express them in the presence of other people who share similar concerns. We have found that talking about death anxiety with an acquaintance or friend can be extremely helpful. Nevertheless, this may be difficult or unavailable because many people are intolerant of the subject. Fortunately, this issue can be addressed in seminars, workshops, and group or individual therapy in private psychotherapy practices or at universities and institutes (Furer & Walker, 2008; Schneider, 2007; 2009; Yalom, 1980) (Note 7).

My associates and I have used deep breathing exercises to facilitate the expression of such intense emotions. We asked people to make themselves comfortable (usually in the prone position) and try to make sounds when they exhaled. When they followed the suggestion, most often people were able to access their deepest emotions. During this exercise, I observed numerous individuals expressing anger, grief, and sadness in regard to the realization that life is terminal. In a sense, they were involved in a process of anticipatory grief or mourning in relation to the fact they will eventually die. When people are able to fully express their feelings of anguish, sorrow, and heartache in this context, they tend to feel closer to themselves and their loved ones. They not only feel a sense of relief from the distress, but also tend to experience their lives more fully.

Feeling sadness openly and permitting its free expression allows us to savor the experience of living. Men and women who face issues of deterioration, dying, and death, rather than living a life of denial, experience richer, fuller, more meaningful lives, and generally do not infringe on the rights of others. They have a sense that all human beings are fragile, life is precious, and that we are all in the same boat.

Learning to Love

If death anxiety is the poison, then love is the antidote. Love and loving make life bearable in relation to the dreadful predicament faced by the human race. Romantic love, loving friendship, love of self, love of nature, and love of humankind—each contributes to making life worthwhile and valuable. Both loving and being loved make people acutely conscious of their existence; they experience a heightened awareness of themselves and an enhanced sense of being and becoming. Paradoxically, these uniquely positive feelings come with a price—that of an especially poignant appreciation of a life that one knows is terminal. Thus, any movement in the direction of expanding the experience of love in one's life and increasing one's options is exhilarating as well as painful and anxiety provoking.

The awareness of their personal mortality has inspired people in the psychological community to take their lives more seriously. These people have recognized the importance of making a serious commitment to life and love. They have placed great value on their personal freedom. This emphasis on freedom and responsibility has been manifested in a strong desire **not** to become embedded in a symbiotic relationship, what Erich Fromm (1956a) referred to as:

> An egotism à deux; they are two people who identify themselves with each other, and who solve the problem of separateness by enlarging the single individual into two. They have the experience of overcoming aloneness, yet, since they are separated from the rest of mankind, they remain separated from each other and alienated from themselves; their experience of union is an illusion (p. 55).

As my friends and associates have expanded their awareness of aloneness, of life and death, and of the essential dilemma and mystery of existence, they have come to express a deep and abiding respect for people's feelings and their well-being. These sentiments have been translated into extraordinary acts of kindness, sensitivity and compassion toward one another as well as toward anyone who crosses their path. These people have elevated the concept of love and loving to a high level that continues to play a central role in their everyday lives.

Because children are hurt to varying degrees in their upbringing, they are negatively affected in their capacity to give or receive love. Faced with these limitations to self-love and love for others, one must develop oneself psychologically to regain these feelings. People can learn to love and to be loved, but like any other skill, it must be approached with discipline, effort, and passion in order to be mastered. By acknowledging death as a reality instead of resorting to defensive denial, we can best meet the challenge and embrace love and life more fully.

CONCLUSION

A number of theorists subscribe to the view that death anxiety masks unfulfillment and dissatisfaction with one's life. However, my clinical experience supports the converse proposition: Death anxiety is positively correlated to the degree of individuation and self-actualization. My clinical data support the hypothesis that death anxiety increases as people relinquish defenses, refuse to conform to familial and societal standards, reach new levels of differentiation of the self, or expand their lives. As I have shown, most people, beginning in early childhood, try to deny death on an immediate, personal level and gradually adapt to the fear of death by giving up, or at least restricting, their lives to a certain extent.

Society reinforces the defense of self-denial by maintaining certain standards regarding "age appropriate" behavior for people who have reached "maturity." Consensually validated attitudes on the part of most members of our society support disengagement from life in every area of human endeavor: early retirement, segregated retirement communities, a premature giving up of participation in athletics and other physical activities, a diminished interest in sex and a reduction in sexual activity, and a decline in social life.

Many individuals never reach an optimal level of differentiation or individuation because they stubbornly refuse to step outside of their customary defenses (Kerr & Bowen, 1988). They fear that they will experience a recurrence of the full intensity of terror and dread that tormented them as children when they first learned about death. Paradoxically, humans who live defended, constricted, unfulfilled lives in an attempt to minimize death anxiety are often tortured by ontological guilt about a life not fully lived.

In essence, we attempt to escape from death concerns by avoiding life. Most people spend their time on this earth without a great deal of self-awareness, living routine lives of emptiness and monotony based on their early programming. They rarely reflect on their circumstances, but rather are addicted to an existence of form and routine. Few develop a life plan or project that gives value and substance to their daily lives.

In the examined life, there is the possibility for powerful changes that can become part of a continuous progression toward a more meaningful and fulfilling existence. As we become increasingly emancipated from destructive remnants of our past, we are better able to confront death with equanimity, to be more aware, to live in the present, to experience both the joy and pain of existence without resorting to defenses or comforting illusions. In being more open and vulnerable, we are able to more fully embrace love and life. As James Baldwin (1963) suggested in *The Fire Next Time*, "It seems to me that one ought to rejoice in the fact of death—ought to decide, indeed, to earn one's death by confronting with passion the conundrum of life. One is responsible to life: It is the small beacon in that terrifying darkness from which we come and to which we shall return. One must negotiate this passage as nobly as possible, for the sake of those who are coming" (Loc. 822-827).

Notes

1. For an in-depth exploration of the effects of conscious and nonconscious fears of death on people's lives, see *The Worm at the Core: On the role of Death in Life* by terror management (TMT) researchers Solomon et al., (2015).

2. See Mikulincer and Florian (2008), and the discussion of my approach to defining death anxiety in "Death Anxiety: An Analysis of an Evolving Concept" by Lehto and Stein (2009).

3. In *the Denial of Death,* Ernest Becker (1997) identified the origins, in early childhood, of vanity as a defense against death anxiety, "According to psychoanalytic theory, the child meets the terror of life and aloneness first by asserting his own omnipotence and then by using the cultural morality as the vehicle for his immortality (p. 120).

4. For a review of TMT research in relation to cultural defenses against death anxiety, see Solomon et al. (2004) "The Cultural Animal: Twenty years of terror management theory and research" in Greenberg, Koole, & Pyszczynski (Eds) *Handbook of Experimental Existential Psychology.* More recent studies (Schimel, Hayes, Williams & Jahrig, 2007; Hayes, Schimel, Arndt, & Faucher, 2010) also provide converging evidence that various threats to meaning, such as "contemplating separation from a relationship partner, drawing similarities between humans and animals, providing people with evidence that the world is unjust and threatening important aspects of one's cultural worldview" make death thoughts more accessible (p. 802).

5. Re: religious beliefs as a defense against death anxiety: "Research . . . demonstrate[s] that mortality salience produces increased belief in afterlife, supernatural agency, human ascension from nature, and spiritual distinctions between mind and body" (Vail et al., 2010, p.84). Also see Florian and Mikulincer's (2004) analysis of the fear of personal death among American college students who came from diverse religious backgrounds.

6. Re: "group identification", see an alternative theoretical model, Uncertainty-Identity Theory (Hogg, Adelman, & Blagg, 2010), which is similar in some respects to my concept of the merging one's identity with that of the group (the fantasy bond).

Re: See *The Allure of Toxic Leaders,* in which Lipman-Blumen (2005) described existential concerns on the part of followers that allow many destructive and ineffective leaders to remain in power.

7. See Chapter 11 "Facing Death with Equanimity and Appropriate Feelings" in *Beyond Death Anxiety: Achieving Life-Affirming Death Awareness* (R. Firestone & Catlett, 2009a). Also see "Death Anxiety: A Cognitive-Behavioral Approach," by Furer and Walker (2008). Routledge and Juhl (2010) have observed that "People who indicated that their lives were full of meaning did not respond to mortality salience with increased death anxiety (p. 851). Similarly, based on their research Lykins, Sergerstrom, Averill, Evans, & Kemeny (2007) suggested that "Intrinsic goals may allow for growth, instead of immobility or defensiveness, to occur following a confrontation with the inevitability of mortality" (p. 11). Also see Vail et al. (2012), regarding "adaptive and maladaptive coping mechanisms" for dealing with death awareness.

Sources: Psychological Defenses Against Death Anxiety In *Death Studies* (1994) and *Beyond Death Anxiety: Achieving Life-Affirming Death Awareness* (2009a)

Note on Sources: Republished with permission of Springer Publishing Company, LLC from *Beyond Death Anxiety: Achieving Life-Affirming Death Awareness* Robert W. Firestone and Joyce Catlett (2009); permission conveyed through Copyright Clearance Center, Inc.

Chapter 9

COUPLE RELATIONSHIPS

The great aim of every human being is to understand the meaning of total love. Love is not to be found in someone else, but in ourselves; we simply awaken it. But in order to do that, we need the other person. The universe only makes sense when we have someone to share our feelings with.

~ Paulo Coelho (2004, p. 116)

THE CHALLENGE OF INTIMATE RELATIONSHIPS

Interpersonal relationships are a fundamental source of happiness or misery; love has the potential to generate intense pleasure and fulfillment or to produce considerable pain and suffering. Our basic sense of self is originally formed in a relationship constellation that predisposes our attitudes toward ourselves, others, and the world at large. Our feelings about life are developed in the context of a close attachment with a parent, parents, or other significant figures in our early years. Extensive research has shown that these original attachments create feelings of wholeness and security, or states of anxiety and insecurity that can persist for a lifetime and affect the quality of relating in an adult attachment (George & Solomon, 1996) (Note 1).

There is nothing more desirable than for two people to love and respect one another in a close personal relationship. An affectionate style of relating is fulfilling and rewarding and is at the core of positive couple and family interactions. The combination of loving companionship and sexual contact in a long-lasting relationship is conducive to good mental and physical health and is an essential goal for most people (Reis & Shaver, 1988).

As I mentioned in the last chapter, I believe love to be the one force that is capable of easing existential despair and the endemic pain of the human condition. I feel that to develop emotionally as well as spiritually one needs to learn how to love, to continue to search for it throughout life and to not become cynical or despairing when love fails. I feel a sense of kinship with R. D. Laing (1976) in his contention that:

> The main fact of life for me is love or its absence. Whether life is worth living depends for me on whether there is love in life. Without a sense of it, or even the memory . . . of it, I think I would lose heart completely (p. vii).

Sadly, many people find it difficult to love and even more problematic to accept it being directed toward them. It is a significant challenge to develop and sustain a kind, generous, and decent relationship in which there is respect for each person's individuality.

In my study of human relationships, I have not only been fortunate enough to draw upon the personal experiences of numerous clients in psychotherapy and close observations of people in my everyday life, but I have also been exposed to the honest disclosures of the group of men and women in the psychological community described in Chapter 1. The discoveries I made during this longitudinal study of three generations of these individuals have contributed significantly to my understanding of the numerous ways people defend themselves in their intimate associations (R. Firestone, L. Firestone, & Catlett, 2003) (Note 2).

Love is a vital force in life, yet it is not essential for physical survival. Despite this fact, when people feel insecure they tend to cling desperately to each other as though the loss of the other person would be life-threatening. In a misguided attempt to find and maintain safety and security in their relationship, they turn away from pursuing their own destiny. Consequently, they suppress their personal interests, goals, and dreams and may even compromise their ideals and basic values. It appears that, in order to hold on to their fantasy bond and maintain the status quo, people inadvertently deceive themselves, confuse their partners, and manipulate one another in ways that are destructive to their ongoing state of being.

The psychological defenses of each member of the couple constitute the greatest threat to personal satisfaction in an intimate relationship. The more defended partners are, the greater the threat to their having a successful relationship and to their own individuation process. Accepting love leads to a feeling of increased vulnerability and challenges any remaining negative identity formed in the family of origin.

As a relationship becomes meaningful and intimate, being loved and positively acknowledged can threaten to disrupt one's psychological equilibrium by piercing core defenses. This causes anxiety, which can be relieved by utilizing distancing behaviors that adversely affect the closeness of the couple. As the relationship deteriorates, one or both partners unconsciously sacrifice their independence and individuality to hold on to the illusion of being in love.

It is exceedingly difficult to maintain one's unique identity given the numerous agreed upon, implicit rules of "coupledom" that are prevalent in our culture. Even when relationships last, each person's individuality and independence can be seriously compromised. Therefore, responsible marriage counseling and couples therapy would ideally focus on each person as an individual rather the couple as an institution.

There is so much pain and suffering in couple relationships, relative to other aspects of life, that this is one of the primary reasons for seeking psychotherapy (Snyder, Castellani, & Whisman, 2006). As romantic attachments evolve, one tends to progress through different phases of relating. Initially, during the falling in love phase, individuals are more open, more vulnerable, and less defended than they are typically. They are congenial in their interactions, willing to risk more of themselves emotionally, experience a greater sense of aliveness and vitality, and treat each other with consideration and respect.

However, the excitement of being in love is also fraught with emotions that can be frightening. As people become aware that they are loved, they give value to themselves, to their partner and to the relationship and come to realize they that have something precious to lose. The fear of future loss that this evokes is difficult to tolerate, particularly for those who lacked a secure attachment early in life. At the point where people begin to feel anxious or frightened, many unconsciously retreat from feeling close, gradually give up the most valued aspects of their relationships, and instead, form a fantasy bond just as they did in childhood.

Once a fantasy bond has been established within a couple, symbols of togetherness and images of love strengthen the illusion of connection, whereas genuine experiences of love and intimacy intrude on its defensive function. To maintain their psychological equilibrium, people unconsciously act in ways that regulate the amount of love and affection being directed toward them. Their distancing behaviors effectively diminish the positive emotional transactions—the kind and respectful give-and-take exchanges—to a level that each person is able to tolerate. Individuals in a fantasy bond relinquish vital areas of personal interest, their opinions, and unique points of view in order to become a unit, a whole, at one with their partner. To the extent that these individuals progressively lose their personal identities, they suffer a loss of feeling for one another and a diminution of real communication. Instead, they gradually come to rely on habitual contact, routines, and small talk about practical matters.

OPINIONS ABOUT COUPLES OFFERED BY THE REFERENCE POPULATION

Over the past 40 years, I have participated in seminars in which couples have spoken openly about their intimate relationships. Below is a sampling of their opinions on various issues. Some of the information revealed may be controversial and contradict certain commonly held attitudes about love and sex in the culture at large.

Relationships are Central in Affecting a Person's Life

When asked to state what they believed to be fundamentally true about relationships, the overall consensus was that a close, loving relationship is central to their happiness and of the utmost importance in their lives. They indicated that these are worth struggling for because of the potential gratification of being close to someone in a tender, sensitive, respectful manner.

Relationships are Generally Unstable

The participants were of the opinion that most relationships are tenuous at best. This view is supported by surveys showing that although there has been some decline in the divorce rate in recent years, between one-third and one-half of first marriages end in divorce (Copen, Daniels, Vespa, & Mosher, 2012) (Note 3). The negative prognosis for relationships and marriage fosters feelings of disillusionment and cynicism in many people.

There is a Good Deal of Dishonesty in Relationships

The deceptions and manipulations of couples in love are obvious and familiar to outside observers; however, most people are not fully aware of the extent to which they are dishonest with their partners. Duplicity and mixed messages exist in many areas within a relationship, including issues of sexuality, money, preferences, opinions, and feelings. People are reluctant to reveal their lies and deceptions to their mates for fear of losing the relationship.

Relationships are Often Based on Emotional Hunger and Desperation

Many individuals experience feelings of longing and desperation that they mistake for love. They fail to make a distinction between emotional hunger, which is a strong need caused by emotional deprivation in childhood, and feelings of genuine affection and concern. Feelings of emotional hunger can be experienced as deep physical sensations, ranging in intensity from a dull ache, to a sharp painful feeling, to generalized anguish. People often are seeking relief from painful primal feelings of aloneness when selecting a partner, and when they find temporary respite, imagine that they have found love.

Few Long-Term Relationships are Made Up of High-Level Choices

People actually find few potential partners who they truly admire and would choose over all others and who would, in turn, choose them for a long-term relationship. In terms of mate selection, there are high-level and low-level choices. Few people are able to select from a wide range of available prospects where there is a greater opportunity for a high-level choice. Most people must make their selection from a small group of available prospects, and this often leads to a low-level choice.

In an effort to rationalize making a low-level choice, people tend to aggrandize their choice. He/she soon becomes "one in a million;" the relationship becomes "a match made in heaven." This transformation of a low-level choice into an imagined high-level one implies a certain degree of self-deception, as well as deception of the other, as is often manifested in a fantasy bond.

People may consciously or unconsciously recognize that they are not a high-level choice of their mates. This fosters a sense of insecurity. Both sexes are fearful that their partner may someday find a better choice and as a result, they make strenuous demands that their mates indicate a preference for them over all others. This poses an essential contradiction, because when questioned individually as to whether they feel that they are better than most, men and women would say, "No, I'm just your ordinary, average person. Sure, I do some things well. I have some good qualities, but basically, I'm just like everyone else." Yet men and women demand that their partners maintain an illusion that they are superior to others, and tend to be punitive when confronted with any evidence to the contrary.

High-Level Choices Can be Made for Negative as well as Positive Reasons

High-level choices, those based on strong attractions where there were many prospects, do not necessarily imply positive choices. On an unconscious level, the need to relive the experiences of one's childhood in present-day relationships exerts a distinct influence over one's choice of a partner. People are compelled to select mates who are similar to a parent or other family member. This is underscored by the fact that so many people choose a succession of lovers similar to those who previously caused them trouble.

My colleagues and I also noted that the level of maturity and the capacity to relate to another as a separate person affects one's selection of characteristics in a mate. If one is an emotionally mature and independent person, one is more likely to emphasize adult companionship, friendship, and mutual interests. On the other hand, if one is immature, one tends to seek dependency ties and personality characteristics in the other to compensate for one's own perceived negative traits or deficiencies.

Many People Have Difficulty Combining Love and Sex

Many people find it difficult to combine emotional closeness and sexual intimacy in a long-term relationship. People who have suffered painful childhoods are often deeply saddened by experiencing love and tenderness in their sexual lives; therefore, they tend to avoid these deep feelings. The combination of love and sexuality can also precipitate separation anxiety. In fact, the sex act itself is a real, but temporary, physical connection followed by a separation. Physical intimacy manifested by close, affectionate contact is followed by a distinct awareness of aloneness. Separation anxiety often fosters resentment, though the anger and hostility can be unconscious.

Another opinion expressed about sexuality was that both men and women often confuse passionate sex with genuine affection, care, and concern. In particular, during the early phase of a relationship, they tend to mistake the initial excitement and pleasure in sex for love.

People Feel They are a Failure Unless They Succeed in Finding a Mate

People do not generally perceive themselves as being whole; they act as though they are incomplete in and of themselves. They operate under a basic unconscious assumption of core inadequacy. Because people have numerous insecurities and perceive themselves as deficient, finding a mate and/or getting married takes on a surplus meaning. The ability to find and keep a partner gives those with a sense of inferiority and low self-esteem a sense of security and a feeling of belonging. On the other hand, the status of being single, separated, or divorced signifies failure. Societal expectations about what men and women are "supposed to do" support these views and arouse considerable tension.

People Can't Tolerate Love

During the seminars, an important truth emerged: many people are intolerant of real intimacy, the very thing they say they desire. People usually fail to sustain meaningful relationships because love makes them feel vulnerable and open to the threat of potential rejection and loss.

I have found that the key issues in conflicted couples and the corresponding breakdown in relationships are not the customary explanations given for failures in relating: the wrong choice of partner, economic hardship, religious differences, problems with in-laws, breakdown of church and family, sexual incompatibility, and many others. Instead, it is the lack of tolerance for intimacy, based on negative attitudes toward self and others, as well as the deeply embedded inward patterns of psychological defenses manifested by each partner, that are responsible for the failure of most relationships.

Partners' fears of aloneness, abandonment, and rejection are serious factors at the core of relationship distress and family dysfunction. To fully understand these factors, one must examine how children react to stress and pain in their formative years and subsequently resolve to protect themselves against future hurt and vulnerability.

A DEVELOPMENTAL PERSPECTIVE ON THE FANTASY BOND – A BRIEF REVIEW

As noted earlier, I use the term fantasy bond to describe both the original imaginary connection formed during childhood and the repetitive efforts of adults to make fantasized connections in their intimate relationships. Several years ago, I outlined a comprehensive theory of psychological defenses (R. Firestone & Catlett, 1999). Reviewing portions of this material is helpful in elaborating the theory underlying relationship problems:

The primary defense or fantasy bond is formed at a time when the child would be in great danger if he were abandoned by the parent. That's why people are afraid to take a chance again. When they do, they fear that they will be exposed to the anxiety, fear, and pain that they went through at the time when they were helpless and dependent. That is why in adult life, people generally tend to relive rather than live — that is, to unconsciously repeat the patterns of the past and avoid the real gamble or adventure of taking a chance on other prospects. On an unconscious level, it is safer to repeat the same pattern than to try something new.

People who have been damaged in their earliest experiences and are afraid of being hurt or rejected again seek security in repetition. They attempt to recapture the more familiar conditions that existed within their families, the conditions under which they formed their defenses. The more rejected children are, the more desperately they cling to and form an imagined connection with the parent. In a sense, the rejected child has difficulty leaving home to develop an independent life and transfers this abnormal dependency to new persons and relationships. Consequently, he/she tends to avoid or reject any person or experience that is different, even when it appears to potentially offer greater satisfaction.

RECREATING THE PAST THROUGH SELECTION, DISTORTION, AND PROVOCATION

To maintain the fantasy bond and preserve their negative identity, people relive their past by modifying the responses of their loved ones, in a sense "working them over," in an effort to maintain equilibrium and reduce tension and anxiety. In a new relationship, they attempt to recreate the emotional environment that was present in the original family through three major modes of defense: selection, distortion, and provocation (Note 4).

Selection

People tend to select partners who are similar in appearance, behavior, and defense patterns to a significant family member (usually the parent of the opposite sex) because they feel familiar and comfortable with that person. The defended individual externalizes the introjected parental image by using the new partner to maintain the "good" parent/"bad" child system.

Distortion

People's perceptions of their partners are altered or distorted in a direction that corresponds more closely to a particular member of their family of origin. Not all distortions are negative. Positive and negative qualities from the past are assigned to significant people in a person's current life, and both types of distortion are maladaptive. Any misperception, whether an exaggeration of admirable traits or of undesirable qualities, usually generates friction in relationships. People want to be seen for who they are, and being distorted by one's partner arouses hurtful, angry responses.

Provocation

If the first two methods fail to recreate the past and maintain the defense system, partners tend to manipulate each other to elicit familiar parental responses. In this case, their actions provoke reactions similar to those of their parent or parents. For example, partners may incite anger and even rage in each other with thoughtlessness, forgetfulness, incompetency, displays of temper, and other childish, regressed behaviors. Frequently, the closest, most tender moments are followed by provocations that create distance between the partners.

Through these three methods, partners are able to externalize the fantasy bond and recreate negative aspects of the original family in their new attachments. They preserve the internalized parent by projecting his/her image onto their partner. In other words, it appears that many people prefer to maintain their original defenses rather than adapt to a new set of circumstances, so they attempt to mold their current environment to resemble past conditions.

THE FORMATION OF THE FANTASY BOND IN COUPLE RELATIONSHIPS

The universal psychopathology is defined as the attempt to create in real life by behavior or communication the illusion of fusion.

~ Hellmuth Kaiser (in Fierman, 1965, pp. 208-209)

Most people have a fear of intimacy and at the same time are terrified of being alone. Their solution is to form a fantasy bond, which allows them to maintain emotional distance while assuaging loneliness and, in the process, to meet society's expectations regarding coupling and family. Elements of destructive fantasy bonds exist, to varying degrees, in the majority of couple relationships and are apparent in most families. The process of forming an imagined connection greatly reduces the possibility of achieving a successful personal relationship.

By the time they reach adulthood, most people have solidified their defenses and exist in a psychological equilibrium that they do not wish to disturb. Although they may be relatively congenial with more casual acquaintances, there is typically deterioration in the quality of relating within their intimate relationships.

As a relationship becomes more meaningful, the personal attachment threatens to penetrate basic defenses and disrupt the emotional balance each person has so carefully created. Conflict often develops as the partners strive to maintain their defenses, while at the same time attempting to hold on to their initial feelings of closeness and affection. The two conditions tend to be mutually exclusive. Usually, one or both partners eventually chooses to sacrifice friendship and love in order to preserve and maintain their respective defenses.

Early Symptoms

When the affection and friendship in a new relationship contrast sharply with the unhappiness and rejection of the past, people often unwittingly attempt to eradicate the difference. As was evident in the couples I described in Chapter 1, early symptoms of this deterioration include diminished eye contact between partners, less honesty and more duplicity, bickering, interrupting, speaking for the other, and/or talking as a unit. Both partners may begin to manipulate each other by playing on the other's guilt or provoking angry or parental responses. Self-doubts and self-critical thoughts are often projected onto the mate, leading each person to complain about the other.

This decline in the quality of relating is not the inevitable result of familiarity, as many people assume. It is due, instead, to deadening habit patterns, exaggerated dependency, negative projections, loss of independence, and a sense of obligation. As one or both partners begin to sacrifice their individuality to become one-half of a couple, their basic attraction to each other is jeopardized. All of these dynamics have a distancing effect on the couple, and both partners may come to rely on a fantasy of closeness and intimacy that is no longer evident in their behavior toward each other.

As the fantasy bond develops and partners begin to hold back the desirable qualities in themselves that originally attracted one another, they tend to experience feelings of guilt and remorse. Consequently, both begin to behave out of a sense of obligation and responsibility instead of a genuine desire to be together.

Symptoms of a fantasy bond often appear following a commitment that originated as an expression of the partners' genuine feelings toward each other. They use these commitments as guarantees of continued love and security—external indications of a fantasy of connectedness. For those with a poor self-image and strong dependency needs, this sense of belonging to another person, of being loved "forever after," offers reassurance that is difficult to resist (Note 5). On the other hand, for mature individuals, a mutual commitment that expresses the desire to be associated with another person throughout life can remain an expression of deep feeling rather than evolving into a desperate attempt to find ultimate security.

Form Versus Substance

Individuals who form destructive ties usually resist recognizing that they have lost much of their feeling for each other and have become alienated. They attempt to cover up this reality with a fantasy of enduring love, substituting form for the substance of the relationship. This conventional type of relating consists of the convenient habits and superficial conversation that many partners come to depend upon to maintain their fantasy of being in love. Everyday routines, customs, and role-determined behaviors provide the structure and form of the relationship. People's capacity for self-deception enables them to maintain an imagination of closeness and intimacy through these symbols, all the while acting in ways that contrast with any recognizable definition of real love.

Couples often rationalize remaining together in spite of their distress because of the addictive nature of their relationship. They have become so dependent upon each other to preserve the illusion of connection that they cannot bear to contemplate the thought of being separate. As R.D. Laing (1985b) noted when describing a couple who consulted with him:

> They both said they loved each other but were extremely nasty to each other...They were both engulfed by their own miserable mirage of intimacy. They were desperately estranged from each other yet they were terrified to realize that they were simply separate. They could not come together because they could not bear to be apart. They had both become a part of the other (p. 18).

As mentioned in Chapter 5, many partners develop unconscious contracts based on conventional views about the obligations inherent in the roles of being in a committed relationship. A common pattern is one that is derived from traditional gender role expectations that are still prevalent in the world today. These are based on stereotypic views of women as weak, childlike, and helpless and men as logical, practical, strong and masterful (Geis, 1993). The couple's implicit pact could be expressed in more explicit terms. In this instance, the woman's part might be, "I'll defer to your wishes and decisions because I need to be taken care of," whereas the man's part might be, "I'll take care of you because I need to feel big and important."

A COUPLE

Jerry, 46, and Maria, 37, became involved at a time in their lives when both were recently single. They were strongly attracted to each other and, as the months went by, their relationship became closer and more meaningful. In an interview several years later, Jerry described the first year of the relationship:

Jerry: We got involved when Maria first moved here from New York. I was happy when she seemed attracted to me. I liked her energy and enthusiasm; we had a lot in common—hiking, swimming, the outdoor life. But I began to notice that sometimes she talked kind of tough and was little phony.

Maria was born in the Bronx, in a poor, crime-ridden neighborhood; her father was often unemployed. When she met Jerry, she was drawn to his intelligence, honesty, and straightforward manner of expressing himself. However, because of her own insecurity and low self-esteem, at first she couldn't believe that Jerry was really interested in her.

Maria: I was immediately drawn to Jerry; it was a deep attraction. But then, when we started dating, I just couldn't believe that he really wanted to be with me. I would tell myself: *You like him a lot, but he really doesn't have the same kind of feelings toward you. Actually, he's not the kind of person who would be attracted to a woman like you. He's way out of your class. What do you have in common with him, anyhow?*

The patterns of defense that each partner brought to the relationship had their sources in their early childhood experiences. Jerry had grown up in a household that was dominated by a cold, authoritarian father who distrusted women, especially his wife. Jerry's mother was critical of both Jerry and his father. But she also used Jerry as a confidant to complain about her dissatisfaction with life and her husband.

Jerry: The first thing I can remember is my mother's disapproving eyes, always on me. I remember just being ignored by my two older sisters. So here was Maria, very interested in me, and in everything I had to say. She was so different from my ex-wife – I was shocked and really happy to have found somebody who genuinely liked me.

As a child, Maria had learned to deny her own wants and focused her attention on trying to win her father's praise and approval. She also observed and unconsciously imitated her mother's childlike dependence on her father and her deference to his wishes and demands. The only warmth or affection she received was the seductive, somewhat inappropriate attention from her father, which intensified her longing for real love and affirmation.

> Maria: I was desperate to get my father's attention, but I never really got what I wanted or needed from him. I believed that Jerry would give me what I wanted and had missed while growing up. Then I would be okay, acceptable, a "good girl."

This case illustrates a number of manifestations of the fantasy bond in couple relationships and specifically examines the psychodynamics involved in the formation of the addictive attachment between Jerry and Maria. It also shows how each partner brought destructive thoughts and attitudes to the relationship that contributed to a collusive pattern of defensive relating.

Progressive Withholding of Qualities Valued by One's Partner

Men and women who have been damaged in early family relationships often attempt to control the amount of love and satisfaction they receive from their mates. As explained in Chapter 3, one method of taking control is to withhold the personal qualities that were originally valued by the partner. In holding back the lovable traits and actions that originally elicited tender responses, partners in effect manipulate each other into a familiar level of relating, rather than remaining close and learning to tolerate feeling particularly loved and chosen.

As Jerry and Maria's involvement became more serious, their relationship was significantly affected by Jerry's inhibitions. As a child, he protected himself from his mother's intrusiveness by becoming distrustful and pseudo-independent. In his relationships, he tended to hold back his affection and sexual responses, especially when he felt a woman wanting something from him. He revealed how these withholding tendencies were regulated by voices when he was with Maria.

> Jerry: I do feel a lot of affection for Maria, but then something seems to stop me from spontaneously reaching out to her. When we're in bed, I may start to feel sexual, but then I distract myself by thinking things like: *You'd better make her feel good. If you don't she's going to be dis-*

appointed. Look at you, you're not feeling very much. What's the matter with you? Maybe you're just getting too old for sex.

Maria described the types of voices she experienced in the same situations.

Maria: When we're just lying in bed at night, watching TV, I'll start thinking: *Does he want to make love tonight? Maybe you should make a move. No, wait for him to touch you. Don't be so aggressive, don't take the initiative, that just turns him off.* It's a complete inner world and I'm totally removed from feeling close as soon as the voices start up, worrying if he's going to make love to me or not.

Maria's anxious and demanding attempts to find the kind of love and physical closeness that was lacking in her childhood tended to push Jerry away, whereas Jerry's sexual inhibitions and aloofness only increased her feelings of emotional hunger.

Idealization of the Partner

A couple's disappointment in and critical views of each other stem partly from their initial tendency to idealize their partner as they had idealized their family in the past. Often when a partner is made aware of the weaknesses and foibles of the other, he/she becomes angry and resentful because this fantasy is shattered. In this, case, Maria's tendencies to aggrandize men led to many problems in the relationship.

Maria: I always saw myself as coming from a lower class and background, being from a poor neighborhood in the Bronx. Jerry went to Stanford, became a lawyer and was sophisticated but still down-to-earth and straightforward. I was attracted to those qualities, but I felt sure that he wouldn't be interested in me. I had very low self-esteem, so I was really excited that he liked me. But that feeling didn't last very long. Looking back now, I realize I never quite trusted his feelings for me, even at the beginning. I tried to cover up my own inferiority feelings by praising him when he won a case, cooking special dinners, anything to show him how much I cared about him. That made me feel like I was okay and that we were close.

Jerry had ambivalent feelings in relation to Maria's idealized view of him. On one hand, he enjoyed the attention, exaggerated focus, catering, and flattery. He liked that she sought his advice and opinions and deferred to his wishes. On the other hand, when her expressions of adulation became too blatant, he felt embarrassed and angry. Maria's idealization of Jerry and her expectation that all her needs would be met in their relationship placed a tremendous burden on him. Essentially, Maria made Jerry feel that he was the source of all her happiness. Obviously, no one person can fulfill such unrealistic expectations or live up to such a glorified image.

Loss of Independence and a Sense of Separate Identity

Perhaps the most significant sign that a fantasy bond has been formed is when one or both partners give up vital areas of personal interest, their unique points of view and opinions, or their individuality to become a unit, a whole. Maria realized that she had become progressively less independent the more she focused she became on the relationship with Jerry:

Maria: I was always trying to get certain signs from Jerry that he loved me. But even if I got that special sign of love, it was great for the moment, but then it was gone, and I would feel insecure again. In that state, I couldn't stand being alone. I was always focused on him; how I was going to get affection or sex again. I became much less interested in many of the activities I usually enjoyed—working out, going out with my close women friends, even my career—and concentrated my attention more and more on Jerry.

Polarization of Parental and Childish Ego States

As noted in Chapter 5, in relationships largely characterized by a fantasy bond, the partners often polarize, one into a parental posture and the other exhibiting childlike behaviors. In this case, Maria tended to act out the childish role in the relationship, while Jerry responded in an authoritarian, parental manner.

Maria: Every time Jerry and I try to share an activity, I'm always tense. I make a mistake or screw up in some way and he ends up in-variably saying something like, "If you don't want to do this with me, if you're going to be like that, I'd rather do the whole thing myself!"

Jerry: I'll admit I can be critical at times, but with Maria, it's totally ridiculous. She's smart and highly competent, but she's even become a klutz on our hikes, and we used to have so much fun together. She acts like a child every time we try to do something together and I end up feeling like I'm a mean bastard.

In general, by regressing to childish modes of relating, people are able to manipulate others into taking care of them and thereby preserve the imagined security of the original fantasy bond with the parents (Note 6). In analyzing Jerry and Maria's relationship, one can observe how Maria adopted the role of the more childish partner, while Jerry assumed the more parental role. This polarization fostered increasingly defensive behavior on each person's part, especially in the area of sexuality. Maria became more desperate and demanding in her advances, while Jerry became more rejecting and withholding in his responses.

Maria was using Jerry and their relationship to validate negative views of herself all the while complaining that he withheld affection and sex from her. For his part, Jerry persisted in criticizing Maria for what he called her "syrupy" sweetness, phoniness, and lack of independence. This style of relating is common in couples who have formed a fantasy bond. The partners complain ineffectively and avoid directly challenging their mate's defensive behaviors. In this way, they ward off each other's feelings so that neither has to experience the vulnerability and sadness that genuine love, sensitive treatment, and tenderness might arouse.

Jerry and Maria were locked in a collusive, defensive pact with each other until Maria entered therapy and took steps to alter her impact on the destructive cycle. After a number of sessions, Maria became more aware of the part she played in maintaining the confusion and distress that characterized their relationship.

Maria: I recognized that I was seeing Jerry as a bastard who I had to either pursue relentlessly or get away from, a person who wouldn't give me what I want. In my mind, I had become a victim of a man who was mean and who didn't understand my needs. I've had to take a hard look at myself in therapy. I've had to challenge how I've been playing the victimized child with Jerry. As I've become more equal and "adult" in my life and in our relationship, Jerry has responded and been more giving and demonstrative. I've found that hard to take. I hate to admit it, but it's the truth, I can feel the discomfort and anxiety in my bones when he's loving toward me.

Maria's insight into her part in perpetuating Jerry's tendencies to withhold his affection and sexual responses helped disrupt the couple's habitual style of relating. She began to change the behaviors that had reflected her constant focus on Jerry, especially her desperation towards him sexually. This development enabled both of them to explore other ways they had been attempting to find security by reliving patterns of the past. Maria gradually emerged from the childlike, dependent role she had assumed during the earlier phases of their relationship, causing a shift in the dynamics between them. Jerry learned to relinquish the critical, parental role he had taken on. Both partners developed more emotional maturity, and the communication between them became more equal (Note 7).

THE ROLE OF THE VOICE IN MAINTAINING A DESTRUCTIVE PSYCHOLOGICAL EQUILIBRIUM

> The partner carries parents inside the self, and is not aware when their voice takes over.

> ~ Wym Bramley (2008, p. 5)

The nature of the fantasy bond as it manifests itself in couple relationships is that both individuals more often than not are "listening" to the dictates of their respective voices. Their communications are filtered through this biased, alien point of view that distorts their partner's real image. Both parties, to varying degrees, ward off loving responses from the other, using rationalizations promulgated by the voice to justify their anger and distancing behavior. Men and women project their specific voice attacks onto one another and, as a result, respond inappropriately, i.e., as though they were being victimized or depreciated by their mates.

Externalization of the voice represents an end in itself because partners are able to avert or reduce anxiety by misperceiving the other as their critical parent to affirm their own negative identity. For example, a man identified voices that women did not see him as a real man and revealed disparaging thoughts concerning his body, general appearance, and sexuality. Overtime, his girlfriend became increasingly irritated by his insecurity, desperation, and self-depreciating comments, and basically came to see him as he saw himself.

By using one's partner as the agent of attack rather than being at the mercy of one's own self-accusations, one diminishes internal feelings of anxiety and self-hatred. Often, it is less painful to defend oneself against an outside attack than to experience the torment and internal sense of division in recognizing the enemy within (Willi, 1982) (Note 8).

In this process of projective identification, an intimate relationship not only provides the conditions for reinforcing destructive voices already existing within a person, but they may also generate new critical voices in the partner. Thus, partners become engaged in a spiral of attack and counterattack that is demeaning and destructive to each person's sense of self.

THE IDEAL COUPLE RELATIONSHIP VS. RELATIONSHIPS CHARACTERIZED BY A FANTASY BOND

It is valuable to consider the psychodynamics that characterize a healthy couple relationship and contrast them with destructive machinations of the fantasy bond. The primary indication of a healthy relationship is the positive impact it has on the lives of the individuals involved, as well as the degree of self-actualization and fulfillment they experience.

Relationships can be conceptualized in terms of the differential effects they have on each person's sense of self. In "healthy" relationships, each person's self-esteem is affirmed and nurtured, as contrasted with "toxic" relationships in which the negative attitudes and voices of the anti-self system of each partner are reinforced. In our study of couples and families, we discovered that any personal communication or interaction between partners could be evaluated as being either supportive of the self or as interfering with each person's positive sense of self and personal development.

The longevity of a relationship is not necessarily a good measure of the well-being of a couple; people may choose to maintain destructive relationships over an extended period of time. In many cases, the relationship has endured, but the individuals are suffering. In considering the kinds of nurturing exchanges that best support the individual lives of the people involved, specific positive and negative modes of interaction that are conducive to success or failure can be operationally defined (see Figure 9.1).

Figure 9.1
Couples Interactions Chart

Interactions in an Ideal Relationship	Interactions in Fantasy Bond
Nondefensiveness and openness.	Angry reactions to feedback. Closed to new experience
Honesty and integrity	Deception and duplicity
Respect for the other's boundaries, priorities,	Overstepping boundaries. Other seen only in relation to self
Physical affection and personal sexuality.	Lack of affection; inadequate or Impersonal, routine sexuality
Understanding--lack of distortion of the other	Misunderstanding—distortion of the other
Noncontrolling, nonmanipulative, and nonthreatening	Manipulations of dominance and submission

STEPS THAT PARTNERS CAN TAKE TO DISRUPT THE FANTASY BOND IN THEIR RELATIONSHIP

There are a number of steps that individual partners can initiate to break into the fantasy bond they have formed with each other and help recapture some of their original love and intimacy in their relationship. All of these suggestions must be taken with the utmost consideration, respect and kindness towards one another. Partners can: (1) admit the existence of a fantasy bond and stop denying that they have become distant and their actions are no longer loving; (2) reveal feelings of anger, hostility, and withholding patterns and admit critical, hostile voices toward themselves and their partner; (3) face the psychological pain and sadness involved in attempting to resume intimacy; (4) expose their fears of individuation and separation, including the fear of loss or death of their partner as well as their own death; (5) move toward independence and respect for each other and establish true equality disrupting reciprocal patterns of dominance, submission, and defiance; (6) develop a non-defensive posture toward feedback and an open and honest style of communication (Note 9); (7) move toward increased interaction with others, extending circle of family and friends to provide better reality testing; and (8) if necessary, plan temporary or long-term separations.

RESISTANCE TO DISRUPTING FANTASY BONDS IN COUPLE RELATIONSHIPS

Intense reactions and strong resistance are inevitable when clients separate from illusory connections with their mates or families. A major problem with many psychotherapies is that both the therapist and the client more or less are unconsciously reluctant to challenge the fantasy bond.

Many clients incorrectly equate breaking the fantasy bond with terminating the relationship itself. In actuality, exposing destructive ties opens up the possibility of a renewed and better relationship. Unless manifestations of this fantasy connection are identified and consistently challenged, there will be no sustained therapeutic progress. Therefore, in an effective couples therapy, fantasy bonds are exposed and understood in the context of each individual's fears and anxieties. This approach assists both partners in relating to one another on a more positive basis and frees them to experience genuine loving feelings. Indeed, there is no defense or relationship problem that is impervious to change, providing the parties are willing to risk being vulnerable in their close associations rather than remaining imprisoned by early programming and illusions of connection.

CONCLUSION

The nature of a fantasy bond explains people's compulsion to relive the past with new persons and relationships. Once the imagined merger is established, individuals are reluctant to take a chance again on gratification from others. This process of reverting to one's original defense patterns interferes with the establishment of secure and satisfying adult relationships characterized by feelings of respect, compassion, and equality. It has been my experience that when these imaginary connections were understood and relinquished, men and women in the reference population manifested new energy, self-possession, and vitality and were able to reestablish affectionate and loving companionship. They learned to respect one another as individuals and to take pleasure in seeing the other person grow and flourish.

Notes

1. See George, Kaplan, & Main's (1984) *Adult Attachment Interview*. The coding scheme for the AAI focuses on predictive clues in the interview narrative such as narrative coherence in secure adults and idealization of caregiver in avoidant/dismissing adults. Hazan and Shaver (1987) found that the three attachment patterns seen during infancy would likely emerge as three primary interpersonal styles during adolescence and adulthood.

2. "Discoveries during the longitudinal study": See Chapter 1 this volume: "Many people are resistant to love and intimacy" (p10).

3. Marriage and divorce rates: Since the 1980s, the divorce rate has declined to a certain extent. Nevertheless, "current estimates of divorce indicate that about half of first marriages end in divorce" (Copen et al., 2012, p. 1).

4. Hazan and Shaver (1987) proposed that "Attachment style (in an adult romantic relationship) is related in theoretically meaningful ways to mental models of self and social relationships and to relationships experiences with parents" (Abstract, p. 511). The tendency to recreate an insecure attachment in one's style of relating with one's partner is mediated by these models. Feeney (2016) asserted, "In terms of functions, working models shape our cognitive, emotional, and behavioral responses to others…" (Loc. 16755).

In empirical studies, Mikulincer and Shaver (2016) explored associations between individual differences in attachment-system functioning and people's perceptions of others and of themselves oneself, both positive and negative. Bartholomew (1990) re-conceptualized adult attachment styles in terms of "positive and negative working models, (destructive inner voices) of self and relationship partners" (p. 147).

5. "Reassurance that is difficult to resist": In *The Transformation of Intimacy* (2013) philosopher Anthony Giddens provides an in-depth analysis of "codependent" and "fixated" couple relationships. His notion of a "fixated" relationship has several elements in common with manifestations of the fantasy bond in an intimate relationship.

6. When relationship partners are involved in complementary parent/child roles, they often elicit, in each other, the exact voice attacks that they are experiencing internally through projective identification. There is an extensive literature regarding the dynamics operating in polarized couple relationships and how the process of projective identification maintains the dysfunctional couple "dance." For example, see Middelberg (2001).

7. In their work, Shaver and Clark (1994) described two types of insecure attachment patterns and the associated internal working models that appear to fit closely the case of Jerry [avoidant] and Maria [preoccupied]:

    The avoidant type seems to cope with attachment needs and a variety of threats and stresses by using emotion-avoidant strategies, denial of vulnerability, and repression. . . . The anxious-ambivalent, or preoccupied, type is . . . perpetually vigilant, somewhat histrionic and anxiety-amplifying rather than anxiety-denying (p. 123).

8. Willi (1982) suggests that "couples in collusion" are resistant to changing their nonproductive behaviors because changing roles is tantamount to breaking up the mutual defensive pact, which arouses suppressed fears.

9. "Honest style of communication . . . ": See related subscale on "The Development of the Functional Analytic Psychotherapy Intimacy Scale" by Leonard et al. (2014).

Sources: *Fear of Intimacy* (1999). Inclusive pages: pp. 3-31; pp.53-69; pp. 163-180.

Note on Sources: Reproduced with permission © 1999American Psychological Association from *Fear of Intimacy* by Robert W. Firestone and Joyce Catlett.

Chapter 10

SEXUALITY

The sacred meaning of sexuality is not located in sexuality itself, but rather in human mutuality. Sexuality is a mode in which mutuality is expressed.

~ John Buehrens

Sex is one of the strongest motivating forces in life. A fulfilling sex life is central to one's sense of well-being and a potential source of pleasure, happiness, and fulfillment. The enjoyment of eroticism and passion, and the giving and receiving of affection are fundamental aspects of life. The special combination of loving sexual contact and genuine friendship that can be achieved in a close relationship is conducive to good mental and physical health and is a highly-regarded goal for most people.

On the other hand, sexual relationships also have the potential for causing considerable distress and unhappiness. Indeed, a good deal of human misery centers around sexually and the difficulties that most people encounter in attempting to achieve and sustain satisfying erotic relationships. Disturbances in sexual relating have serious consequences, affecting every aspect of a person's life, including activities and pursuits far removed from that domain (Laumann, Gagnon, Michael, & Michaels 1994; Laumann, Park & Rosen 1999)

NATURAL OR HEALTHY SEXUALITY

I have defined healthy sexuality as a natural extension of affection, tenderness and companionship between two people. When both partners are spontaneous, fully present and in close emotional contact with each other, their lovemaking contributes significantly to their emotional welfare and overall satisfaction in life.

In my work, I focus on the psychological factors that tend to give sexuality its depth and meaning. From this perspective, healthy physical intimacy involves two individuals who have mature attitudes toward sex and do not view it as an activity isolated from other aspects of their relationship. They see sex as an opportunity to offer pleasure to each other and to experience it for themselves. Both partners have an active desire for sex, a positive body image, and congenial attitudes about themselves and their partner that are relatively free of distortion (Note 2).

Healthy sexuality also implies incorporating eroticism into one's daily life rather than consigning it solely to the sex act itself. Sexual desire adds zest to people's lives, whereas diminished or inhibited desire can detract from their enthusiasm for living and make life seem bland and uninteresting. Indications of one's desire and lively interest in sex are evident in one's facial expression, smile, friendly manner, sense of humor, playfulness, spontaneity, and enthusiasm.

"Natural" or "healthy" sexuality includes an acceptance of one's animal nature and a positive attitude towards one's body, nudity, and sexual urges. It implies seeing sex as a simple and enjoyable act and giving it a high priority in our lives. Sexual feelings, like all feelings, arise involuntarily and are experienced as sensations in the body. In this regard, I believe that people who are close to these feelings are better able to respond positively to loving and being loved in an intimate relationship than those who have less access to their feelings.

Along with the dimensions described above, healthy sexuality affects the basic identity of each individual. The ways that people express their sexual nature play a significant role in all of their relationships, including those between women and men, women and women, and men and men. As Celia Harding (2001) cogently noted: "Whenever two people find themselves together they have to negotiate the hetero-erotic or the homo-erotic potential of their relationship in some way" (p. 1).

This chapter refers to all aspects of interpersonal relationships and sexual encounters between adult partners, and makes no distinction between same-sex and opposite-sex preferences. By assigning men and women to discrete categories in terms of their sexual functioning or preferences, an important truth is being overlooked: like other aspects of human functioning, an individual's sexual functioning—including the dimensions of masculinity, femininity, and androgyny, gender identity, and sexual orientation—ranges along a continuum. Both psychological and biological/genetic factors enter into determining where a person is on this continuum at any given time.

Whereas some people's sexual preferences are determined primarily by genetic factors, others are affected by specific family dynamics and/or sexual child abuse. There is extensive evidence for both genetic/biological predispositions and for environmental factors. In addition, recent research suggests epigenetic influences, which involve interactions between genetic and pre-and post-natal conditions, on both gender identity and sexual orientation (Note 3). In the following pages, I explore various psychological and social factors that influence a wide range of physically intimate experiences and associations.

BARRIERS TO AN IDEAL SEXUAL EXPERIENCE

What are the parameters of a sexual encounter that contribute to its being satisfying both physically and emotionally? Based on extensive interviews and focus groups, the general consensus seemed to indicate that in order to be the most fulfilling, the sexual experience would include personal intimacy. Both partners would be spontaneous in their responses, and neither would try to control any aspect of the sex act. Because both people would take responsibility for their own desires and needs and indicate their wants, there would be a feeling of equality inherent in their interaction. Afterwards, partners would tend to experience a mixture of happiness, sadness, relaxation, and fulfillment, and might well express their mutual appreciation, both verbally and nonverbally, for the gratification they shared.

In listening to individuals talk about their sexual experiences, my associates and I learned a great deal about what interrupts the smooth flow of feelings and sensations during lovemaking. Men and women described the kinds of voice attacks that intruded into their thinking at critical moments, distracting them from the full enjoyment of the experience. In many cases, these critical inner voices were directed toward their performance and increased any anxieties they might have had regarding having an orgasm and/or satisfying their partner. These will be discussed in more detail later in this chapter.

As noted in the previous chapter, in relationships where the partners have formed a fantasy bond, their physical intimacy can gradually devolve into a routine, habitual pattern of lovemaking that is used to cut off feeling, which progressively diminishes the closeness in the relationship. This type of impersonal or mechanical sexuality is an obstacle to gratifying experiences and healthy sexual relating, and has a negative prognosis for the overall relationship.

MY VIEWS ON THE ETIOLOGY OF SEXUAL DYSFUNCTIONS

In general, the way people relate in their intimate relationships reveals a great deal about where they are in their development psychologically. Their attitudes toward sex, as well as their mode of sexual relating, indicate the extent to which they are defending themselves against becoming fully autonomous adults (Note 4).

The major threat to physically and emotionally fulfilling sexual relations can be traced to the developmental history of each partner and to experiences that necessitated the formation of psychological defenses. As mentioned in previous chapters, all people exist in conflict between tendencies to pursue real gratification in their closest relationships and tendencies to depend on internal sources of gratification, including fantasy, excessive use of substances and inward, routinized behavior patterns. It has been my experience that healthy, mature sexual relating, in combination with feelings of friendship in a close relationship, tends to arouse anxiety because it represents an intrusion into people's defensive posture, their illusions of self-sufficiency and their pseudo-independence.

The Oral Basis of Sexuality

The drive to be physically close to the mother is one of the earliest determinants of gender identification for both male and female offspring. However, if the child's natural attraction to the mother or primary caregiver is frustrated, healthy sexual functioning may be compromised in any number of ways (Fonagy, 2008) (Note 5).

Sexual functioning can be conceptualized as ranging from the oral phase to mature genital sexuality. To understand where clients are on this continuum, it is valuable to examine both their sexual fantasies and activities because these manifestations symbolically express basic attitudes toward the giving and receiving of love.

Attitudes regarding love-making are closely related to feelings associated with early nurturing experiences and other reciprocal interactions with the mother or primary parenting figure that take place during the pre-verbal stage of development (D. Stern, 1985). Studies of early psychosexual development have also emphasized the pre-Oedipal stage as being a critical period for establishing one"s sexual identity as well as one's basic feelings of trust in attachment figures (Schoenenwolf, 1989).

When early experiences with the mother or primary caregiver have been characterized by anxiety and deprivation, physical touch and bodily contact with others may come to be perceived as threatening. Sexual dysfunctions such as premature ejaculation, retarded ejaculation, or erectile difficulties in the male and hypoactive sexual desire disorders and arousal and orgasmic problems in the female may, at times, reflect a movement away from love-making as a close, emotional exchange between two people and a movement toward relying on it more as a means of self-gratification.

Parental Attitudes Toward Sex and the Human Body

Parents tend to pass on to their children, both directly and indirectly, the same values and views of sexuality that were passed on to them. This has a negative impact when these views are restrictive, narrow or distorted, i.e. that sex is bad or dirty, masturbation is perverted, and open discussion of it is taboo. In addition, studies have shown that severe, harsh, or intrusive toilet training is correlated with later emotional and sexual disturbances (Fisher & Fisher, 1986). Negative views held by parents in relation to nudity and the human body, contribute to children developing feelings of shame and guilt about their bodies and their sexual feelings. These feelings are retained throughout life, causing problems in intimate relationships.

Although attitudes toward masturbation have changed over the past several decades, some parents still react severely, even punitively, when they discover their child masturbating. The guilt engendered by these overreactions can have serious consequences. Many parents still have strong negative responses to sex play among children rather than recognizing that such play is a natural expression of a child's curiosity. Some families go to the opposite extreme and exploit or overemphasize sex. This focus can be as damaging as the restrictions placed on sexuality in families that are more rigid and repressive.

Societal Attitudes Toward Sex

Distorted attitudes toward sexuality acquired by individuals in their formative years are pooled and combine to form cultural attitudes and social mores. Once established, cultural prerogatives based on these defensive attitudes then reflect back on each member of society in the form of negative social pressure. Social conventions reinforce a collective conscience and form the foundation of social relationships. Cultural imperatives permeate every aspect of daily living and, more often than not, can be inhibiting and repressive.

In society, unnecessarily restrictive attitudes inhibit normal sexual expression, predisposing an increase in aggression, sexual abnormality or perversion, sexual molestation, rape, and other crimes (Prescott, 1996; Zillman, 1998). Paradoxically, in these instances, the overemphasis on sexual morality has immoral consequences. People are not basically evil, harmful, or animalistic in their desire for sexual expression. The negative loading on sexuality stems from ignorance, irrational fear, and prejudices that force men and women to turn on themselves and dehumanize the erotic component of their being.

Although there have been changes in the roles of men and women in our society, there are still residuals of stereotypic views that portray men as masterful, powerful, paternalistic, and uncommunicative, and women as emotionally responsive and communicative, yet childlike, helpless, and incompetent (Brescoll & Ulhmann, 2008; M. Walsh, 1997). Social pressure exerted by these stereotypes and hostile views of both women and men are as damaging to couple relationships as is racial prejudice to the relations of people of various ethnic backgrounds.

Gender stereotyping confuses people's thinking about the differences between men and women by placing them in artificial categories. For example, Prentice and Carranza (2002) stated unequivocally that "Gender stereotypes are highly prescriptive. The qualities they ascribe to women and men tend also to be ones that are required of women and men" (p. 269). Sexist or stereotyped attitudes come into play in many different ways to cut off feelings of sexual attraction and emotional closeness. For example, women may think: All men want is sex. They don't want a commitment. They don't want to be emotionally close. They can't be trusted. Or men may think: Women are unreliable. They are so irrational and overemotional. They can't be trusted. Children assimilate stereotypic views of men and women from their parents, which they then retain throughout their adult lives. These hostile and sexist attitudes cause dissension in intimate relationships and complicate couple interaction.

Competition and Oedipal Issues

Most parents find it difficult to admit feelings of anger, jealousy or rivalry in relation to their children and try to suppress these "unacceptable" emotions. For example, immature and narcissistic parents can be jealous of the attention paid to their child by their partner. Children sense this covert aggression and it has a detrimental effect on them. Later, when they are involved in competitive situations as adults, these individuals may experience irrational fears and self-attacks. Consequently, many people pull back from competing, especially in sexually rivalrous situations.

In some cases, sexual problems can be caused by a fear of competing due to covert or overt sexual rivalry experienced within the family (R. Firestone, 1994a). Children of both genders often feel threatened by retribution from their parent of the same sex. As adults, they tend to retreat from expressions of mature sexuality and hold back their natural responses of affection and love. In many cases, they project the fears of retaliation for competing that they originally experienced in relation to a parent onto their present-day rivals. Many men and women retreat from competitive situations because they anticipate that either winning or losing will arouse self-destructive thoughts and angry self-attacks.

The Development of Opposing Views of Sexuality

As a result of the socialization process within the family, most people hold two diametrically opposed views of sexuality: a natural or "clean" orientation toward sex and a distorted or "dirty" view. From a healthy "clean" point of view, a sexual experience is perceived as a natural extension of affectionate feelings, rather than as an activity separate from other aspects of a relationship. In contrast, from a distorted or "dirty" point of view, sex is seen as an activity that should be kept hidden and secretive; the human body is seen as shameful and those parts having to do with sexual functions in particular are given a dirty connotation. This view of sex takes it out of the realm of a natural human function and relegates it to a separate and distinct area of life. As such, it is seen as a subject unfit for social conversation or discussion, especially with children. Instead, it often manifests itself in hushed conversations or dirty jokes.

On an intellectual level, most people would agree that sexual functions are a simple and natural part of human nature. However, on an emotional level, many men and women still retain negative attitudes toward their sexuality. Nearly every individual in our society has been taught to feel some degree of shame regarding his/her body and sexuality, which has, in turn, generated a variety of sexual dysfunctions and fears related to performance (Calderone & Johnson, 1989; Giddens, 2013).

THE CONTINUUM OF SEXUAL RELATING

As noted, sexual relationships can be conceptualized as ranging along a continuum between two modes of sexual expression: (1) an outward form of genuine contact that is a natural extension of affection, tenderness, and companionship between two people and (2) an inward, masturbatory style of sexual relating in which sex is used primarily as a narcotic (Note 6).

Outward, Personal Modes of Sexual Relating

Characteristics of an outward, personal mode of sexual relating would include close emotional contact with one's partner, a sense of mutual give and take, and feelings of fulfillment and well-being following the experience. There would be a notable absence of inhibition or voices at any point during the process, beginning with the initial expression of physical affection, through foreplay and intercourse, and afterwards. Schnarch (1991) has described this mode of relating in terms of an individual's capacity for intimacy and his/her ability to attach "profound emotional meaning to the sexual experience" (p. 19).

Men and women who are motivated to develop beyond their defenses against intimacy, especially in their communications, are generally not secretive or self-protective in relation to their sexuality, nor are they embarrassed or ashamed to disclose their fears or doubts about personal matters to their partner. Both partners are empathic and capable of communicating with compassion and respect for the other person's wants, attitudes, and values. They are able to candidly discuss their differences as well as their commonalities. As a result, their communications, both during lovemaking and in other parts of their life together, have the positive effect of making each person feel acknowledged and unique.

The special combination of loving, physical contact and genuine friendship that can be achieved in an intimate relationship is difficult to find and even more difficult to develop and sustain over the long term. As mentioned, even though people feel gratified when a sexual experience is emotionally satisfying, they have a good deal of resistance to that combination. This resistance arises in part because genuinely loving sexuality represents a significant intrusion into people's psychological defenses. It can serve to remind people that they are truly alive, that they really do exist. Giving value to their experience tends to make them acutely aware of the fragility of life and the ultimate separation, through death, from loved ones and from the self.

Inward, Impersonal Modes of Sexual Relating

During lovemaking, whenever there is a switch from close, emotional contact to a more self-gratifying style of relating, the transformation is hurtful to the well-being of the individuals involved. Many people report feelings of emptiness, a sense of dissatisfaction, and irritability after a sexual experience in which an inward or a less personal mode of relating predominates.

This type of sexual relating represents a movement away from real intimacy and emotional exchanges between two people and toward a reliance on sex as a mechanism for self-gratification that places a limitation on mature genital sexuality. For this reason, this style of sexual relating can be symptomatic of a fantasy bond. By maintaining a pseudo-independent posture in relation to their sexuality, individuals are denying their need for another person or for anything outside the self-parenting system.

It is important to mention that satisfying, sexual relationships are not restricted to those in which the partners are deeply involved or committed. A spontaneous sexual encounter between two people who are more casually involved can also be satisfying, both physically and emotionally. The crucial differences between the two modes of intimate relating described here is not the stability, longevity, or depth of the relationship. Instead, the distinguishing factors are related to an awareness of one's partner as a separate person, as opposed to an unfeeling or impersonal use of the other as an instrument for one's own gratification. When sex is used for control, power plays, manipulation, security, or self-soothing—that is, for purposes other than its natural functions of shared pleasure and/or procreation—there is deterioration in the quality of relating between the partners in general and in the erotic aspects of the relationship.

Self-gratifying modes of sexual relating are characterized by a number of specific behavior patterns and associated feeling states: (1) elements of control and sexual withholding in one or both partners; (2) increased reliance on fantasy with corresponding emotional distancing; (3) guilt reactions associated with reacting impersonally; and (4) the emergence of negative self-attitudes and critical or hostile attitudes toward one's partner.

Sexual Withholding and Control: The basic characteristics of a self-protective, addictive style of sexuality center on the issues of withholding and control. Sexual withholding refers to inhibiting one's natural sexual desire and its expressions: physical affection, touching, physical attractiveness, and all other aspects of one's sexuality. Habitual patterns of self-denial or self-limiting experiences have a progressively deadening effect on the feelings of excitement and attraction usually experienced at the beginning of a relationship. Although this withholding occurs primarily in the privacy of the bedroom, its destructive effects are not confined there. They are widespread and impact every aspect of family life.

Adults who are sexually withholding experience spontaneous sexual interactions and physical intimacy as threatening to their defended state. Consequently, they try to regulate, control, or direct various aspects of the sex act, i.e., dictate the frequency of love-making, the time, the place, the conditions, movements, positions, and manner of expressing affection. Passive or covert forms of control, such as seductive behavior followed by rejection, appear to be more common than overt, aggressive maneuvers.

Patterns of sexual withholding are regulated or strongly influenced by the voice. Over time, the inhibition of one's responses can become habitual and automatic, and the destructive attitudes may be deeply repressed. The unconscious inhibition of affection and sexual responsiveness has an impact on many marriages and close relationships, as indicated by the increase in numbers of sex-deprived marriages. B. McCarthy (1997) has defined a nonsexual marriage as one in which partners have sex less than ten times a year. According to this definition, "approximately 20% of married couples and 40% of non-married couples who have been involved more than 2 years have a nonsexual relationship. This is a major mental health problem that poses a threat to marital satisfaction and viability" (p. 231).

Fantasy, Emotional Distance, and Guilt Reactions: Many men and women put emotional distance between themselves and their partner by fantasizing during lovemaking. The compulsive use of fantasy to enhance excitement indicates a denial of the need for the other person. When these fantasies are kept secret, the guilt feelings associated with fantasizing during a sexual experience are intensified. This is particularly true when they contain incestuous, sadistic, masochistic, or other components, which are unacceptable or ego-dystonic to the person who is fantasizing.

As mentioned earlier, individuals who have been damaged in the basic feelings of trust during the oral or Oedipal phase of development may revert to more impersonal, masturbatory modes of relating, use fantasy to enhance their excitement, and lose emotional contact with their partner. When men and women defend themselves against painful feelings aroused by a close personal relationship, they are aware, on some level, that their retreat is hurtful to their loved one. Attempts to control one's partner, the holding back of affection and sexual responses, and other manipulations that create emotional distance also tend to precipitate strong guilt reactions in the withholding partner.

Environmental Factors Affecting Sexual Withholding and Control

Parents' Inability to Accept Loving Responses from Their Child: One environmental factor strongly related to the child's developing a posture of self-denial and withholding is the parents' inability to accept expressions of love and affection from their offspring. Surprisingly, many well-meaning parents unconsciously discourage loving responses from their children because the affection threatens long-standing defenses. When parents find it difficult to accept expressions of love from their offspring, their children learn to gradually disengage from and suppress their positive feelings. Many come to believe that there is something wrong with their loving feelings and that their affection or their physical nature is somehow unacceptable. The resultant shame they experience causes them to unconsciously resolve to hold back their warmth, tenderness, and affection in future interactions.

As the child matures, other parental behaviors also contribute to the tendency to be self-denying. For example, when parents respond with rejection to children's wants and humiliate them for expressing their wants and needs children learn to suppress wanting feelings. Parental withholding of affection instills a deep sense of shame in the child, which later in life is transformed into feelings of embarrassment, self-consciousness, and a sense of degradation about having sexual wants and desires. In addition, mothers and fathers who are self-denying and hold back affection from each other serve as poor role models for their daughters and sons. Children observe the withholding behaviors acted out between their parents and later imitate these same behaviors in their adult relationships.

The Relationship Between Sexual Child Abuse and Sexual Withholding: When men and women have suffered from overt sexual abuse or over-sexualized interest (emotional incest) during their formative years, they are predisposed to developing sexual problems. For those who were sexually abused, when they experience intimacy that combines emotional closeness and sexual passion, fragmented memories or emotional flashbacks of earlier sexual abuse can often break through to consciousness during the sexual encounter or afterward (Courtois, 1999; 2000; Herman, 1992; Roth, Newman, Pelcovitz, van der Kolk, & Mandel, 1997). In many cases, they avoid the emergence of these images and emotions by either withholding their responses or trying to control aspects of the sex act. In most cases, they have little or no conscious awareness of their fear or anxiety prior to instituting these defensive behaviors (Sawrer & Durlak, 1996).

VOICES THAT AFFECT SEXUAL RELATING

Nowhere are destructive thoughts or voices closer to the surface and more directly connected with behavior than in the area of sexuality. The intrusion of negative cognitions and attitudes into a sexual relationship can have a debilitating effect on each partner's ability to achieve satisfaction in this most intimate aspect of the relationship. These self-attacks affect people's sexual identity, their ability to both give and receive gratification and pleasure, and create tension in the sexual situation. Therefore, becoming aware of one's voices, identifying their content, recognizing their irrationality, and understanding their sources, are valuable in helping partners achieve more satisfying physical intimacy in their relationship.

Many men and women have negative attitudes toward nudity and critical feelings about their bodies that cause them embarrassment in sexual situations. Interestingly, people's self-depreciating thoughts in relation to specific parts of their bodies more often than not are sensed on a subliminal level by their partners, who become less responsive and even tend to avoid touching those areas (Note 7).

Feelings of affection and attraction that lead to a couple's mutual desire to express their feelings sexually are easily dispelled by negative thoughts about sexual performance. Often, when the transition has been made from an affectionate embrace to a sexual caress, people's voices gain ascendancy and can significantly diminish sexual desire as well as positive personal feelings. Every aspect of lovemaking is subject to attack by the voice process— for example, men's and women's level of excitement, their movements or their ability to please their partner (R. Firestone, 1990d).

Prior to an intimate encounter, the voice may take the form of self-protective warnings against becoming involved sexually and emotionally with another person, which can effectively destroy one's erotic interest, excitement, and desire. For example, on the basis of extensive clinical and empirical research with 2,109 patients and couples "with . . . deficient sexual desire," H. Kaplan (1995) asserted, "The psychogenic form of this syndrome is caused by their active, albeit unconscious selectively negative cognitions and perceptual processes by means of which they literally 'turn themselves off'" (p. 4). Kaplan observed that, "The negative feelings of desire disorder patients typically surface *before* they enter the bedroom, thereby destroying any possibility of a normal build-up of their sexual desires" (p. 118).

As a response to the various inhibiting aspects of the voice process during sex, people often shift their focus to concerns about performance and concentrate on the technical aspects in an effort to circumvent these inhibitions and complete the act of intercourse. However, if a sexual experience has been particularly gratifying and emotionally meaningful, negative self-protective voices may also arise. These thoughts are often degrading to one's partner or to oneself. As a result, some people may appear to change character immediately after being sexual, for example, becoming cool and aloof or argumentative.

In responding to the negative prescriptions of their voices, men and women may inhibit their spontaneous, natural responses prior to, during, and/or following a sexual experience. Even the mildest voice attack can interfere with an individual's ability to take pleasure in making love. Internalized voices also reinforce feelings of shame and guilt that, in turn, effectively tone down or dampen desire and arousal.

For example: *You've had such a hard day.* Or, *He (She) is so awkward! Why would you want to make love to him (her)?* Or, *What's the big deal about sex? There are other, more important things in life.*

During sex a person might think: *(He) She is grossed out by you!* Or, *He (she) is not attracted to you. You're not feeling enough.*

After sex, one might think: *You were too tense! He (she) didn't enjoy it.* Or, *Once again you failed to satisfy her (him).*

After being married for a while, a person might experience voice attacks such as: *The honeymoon is over. He won't like you. You should give up.* Or, *It's just the same all of the time. Just get it over with!*

After having a baby: *All he wants to do is have sex. Can't he understand you've been up all night with the baby?* Or, *All she cares about is the baby. She never wants to make love with you anymore.*

When both partners are focused on their careers and/or children: *All he thinks about is work. Since her promotion, she never wants to make love.* Or, *All she thinks about is the kids. She's never as interested in sex as you are.*

As a person ages: *You won't be able to get an erection.* Or, *You'll just be dry and turn him off. Besides, people your age don't need sex. Sex isn't fun for you anymore.*

Men and women can utilize Voice Therapy techniques (as discussed in Chapters 12 and 13) to interrupt their negative thoughts and stop them from influencing their sexual relating. By taking the time to analyze their negative thoughts and express their anxieties to one another or a close friend, they are better able to sustain feeling while making love and maintain closeness with their partner rather than becoming cut off. If the situation is more serious, a person can develop insight into the voice attacks in Voice Therapy sessions and gain insight into deep feelings from the past that may be aroused during sex.

JEALOUSY AND SEXUAL RIVALRY IN COUPLE RELATIONSHIPS

In all of us there still lives the child's unregarding possessiveness—the longing for an absolute, certain, and exclusive love.

~ C. Downing (1977, p. 74)

Jealousy, sexual rivalry, and competitiveness arise naturally in interpersonal relationships. In fact, one of the primary reasons people seek therapy is because of the extreme distress they experience upon discovering that their mate is sexually involved with another person (Glass, 2003). The feelings aroused by this crisis are often even more distressful and emotionally painful than those experienced by people facing rejection or loss when a third party is not involved.

Initially, pledges of fidelity may be based on real desire or mutual agreement; however, these vows can become part of a destructive bond. This is most likely to occur when the vows are based on the false premise that people have proprietary rights over each other, particularly over each other's bodies and sexuality. Within a relationship, monogamy imposed by external social mores routinely assumed or expected by partners is very different from sexual fidelity based on freedom of choice, genuine personal commitment, and the desire to share one's life with another person.

In relationships characterized by a fantasy bond, each partner has an exaggerated need for reassurance that he/she is always the first and only choice of the other. In general, one partner's sexual involvement with a third party disrupts the illusion of fusion operating within the couple and shatters the false sense of security both partners derive from their merged identity. I suggest that the feelings of anxiety, anger, and grief experienced by the betrayed party are more often due to the destruction of the fantasy bond with the partner than to the threat of the relationship actually ending or the loss of the partner to a rival.

The threat of losing one's mate or lover to another often precipitates self-destructive thoughts and profound feelings of shame and humiliation that, under extreme conditions, can lead to thoughts of self-harm or suicide. On occasion, sexual infidelity can trigger vicious thoughts against one's mate and/or rival including a strong desire for revenge that may lead to violent acting-out behavior or even homicide (Felson, 2002).

The Subjective Experience of Jealousy

When men and women describe their subjective experience of sexual jealousy, they usually indicate feelings of fear, anger or depression. They tend to imagine or compare themselves unfavorably with their rivals to their own detriment, especially when their rivals are unknown. According to Pines and Aronson (1983), intense jealousy is an extremely painful emotional state that is associated with physical sensations, such as "feeling hot, nervous, and shaky; and experiencing fast heartbeat, and emptiness in the stomach" (p. 131). Pines (1998) noted that participants in her study on jealousy reported that, "the emotional reactions felt most strongly were anxiety, fear of loss, pain, anger, vulnerability, and hopelessness" (p. 131).

Feelings of jealousy are natural, yet behaviors based on jealous feelings can often be damaging. They may be morally offensive or against one's best interest. They can be misdirected against one's object of affection or acted out in a manner that leads to being rejected. Abnormal feelings of jealousy usually indicate deep-seated feelings of insecurity and inferiority. On the other hand, it is logical to have competitive thoughts and do your best to win in the competition.

When jealousy is intense, people tend to have exaggerated, dramatic emotional responses, which they themselves often perceive as abnormal. They may feel overwhelmed by torturous images of their mate and their rival in a sexual situation or they may obsessively ruminate about the whereabouts of their mate, suffer severe constriction of thought and emotion, avoid situations where their jealousy might be intensified, lose interest in other people and activities, become hyper-vigilant, or suffer from insomnia, all of which are symptoms of PTSD as described in DSM-V (American Psychiatric Association, 2013).

When men and women unconsciously inhibit their sexual desires or hold back their physical responses, they come to feel that they are at a disadvantage as competitors. Their sense of being unable to compete makes them inclined toward morbid, jealous brooding over imagined losses instead of actively relating to their partner, i.e. staying competitive. In pulling back in this way, people imagine others as being more attractive, powerful, and better than they are. Often, jealousy disguises the fact that it is the person's own withholding that is preventing him/her from succeeding in a romantic relationship, not the presence of a rival or competitor.

Deception and Jealousy

Deception may be the most damaging aspect of infidelity. Deception and lies shatter the reality of others, eroding their belief in the veracity of their perceptions and subjective experience (Bader & Pearson, 2000). The betrayal of trust brought about by a partner's secret involvement with another person leads to a shocking and painful realization on the part of the deceived party that the person he/she has been involved with has had a secret life and that there is an aspect of his/her partner that he/she had no knowledge of.

Many men and women who originally commit to a monogamous relationship later violate the agreement. In these cases, the violation of trust can have a more damaging effect on the relationship than the sexual infidelity itself (Glass & Wright, 1988; 1997). In her book, *Not "Just Friends,"* Glass (2003) emphasized the point that lies, dishonesty, and deception in personal relationships invariably destroy the trust between partners. She asserted that:

> Intimate relationships are contingent on honesty and openness. They are built and maintained through our faith that we can believe what we are being told. However painful it is for a betrayed spouse to discover a trail of sexual encounters or emotional attachments, the lying and deception are the most appalling violations (p. 60).

In light of the damage to a person's feelings and sense of reality caused by lies and deception, honesty in personal relationships becomes a moral imperative. Therefore, it is essential for partners who claim to love and respect one another to agree to maintain an open and honest dialogue about their feelings and behaviors in relation to sexual fidelity.

In general, the best policy for individuals in a couple relationship is to support their partner's freedom, including sexual freedom. Imposing unnecessary rules and restrictions in a marriage violates the policy of supporting the autonomy and independence of one's partner and, in that sense, tends to have a damaging effect on the relationship. This policy may seem scary, dangerous and difficult to follow because most people are insecure and possessive in this area. If this policy is too difficult, one can at least respect the personal freedom of his/her partner in every other aspect of his/her life (Note 8).

CONCLUSION

When sexual love persists and becomes a vital part of a fulfilling long-term relationship, erotic feelings and responses represent an extension of the affection felt by the partners. In contrast, defensive patterns of sexual expression manifested by many adults, including withholding, depersonalized relating, and excessive reliance on fantasies, are detrimental to healthy relating. In addition, stereotypic views about the differences between men and women lead to distortions and misinformation about men's and women's sexual nature, and perpetuate myths that support neurotic dependency and/or alienation between men and women.

People have both a healthy, "clean" orientation to sex as well as an acquired unhealthy, "dirty," or distorted view that can be verbalized in the form of the voice.

A large majority of problems in sexual relationships would never arise if there were not other, more basic, disturbances in the early parent-child attachment patterns. Children who grow up in an emotional climate where they feel secure, loved and accepted, especially in relation to their physical nature and bodily functions, would not be as likely to develop sexual dysfunctions as adults and would feel more confident in their sexual identity (Note 9).

Lastly, in recognizing and effectively challenging destructive voices, people can begin to differentiate themselves from negative attitudes toward sex learned in their families-of-origin. This understanding helps them achieve a natural, more positive point of view regarding their sexuality, and develop more fulfilling relationships.

Notes

1. Laura Kipnis (2009) cited "a 1999 report in the *Journal of the American Medical Association* . . . that more than 43 percent of women and 31 percent of men regularly have no interest in sex, can't have orgasms, or have some other sexu-

al impediment" (Loc. 1296). In their report of the "Prevalence of Sexual Dysfunctions," Simons and Carey (2001) noted, "sexual dysfunctions are believed to be among the more prevalent psychological disorders in the general population" (p. 177). DeRogatis and Burnett (2008) found that, "Sexual dysfunctions are highly prevalent in our society worldwide" [Abstract].

2. The University of Illinois website (University of Illinois Board of Trustees, 2004) used sex therapist Wendy Maltz's definition of healthy sexuality: "Healthy sexuality is positive, enriching, and about how we communicate and accept and give love. It means having the ability to enjoy and control our sexual and reproductive behavior without guilt, fear or shame. Sexual expression is a form of communication through which we give and receive pleasure and emotion. . . . Healthy sex requires that these conditions be met: Consent, Equality, Respect, Trust, and Safety" (p. 1).

3. For research in genetic and epigenetic antecedents of same-sex preference, see Rice, Friberg and Gavrilets (2012). For studies in factors involving family dynamics and sexual child abuse, see Friedman et al. (2011). Also see Ritter and Terndrup (2002).

4. According to Wallerstein and Blakeslee (1995), the first task of intimate partners is separating emotionally from the family of origin. In explaining what this entails, they wrote: "Psychological separation means gradually detaching from your family's emotional ties. . . . This emotional shift from being a son or daughter to being a wife or husband is accomplished by *internally* reworking your attachments to and conflicts with your parents" (p. 53) (italics added).

5. See Fonagy (2008) where Fonagy proposed a new model of human sexual experience "that once again places sexuality at the center of psychoanalytic clinical inquiry. Because emotion regulation arises out of the mirroring of affect by a primary caregiver, (usually the mother) and sexual feelings are unique in that they are systematically ignored and left un-mirrored by caregivers, sexual feeling remain fundamentally dysregulated in all of us. Adult sexual experience serves as a way of coming to organize the psychosexual" [Abstract].

6. Otto Kernberg (1980) has also conceptualized a continuum of sexual love largely determined by "the capacity—or rather, the incapacity—to fall and remain in love" (p. 278). According to Kernberg (1980; 1995), Fromm (1956a), and others, "immature" sexuality and love relations also reflect an individual's failure to extend "self-love" (primary narcissism) to the love object. In a somewhat similar vein, one of my criteria for "mature" sexuality and intimate relating would imply a transformation from self-gratifying forms of sexuality into a reliance on others for satisfaction in interpersonal relations.

7. In these cases, the process of defensive projective identification may be operating. Scharff and Scharff (1991) have applied the concept of projective identification to treating couples' problems in sexual relating. Scharff and Scharff (1991) and Zinner (1976) have suggested that through the process of projec-

tive identification, *feelings* of sexual inadequacy in one partner can be defensively and unconsciously transferred to the other.

8. See philosopher Anthony Giddens' (2013) essay on *confluent love*, which "presumes equality in emotional give and take. . . . Love here only develops to the degree to which intimacy does, to the degree to which each partner is prepared to reveal concerns and needs to the other and to be vulnerable to that other" (Loc. 969). "Unlike romantic love, confluent love is not necessarily monogamous, in the sense of sexual exclusiveness. What holds the pure relationship together is the acceptance on the part of each partner, 'until further notice', that each gains sufficient benefit from the relation to make its continuance worthwhile. Sexual exclusiveness here has a role in the relationship to the degree to which the partners mutually deem it desirable or essential" (Loc. 983).

9. According to Schachner and Shaver (2004), individuals identified as securely attached "are open to sexual exploration and enjoy a variety of sexual activities, including mutual initiation of sexual activity and enjoyment of physical contact, usually in the context of a long-term relationship" (p. 180). In contrast, individuals categorized as "anxious/ambivalent" or "preoccupied" lovers (approximately 20%), "show a greater preference for the affectionate and intimate aspects of sexuality than for the genital aspects (e.g., vaginal or anal intercourse)" (p. 180). Avoidant or dismissing lovers, who make up approximately 25% of couples "are less likely than their less avoidant counterparts to fall in love...and their love style is characterized by game playing. . . . Avoidant adults express dislike for much of sexuality, especially its affectionate and intimate aspects" (p. 181). Also see Timberlake et al. (2016).

Sources: *Sex and Love in Intimate Relationships* (2006) Inclusive pages: pp. 11-27; pp.111-132; and pp.197-225.

Note on Sources: Reproduced with permission © (2006) American Psychological Association from *Sex and Love in Intimate Relationships* by Robert W. Firestone, Lisa A. Firestone, and Joyce Catlett.

Chapter 11

OPTIMAL CHILDREARING

Whenever parents feel besieged or anxious about a small child's behavior, it is time to reflect upon the ghosts from their own nursery . . . important experiences from the past that can dominate parents' behavior. These ghosts influence the biases and approaches of the parent. . . . Biases dominate our behavior much more completely if we aren't aware of them. Bringing them to consciousness gives us a choice: conform to the bias or resist it.

~ T. Berry Brazelton and Joshua D. Sparrow (2001, pp. *xxi-xxii*)

After all, behind all our actions in a given situation is the whole of our past life experience, which soon begins to influence our view of what we are doing to our child and of what he is doing to us. The same is true for our child; he, too, reacts to our intervention in terms of his past experiences, many of which we ourselves have provided or shaped.

~ Bruno Bettelheim (1971, p.14)

Traditionally, in our culture there is a tendency to idealize the couple and family, which limits or prohibits open scrutiny of family practices. In breaking through this barrier and coming to terms with parental behaviors that are detrimental to a child's well-being, the object is not to criticize or denigrate the institution of the family, but rather to explore and better understand issues of child development and find optimal ways of improving parent/child relationships. Parents who were damaged in their upbringing will inadvertently pass on this damage to their children in spite of their best intentions, unless they work through their own developmental issues. Both parents and children should be viewed with compassion (R. Firestone, 1997a; Fraiberg, Adelson, & Shapiro, 1980; Lieberman & Zeanah, 1999).

To understand the basic problem involved in raising children, we need to understand the fundamental ambivalence with which we view life, other people, and ourselves. All of us have strong desires to live and fulfill our potential on the one hand, while at the same time, we have self-destructive tendencies that compel us to limit our lives. These self-limiting propensities generally exist on an unconscious level.

Parents exhibit the same mixed feelings and attitudes toward their children that they have toward themselves. They have strong desires to nurture their children and help them fulfill their potential and, on the other hand, parents often limit their children, stifle their excitement, and cut off their emotional responses in order to protect their own defenses. People who have themselves suffered deprivation and rejection and have shut down emotionally cannot help but pass on this damage to their offspring. This form of destruction is the daily fare of most children, despite their parents' good intentions and efforts to love and nurture them. However, through a growing awareness of significant aspects of childrearing, parents can strive to avert this repetition of trauma and to cope more effectively with the core issues that may have limited and demoralized them.

In this chapter, I describe my basic philosophy of childrearing, with principles similar to those underlying effective psychotherapy: a basic respect for the individual, open-minded and non-judgmental attitudes, warm regard and desire to help, empathy and compassion, and support for the uniqueness of the individual. Many traditional childrearing books suggest specific techniques or methods for people to use to improve their parenting skills. Yet these cannot have a long-lasting or profound effect on the ways parents treat children, because any attempt to play out roles that are "proper" or "constructive," rather than being authentic, inadvertently causes more damage. Children are able to discern the real emotional state of their parents, and their sense of reality is distorted by duplicitous communications (Bateson, Jackson, Haley & Weakland, 1956; Bugental, Love, Kaswar & April, 1971; Laing & Esteron, 1970) (Note 1).

Furthermore, children tend to idealize or protect their parents at their own expense. Clients in therapy often feel guilty about exposing the truth of what happened to them in their families because they feel sensitive about hurting others and being disloyal for revealing family secrets. However, coming face-to-face with painful issues in one's development can lead to deeper self-understanding and can break the chain of damage that links the generations, despite the inclination to rationalize and defend one's family.

THE ESSENTIAL NATURE OF THE CHILD

The infant at birth is unusually sensitive and vulnerable to sensory inputs (Bertin & Striano, 2006; Tronick, Cohn & Shea, 1986). From the beginning, babies are highly reactive to their immediate surroundings. As noted in Chapter 5, the parental environment has a profound impact on them, and they respond with their whole being to painful intrusions from the outside world. The prolonged dependence of human infants on their parents for physical and psychological survival provides the first condition for the development of defenses (A. Freud, 1966) (Note 2). Guntrip (1961) has noted that, "The infant's need for 'reliable maternal support' is so absolute and failure to provide it so nearly universal that 'varying degrees of neurotic instability . . . are the rule rather than the exception'" (p. 385).

Parents feel and are very much aware of the responsibility implied by their child's utter dependence on them. At the same time, they are awed by the unique capacity for human response in their baby. From the neonate's first smile of recognition, parents sense its capability for deep feeling. Later, they become aware of the child's potential for imagination and creativity in his/her underdeveloped mind. All of these latent qualities make the child especially precious, and they inspire unusually strong and tender feeling responses from parents and other family members.

Because so many parents have difficulty tolerating these emotions, the child is not born into a neutral atmosphere. Due to their own defensive limitations, most parents unintentionally transform this extraordinary creature into an ordinary creature. They offer the gift of life and then unconsciously take it back. In attempting to socialize their children according to their own defensive, self-protective prescriptions for living, they unwittingly deprive them of significant aspects of their human heritage.

In my experience, most mothers and fathers feel love for their children, are fond of them, and wish them the best. My concern has always been with understanding why, despite their best intentions for their children, parents so often behave in ways that are not sensitive, loving, or even friendly. Why, despite their wishes to instill a sense of independence and self-reliance in their offspring, do parents demand conformity and submission? And why, despite their desire to foster spontaneity and vitality in their children, do they actually create deadness and dullness in them?

Although I focus attention on parental interactions and the psychological and emotional issues in child development, I do not minimize other powerful influences on the psyche of the child. As noted earlier, biological tendencies, inherited temperamental differences, and physiological predispositions combine with personal environmental influences to form unique and complex phenomena. There is no single cause of specific symptoms or mental aberrations. All psychological functions are multi-determined. In some cases, somatic aspects clearly outweigh environmental components in the etiology of ego weakness, maladjustment, and psychological disturbance. However, in most cases, the impact of environmental conditions on the child's development in all probability exceeds the influence of innate predispositions (Note 3).

Moreover, the view that developmental influences play a central role in the mental life of children and in their subsequent adjustment as adults, as well as being true, can be optimistic. As the founder of attachment theory John Bowlby (in filmed interview) emphasized:

> One important finding has been this: that, with few exceptions . . . sensitive, responsive mothers are capable of enabling an infant who is, by any standards, rather touchy or difficult in the early days, to become a securely attached child by twelve months. That's very heartening. So the notion that these patterns of attachment correlate with temperament does not stand up (May & Solomon, 1984) (Note 4).

Remedial action and preventive measures can be taken in relation to many of the psychological factors that cause human misery. By contrast, it is difficult, if not impossible, to alter hereditary patterns that originate in a biological substrate. Thus, it is our fundamental responsibility to give full weight to those causative agents within the family structure that are within our power to change.

WHY PARENTS OFTEN HAVE DIFFICULTY
LOVING THEIR CHILDREN

Parental love enhances the well-being and development of children. As such, love encompasses all that is nurturing and supportive of the evolution of a child's unique personality. Conversely, it would be a distortion to define as loving those responses that are in any way detrimental to the child's psychological growth, cause painful wounds to the child's psyche, or predispose a lifetime of maladaptation and pain.

Parental love includes genuine expressions of warmth—a smile or friendly look that conveys empathy and good humor—as well as physical affection; respectful, considerate treatment; tenderness; a willingness to be a real person with the child as opposed to acting the role of "mother" or "father;" and a sensitive attunement and responsiveness to the child.

Almost all parents feel that they love their children. But, in order to have a positive effect on their children, what parents feel internally must also have an external manifestation in actions that are loving. Their good intentions are not a substitute for nurturing love, which can only be provided by a psychologically healthy and independent adult. Both the intention and the capacity to love are necessary to sustain the small child in his/her growth toward maturity.

In my observation of nuclear families, I have noted countless examples of well-meaning mothers and fathers engaging in behavior that is insensitive, misattuned, or otherwise harmful to their children, while earnestly believing that they love them and have their best interests at heart. These parents are being honest, although on a defensive level, when they tell their adult children who have been emotionally hurt that they loved them and did the best they could for them. It's true: they did the best that they were capable of but, more often than not, they simply weren't able to really see their child as a separate person and meet his/her needs. Unfortunately, no matter how well intentioned they are, many people are not prepared for the task of raising children.

There are a number of reasons why it is often difficult for people to love their children:

(1) Many parents have a negative self-image that they unwittingly extend to their children. If they cannot love themselves, or have developed a nega-

tive conception of themselves and their bodies, they cannot pass on love and tenderness to their offspring. In fact, they are more likely to project their negative feelings onto others, and there is no more convenient dumping ground for our negative perceptions of ourselves than our children.

(2) Parents who are narcissistic, self-nurturing or immature experience their children as an unwanted, intimidating dependency load. They find it threatening to bear the responsibility of offering the extensive care that the baby and developing child require, and may even come to resent their offspring.

(3) Many people find it difficult or intolerable to accept love—in particular, the simple loving expressions of their children. If they were hurt in their own developmental years, they will have problems accepting love and warmth from their children. Faced with the emotional pain that it causes them, parents will unconsciously distance themselves from their children.

(4) Most parents have suffered some degree of unresolved trauma or loss in their own childhoods. This will tend to cause parents to be misattuned to their children, especially when their children approach the ages that were traumatic for them. They may react by becoming rejecting or, conversely, overcompensating. Neither reaction is appropriate to, or constructive for, the child's experience.

For example, individuals who cannot bear to be reminded of their own childhood sadness may be vindictive or punishing to their children when they cry. Others may suppress their children's pain in just the opposite way —by over-comforting and over-protecting them. In any case, the child is always more expendable than the parent's defense system. The more defended people are, the more they will act out their defenses on their child, fail to perceive the child correctly and be unable to encourage his/her healthy development.

(5) Having children reminds people that time is passing, thereby increasing their death anxiety. For parents, especially those in a self-protective, defensive retreat from feeling, this can cause tension and even resentment that is directly or indirectly hurtful to their children.

(6) As noted in Chapter 8, parents tend to use their children as immortality projects—that is, as a symbolic victory over death by perpetuating their identity into the future. This misuse has a destructive effect on their offspring. In order to serve this purpose, children must replicate their par-

ent's attitudes and choices. If they differ, their independent actions are often misinterpreted as defiant or rebellious. As each child is genetically different and has a unique personal destiny, impressing this sameness upon them is highly damaging.

(7) Parents' unfulfilled primitive hunger for love and care from their own childhoods causes them, in turn, to focus these strong desires on their children. They confuse powerful feelings of longing and possessiveness that they have toward their offspring for genuine feelings of love. They offer affection and love when they feel the need for it themselves and inadvertently take *from* their children, rather than give *to* them. In acting on their own desperation and desire to be taken care of, they tend to make parents out of their own children (Parker, 1983) (Note 5).

Children who are caressed by a hungry, needy parent will not feel seen, understood, or secure, but instead can become refractory to physical touch. The "loving" fingers of this type of immature parent are felt as possessive, sucking tentacles, which drain children rather than nurture them. This causes them to have feelings of being trapped or suffocated by close relationships in later life. As adults, they may experience affection as physical or psychological pain.

(8) Due to inadequate or problematic parenting styles, many children develop traits that are unlikeable or intolerable. They may become unruly, defiant, disobedient, obnoxious, demanding, hostile or generally unpleasant. Even though parents are a primary cause of these behaviors, they find it difficult to love, or even like, a child who exhibits these traits.

THE MYTH OF UNCONDITIONAL PARENTAL LOVE

The assumption that parents, especially mothers, have a "natural" love for their child is a fundamental part of our belief system which is at the core of family life and society (Note 6). Very often this myth has an adverse effect, in that it leads to a failure to identify and challenge negative behaviors within the family. It also intensifies parents' guilt when they do not experience these "natural" feelings. These guilt feelings further contaminate the situation for those individuals who, because of their own upbringing, may be unable to provide their children with the love and care they need.

Children do need and deserve love, and to the degree it is not available they will suffer emotional pain. As noted in Chapter 5, research in the neurosciences has shown that the way parents interact, or fail to interact, with their children forms strong neuronal connections in their children's brains, often before children are capable of formulating words to describe what they are experiencing. As they grow older, children find numerous ways of defending themselves in order to relieve or numb their pain. In the process, they close off many other aspects of themselves and, to varying levels, become emotionally deadened.

Indeed, it would be better for all concerned if the illusion of unconditional parental love were withdrawn from the childrearing scene. It serves no constructive purpose for parents to try to live up to the fantasy and then, even worse, to conceal their inadequacies from their child. An honest acceptance of their deficiencies would enable both parent and child to better cope with reality devoid of additional defensive pressure. With a lessening of this pressure and the subsequent relaxation for both parent and child, they may even regain or be able to develop genuine loving feelings and regard for one another.

PARENTAL AMBIVALENCE

My clinical findings and observations of family interactions indicate a fundamental ambivalence in parental reactions. Parents' feelings toward their children are both benevolent and malevolent (Note 7). Sometimes they are warm, affectionate and attuned to their child; at other times, they can be misattuned, cruel, or unfeeling. Children, however, are highly sensitized to painful experiences and, therefore, form their defenses at times of undue stress (Note 8).

When parental figures are inconsistent or erratic in their responses, children become hypervigilant, anticipating frightening reactions at unexpected times. These children tend to withdraw from pleasant interactions before they can be hurt. This expectation of hurt, rejection, or punishment persists into adulthood, influencing their responses in interpersonal relations. As a result, they frequently avoid closeness and intimacy because they anticipate future rejection, loss, or other negative consequences.

Because negative and hostile feelings toward children are generally considered socially unacceptable, parents often show a strong resistance to recognizing those negative emotions in themselves. However, to be effective, any childrearing approach must take into account the fundamental ambivalence of parents and its sources.

Parents can successfully repair disruptions in in their interactions with their offspring. Repair involves the parent acknowledging the disruption, taking responsibility for it, and providing a reasonable explanation for what happened which would validate the child's reality. The child is then able to make sense of his/her emotional reactions and can begin to construct a coherent narrative of the event (Note 9). When mothers and fathers admit their errors and try to make restitution, their child is also less likely to blame himself/herself, idealize the parent, or internalize an image of being the "bad child." Observing this process also helps children learn to how regulate their emotions.

THE TRANSMISSION OF PARENTAL DEFENSES

Although most parents remain largely unconscious of the fact that their defenses operate to the detriment of their child, parental defenses have a profound influence on the developing child's disposition and attitudes toward life. As explained in previous chapters, young children incorporate both the defenses of their parents and the critical or hostile attitudes that were directed toward them, consciously and unconsciously, by their parents. In the process, they incorporate an internal parental figure, which is represented by the critical inner voice. Children carry this destructive voice with them through life, restricting, limiting, and punishing themselves, and eventually pass on the same defensive adaptations to their children (Note 10).

In addition, most people feel obligated to teach their children the information necessary to "get along in the world" and to instruct their offspring in the basic ways they have learned to cope. These "survival techniques" are passed on to the child not only directly through instruction, reward, and punishment, but they are also transmitted indirectly through nonverbal cues and the process of imitation. The latter is by far the most significant means of transmission and has more extensive effects because children automatically model themselves after parental figures.

THE EFFECT OF THE FANTASY BOND WITHIN
THE FAMILY ON CHILDREN

Genuine closeness, love and intimacy, combined with independence and strength in each of the parents, are qualities that foster children's development. Often, however, this support is absent. With parents who have cut off feelings for each other but who imagine they are still close, the child is starved for affection and emotional gratification.

Children whose basic needs for warmth, affection, direction and control are not met are faced with overwhelming anxiety, fears of annihilation, and physical and emotional pain. As described in Chapter 3, they must then employ defenses to ensure psychological, and perhaps even physical, survival. They form a fantasy bond in an attempt to parent and take care of themselves. To compound this lack of emotional sustenance, the family situation tends to be complicated by the rules, regulations, and obligations that are determined by the family's role-playing. Even when two people have strong potential for genuine caring, they often lose it within the traditional family structure.

Parents in a fantasy bond inadvertently create an unpleasant atmosphere by the incessant arguments, snide remarks and dismissive attitudes they typically engage in. Even adults feel uncomfortable in the company of a bickering, warring couple. The small child, however, is tortured and torn apart by fights and arguments between his father and mother. Many children live in cringing anticipation of hostility and explosiveness that can erupt at any moment. These outbursts only temporarily dispel the paralyzing routine tension of the home. In some families, the underlying tension and hostility persist without clearly surfacing, and there is no relief, only anticipatory fear. In addition, children are forced to see their parents as fallen heroes during their parents' childish, irrational moments.

Children feel excluded not only by the obvious negative aspects of a fantasy bond, but also by its ostensibly positive aspects. They are left out of long conversations that take place between their parents behind the closed bedroom door. The secrecy of their parents' sexual relationship along with the contradictory types of interactions between them, are confusing to the innocent child.

The fantasy bond leads to the curtailment of freedom of speech within the family, because certain topics are forbidden. Any communication or conversation that threatens to disrupt the bond or interrupt the illusion of enduring love between parents and family members is not permitted. Restricting personal communication creates a toxic environment for the developing child that fosters anger and resentment. The child must not show this pain or unhappiness, because this would betray the destructiveness of the family. Perceptions and emotional responses that disrupt the illusion of closeness are suppressed. This, in turn, increases the child's tendency to become inward, secretive, and cynical.

When a fantasy bond exists between parents, it is usually extended to their children as well. Family members then share the illusion that their family is superior to others. However, to sustain this fantasy, each one must subscribe to family beliefs and points of view, and learn that it is wrong to deviate from this tradition. Therefore, free speech and honest perceptions are controlled in typical family life. In this sense, many family constellations take on the dimensions of an oppressive dictatorship that is hurtful both to its members and to outsiders.

GENERAL PHILOSOPHY OF CHILDREARING

In my work with clients and parenting groups, I have been continually concerned with the toxic aspect of interpersonal relationships that contribute to the defensive process in the child and the subsequent development of character neurosis in the adult. Recognizing how clients were hurt in their upbringing and how they, in turn, go on to damage their children has significant implications for childrearing. In identifying the trauma that children suffer, I have formulated some basic philosophical guidelines to childrearing practices that I feel could minimize the damage. These basic principles are directly analogous to the feeling and tone that I consider to be essential elements of an effective psychotherapy (Note 11).

First, a basic principle of psychotherapeutic practice is that the client is being offered a "sound listening-formulating process"—with subsequent "working through of the unique insights . . . improved adaptation, symptom resolution, and growth" (Langs, 1982, p. 26). In this process, the therapist listens with empathy and compassion, attempting to understand both the "manifest and latent" content of his client's communications. Therefore, the therapeutic process is essentially one of inquiry; the therapist suspends judgment while he intuitively searches, wonders, and questions himself concerning his client and the genesis of her disturbance. "Why is she depressed?" "What events cause her to respond inappropriately?"

In the same sense, parents who develop a sense of inquiry in relation to their child are both fascinated by and alive to the emergence of a unique personality. When things appear to be going badly, they wonder what is troubling their child rather than automatically punishing inappropriate or "bad" behavior.

Second, in most effective therapies, there is a strong emphasis on freedom of speech and emotional expression. For example, the technique of free association utilized in psychoanalysis allows the client to let her thoughts flow in a stream of consciousness unencumbered by the rules of logic. Within this framework, the client not only learns to think creatively but also gradually comes to recognize that any thought or feeling is acceptable. Thus, in psychoanalysis and other psychodynamic therapies, the therapist directly and implicitly teaches his client that feelings are not equivalent to actions: that is, that any feeling, thought, dream or fantasy is morally acceptable and valid subject matter.

The analogy to childrearing is clear; ideally, parents would permit and accept all of their child's feelings uncritically and, at the same time, teach their children to control undesirable actions. They would learn to encourage the verbal expression of hostile or destructive attitudes while rejecting nasty or abusive behavior.

Third, a good working relationship between the therapist and the client is necessary for a successful outcome (Ackerman & Hilsenroth, 2003; Angus & Kagan, 2007; Grencavage & Norcross, 1990). Effective therapy takes place in the context of a respectful, equal, therapeutic alliance between two individuals and not within a doctor-client role-playing, unequal relationship. Ideally, the good therapist does not assume a posture of omnipotence and superiority; for example, he would not utilize his technical expertise to confound his clients with "all-knowing" interpretative statements. This tendency can lead to feelings of inferiority in the client and, concomitantly, to the client's idealization of the therapist. Harry Guntrip (1969) addresses this in his remarks concerning the curative factors in the healthy therapeutic relationship:

> The psychotherapist must be primarily a human being who has faced
> and sufficiently understood himself to be worthy to be admitted into

the client's private pain and sorrow. . . . He knows, not just theoretically but in his own experience, what the client is passing through (p. 353).

The same conditions are applicable to parent-child relationships. Although the child is obviously not the equal of his/her mother or father in terms of physical size, power, knowledge, or competence, it is imperative that people not utilize these differences to exploit, overpower, or intimidate their offspring. Parental "omniscience" tends to make the child feel unnecessarily small, weak, or inferior.

A fourth principle or characteristic of good psychotherapy is the therapist's consistency and stability; the therapist refuses to be alienated and maintains a relating posture. In addition, the rule of confidentiality encourages trust and a sense of safety in the client. The therapist refrains from punishing or rejecting the client for her communications, no matter how distorted or negative they are. This implies a maturity that allows the therapist to suspend his own needs and priorities during the session so that his responses to the client's communications are consistently helpful.

In relation to childrearing, I place considerable emphasis on parental maturity and consistency. Parents need to resist regressive trends in their own personalities in order to foster security in their offspring. Obviously, in the parenting situation, this task is even more formidable than in the therapy session.

Lastly, a key dimension of psychotherapy lies in its non-intrusiveness; that is, the therapist acknowledges the basic worth of the client and his/her right to an individual existence. Many clients enter therapy with the complaint that they feel unseen or invisible as a result of having grown up with parents who failed to respond to them as persons in their own right. Others have described how their boundaries were ignored and intruded upon as children, which violated their basic rights as human beings.

The preservation of a sense of self is vital in psychotherapeutic interactions, as well as in parenting. In this regard, selective or conditional acceptance of the child is unacceptable. Part of a child's feeling of not being seen is often related to the lack of positive acknowledgment of his/her bodily functions, sexuality, or gender identification. Therefore, the therapist's implicit validation of clients' sexual identity is important. In much the same manner, child-rearing practices that lead to the child's developing a healthy attitude toward his/her physical nature, as well as a strong sexual identity, are crucial to the child's overall development (Whitaker & Malone, 1953).

PHILOSOPHY OF DISCIPLINE AND SOCIALIZATION

My philosophy regarding childrearing practices refers to attitudes that predispose action, rather than specific how-to-do-it practical techniques. It is my view that the ultimate purpose of discipline is to help the child develop into a decent, likeable adult, capable of survival in a social milieu, rather than one who is submissive to the socialization process. With this goal in mind, I would recommend that parents with a similar interest try to: (1) avoid unnecessary restrictions, rules, and standards, (2) act as positive role models, (3) reward rather than punish, (4) avoid physical punishment, (5) avoid cynical, judgmental attitudes that reinforce a child's sense of badness, and (6) attempt to control their children's acting out of hostile, manipulative behavior.

Avoidance of Unnecessary Restrictions, Rules, and Standards

It is remarkable how few rules or restrictions are really necessary to accomplish parents' goal of effectively socializing their child; however, their goal can be better realized when those rules that are necessary and useful are consistently upheld. They need to clearly state their standards and restrictions to the child. As the child matures, fathers and mothers can explain the reasoning behind placing limits and emphasize the beneficial results of leading a disciplined life.

In situations where definite rules apply, parents would not act as though the child had a choice in the matter. For example, if they predetermined their child's bedtime, they would not ask him each night if he wanted to go to bed, and then when the answer is "no," insist that he go anyway. Authority would be administered in a straightforward manner. Parents would state, "Now it's time for bed," not, "Would you like to go to bed?"

Parents as Role Models for Their Children

More powerful than specific training or disciplinary measures is the modeling effect derived from the child's living day-in and day-out with adults who themselves consistently behave in a responsible manner. For example, there is no better method for teaching a child to be considerate of other people than for his parents to be considerate of him and of each other. The psychological processes of identification and imitation eclipse parents' verbalizations and prescriptions for good behavior.

Toxic personality traits in parents not only have a profoundly destructive effect on children directly, but these negative qualities are passed on to succeeding generations through role modeling. For example, a harsh, judgmental, or disrespectful father is likely to have a strong negative impact, particularly on a son, causing him to feel worthless and unlovable. In addition, these undesirable traits will tend to become a part of the boy's emerging personality; as an adult, he would tend to become authoritarian and parental with his own child.

An individual who is congenial, non-defensive, non-intrusive, consistent and generous will have a positive impact on his child's personality. Parents who reflect on their negative traits may become motivated to further develop themselves personally. Parents can best help their offspring not by "sacrificing themselves for their children," but by attempting to fulfill their own lives, thus offering a healthy role model of a person seeking a meaningful life.

Reward Rather than Punishment

Positive reinforcement responses such as smiling, taking pleasure in the child's company, verbal praise, and physical affection, are integral parts of the learning process. It is surprising how easily discipline is achieved in a family characterized by love and understanding. Withdrawal of these positive expressions of displeasure can also mold the child's behavior. In general, a combination of verbal approval, tangible rewards, affection and genuine acknowledgment, along with some form of reasonable consequence for misbehavior, is conducive to successfully disciplining children.

Avoidance of Physical Punishment and Threats

It is never appropriate for a parent to beat or otherwise physically abuse a child. If restraint is needed, parents can hold the child firmly and talk to him sternly or even move him physically to get him to go where they wish, without striking the child. Those individuals who are sure of their own power and accepting of their own angry feelings can effectively stop their children's annoying behaviors and physically hurtful actions without hitting, spanking, or violently shaking them.

It is ineffective to use idle threats of future punishment to enforce rules and standards. Most parents fail to back up their threats with action, which undermines their authority. The use of frightening ultimatums is damaging to children. For example, the parent who sadistically warns his child, "If you're not good, I'm sending you to boarding school," inflicts an untold amount of misery.

Avoidance of Judgmental Attitudes

As much as physical punishment damages the children's psyches, parents' harsh, judgmental attitudes act to destroy their self-esteem. Most children grow up feeling that they are somehow bad. They ascribe many reasons to why they feel that way: because they cry or feel sad, because they have wants or desires, or because they feel angry or resentful. They also have a critical view of themselves for feeling anger at being harshly judged, as well as for feeling hatred toward those who are judging them.

Labeling or categorizing children's behavior as "good" or "bad" is not recommended; for example, using remarks such as, "Were you a good boy today? Did you do your homework?" or "You're bad if you don't listen to your mother!" Evaluative statements differentiating good and bad behaviors tend to support the formation of a narrow view of human nature and to discourage the child from developing his/her own standards.

In addition, parents should avoid negatively comparing their children to others. These comparisons leave a strong impression of unworthiness. The negative identity that is formed in the family and integrated into the child's self-concept will become a functional part of the child's and later the adult's personality dynamics. In many ways, this conception of self remains irrefutable in spite of evidence to the contrary. It is implanted on a deep level and becomes part of the substructure of a person's attitude toward self and others.

Moralistic training procedures in which children are viewed as bad or sinful, have a negative effect: Children are not born inherently evil or bad. Some people, while not conscious of this attitude, implicitly believe that children are bad and tend to treat them accordingly. Children who are fortunate in having decent, moral parental figures do not need to be taught moralistic prohibitions or principles; they will learn ethical behavior and decency through observing and imitating their parents.

Teaching children that it is moral to be selfless in the sense of being self-denying and unnecessarily deferring of their wants can be damaging and, later, may seriously interfere with their pursuing goal-directed behavior. Children's desires and wants are an important part of their personal identity, and should be encouraged and supported. People are defined by their feelings, perceptions, thoughts, wants, and unique ways of coping with their environment and pursuing their priorities.

Reassuring children that they are not bad after disciplining them helps them regain their self-esteem: Responsive parents stress the fact that it is their child's *behavior* that is irritating or offensive, not that the child is inherently bad or offensive. They also emphasize that the unacceptable behavior can be changed. Most important, after disciplining their children, they reassure them of their love with a hug or other expressions of affection, which helps repair any break in their attuned relationship. Since the point of discipline is not to punish but to teach, it also helps to have a follow-up conversation with the child about his/her thoughts and feelings regarding the situation.

Parents can also use humor to help their children get out of a bad mood and stop misbehaving: Optimistic good humor about negative events or about a child's mistakes can often dispel the seriousness and drama of an otherwise painful or unpleasant situation. This humor does not involve the sarcasm or hurtful barbs that some parents use to control, degrade, or humiliate their children; on the contrary, this style of humor is respectful of the child. Not only is humor a useful adjunct to discipline, but children really enjoy their parents being playful and spontaneously fun-loving. To illustrate, when a group of 10-year-old school children were asked to write down their answers to the question, "What's wrong with grownups?" One child wrote, "Grown-ups almost never like to get silly. And when we have fun and get silly, they always say 'settle down.' When they *do* get silly, it is the most fun we have" (Buscaglia, 1987, p.10).

Controlling Children's Hostile, Manipulative Behavior

It is a good idea for parents to interrupt the behavior patterns in their child that are irritating or provoking before they find themselves starting to dislike or even hate the child. It is more constructive for them to identify the cause of children's disruptive behavior than to continually punish its manifestations. It is never advisable to allow a disruptive situation to persist within the family. It is much more productive to get at the core problem by talking things out.

Negative power on the part of children needs to be dealt with firmly: Negative power can be defined as an attempt to control and manipulate through weakness. This includes behaviors such as continually crying, falling apart, behaving in a self-destructive manner, playing the victim, trying to make others feel guilty, having temper tantrums, behaving selfishly, displaying intrusive behavior, or acting paranoid and mistreated. Parents need to be aware that children do not typically outgrow these characteristics. Unless they are addressed, they become life-long habits that interfere with future personal relationships.

Children can be taught that it is never appropriate to castigate or hate themselves for wrong-doing: It is much more functional and appropriate to change their behavior in the future. Self-attacks generally lead to more negative behavior. Children can be taught that no matter how reprehensible their behavior was, it serves no purpose to rip into one's self and ruminate obsessively about the past. Parents can let their child know that everyone makes mistakes or acts badly at times, yet these behaviors are correctable.

Battles of the will are best avoided: Unnecessary power plays on the part of the parents that degrade the child and force conformity and submission can be prevented. It is not advisable to issue ultimatums or arbitrarily take a rigid stand. This type of posture sets up situations that invariably lead to power struggles. Both parents and children suffer from this kind of exchange.

I am not suggesting, however, an overly permissive attitude that allows regressive behavior, destructive acting out, or parent abuse. There is an obvious balance that is required that depends primarily on parents' maturity and self-control. If circumstances do arise where parents find themselves in a battle of this sort, they can learn to assert their power over the child without causing him/her to lose self-esteem or to feel devastated by the interaction. They can refrain from exploding in anger at their child, although this is a strong temptation once the child stubbornly refuses to behave. Irrational expressions of rage are frightening to children; they tend to perceive that their parent is out of control, and terrifying, while at the same time, ineffective and weak. On the other hand, parents who have access to their anger, and feel comfortable expressing it in a controlled manner are neither feared by their child nor seen as ineffective. Rather, they are respected and seen as allies.

To summarize, discipline is best practiced with firmness, not cruelty; with understanding, not condemnation; and from an underlying motive of helping children not only to become the kind of people who like themselves, but also the kind of person whom other people like, respect and enjoy being with. Indeed, the ideas for discipline and socialization described here are based on a philosophy that allows the gradual unfolding of the child's unique personality, vitality and enthusiasm for life.

EFFECTIVE PARENTAL TRAITS AND ATTITUDES

It is essential that parents take steps to minimize the types of experiences that contribute to their children's confusion, pain, and suffering and to reduce the necessity for them to form personal defenses. These steps and the principles upon which they are based are similar in most respects to the dimensions of the positive therapeutic process described earlier.

Parental Honesty: Just as it is necessary for therapists to maintain a high level of personal and professional integrity in relation to their clients, it is also vital that parents not mislead their children. Confusing their children's perception of reality can be more damaging than the negative experiences that are covered over. Distorting a child's perception leads to distrust and suspicion and is a key factor in mental illness.

Parents can try to represent themselves honestly to break the process of idealizing the family. It is damaging for parents to try to conceal their limitations and fears from their offspring. For children who have grown up in a less-than-ideal emotional climate to be told by relatives and acquaintances how wonderful and special their family is, only makes matters worse. This build-up serves no constructive purpose and distorts the child's reality. On the other hand, helping children from their earliest years onward to develop an objective, realistic picture of their parents contributes to their forming a realistic, non-defensive view of themselves as well.

Respect for Separateness: It is beneficial for children to be seen as human beings with respect for their separate identities. They do not belong to their parents or their families, but to themselves; therefore, it is vital that people refrain from patronizing their children, categorizing them, or speaking for them. Parents often talk about their children as if they were not there. "She's such a shy child," or "I just don't know what I'm going to do about him!"

It is helpful for parents to learn the meaning of "leaving the child alone" or "letting him be." To let children be is to allow them to feel that they are people in their own right, distinct from other persons or family members. Parents who are respectful of personal boundaries avoid intruding into the lives of their children by identifying too closely with their interests and aspirations or by making them feel that they must report their thoughts, feelings, and behaviors. Children who are "not seen" or responded to as separate individuals often grow up to be mere reflections of how their parents viewed them and never discover who or what they might have become.

The Value of Being Personal: It is vital for parents to respond as real people to their children, rather than role-playing or acting condescending, strategic, or phony in their interactions with them. Children need adults who relate to them directly; they need people who are open with them about *their* thoughts and feelings. They search the faces of their parents for a source of genuine feeling contact. They have strong needs to feel the humanity of their parents, to see beyond the roles of "father" and "mother." When people behave in a manner that is natural or personal and dispense with roles, their children experience them as human and lovable.

Children desperately need to feel love for their parents, and if they are deprived of this opportunity, it causes them unbearable pain. Children who are kept at a distance or provoked into a negative or hostile posture toward their parents feel alienated and suffer intense guilt reactions. In a sense, they are bent out of shape psychologically and lose contact with themselves. In addition, they are often defined as or accused of not being loving people, and are punished for this "flaw."

In general, I encourage parents to be personal in relating to their children, to talk about their own feelings and life experiences, much as they would to a friend. This does not imply that they would "dump" their problems on their children or make immature demands on them for comfort or reassurance; rather, it implies that they would share their world with their children and allow their children to share their world with them.

In summary, by respecting their children as separate individuals, supporting and encouraging their independence, and relating to them directly with real feeling, rather than hiding behind roles, parents can offer their offspring a firm foundation on which to build their lives, rather than forcing them into an inward, defensive posture. Parents' honesty and maturity are far more effective in determining the healthy development of their children than any particular technique or routine.

CONCLUSION

Today's parents are attempting to raise healthy, productive individuals in a confused age of alienation. The movement away from feeling in our society has increased anxiety and led to considerable stress, making genuine personal relationships progressively more difficult. With the changes in traditional family life, these symptoms have come more to the surface in the form of increased divorce rates and a partial breakdown of the nuclear family and other social institutions. The erosion of these traditional structures has been incorrectly considered by many to be the principle cause, rather than the effect of, emotional distress and neurosis.

The true sources of the difficulty, however, are deeply rooted in the individual defensive process, which manifests itself in the formation of destructive couple and family bonds and their extension into the institutions of society at large. Environmental factors such as parental ambivalence, duplicity, and role-playing in the family, the illusion of connection between family members, along with the myth of unconditional parental love, all have a negative effect on the minds and feelings of young people.

Without exception, we have all suffered a certain amount of trauma during our developing years. Despite parents' desires to do the best for their offspring, remnants of this trauma hurt their children at a time when they are particularly vulnerable. My efforts have been devoted to trying to understand the sources of this incidental harm and to developing a psychotherapy that could minimize and repair the damage.

As a father, I have come to recognize that there are no easy solutions, no short cuts, to good parenting practices. As a psychotherapist, I have learned that there are methods that parents can utilize to develop understanding and compassion for themselves and feeling for what happened to them as children. They can achieve better relationships with their children by recovering feeling for themselves and their own lives.

It is critical that we remember that children are not our possessions; they are not ours in the proprietary sense of the word; rather, they belong to themselves and have the right to an independent existence. Lastly, in learning to value their own lives, parents are better able to allow their children to preserve their human heritage. My optimism in writing about childhood suffering stems from my belief that by *not* surrendering to their internal processing and their parents' fears and anxieties, people could break the chain of pain and neurosis that is passed from generation to generation. Perhaps, in future generations, parents will no longer be the lost children.

Notes

1. Duplicitous communications are characterized by verbal statements that are contradicted by nonverbal messages, that is, the sender's behavior, posture, facial expressions, and tone of voice. In many families, there are implicit rules forbidding any commentary on this discrepancy, which further confuses and mystifies the child. See Bateson et al.'s (1956) concept of the "double bind," and Laing and Esteron's (1970) interviews with eleven families, each of whom had an identified "schizophrenic" family member. These families exhibited a preponderance of double messages, exemplifying Bateson's "double bind" theory.

2. The formation of psychological defenses to reduce overwhelming emotion and anxiety states experienced by the child increases the probability that he/she will attain sexual maturity, reproduce, and contribute to the gene pool. In his book, *Human Nature and Suffering,* Paul Gilbert (1989) pointed out, "All life forms are equipped to defend against threat and also to advance their own life form" (p. 79). Similarly, Bowins (2004) argued that, "Psychological defense mechanisms represent a crucial component of our capacity to maintain emotional homeostasis. Without them the conscious mind would be much more vulnerable to negatively charged emotional input, such as that pertaining to anxiety and sadness" (p. 1). George Vailliant's (1977; 2011) essays make an important distinction between "mature" (adaptive) and "immature" (maladaptive) character defenses. Also see David Shapiro's (2000) *Dynamics of Character* that link defense mechanisms to self-deception.

3. Extensive research supports this hypothesis: for example, Jacobson (2009) reported, "Emerging lines of research from epigenetics suggest that not only can nature alter nurture, but nurture, in turn, has the power to modify nature (p. 2). Tremblay and Szyf (2010) found that, "Epigenetic mechanisms are especially important because they provide a powerful explanation for maternal transmission of behavior disorders that extend beyond the traditional genetic transmission explanations. The mother, through her maternal behavior, can affect DNA methylation of critical genes in the offspring" (p. 497).

Also see Varese et al. (2012) who found that "patients with psychosis were 2.72 times more likely to have been exposed to childhood adversity than controls" [Abstract]. These findings indicate that childhood adversity is strongly associated with increased risk for psychosis.

sAlso of interest are Belsky and de Haan's (2011) and Whittle et al. (2009), who studied less extremely abusive or more "normative" parenting environments and their effect on adolescents' brain functioning.

4. John Bowlby's statements were transcribed from a videotape titled *Theoretical Aspects of Attachment*, produced by David Scott May, M.D. and Marion Solomon, Ph.D. (1984).

5. Emotional hunger, based on a parent's unresolved dependency needs, is often manifest in overprotection and has detrimental effects of infants and young children. DeRuiter and van IJzendoorn (1992) found that "adults with agoraphobia were also more likely to rate their parents as low on affection and high on overprotection than controls" (Loc. 27088). Also see Murray Bowen's (1978) studies on parental overprotection which showed that some forms of over-solicitousness are linked to "the family projection process," which "begins with anxiety in the mother" (p. 381). In their work, Parker (1983) and Tronick et al. (1986) discussed several manifestations of emotional hunger, including parental overprotection and the notion of "affect hunger." D. Stern (1985) described 'over-attunement' on the part of some mothers, as a "counterpart of physical intrusiveness.... Maternal psyche hovering, when complied with on the infant's part, may slow down the infant's moves toward independence" (p. 219). Nervous over-concern, another manifestation of emotional hunger, has been identified by other clinicians as common in "psychosomatic" families (Minuchin, 1984).

6. Re: unconditional parental love, see Elizabeth Badinter (1981) who wrote, "Intellectually and—more to the point, in fact—emotionally, people continue to think of mother love as an absolute" (pp. xxii). On a similar note, Robert Harper (1981) observed, "That most marriages are not deeply satisfying relationships hardly needs documentation. A lot of praise and sanctification floats about us, however, on the matter of families. I think we engage in a lot of repression and denial. Put more simply, we double-pretend: we pretend families are mostly wonderful and then we pretend we are not pretending" (p. 5).

7. Re: Parental ambivalence. Research shows that these conflicting feelings and attitudes toward children coexist within all people in all societies (Rohner, 1986; 1991). Rohner conceptualized parents' attitudes as existing on a continuum ranging from parental warmth and acceptance to indifference, rejection, and hostility. On the basis of cross-cultural studies encompassing 35 cultures, he concluded that parental rejection has a universal effect on children and that it can be measured intergenerationally (in both parent and child).

8. According to Baumeister, Bratslavsky, Finkenauer, and Vohs (2001), painful, aversive, or negative stimuli often arouse more powerful reactions than do pleasant or positive stimuli. This is evolutionarily beneficial because stimuli that arouse pain or negative emotions are often dangerous or even life-threatening.

9. See D. Siegel & M. Hartzell (2003): "Try to see the interaction from your child's point of view... Being able to focus on both your own experience and that of your child is a central feature of effective repair" (p. 199).

10. I have conceptualized the voice as a fundamental part of the "internal working models" that explains the dynamics involved in insecure adult attachment relationships. Clinical studies into the origins of the destructive inner voice have clarified its role in the intergenerational transmission of negative parental attitudes, behaviors, and defenses. The voice is the intrapsychic mechanism primarily responsible for the perpetuation of parental defenses in succeeding generations and it also influences the type and quality of attachments formed by adult individuals in their couple relationships.

See also Fonagy, Luyten, Allison & Campbell (2016): "The central feature of the IWM (internal working model) concerned the infants' encoding of interactions in terms of what they implied about the expected availability of the attachment figure. Bowlby (1980) described how an individual defensively excludes stimuli that are incompatible with the IWM, leading to an inability to accommodate external reality, often in relation to other people's emotional states or attachment needs" (Loc. 48333).

11. See *The Science of the Art of Psychotherapy* (2012) by Alan Schore, who quotes a statement by Ginot (2009): "The analyst's sensitivity, or her right brain readiness to be fully attuned to nonverbal communication, is a necessary therapeutic skill" (p. 297). Schore continues, "…and so there are direct commonalities between the spontaneous responses of the maternal intuition of a psychobiologically attuned primary caregiver and the intuitive therapist's sensitive counter-transferential responsiveness to the patient's unconscious nonverbal affective bodily based implicit communications" (Loc. 3441, 3540).

Sources: *Compassionate Child Rearing: An In-depth Approach to Optimal Parenting* (1990); Chapter 2 *Combating Destructive Thought Processes: Voice Therapy and Separation Theory* (1997); Chapter 2 *The Self Under Siege: A Therapeutic Model for Differentiation* (2013) and *Psychology Today Blog* "8 reasons Parents Fail To Love Their Kids", October 7, 2015.

Chapter 12

MY APPROACH TO PSYCHOTHERAPY

The criterion of mental health is not one of individual adjustment to a given social order, but a universal one, valid for all men, of giving a satisfactory answer to the problem of human existence.

~ Erich Fromm (1956b, Loc. 277)

When I was a graduate student in clinical psychology working for my Ph.D., I invested time and energy in my own personal psychoanalysis. It was not a requirement at the university I attended, but I could not imagine becoming a psychotherapist without that experience as part of my training. The sessions opened up a new door to my self-understanding and insight.

The experience was not always pleasant; my analyst's general line of interpretation was Freudian with an emphasis on Oedipal issues. His primary concern was about competitive feelings and fears. He recognized that many of my anxieties were associated with a fear of reprisal for aggressive or rivalrous thoughts and actions. This core interpretation was valuable to me in understanding myself. My family demanded success and achievement, and a degree of perfection that was all but impossible to attain. How could I get their approval?

In my sessions, I kept trying to get the good doctor's approval. I gave him a copy of my dissertation, but he said nothing. I demonstrated my clever insight into psychoanalysis and still no response. I free associated, analyzed my dreams and brought up significant sexual material, all to no avail. There was absolutely nothing I could do to get a positive reaction, which explained a good deal of my rage. The entire situation fit the analytic model. The assumption was that when I projected these transference feelings from my family onto my therapist, I would be able to work them out and this would cure my neurosis. His failure to praise me or respond to my demands would naturally arouse my anger, and I would have an opportunity to learn to handle my aggression.

One day after my session, I was so angry at my analyst that I closed the car door on my head as I was getting in. I just sat in the car laughing out loud. I realized that my self-destructive action was caused by my guilt feelings for expressing my hostility toward him. Aside from humor, there was a basic problem in all of this: in his treatment of me, the doctor consistently behaved as a "non-person" as per his assigned role. However, this style of relating was very similar to my father's way of relating to me. On an unconscious level, in the current re-parenting experience of the analysis, I was being reconditioned along the same lines that had originally damaged me.

The analytic procedure can be problematic if the new interpersonal relationship with the therapist replicates the atmosphere of the client's family environment. In that case, the therapist's studied neutrality and lack of feeling can have destructive side effects. Fortunately, at times, analysts sidestep the traditional procedure, break the rules and appropriately reveal honest emotions to the ultimate benefit of their clients (Note 1).

Although it was a difficult period, I discovered so much about myself and I was impressed with the realization that there was no other conceivable means to have digested what I had learned in those three years. After concluding my analysis, I spent many years involved in self-analysis with a group of colleagues, in which I utilized my analytic work as a teaching device. During that time, I continued to develop my personal insights and considerably improved my life circumstances. I had great respect for the psychoanalytical approach to psychopathology.

Aside from the curative aspect for those with special problems, the process of psychotherapy offers the maximum potential for an individual to live an insightful, adventurous, and creative life. Self-limiting psychological defenses can be identified and challenged in the talk therapy context. In sessions, specific defenses against early trauma and, later, against death anxiety can be recognized and addressed directly. The therapeutic experience offers a unique opportunity for a new, more fulfilling life.

PRINCIPLES OF AN EFFECTIVE PSYCHOTHERAPY

> The psychotherapeutic alliance is a unique human relationship, wherein a devoted and trained person attempts to render assistance to another person by both suspending and extending himself. Nowhere in life is a person listened to, felt, and experienced with such concentrated sharing and emphasis on every aspect of personal communication. As in any other human relationship, this interaction may be fulfilling or damaging to either individual.

> To the extent that a new fantasy bond or illusion of connection is formed (doctor-client, therapist-client, parent-child), the relationship can be detrimental; whereas in a situation that is characterized by equality, openness, and true compassion, there will be movement toward individuation in both parties. My therapy helps a person to expose and challenge dependency bonds and destructive "voices," remnants of negative childhood experiences that seriously impair people's sense of self, spirit, and individuality.

> ~ R. Firestone (in Zeig & Munion, Eds., 1990c, p. 68)

The techniques or treatment strategies utilized in psychotherapy are based on fundamental philosophical assumptions held by the therapist about human beings and their institutions. As Robert Langs (1982) emphasized in *Psychotherapy: A Basic Text*, "The nature of this therapeutic relationship, and of the transactions between the two participants, is structured and shaped by the *implicit and explicit attitudes* and interventions of the therapist" (p. 3).

As noted in Chapter 2, a basic assumption underlying my approach to psychotherapy reflects my personal view of people as being innocent rather than inherently destructive or self-destructive. My focus is on the development of a sense of self in opposition to the invalidation of self that is caused by maintaining destructive voices and self-limiting defenses. As a therapist, I have always viewed hostility and aggression as part of the defense system that people form to cope with life's adversities. They are an overlay on the personality that can be dealt with in therapy with compassion and understanding. When one is hurt or suffers personal abuse, there is a reflexive reaction of anger and outrage that must be addressed and worked through in the therapeutic setting.

I believe that an acceptance of one's sexuality and sexual identity is a vital part of the therapy process. This can be difficult in a society that promulgates distorted views of the body and sexuality through its social mores, institutions, and media. I also believe that people need to develop their sense of self and their own personal value system. When individuals formulate values and ethics from within themselves rather than from without, they can chart the course of their lives in a manner that is harmonious and well integrated. As described earlier, my approach also emphasizes the pursuit of transcendent goals that go beyond the narrow confines of self and family. By involving themselves in goals that have a deeper meaning than immediate gratification, people increase their capacity for feeling worthwhile and expand their life space.

Lastly, I believe that the therapist must not impose his theoretical orientation on the client but, instead, should attempt to develop a personalized theory for each individual. This does not negate the therapist having a theoretical orientation or background of understanding, but rather emphasizes his/her flexibility and openness.

DEFENDED VS. UNDEFENDED LIFESTYLES

A comprehensive theory of psychopathology and a comparative mental health model combine to help clinicians develop a treatment strategy for their clients. As noted in Chapter 1, human beings exist in a state of conflict between the active pursuit of their goals in the real world, and the urge to live within an inward, self-protective defense system, characterized by reliance on fantasy gratification, addictions, and negative attitudes towards self and others. The more an individual is damaged in early life experience, the less willing he/she is to undertake the risks necessary for self-actualization.

The defended person's life is significantly distorted by desperately clinging to addictive attachments, strong guilt reactions, low self-esteem, a rigid approach to life and a distrust of others whereas, ideally, a less defended individual exists in a state of continual change, moving toward increased autonomy, and enjoying more satisfying relationships. Both approaches to life have certain advantages as well as certain disadvantages. On the surface, "adjusted," albeit defended people may feel less anxious and more secure; however, their adaptations have negative consequences, which are manifested in a loss of freedom and feeling and a more constricted life. Moreover, at some point, this condition can lead to a recurrence of neurotic symptoms.

Comparatively less defended individuals generally feel more integrated, have a stronger identity, a greater potential for intimacy, and tend to be more humane toward others. They are relatively asymptomatic and free of the compulsion to repeat familiar destructive patterns, but they must live with a heightened sense of vulnerability and sensitivity to both joyful events and emotionally painful situations. They are more responsive to circumstances in their lives that impinge on their well-being, and they experience more feeling for life's tragic aspects, along with a greater awareness of death. They are cognizant that they are investing in a life that they must certainly lose.

The choice to live non-defensively is partially an ethical one, given the inherent damage caused by defenses that limit people's capacity for living and feeling, causing corresponding damage to self and loved ones, especially one's children. The dilemma facing the therapist, as well as the client who has progressed in therapy, brings these two alternatives to the foreground.

HISTORICAL DEVELOPMENT OF METHODOLOGY

The cumulative effects of interpersonal relationships . . . typically in childhood—has made the client "ill" and . . . another human relationship, with a professionally trained person and under particularly benign circumstances, can provide corrections in the client's self-esteem and in the quality of his/her relationships with significant others.

~ Hans Strupp (1989, pp. 717-718)

My treatment strategy is based on my 60-year study of resistance to change or progress in psychotherapy (Note 2). As I described earlier, I began working with schizophrenic clients under the auspices of John N. Rosen (1953). At that time, I developed the basic concepts of my theoretical approach to schizophrenia (Note 3). Later, I extended and applied these concepts to the neuroses. In my doctoral dissertation, *A Concept of the Schizophrenic Process* (R. Firestone, 1957), I described the dimensions of the fantasized, self-mothering process that the schizophrenic client relies on for gratification at the expense of interpersonal relationships.

In effect, schizophrenic patients are split between being the powerful parent and the weak, helpless child and experience varying degrees of ego fragmentation. To counteract the self-mothering process, my colleagues and I provided an interim form of parenting that helped these patients compensate for their early emotional deprivation. Our therapy was a direct attack upon their internal source of gratification through fantasy, combined with an attempt to make reality more inviting. These patients were fixated on an oral level of psychosexual development. We directly analyzed and interpreted their schizophrenic productions accordingly. The methodology challenged patients' idealization of the mother, while at the same time we provided emotional support that enabled them to progress through the early stages of development at which they had been fixated.

Rosen's treatment of patients in a non-institutional atmosphere where they lived with their therapists, as well as the wealth of information I gathered in this setting, left a lasting impression on me. My attitude toward these patients suffering with schizophrenia was one of respect for their attempt to maintain some form of integrity in the face of severe trauma and support for the fact that their symptoms made logical sense. I believed that these people had come by their symptoms honestly; that is, I felt that real events harmful to their psyche had occurred to have fostered this level of regression.

After leaving Rosen's and receiving my Ph.D., I entered into private practice and utilized a psychoanalytically oriented therapy model for many years. Essentially, I used the technique of free association and interpretation of my clients' material. I worked diligently coping with their resistance and helped them resolve their transference reactions. My therapeutic approach progressed further as I integrated what I was learning in my practice with the knowledge gained from my work with the schizophrenic patients and the discoveries that I made while working at Rosen's.

Later, I found the work of Arthur Janov (1970) and Primal Therapy to be of interest. My goal was to help my clients develop a depth of feeling to match their intellectual understanding. Janov's methods presented a means for clients to express deeper feelings, so I developed a modification of Primal Therapy, which I called Feeling Release Therapy. My associates and I applied the method to over 200 clients. We found that as clients released powerful feelings and relived core incidents in their lives, they formulated powerful insights (Note 4). This technique became an integral part of my treatment approach. My experience with this form of psychotherapy, together with the psychoanalytic approach, proved to be very effective in helping my clients.

Finally, these studies led to my investigation of Voice Therapy techniques. Understanding destructive thought processes, developing methods to allow these voices to come to the surface, understanding their sources, and helping individuals to cope with their destructive thoughts greatly added to my therapeutic methodology. All of the above-mentioned procedures have contributed to maximizing a positive therapeutic outcome.

STAGES IN THE THERAPEUTIC PROCESS

The ultimate aim of therapy is to encourage the client to challenge his/her defenses and inner world of fantasy and risk seeking satisfaction through goal-directed behavior. To this end, I have utilized the techniques and procedures noted above, and they have proven to be valuable and consistent with respect to Separation Theory.

This multidimensional methodology has proved most beneficial in overcoming resistance and promoting therapeutic movement. I have utilized all of these procedures in my work, but not as a rigid system applied to all persons seeking help or therapeutic intervention. The techniques may or may not be used in the order described, and there is no regimented treatment plan implied for all clients. My approach is adapted to the specific requirements of the individual.

FEELING RELEASE THERAPY

Historically, psychoanalysts were concerned with developing a method whereby they could obtain a free release of thoughts as well as an emotional catharsis. They turned to free association as the "royal road to the unconscious" and believed that if the unconscious material—the impulses, repressed feelings and memories—were recovered, it could be integrated into the ego and the client would be cured in the process.

Feeling Release Therapy utilizes techniques that elicit deeply repressed feelings and reawaken emotional pain from the past. After re-experiencing this pain, individuals usually have a flood of intellectual insights and are able to understand the meaning of their present-day neurotic symptoms and behaviors. This therapy utilizes techniques similar in many respects to those of Arthur Janov's (1970) Primal Therapy, as described in *The Primal Scream*.

When applied appropriately, Feeling Release Therapy can be a significant advance over free association as a technique for recovering memories and experiences from one's childhood. It is more direct than traditional methods aimed at bringing unconscious material to the client's awareness. The material that is unearthed provides valuable information and feeling about both the clients' history and their present day symptomology, in a straightforward manner that they can clearly understand for themselves.

In addition, when I began working with clients using techniques of Feeling Release Therapy, I found that many of my concepts about the neurotic process were validated by the revelations and insights of clients who interpreted their own material and integrated it without assistance or interpretation from me. Because of the lack of therapeutic interference in the process, Feeling Release Therapy has excellent research potential, which has been largely neglected by practitioners and theorists in the field.

Prior to the first feeling release session, individuals are asked to avoid painkillers—cigarettes, alcohol, and other self-soothing habits—and are encouraged to spend 24 hours in isolation and self-contemplation while writing down their thoughts and feelings. The combination of prohibiting the use of substances and interrupting routines has the effect of creating an immediate state of heightened tension and deprivation. This warm-up period generates anxiety, and feelings tend to become more easily accessible.

In the sessions, clients are encouraged to breathe deeply, to allow sounds to emerge as they exhale, and to verbalize any thoughts that come to mind. Feelings gradually escalate until powerful emotions are released. Afterward, clients form their own insights and spontaneously relate irrational or primitive emotional responses, as well as present-day limitations, to early negative experiences in the family. Most describe their memories with unusual clarity and appear to genuinely relive events and feelings from early childhood. Clients generally interpret their own material and integrate it without assistance or intervention from the therapist; thus, transference reactions tend to be minimal during this phase.

Janet, thirty-five and the mother of three, had lived the better part of her life subordinating herself to her husband and living through his accomplishments, never fully developing her own capabilities and intellect. She had hoped to gain a greater sense of self through therapy and to become more independent in her relationship with her husband. In her first sessions, she recalled vivid scenes of her early years spent in a large lonely house on a ranch in the Southwest. The following are excerpts from her journal during this part of her feeling release sessions:

Session 3: Why am I such a coward? What am I afraid of? Of him, my father. Why? I see him with his hand raised (I often picture him that way)—he is going to hit me! Why? Then I see an awful veiny thing hanging down between his legs at my eye level. I feel disgusted. It's red and veiny and I don't seem to know what it is. It is dripping a sticky, colorless liquid. He has been making love to someone! Then I see two bodies on the bed, very clearly, from the rear—I see his behind. I walk into my parents' room. He is screwing and then I see her lying on the bed. I don't want to look, but I see that it is the Hispanic maid in our house. She is young and slight, slim and thin. (My mother is fat and ugly—I always feel fat. I always feel awkward around women shorter than I am, especially if they are slim.) My father raises his hand to me and chases me back to my bed in my own room. I cower on the bed and let him hit me! I feel like a coward, but I got his attention away from her—I get my husband Jim's attention by provoking him to be angry. Then he doesn't have any heart for anyone else, even though the attention focused on me is negative attention.

Session 9: I was a baby calling for mommy to come and pick me up. After many screams, she came. She put something in my mouth—I didn't want it (a bottle?)—I felt smothered. I imagined what it would be like to be held in someone's arms, and felt warm and safe. I liked it so much and felt it for a long time. Then I remembered what it was really like. I felt lost, held myself, tried to comfort myself and could not keep myself warm, it was a cold feeling, I was anguished. I am still trying to care for myself by stuffing myself with food or indulging myself by buying things for myself. When I was ungenerous about serving people in my house, I remember an irrational feeling that there would not be enough food left for me—I would starve.

Despite her regression in the sessions themselves, Janet functioned in an adult and rational manner during her everyday life. Other sessions, similar to session 9, touched on themes from a primitive stage of development, where Janet relived memories pertaining to the frustration of her needs on an oral level. She became aware that this was the source of her current underlying dependence on her husband. Direct oral material of this nature, such as memories of early feeding experiences and frustration at the breast, are usually not accessible in traditional insight therapy, even to a person with the ego strength of this particular client.

The knowledge of self and personal understanding gained through feeling release sessions is unusually direct and pure. It is as though clients are able to envision their childhood situations, seeing through their present-day problems to their source, rather than intellectually figuring them out or analyzing them.

Much time was spent evaluating the results, recording and transcribing the vast amounts of material from individual and group sessions, and assessing the advantages and disadvantages of this form of therapeutic intervention. My associates and I came to realize that everybody has a considerable amount of deep-seated pain and sadness that they are continually suppressing and, indeed, may be completely unaware of in their everyday lives. It seemed that no one was immune to this intense primal pain and that no one had escaped childhood without being scarred to some extent.

Our results confirmed Janov's (1970) findings, as well as his view that defenses are basically a protection against feeling primal pain. However, in contrast to Janov, who felt that repeated expression and release could empty the reservoir or "pool" of primal pain and lead to a "cure", our investigations showed that this "pool" cannot be emptied, as such. If defenses formed early in relation to interpersonal traumas stood alone, and were not reinforced by reactions to death anxiety, Janov's assumptions and hopes might have been realized.

Moreover, I found that the techniques of Feeling Release Therapy were not in themselves sufficient to alter an individual's basic attitude or defense. As necessary as it is for people to understand the connection between their current behavior and past trauma and have access to their deepest feelings, this methodology in and of itself does not necessarily change the compulsive reliving of destructive patterns, restricted lifestyles, the negative self-concept, or the preference for fantasy gratification and self-parenting defenses.

Feeling Release sessions offer a heightened awareness of those childhood experiences that affect current behavior. They help a person become far less defensive, and contribute to a perceptible reduction in tension and anxiety associated with repressed feeling. In addition, feeling release sessions can help clients cope with the intense emotional reactions linked to the verbalization of negative thought patterns in the next phase of treatment.

Verbalization and Identification of Negative Thought Patterns

My specific orientation and approach to psychotherapy is known as Voice Therapy because it is a process of giving language or spoken words to the negative thought process at the core of an individual's maladaptive or self-destructive behavior. Expressing voices in the second person format facilitates the process of separating the client's point of view from negative thought processes antithetical to self and hostile toward others that had been incorporated during the developmental years. It also serves to facilitate the expression of affect associated with negative introjects. My conclusions regarding the sources of the voice were not the result of an *a priori* hypothesis on my part as the therapist; rather, the clients themselves spontaneously developed insight and made the necessary connections.

The Voice Therapy process is an effective tool in unearthing the sources of people's feelings of self-hatred. It increases their understanding of the origins of their self-destructive urges and helps them separate from the incorporated parental view of themselves that is an overlay on their real self-image. The emotional catharsis that accompanies this exposure of the voice relieves tension and promotes positive feelings similar to the results I have observed following sessions of Feeling Release Therapy.

My approach to eliciting and identifying the contents of the voice is *not* didactic; that is, I do not directly try to persuade people to think or behave rationally. Rather, I help them discover the contents of the voice's malicious "coaching" in various situations and attempt to assist them in moving away from these negative attitudes and prohibitions. Even though presented as five steps, the stages in this treatment strategy are not discrete, and they often overlap one another.

THE FIVE STEPS OF VOICE THERAPY

(1) Identifying and verbalizing the hostile voice attacks on self and others in the second-person format, and releasing the associated affect. Attacks are presented in the form of negative statements directed toward the self as though someone were speaking to you, such as: *You're are so foolish; you can't do anything right, who do you think you are?*

(2) Identifying the sources of the voice in the client's background.

(3) Answering back to the incorporated point of view and to the attacks on self and others. There are two aspects of the answering back process: (a) offering a rational and realistic evaluation of one's actual point of view; and (b) countering the charges by answering back with strong emotions of anger, and sadness.

(4) Understanding the impact of the destructive thoughts or voices on present-day behavior, therapeutic goals, and the desire to change.

(5) Challenging the negative traits and behaviors dictated by the voice by collaborating with the therapist in the planning and implementation of corrective suggestions.

As these steps are explained, they will be illustrated with a session with a 25-year old man, Bill, who attacked himself about his awkwardness with women.

Step 1: Clients learn to identify and analyze self-attacks and defensive negative prescriptions and to restate them in the second person, as "you" statements, as though someone else were addressing them. The process of verbalizing voices can be approached intellectually as a primarily cognitive technique or more dramatically using cathartic methods. In the latter technique, there is an emphasis on the release of affect accompanying the expression of the voice attacks.

Bill: I want to feel comfortable relating to women, but I'm always so uncomfortable and awkward. All I do is attack myself.

Therapist: What are some of your self-attacks?

Bill: I'm so awkward. I don't know what to say to women. And they can tell and they think I'm so weird. Other guys are so relaxed and funny. I wish I could be like them.

Therapist: What if you said those as voice attacks. Say the same things, but say them as "you" instead of "I." Like *"You're so awkward."*

Bill: Okay. *You're so awkward. You don't know how to talk to women. They think you're so weird.*

Therapist: Keep going. Say whatever comes to mind.

Bill: *You're not like other men.* [with more intensity] *You're a freak. You're repulsive! No one could ever love you!*

Many clients voluntarily adopt an emotional style of expression when articulating their voice. They often release intense feelings of anger and sadness as they reveal the self-derogatory thoughts and attitudes that hold special meaning for them. When people verbalize the voice in this form, it is remarkable to witness the scope and intensity of angry affect directed toward self that is so close to the surface.

When clients get to the emotionally charged content of their voice attacks, there is often a remarkable change in their physical expression. Their body often takes on the posture and mannerisms of a strict parent delivering a lecture or issuing an ultimatum. Their tone of voice sometimes expresses the accent of one of their parents. This phenomenon is especially obvious if the parent is of foreign birth. Often, entire phrases and colloquial expressions are blurted out that are replications of the parent's speech pattern, or even in the parent's native language.

Step 2: Clients rapidly achieve their own insights and draw their own conclusions from saying the voice and then formulate their own ideas about the sources of their distorted views and attitudes. They connect specific voices with discrete parental attitudes and interactions that defined them, either explicitly or implicitly. In Step 2, they discuss and develop these insights with the therapist.

> Bill: I was shocked by how vicious my voice attacks became. I had no idea those feelings were there. They immediately reminded me of my father and how he felt toward me. I was small and sickly, and he ridiculed me for not being athletic like the other boys. He was so critical.
>
> Therapist: That's what you thought of from saying your voices?
>
> Bill: Yeah, he acted like I was a freak!

Step 3: Clients formulate an answer back to the voice and challenge it directly as though they were addressing an actual person. Since people tend to identify the voice in relation to parental figures during Step 2, they often end up talking back directly to their parents in a form of psychodrama. There are two approaches to answering back. In the analytic approach, clients respond rationally with a more realistic, objective self-appraisal. In the cathartic method, they respond emotionally with anger and forcefulness, and often sadness.

> Therapist: How would you answer back to those voice attacks?
>
> Bill: You're wrong about me. There's nothing wrong with me. When I get in my head and listen to you, I get self-conscious. That's when I'm awkward. But otherwise, I'm a nice guy and I like women.
>
> Therapist: Say it louder. Stand up for yourself.
>
> Bill: You don't know what you're talking about [emotionally]. I'm not different from other men. I'm not a freak. I'm not repulsive! I'm a normal man and I'm sick of your way of ridiculing me. You were wrong about me!

Contradicting one's voice by defending one's own point of view represents an attack on the introjected parental images and is often akin to attacking the parents themselves. As such, it can cause considerable tension and self-recrimination. Voicing these angry, hostile feelings toward parental introjects in a session tends to disconnect a person from imagined or symbolic sources of security, and regressive trends may follow. Therefore, I tend to discourage dramatic answers to voice attacks for clients who appear to lack sufficient ego strength to cope with the resultant guilt and anxiety. In these cases, a non-dramatic evaluation of voice attacks on a cognitive level is less threatening and partially serves the purpose of separating out destructive elements and improving the client's self-concept. In challenging the power of the voice over their lives, behavior, and emotional state, people can make objective statements about traits and actions they like in themselves and those they wish to change.

Step 4: Clients attempt to understand the relationship between their voice attacks and their self-limiting and self-destructive behavior patterns. They identify how the voice has influenced the limitations that they impose on themselves in everyday life. Becoming aware of one's self-imposed restrictions reduces paranoid reactions to others and feelings of victimization.

Clients also evaluate the truth of their self-criticisms, that is, subjecting the content of voice attacks to a process of reality-testing. Although in many cases people's negative thoughts toward themselves are made up of real components regarding their undesirable behaviors or personality traits, angry affect and malicious attacks on the self are always unjustified. Self-evaluations that are realistically negative, yet objective, based on the underlying premise that people can change even long-standing character traits are very different from voices that categorize the client as inherently defective. During this phase of therapy, individuals learn that it is not appropriate to attack themselves for shortcomings or weaknesses; rather, it is more productive to work on modifying behaviors they dislike.

> Bill: I can see how listening to the voices about not being a real man and being a freak makes me feel so awkward around women. Then I act shy, like a nerd, and that's not very attractive. So it's been like a self-fulfilling prophecy. There's nothing wrong with me as a man, but I am acting like there is.
>
> Therapist: So you're believing your voice and acting accordingly?
>
> Bill: Yeah.

Step 5: Client and therapist attempt to interrupt the client's maladaptive behavior patterns through collaboratively planning for behavioral changes that are in accord with the client's personal motivation. These behavioral changes fall into two categories: (1) those that help control or interrupt self-feeding habits and disrupt dependency bonds; (2) those that expand the client's world by taking risks and gradually overcoming fears related to pursuing wants and priorities.

Bill: I'm going to take action to change this way of thinking about myself. For one thing, I'm not going to isolate myself anymore. I'm going to seek out friends to do things with, men and women. Avoiding my men friends keeps me feeling like I'm different from them. And avoiding women makes me feel more and more awkward around them. I want to challenge these voice attacks; they're ruining my life. And if it makes me feel anxious or makes me have voice attacks, I'll deal can deal with them in therapy.

Therapist: Yes, it's a process, but you can change your negative thinking and feeling.

During this final step in Voice Therapy, clients formulate the unique values that give their lives special meaning. Then they plan, with the therapist, means of supporting these goals. And lastly, as they move toward risk situations and a new level of vulnerability, they learn to tolerate the anxiety involved in positive changes. The overall procedure has an experimental flavor and is undertaken in a cooperative spirit.

The new set of circumstances, albeit more positive, is unfamiliar and initially leads to anxiety. Clients report that, although there are often strong voice attacks after significant movement, these self-attacks gradually diminish after the new behavior has been maintained for an extended period of time. The importance of teaching people to "sweat out" any major changes in their identity and style of relating cannot be overstated. In this sense, clients must relinquish their crutches *before* they learn that they will not fall without them. Only by coping with the anxiety generated by positive change can people hold on to the psychological territory they have gained.

People are understandably disconcerted and frightened to feel the depth of their animosity toward themselves. In an effort to achieve integration and appear more consistent in their behavior and attitudes, they frequently side with the alien point of view represented by the voice. Helping clients externalize negative thoughts enables them to cope more effectively with self-defeating, self-limiting, self-destructive tendencies. By identifying the destructive effects of internalized voices, discovering their source, and understanding the role they play in restricting one's current life, individuals can separate from the dictates of the voice and act in their own interest.

The technique of verbalizing the voice is an effective tool in unearthing the sources of people's feelings of self-hatred. It increases their understanding of the origins of their self-destructive urges and helps them separate from the incorporated parental view of themselves that is an overlay on their real self-image. The emotional catharsis that accompanies this exposure of the voice relieves tension and promotes positive feelings similar to the results I have observed following sessions of Feeling Release Therapy. By the time clients reach the ending phase, their personal goals have become clear and self-evident. They are acutely aware of the factors that are limiting their freedom, have compassion for themselves, and are focused on maintaining a concerted effort to change their actions.

GOALS OF VOICE THERAPY

In my book, *Voice Therapy* (1988), I delineated what I consider to be the ultimate goals of psychotherapy, which are to help individuals: (1) remain vulnerable and open to experience and feelings; (2) maintain the ability to respond in a realistic manner to both positive and negative events in their lives; and (3) achieve a free and independent existence.

In addition, because of its emphasis on taking action, Voice Therapy is practically oriented in that it directly challenges repetitive patterns of compulsive and self-defeating behaviors, allowing clients to develop and progress beyond results they may have achieved in other therapies. Voice Therapy sessions provide an opportunity for individuals to develop and practice countermeasures—ways of living and being—that they will continue to use throughout their lives in challenging their defenses. Some of these are as follows:

Remaining vulnerable and open to experience and feelings

Many people conceptualize vulnerability as a negative trait or weakness and view invulnerability as a strength. In contrast, I conceptualize vulnerability in positive terms and perceive openness to the possibility of being emotionally hurt as a powerful position to take in life. Living a relatively undefended, vulnerable life implies self-acceptance, inner strength, and the capacity to deal with uncertainty.

To achieve the goal of remaining open and undefended, clients should refrain from overreliance on substances and habit patterns that alter their experience or suppress feelings. This implies taking actions based on psychological insights that go beyond simply being receptive and open to feedback: it involves continually confronting addictive patterns, routines, and other self-protective behaviors that cut one off from truly experiencing one's life.

Maintaining an open, receptive stance entails the ability to uncritically accept all thoughts and feelings, including anger. In Voice Therapy, clients are encouraged to freely express their angry feelings as they arise. Therapist and client then evaluate the meaning or the underlying cause of their anger, explore the primal components, and discuss ways of dealing with anger in the current situation. This approach to anger offers clients relief and an understanding of their emotions, thus enabling them to act responsibly with regard to their feelings.

A related goal is learning to experience deep sadness without resorting to defensive maneuvers. As a therapist, I have found that many clients have an initial reluctance to experience or express sadness. Prior to therapy, they tend to confuse sadness with depression, a state that generally involves self-castigation, attacks, and anger turned against the self. Anticipating sad feelings appears to arouse primal fears and considerable tension, whereas the actual experience of feelings the sadness frequently brings relief. After expressing emotional pain or deep sadness, people usually feel more integrated and report a stronger sense of identity. When these feelings are accepted and allowed full expression, people experience fewer feelings of depression and have less need for the compulsive reliving of past trauma.

When individuals are open to their emotions and able to tolerate irrational, angry, competitive, or other so-called unacceptable feelings, they are not compelled to act these out on other people. This manifestation of mental health has broad implications. For example, in cases of emotional and physical child abuse, the inability to accept feelings of anger, hostility, and resentment causes many parents to extend these feelings to their children. As noted in the previous chapter, when parents are able to recognize and accept the destructive feelings they have toward their children, tension is reduced and damaging responses are minimized. In general, people who remain vulnerable and open to experiencing all emotions tend to be more willing to take reasonable risks in life and are more humane toward others.

When Voice Therapy techniques are used as an adjunct to a psychoanalytically oriented therapy, clients gradually become aware of their needs and desires within the transference relationship. They develop trust in the therapeutic setting and are able to risk asking directly for what they want. The inevitable limits to personal gratification inherent in the boundaries and discipline of psychotherapy necessarily lead to frustration of the client's primitive wishes. This provides a corrective emotional experience because, on a deep level, clients learn that they can survive without the gratification of their primal needs and are able to come to terms with their anger at being frustrated.

This is the crux of the analytic therapeutic process because in the course of facing their anger at the inevitable frustration, clients strengthen their independence and sense of self. This is a critical step in psychotherapy, which contributes to the development of a mature orientation to life. Clients recognize that, as adults, they can afford to be vulnerable because they are no longer helpless and powerless children, nor are they dependent on their parents for survival.

Maintaining the ability to respond appropriately to both positive and negative events

Prior to therapy, many clients, especially those who are cut off from their feelings, have melodramatic overreactions to personal slights yet display a curious lack of feeling in response to real adversity. In Voice Therapy, they are able to reconnect to long suppressed feelings and explore both the primal and realistic elements of the anger, sadness, and grief they are experiencing during sessions. They become increasingly aware of the specific events that trigger overly intense reactions, which are inappropriate to their present-day lives. They gradually learn how to respond with appropriate feelings to both positive and negative events. Moreover, by fully feeling their emotional reactions and then responding from an adult perspective, they are better able to cope with anxiety and stress, and are far less susceptible to regressing and forming neurotic symptoms.

Learning to live without illusions of connection—achieving a free and independent existence

In Voice Therapy, individuals alter their self-concept in a favorable direction and give up the previously held negative identity formed within the family system. In addition, they break with their idealization and protection of family members. In breaking with the idealization process, they are free to develop a more realistic view of themselves and their parents. This frees them to form better, more rewarding, personal relationships.

EVALUATION OF VOICE THERAPY

Voice Therapy was originally developed as a means to elicit and identify clients' negative thoughts and attitudes toward self, bringing them more into conscious awareness. As a psychotherapeutic methodology, it has proven to be largely effective in gaining access to core defenses and in facilitating changes to maladaptive behaviors. The procedures are relatively simple and easy to apply; nonetheless, the techniques deal with deep-seated character defenses and crucial psychological issues. Therefore, their application requires the skill of a professional who is sensitive to the guilt and anxiety involved in breaking away from habitual defenses and symbiotic relationships.

As is true in most depth psychotherapies, at the point where the client becomes aware that present-day limitations are closely related to early experiences in the family, intense feelings of anger, grief, and outrage are aroused, and clients sometimes experience a strong tendency to turn this rage against themselves. At this stage, serious regression may occur and there may be a corresponding breakdown in the therapeutic relationship. Therapists working with these specialized techniques should have a thorough understanding of the underlying theory to be able to help individuals through critical phases in their development (R. Firestone, 1990c).

SIMILARITIES AND DIFFERENCES BETWEEN VOICE THERAPY AND OTHER THERAPEUTIC METHODS

Separation Theory integrates aspects of several diverse approaches including psychoanalytic, cognitive-behavioral, emotionally focused methodologies and existential psychotherapies. The specialized techniques of Voice Therapy are similar in certain respects to Cognitive-Behavioral Therapy (CBT) (Beck, Rush, Shaw, & Emery, 1979), Rational-Emotive Therapy (RBT) (Ellis & Grieger, 1986), Dialectic Behavioral Therapy (DBT) (Linehan, 1993), and Gestalt Therapy (Oaklander, 1979; 2006); however, there are a number of noteworthy differences.

Most cognitive-behavioral therapies are short-term or time-limited interventions and are largely concerned with clients' reactions to present-day events. For example, Beck (1976) believed that it was unnecessary to explore causes of clients' distorted thinking, and asserted that, "the therapist focuses more on how the client misinterprets reality rather than on why." (p. 319). My approach is at variance with Beck's in that I *am* concerned with the dynamic origins of the voice. In Voice Therapy, clients automatically make connections between current destructive thought processes and early family experiences (Note 5).

My theoretical approach and methodology are more deeply rooted in the psychoanalytic approach than in cognitive-behavioral or Gestalt models. My theoretical focus is on understanding the psychodynamics of the client's disturbance in the present, and my methods are based on Separation Theory, which emphasizes a primary defensive process.

Both Beck (CBT) and Ellis (RET) recommend pointing out the illogic of the client's thinking, whereas in my approach, the therapist neither refutes the client's logic nor focuses on it. Instead, clients make their own symbolic or direct memory connections to the sources of their disordered thinking. When utilizing Voice Therapy techniques, therapists do not take an educational, analytical approach, nor do they directly persuade their clients to think or behave rationally.

As noted, the goal is to help individuals discover what they are telling themselves about situations in their everyday lives and to assist them in moving away from destructive parental attitudes and prohibitions. Gestalt Therapy is similar to Jungian analytical psychotherapy in that its practitioners try to integrate negative elements—the shadow self—into the client's personality, whereas Voice Therapy methods help the client identify and separate from these destructive elements.

In recent years, cognitive-behavioral therapies have begun to deal more directly with feelings, at times even employing exercises that elicit emotional responses. However, their focus is still primarily on correcting clients' disordered thinking. In contrast, Voice Therapy techniques concentrate on bringing clients' strong emotions to the surface. In addition, the overall approach incorporates deep feeling release sessions that access clients' most intense and primitive feelings. This helps free them from the constraining influences of destructive self-parenting. Clinicians trained in Separation

Theory and Voice Therapy methodology have reported that utilizing these techniques tends to create a sensitive and moving atmosphere in the session that enhances the client's ability to feel and relate to others.

QUALITIES OF THE EFFECTIVE THERAPIST

The personality of the therapist largely determines the emotional quality of the interaction that takes place between client and therapist. Research has shown that a number of specific personality characteristics of the therapist are correlated with the ability to form and sustain a constructive therapeutic alliance (Beutler & Harwood, 2000; Wampold, 2001). These characteristics are common to therapists across a wide range of treatment modalities.

Although all forms of psychotherapy challenge defenses to varying degrees and in general have positive results (Chambless & Ollendick, 2001; Hansen, Lambert, & Forman, 2002), there are certain elements that are crucial to a psychotherapeutic endeavor achieving a successful outcome. First, the therapeutic process must support the truth and place it above any form of protecting false assumptions about the family, society, or human beings. Therefore, therapists must be open to the painful realities that clients reveal and must refuse to place social conformity over the interests of their individual clients.

Ideally, the therapist would have integrity and personal honesty and be uncompromising in his/her approach to defenses that limit and debilitate clients. As a catalyst and facilitator, he/she must also be sensitive to the wide range of addictive patterns that may be manifested by clients and have the courage to help expose and interrupt these patterns.

Therapists must be exceedingly skillful in helping their clients reconnect to themselves and their lives. To move toward this goal, the therapist, like an artist, must be sensitive to clients' real feelings, qualities, and priorities, and distinguish them from the overlay on the personality that prevents the clients from reaching their full potential. Effective therapists do not try to fit their clients into a particular theoretical framework or model. Instead, they are willing to experience the truths that their clients reveal over the course of treatment and to respond as clients' individual needs dictate. Otto Rank (1935, quoted in Kramer, 1996) asserted that:

> No therapy can succeed unless it is flexible enough to allow for whatever approach seems to be necessary for different individuals.

After all, it is the client who counts and it is his psychology that we have to study and follow instead of creating therapeutic ideologies to suit certain individual therapists or special schools (p. 262).

Rank further explained that although each client obviously possesses a number of human elements common to all people, these human potentialities should only be used as hypotheses when getting to know a particular client. According to Rank, effective therapists base their understanding of each client on the contents of his/her unique productions (e.g., dreams, fantasies, narratives, and mode of relating to the therapist) rather than on a specific conceptual model of human behavior.

In my work as a psychotherapist, I view the psychotherapy experience as a personal adventure and significant learning experience. I want to learn a great deal about the client in the first session because I will typically be involved with this person for a long time. The session is not only diagnostic—an attempt to determine the primary issues and correct therapy application—but also personal. I want to know how I feel about this individual. I particularly want to test how he/she responds to feedback and interpretation in order to determine the prognosis for a good working relationship. For this reason, the initial sessions are very exciting and there are a number of personal exchanges back and forth. When the overall interaction has a positive valence and I accept the client, I know that both of us are about to have a unique and profound experience.

Good therapists never predetermine or set their own personal agendas for clients, nor do they impose their values and biases on a client's development. Instead, they attempt to gain greater access to the client's point of view. Although strong in their optimism and belief in the possibility of personal growth and change, they do not underestimate the strength of a person's defense system and are sensitive to the fear underlying resistance (Note 6).

As much as possible, therapists should avoid establishing a doctor/client dynamic. Instead, they are open to investigating voices within themselves as part of the counter-transference reaction and are aware of their own self-limiting behavior patterns. In this respect, Voice Therapy tends to be a great equalizer; that is, the therapist is a real person in the therapeutic relationship, not a superior human being applying a predetermined technique.

In addition, the ideal therapist would be capable of relating to the client in empathic exchanges in which the interpersonal contact resonates phenomenologically with the intrapersonal. The therapist responds by reaching into him/herself and reaching out to the client. Simultaneously maintaining internal feelings for him/herself and external feelings toward the client allows for real communication and rapport, or "co-presence." Laing (1985a) specified that this condition is an essential ingredient of a positive therapeutic encounter. The communication that takes place during these moments is largely nonverbal, yet potentially curative. The combination of empathy, compassion, and insightfulness all work together to produce positive therapeutic movement.

The therapist can be conceptualized as a transitional object in that he/she provides a genuine relationship for the client during the transition from depending on self-nurturing processes to seeking satisfaction in real relationships in the external world (Winnicott, 1958; 1971) (Note 7). In serving this function, therapists would remain human—that is, they would be interested and warm as well as direct and responsible. This would support or sustain the client as he/she moves away from fantasy gratification toward authentic relationships and the pursuit of personal and vocational goals.

The good therapist also anticipates the termination phase by continually encouraging the independent development of healthy ego functioning. Excessive dependence on the therapist and attempts to seek fusion are discouraged; instead, transference reactions are interpreted and worked through with sensitivity and proper timing. In regard to the final phases of psychotherapy, working on termination addresses transference reactions, resolves the dependency bond between the client and therapist, and establishes equality between the two participants. Positive therapeutic outcome involves successfully coping with the anxiety of separation, signaling an end to the need for office visits and indicating the person's potential for a self-support system.

Because there is a great deal of controversy in the field of psychology regarding the most effective methods of psychotherapy, at the least the therapist *can* offer the client an honest interaction, marked by personal integrity, strength of character, and the moral courage to challenge the status quo. The therapeutic process offers the client a renewed opportunity for personal development that transcends virtually any other mode of experience. Therefore, this opportunity for growth must not be limited or interfered with by the therapist's defenses or tendencies to deny unpleasant truths that may be uncovered by the client over the course of treatment.

THE DILEMMA OF PSYCHOTHERAPY

Most people have very little awareness of how much they are afraid, or even terrified, of freely pursuing their goals, achieving personal power, and finding satisfaction in loving interactions. Prior to therapy, the client may have underestimated the distress and anxiety involved in establishing a new identity and long-lasting relationships that are free from a fantasy bond. The essential dilemma of cure may be stated as follows: the individual who progresses in therapy faces an increased awareness of death and intensified feelings of death anxiety. As he/she reaches out to life, there is a greater realization of a finite existence.

Yet, the problem facing the client is basically no different from that faced by every human being. As one studies the situation, the alternatives become clear: without challenging destructive aspects of ourselves, we will gradually submit to an alien, inimical point of view and shut down our authentic self and unique outlook; on the other hand, disrupting these self-protective defenses intensifies our awareness of life's tragic dimensions and threatens at times to overwhelm us with feelings of helplessness and dread.

Clients' fears of change are related to each dimension of life: an increased potential for feeling both happiness and sorrow, the problematic nature of intimate relationships, the circumstances of a troubled world, destructive societal forces, and the fear of losing through death everything gained through expanding one's boundaries. Juxtaposed against this fear is the knowledge that only by abandoning defenses and fantasy bonds can one avoid inflicting incidental damage on other people. In addition to expanding opportunities for personal gratification and becoming better adjusted, remaining vulnerable and undefended becomes an ethical choice, given the alternatives.

CONCLUSION

The ultimate goal of my therapeutic approach is to help individuals find satisfaction in life. To this end, the process of identifying the voice and the associated feelings of self-hatred and rage toward self, combined with corrective strategies of behavioral change, significantly expand the client's boundaries and bring about a more positive image of self.

In recognizing and gradually giving up the authority of the voice as an anti-feeling, anti-life, regulatory mechanism, a person feels far less victimized or blaming and far more compassionate toward self and others. One becomes, in the best sense of the word, an explorer, an investigator, as it were, uncritically accepting and examining one's most irrational thoughts and feelings, while at the same time viewing others and the world with a very real curiosity and concern. As Thomas Malone (1981) said:

> The task of psychotherapy is to make the ordinary a full experience
> . . . to uncover, or reactivate . . . the experiential dimensions of the
> ordinary experience (p. 91).

The examined life is rich with opportunities for personal growth and offers a unique and powerful approach to self-understanding. Yet, psychotherapy is much more than a methodology designed to cure neuroses; it offers an unparalleled opportunity to open one's eyes and expand one's world.

Notes

1. Ginot (1997) emphasized "the contribution that the analyst's self-disclosure may have for the patient's struggle to integrate unconscious aspects of the self" (p. 365). Also see Arnold Lazarus (1994) who contended that, "those therapists who always go by the book and apply predetermined and fixed rules of conduct (specific dos and don'ts) across the board will offend or at the very least fail to help people who might otherwise have benefited from their ministrations" (p. 257).

2. In terms of the neuronal basis of the fear of change, see Louis Cozolino (2015), who suggested, "What we usually call resistance may simply be primitive brain circuitry engaging in anxiety reduction by holding onto the beliefs that make us feel safe. As bad as your life may be, your amygdala pairs it with survival every moment you avoid death—change, even for the better, activates anxiety" (Loc. 455).

3. John N. Rosen (1953) communicated with hospitalized schizophrenic patients in a way that led to observable changes, especially with patients who were in the early stages of schizophrenia. He helped these people to change very serious conditions, for example, states of extreme catatonic excitement when the patients would normally develop high fevers and die.

4. For a historical development of perspectives held by major theorists in the field of psychology regarding the importance of accessing emotions in psychotherapy see L. Greenberg and Safran (1987) and L. Greenberg, Rice and Elliot (1993) who proposed that "Direct emotional experience has a salience that overrides other cues or concepts to reorganize and restructure people's views of themselves and the situation" (p. 192). EFT's focus on accessing emotion and providing clients with a "corrective emotional experience" is similar to my focus on clients' expressions of deep emotion in Feeling Release Therapy and Voice Therapy.

5. The major differences between Cognitive-Behavior Therapy, Rational-Emotive Therapy, and Voice Therapy can be found in (1) the importance that each system places on investigating the etiology of the patient's illness; (2) the theory of personality upon which the therapeutic methodology is based; (3) the techniques utilized to identify and correct dysfunctional thinking; and (4) the view of emotion or affect. Phil Shaver (2013) noted: "[In] Voice Therapy, the emotional impact of stating the thoughts out loud and directing them at oneself is much more powerful and insight-provoking than the general `cognitions' or statements one finds, for example, in Albert Ellis's books (e.g., 2001) about rational-emotive therapy" (p. x).

6. In his practice of relational therapy, Paul Wachtel (2008), approaches clients in a manner that is similar in many respects to my own approach. According to Wachtel, relational therapy "aims to *expand* his [the client's] conscious experience…The key to effective psychotherapeutic practice lies in embracing and working with the dialectical tensions between the patient's need for affirmation and his need for change" (Loc. 5157).

7. The term "transitional object" was introduced by Winnicott in *Collected Papers* (1958) and later elaborated in *Playing and Reality* (1971): "The term 'transitional object,' according to my suggestion, gives room for the process of becoming able to accept difference and similarity. I think there is use for a term for the root of symbolism in time, a term that describes the infant's journey from purely subjective to objectivity; and it seems to me that the transitional object (piece of blanket, etc.) is what we see of this journey of progression towards experiencing" (1971, pp. 6-7).

Sources: *The Evolution of a Psychotherapist* (unpublished manuscript); "Voice Therapy" in *What is Psychotherapy? Contemporary Perspectives* (Zeig & Munion Eds.,1990); "Prescription for Psychotherapy", (1990b); Chapter 9 "The Value of Psychotherapy' In *Beyond Death Anxiety: Achieving Life-Affirming Death Awareness.* (2009); Chapter 10 "Approach to Psychotherapy and Chapter 15 "The Essential Paradox in Psychotherapy" in *"Combating Destructive Thought Processes: Voice Therapy and Separation Theory.* (1997); Chapter 17 "Psychotherapy Overview" in *The Fantasy Bond* (1985); and Chapter 12 "The Dilemma of Psychotherapy" in *Voice Therapy: A Psychotherapeutic Approach to Self-Destructive Behavior.*

Chapter 13

VOICE THERAPY APPLICATION TO COUPLE RELATIONSHIPS AND PARENTING GROUPS

Love takes off the masks that we fear we cannot live without and know we cannot live within.

~ James A. Baldwin (1963)

Voice Therapy is both a laboratory procedure and a psychotherapy technique. In the laboratory setting, it has provided the means for eliciting and identifying partly conscious or unconscious negative thought patterns that impair personality functioning and damage relationships. The technique has been effectively applied in evaluating suicide and violence potential, individual therapy, group therapy, couples therapy, problems in sexual relating, and specialized parenting groups as a form of preventive psychotherapy.

APPLICATION OF VOICE THERAPY TO COUPLES

Voice Therapy techniques are particularly applicable to couples' therapy and problems in sexual relating. They are effective in uncovering defenses that directly affect the compulsive reliving of the past with new persons. In applying the principle technique of Voice Therapy to couples, individual partners verbalize their self-critical thoughts in the second person format, as was explained in the previous chapter. For example, attacks such as "I feel unattractive; I'm unlovable", would be voiced as, *You're unattractive; You're unlovable.*

Destructive attitudes in couples can be described as a malignant form of coaching, telling clients negative things about their mates and themselves. People's cynical attitudes toward their partners are verbalized in the third person format, as though someone else were imparting the information to them about their partner. For example, thoughts like, *Don't get seriously involved with her, she's so childish.* Or, *He's cold and rejecting. He doesn't really care about you.* Or, *She's so vain, why would you want to get involved with her?*

The Therapeutic Process in Couples Therapy

In conjoint sessions or couples' groups, partners generally progress through the following steps over the course of treatment: (1) formulating the problem each individual perceives is limiting his/her satisfaction within the relationship; (2) learning to verbalize self-critical thoughts and negative perceptions about their mates in the form of the voice and releasing the associated affect; (3) developing insight into the origins of the voice; (4) answering back to the voice from one's own point of view; (5) making connections between past experience and present conflicts; and (6) altering behaviors and communications in a direction that counteracts the dictates of the voice. This process helps both individuals take back their projections and allows them to stop blaming and criticizing each other

In the sessions, both partners are present as each reveals the self-attacking voices as well as the voice attacks they have toward their partner. In a real sense, they are sharing in each other's individual psychotherapy. In tracing back the source of their self-criticisms and cynical views to early family interactions, each gains perspective about the other's problems and feels more compassion for their partner, as well as for themselves.

Partners can participate in sessions together from the beginning. However, the therapist may determine that the couple would first benefit from having individual sessions where they might feel less inhibited in expressing their angry, hostile voice attacks about their partner. After they have learned to separate incorporated attitudes from their own point of view, conjoint sessions are more productive.

When exploring their voice attacks toward their partner, people often speculate about which critical statements their parents or other significant early figures might hold regarding their mate's behaviors and personality traits. For example, *He's so weak and pathetic!* Or, *She's so overbearing and bossy!* Partners should attempt to be sincere and sensitive when giving away their negative thoughts. The point of this step is to give away the inner voice attacks. Partners must try to relinquish critical views and grudges along with any underlying hostility, even when the voice attacks have some basis in reality.

Case Example of Utilizing Voice Therapy with a Couple

For the first two years that Don, 30, and Rachel, 37, lived together, they enjoyed an intimate, loving relationship. However, after that time, they became increasingly alienated and their interactions were characterized by arguments, which were stressful to both of them. They sought professional help to confront these problems with the goal of recapturing the feelings of companionship, emotional closeness and passion they had initially enjoyed.

Step 1: Formulating the problem. In this step, partners are encouraged to listen respectfully to the other person as he/she expresses feelings, thoughts and opinions about the problem they are experiencing in their relationship. In their first conjoint session, Rachel describes a typical interaction with Don:

Rachel: Every time Don and I try to talk things over, I start feeling bad. Even if we're just trying to decide something simple like where to go for dinner, or something more complicated like our finances, I start feeling tense and agitated. Then Don reacts to me and says, "Look, if you're going to act nervous, like I'm criticizing you, then I'd just as soon not talk at all."

Don's so judgmental these days, but he didn't used to be this way. A few months ago, we were getting closer and closer and even thinking about getting married. Then I was promoted at work. Maybe that's what changed everything. Now he acts like I'm lording it over him somehow, because I'm making more money than he is.

I feel totally misunderstood, because I don't feel superior at all. But I do get angry at him and try to argue my side. Sometimes I just walk out of the room crying, and that makes him even angrier. I end up feeling powerless, like a little girl. The thing that's really puzzling to me is I don't feel nervous or insecure in other areas of my life. I'm a really level-headed, confident person at work, so it has something to do specifically with our relationship.

Don describes how he conceptualizes their difficulties:

Don: I realize that I *am* critical at times. I guess I do feel resentful about Rachel making more money than me, but she's also spending a lot more. Sometimes I get so frustrated with her. [turning to Rachel] I know that you're smart, look at what you've accomplished at work! But with me, you act all nervous. Sometimes you talk so fast trying to defend yourself I can't get a word in edgewise. That really irritates me. And it's provoking when you act childish about our finances, asking dumb questions. If I even mention any concern about our finances, I end up feeling like I'm the meanest guy in the world. And we used to have so much fun doing anything together. [sad]

Whereas initially their relationship had been more equal, Don and Rachel had become polarized in a collusive parent/child pattern of interaction. This polarization fostered defensive reactions and counter-reactions in both people. Their relating became increasingly characterized by bickering and outright hostility, and there was a reduction in the respectful exchange of thoughts, opinions, and feelings between them.

Later in the session, Rachel said that she had begun to doubt Don's feelings for her. She revealed that he wasn't very affectionate anymore and didn't seem interested in being sexual, which left her feeling insecure and self-hating. She admitted feeling a little guilty about making more money than Don, who was just starting out in a new career. Don admitted feeling slightly self-conscious about the fact that Rachel earned more money than he did, but he strongly disapproved of her spending habits and her "careless disregard of money and of my feelings."

Step 2: Verbalizing destructive thoughts and releasing feeling. In this step, both partners, in turn, verbalize (a) voice attacks toward themselves and their partner, and (b) negative attitudes they believe significant family members have about them, their partner, and their life. They also express any feelings that surface while articulating these destructive thoughts and attitudes. It is important for each partner to openly admit and take responsibility for his/her negative attacks in a nonjudgmental style and not to react to the voice statements of the other as personal criticism.

A frequently asked question is whether or not the partner feels personally attacked, hurt, or angry when these negative voices are verbalized by the other. In truth, most people are relieved to hear their partner's hostile statements spoken aloud. It often makes explicit attitudes they have picked up from their partner nonverbally. Further, in the process of listening to their mate express the cynical, distrusting attitudes, it becomes clear to each partner that these are alien attitudes that neither one agrees with.

Dr. Firestone: What are your voices about Don?

Rachel: They sound sort of like: *He's so critical of you! You can't do anything right in his eyes. And he's so rejecting. He doesn't care about you the way he used to. And who is he to criticize you about money? He's such a loser!*

Dr. Firestone: Whose point of view do you think that represents?

Rachel: That's definitely my mother's view of my father. She always complained about him being cold and unavailable. And she hated that he didn't have a better job and make more money. But I liked him; he was warmer and more loving to me than she was. I hated seeing the way she treated him.

Dr. Firestone: And that hurt you.

Rachel: Yes. When I was little he doted on me and I had the feeling that he liked me more than he liked my mother. But I felt like it was only for my looks; he was critical of everything else, my schoolwork, how I was at sports, my friends. He wanted me to be perfect.

My relationship with my mother was horrible. She always said we were so different. We were always fighting. But if it ever came down to where it was either her or me, my father always supported her. Even though she treated him badly too, as much as she treated me that way.

Dr. Firestone: It's like you've incorporated your father's critical attitudes toward you as well as your mother's feelings toward your father; that's the part you're directing toward Don. What about yourself? What are your voices toward yourself?

Rachel: I'm not feminine. I'm not a real woman.

Dr. Firestone: Say it as a voice.

Rachel: It's like: *You're not a real woman. You're not pretty. You're . . .*

Dr. Firestone: Say it with feeling. Really listen to it. Let yourself feel this. It's okay. Just really let yourself feel it.

Rachel: *You're not like other women. And you're getting older. Why would Don still be attracted to you? He's way more interested in younger women. You're not like them. You're not feminine. You're not lovable like other women.*

I can also feel my mother's view of me; it's like she would say: *I hate you. I hate your face. You're not right. You don't look right. You're not cute; you're not pretty, even though your father thinks so. You don't act right. You're different from anybody in this family. I'm embarrassed by you.*

Dr. Firestone: It looks like you're feeling a lot.

Rachel: It's interesting that you said that, because one of the attacks she made on me was like: *You're cold. You don't feel anything. You don't care about anybody but yourself.*

Dr. Firestone: Do you have any other voices about Don?

Rachel: The other voices I have about Don are about his holding back affection. *He never takes the initiative when you make love. He's so passive. He's not going to make things happen. You have to make it happen. You have to go after him.*

Rachael (*to Don*): It's hard to say these voices because I care so much about you.

Dr. Firestone: What about you, Don? What are your voices about yourself?

Don: I don't think of them in terms of attacks on myself but I definitely attack the relationship.

Dr. Firestone: Do you want to say your attacks on the relationship?

Don: Lately, for instance, she's been expressing her affection by saying that she loves me, and I know that I have a really hard time believing it. I think that she's lying. *She doesn't feel it. She doesn't really love you or respect you. She's just trying to get something from you. She's trying to suck you in so you'll believe her. She's just trying to pull a response out of you. I* don't think this part clearly, but I'm pretty sure I don't feel worthy of being loved.

Dr. Firestone: Say that as a voice. You're not worthy of being loved.

Don: It's like, *There's no way somebody could really love you.*

Dr. Firestone: That's right. Go ahead. Like that.

Don: *You're no good. You're pathetic. You're a failure. How the hell could somebody be interested in you?* [angry, loud voice] *You may be able to fool them for a little while but they're going to find out you're really bad, that you'll never amount to anything!* [sad] I know my father always thought I was a bum, a troublemaker, through and through.

My mother questioned me endlessly about school and especially about any girls I dated. She intruded into my life so much it was ridiculous. She and my father had no sexual life as far as I could tell. I felt like she was focused more on me than on my father.

Dr. Firestone: What are your voices when you and Rachel have those arguments?

Don: When we get into an argument, it's like I can hear my father's voice in my head, saying: *You'll never get anywhere arguing with her. She's like a stubborn child! Look, just give up on her. She'll never grow up. Sure, she was a good companion and friend for a while, but look what's happened now. She's just like your mother!* I had to put up with her childishness, over-spending and lies for years.

Those are the attacks I have on Rachel, but mostly I turn on myself and have attacks like: *You don't care about anybody but yourself! You don't give a damn about her, or about anybody! You're incapable of loving anyone. You're just like your father!* Obviously, that's my mother's point of view.

Dr. Firestone: Rachel, you really *do* think that you are different and peculiar and disgusting and not right. You really believe it. And you weave in the age difference to put yourself down. It affects your whole relationship and your attitudes toward yourself and toward Don, both. With you, Don, you have your father's attitude toward women: that you can't give them what they need. You just can't give them all that they want or that they're demanding of you.

The dynamics operating in this relationship underscore the fact that both partners were using the other to validate the negative identity formed in their families of origin. Rachel was using Don to confirm a view of herself as unlovable, desperate and childish. She was holding on to low-grade anger and hostility toward her husband and she acted out a child-like, victimized role in relation to him. For his part, Don was using Rachel to support his view that he was mean by being critical and condescending toward her, especially when discussing their finances. It appeared that they both had become anxious as their relationship became more meaningful and had retreated to a less vulnerable, more defended posture.

Step 3: Discussing insights achieved from partners expressing their voices. In this step, each partner discusses the insights they have achieved regarding the origins of their voices. As a result of saying their voice attacks and separating from a point of view that is not their own, people gain more clarity about their lives. Releasing feelings often leads to recovering implicit memories of early attachment trauma and loss. These new insights allow people to make sense of their childhoods and develop an understanding of their personal history. This helps them keep their past out of their current lives.

> Rachel: I remember that things got really horrible after my parents divorced when I was around seven. There were times that we had absolutely no money. Then my mother would get really panicky. So those are the feelings that come up in me whenever Don and I have a discussion about finances. I get into such a guilty, anxious state that I don't make any sense. I just start talking fast or crying and he gets furious.

> Dr. Firestone: That distortion really cuts into your relationship with Don. It's hard to have an equal relationship when you are thrown back into reliving your childhood. If you could learn to recognize that your emotional reactions are exaggerated because they pertain to old situations and old fears, then you and Don would be able to talk in a more rational way, as two adults.

After listening to Rachel describe her childhood of financial insecurity, Don felt empathic toward her and more optimistic about their relationship.

> Don (*to Rachel*): For the first time, I understand how you must have felt back then. I feel sorry for whatever I do to make you feel more

afraid. It's amazing how our voices fit together. And once I'm angry, I'm back to where I was as a kid: critical of you like my father was toward my mother, and then feeling like the angry, mean person my mother accused me of being for not telling her everything about my life.

Although Rachel and Don originally came to therapy to improve their relationship, an additional benefit was that both partners became stronger personally, more centered in themselves. In the sessions, they discovered that they had begun living their lives largely based on destructive thought processes and parental prescriptions rather than on fulfilling their personal desires and goals. After realizing the influence of the negative voices, they began to challenge the thought processes that were causing conflict in their relationship.

Step 4: Answering back to voice attacks. In this step, partners formulate responses to their self-attacks and distorted views of the other person.

Dr. Firestone (*to Rachel*): What would you say back to the voice, to your mother's view of you?

Rachel: My answer feels really angry. "You lived like a victimized child. You were bitter and blamed everything on your husband. Well, that's not my life. I'm strong and I'm not a victim of anything. Don loves me and I love him. And he's not mean and critical toward me like you were. I always thought I had to take punishment from you. I felt like I deserved it, but I was wrong. You're a self-centered, punishing bitch! He's so different from you. I have such a different life than I had living with you, especially the way it was after Dad left. I'm not going to repeat that today in *my* life!"

Don said that he felt touched to hear Rachel standing up for herself and defending him against her mother's point of view. He then answered back to his own voice attacks.

Don: I feel like standing up for myself too and saying back to my mother's voices, "Leave me alone! Stop asking me questions. I'm not a mean person just because I don't answer all your questions or because I get angry sometimes! Everyone gets angry."

And my answer to my father's point of view would be like, "I'm not a failure. I'm not a bum. I'm not worthless . . . I'm not bad! [sad] *You* were a failure. As a husband and father."

It feels good just to hear my voice sounding loud. I used to feel louder and more self-assured. That was more like the real me. I used to express my feelings and my anger more directly and not get so wrapped up in it. But after we started to have these problems, I got worried that I was becoming an angry, mean man like my father. I began believing my mother's attack on me.

My rational answer to her attack is, "I'm not mean, I'm not a failure, and I don't have to be judgmental with Rachel. I can just express myself directly without being condescending." *(to Rachel)* I know within myself that I really care about you, Rachel, I really love you.

Rachel *(to Don)*: I felt a lot when you were talking. I felt sad about how you were treated when you were a kid. I felt a lot of pain for you.

Don: Thanks for saying that. I realize that I've had a block against looking at my part in keeping this whole thing going. As long as I believed that you saw me as mean and judgmental, I couldn't see that I was making those attacks on myself. And I couldn't see that they were really how my mother saw me. I sort of understood it intellectually, but I haven't been able to really see it until now.

Step 5: Making connections between past experience and present conflicts. In this step, clients reflect on what they have learned from saying their voices, identifying their sources, and answering back to them, and then apply their insights to their current relationship problems.

Rachel: Our relationship used to be equal, but now we're relating more like a parent and child. We've been stuck in this polarized pattern for a while. And we trigger each other. I'm childish and insecure, and he feels angry and pulled on. He's parental and critical, and I feel rejected and unloved. It's clear to me that I've been reliving my relationship with my mother, reacting like I'm being disapproved of and hated. Then I get desperate toward Don, which makes things worse.

Dr. Firestone: Don, what are your thoughts?

Don: I've been feeling angrier and angrier in this relationship, like I really *am* a mean bastard. But from saying my voices, I recognize that this feeling was how I experienced my father, and it was also the feelings my mother had toward me. I've been reacting to Rachel's insecurity just like I did to my mother's hunger and intrusiveness. But Rachel isn't my mother and I'm not a helpless child, either. Listening to Rachel in these sessions has made that apparent to me. Instead of hating her insecurity, I feel for her and see that it doesn't really have anything to do with me.

Step 6: Planning and implementing suggestions to change behaviors dictated by the voice. In this final step, the couple and therapist collaborate to identify specific behaviors based on each partner's voices that interfere with them having a close relationship. Then they plan actions to take that would counteract what their voices are directing them to do. As they implement their plans, they discuss any resistance they encounter or that arise as a result of their taking the actions to challenge their voices.

Dr. Firestone: It seems like things are going in the right direction. If you both continue to be aware of your voices, you'll be able to communicate better, instead of using each other to feel bad. That's the most important part, to actually be friends and allies by not being on the defensive in your conversations.

Rachel: *(to Don)* I feel so much more on my own side right now. I can certainly be as adult here with you as I am at work. I can stop acting so nervous and insecure now that I know where those feelings are coming from. Also, I'm determined to stop focusing so much on what you're thinking and feeling toward me, and pay more attention to what I'm thinking. I want to know how I feel toward myself and toward you. I just want us to be close again.

Don: *(to Rachel)* From talking together like this, I've begun to feel closer to you, more affectionate and sexual. I really want our relationship back the way it was! I'm determined to be more respectful and direct in our conversations. I want to be more compassionate toward you about the things you are struggling with. I know that I can stop being so parental and listen to what you're saying without being condescending.

Tracing the origins of their self-attacks to childhood experiences ena-bled Rachel and Don to take back their projections and opened up the pos-sibility for real communication. Prior to therapy, Rachel and Don had been acting out complementary parent/child roles and inducing the same nega-tive thoughts and disturbing emotions in each other that they were experi-encing within themselves. In explaining this process, Scharff & Scharff (1991) noted that the partner who disowns undesirable traits in him/herself and projects them onto the other person, "so convincingly identifies the part of the self in the external object that the feeling state corresponding to that part of the self is evoked in the spouse" (p. 58) (Note 1).

The cycle of blame and counter-blame had become well-established in Rachel and Don's relationship. In therapy, they were able to straighten out their complicated aversive interactions only after they had gained a com-prehensive understanding of the voices operating within themselves and of how these were influencing their behavior.

In exposing their self-attacks and releasing the accompanying emotions, partners learn the specific ways they distort each other and are then able to take back their projections. By exploring the connections between their ear-ly experiences in the family and their current interactions with each other, they can learn to distinguish between their distortions and the real charac-teristics and behaviors manifested by their partner. They can also learn to realistically assess their own assets and liabilities. This process leads to an acceptance of ambivalent feelings toward themselves and their partner and, therefore, offers a more stable and honest perspective (Note 2).

In summary, Voice Therapy procedures uncover major defenses that di-rectly affect repetitive behavior and the recreation of the past in a new rela-tionship. Understanding that self-attacks are the primary source of misery in one's life takes pressure off of the relationship. Freeing this energy alters and improves partners' attitudes toward each other and enhances each indi-vidual's personal growth.

APPLICATION OF VOICE THERAPY TO PARENTING GROUPS

Utilizing Voice Therapy procedures in specialized parenting groups can help parents uncover the source of their ambivalent attitudes toward them-selves and their children, which enables them to gain control over destructive childrearing practices. The dimension of these parenting groups that sets them apart from other parenting groups is their dual focus on: (1) parents' attitudes toward their children, and (2) the experiences parents went through in their own childhood. This twofold emphasis helps them have more compassion for themselves by developing feeling for what happened to them as children. The goal is for parents to develop an empathic understanding of the sources of their limitations and then to see their child from that same perspective, that is, to pass on this sensitive view to their offspring. Regaining feeling for themselves may well be the key element that enables parents to alter their child-rearing practices in a positive direction (Note 3).

In specialized parenting groups, Voice Therapy methods are used to help the participants express their ambivalent feelings and attitudes about their children, to reflect on relevant events from their own childhoods and to release repressed affect. By acknowledging the inadequacies in their family of origin in this way, parents can then make connections between their own early defenses and their present-day limitations as parents.

Expressing Ambivalent Feelings and Attitudes

Parents first present the problems about their children that concern them. These can be difficulties in the parent/child relationship or complaints relating to a particular aspect of their child's life that is causing them worry or distress. They are encouraged to express their attitudes in relation to their child and then translate them into the third person format of Voice Therapy, as though someone else were telling them something about their child. For example, "He's so defiant. He goes against everything I say. He hates me!" "She's driving me crazy!" becomes, *He's so defiant and he's against everything you tell him!* Or, *She's so irresponsible. You've got to make her take it seriously. She's making you crazy!*

Parents are then encouraged to reveal the negative attitudes that they have toward themselves, and verbalize them in the second person format of Voice Therapy, as though someone were talking to them. For example, statements like "I don't know what to do. I can't make him do what I say." "I'm so ineffective as a parent." "This is all my fault; I've been too indulgent." Are spoken as a voice, *You're so ineffective as a parent. No wonder your kids don't respect you.* Or, *It's all your fault; you've been so indulgent and weak.*

After saying these voices, parents discuss their ambivalent reactions toward their children and identify the specific circumstances, situations, and types of behavior in their children that arouse hostile feelings. Participants are often able to make connections between their self-attacks and the aggressive, resentful attitudes manifested toward their children.

In a parenting group, Mark, who was raised by a harsh, authoritarian father, spoke about the intense emotional reactions he had toward his son, Doug, whenever he sensed the young boy was frightened of trying something new.

Mark: With Doug, situations come up where I want him to do something and he doesn't want to do it. He says either that he doesn't want to do it, or that he doesn't know how. Or he is scared about it—whatever it is. But I think that he could and should do it. And when he doesn't do it, I get so angry, because [pause]—

I know that I have this same feeling in myself that if I feel like I'm supposed to be able to do something, then I've got to do it! [angry tone] I think things like, *You've got to do it. Do it now! What's the matter with you?* Then if I don't do it, I feel extremely critical of myself for not doing it.

I feel exactly the same way with Doug. I feel furious because he won't do it, and then I feel like it's some basic failure in his life and failure in my parenting him. Then I feel like I have to make him really do it.

It becomes really crucial. Those are the worst times between us. I make issues of things like, 'Cut your meat the right way!' or, 'You just climb the ladder, you can climb it.' [Yelling] 'Climb the ladder!' And he would be so afraid. [sad] Thinking about it like this, I know I have exactly the same set of feelings toward myself.

While describing the turbulent feelings aroused in him by his son's timidity, Mark recalled feeling terrified as a child in similar situations with his own father. However, not until he talked about the specific characteristics and behaviors in his son that had triggered his fury did he develop insight into both himself and their relationship. Connecting his self-censure with the harsh feelings he had toward his son led to a sense of compassion and kinship with the boy.

Participants reported experiencing a sense of relief from feeling guilty about the negative attitudes they held toward their children after expressing them in the accepting, nonjudgmental atmosphere of the group. As other parents revealed similar feelings of resentment and anger toward their children, they felt less ashamed and more curious about these feelings within themselves.

Recalling Significant Events

Participants are asked to remember and refer to experiences in own their families that had caused them pain or anxiety. As they reveal stressful or traumatic incidents from their past, they often become aware of uncanny parallels between the specific abuses they suffered in their development and their own faulty patterns of childrearing.

One woman described having been abandoned by her mother when she was two years old. In a repetition of the mother's desertion, this woman had left her own son when he was a toddler due to overwhelming feelings that she was unfit as a mother. However, at the time, she failed to connect the two events in her mind. Later, in sharing her experiences with others in the parenting group, she recognized the full impact of her mother leaving her and understood that she had unconsciously and compulsively repeated her mother's pattern. She also realized that she had somehow blamed herself for her mother's desertion. When she became a mother, this repressed guilt had emerged and manifested itself in her own feelings of being unfit.

Releasing Repressed Affect

Most people tend to deny the traumas from early interactions within their families, as well as to minimize the emotional impact these incidents had on them as children. However, these memories are validated if people feel the emotions associated with the painful events. For parents, experiencing these feelings is necessary to develop compassion for themselves and their children. In the group setting, one person's revelations often stimulate the recovery of memories in others because of the commonality of experiences that occur during people's formative years.

Making connections between present-day limitations and early defenses

As parents talk more openly about themselves in this setting, they become cognizant of areas in their lives where they feel limited. They often bring up material relating to patterns of inwardness, passivity, forms of withholding, and passive-aggressive responses that they have found difficult to overcome. They are able to link these habit patterns and behaviors to specific events in childhood or to the emotional climate that originally caused them to construct dysfunctional defensive patterns. As individuals learn how they were limited in their early lives, they recognize that they were implicitly taught to blame themselves for their inadequacies. As they come to a deeper awareness of the sources of their weaknesses, they begin to adopt a more compassionate attitude toward themselves and their children.

Exposing inadequacies in their family of origin

As parents develop more sensitivity toward themselves, it is inevitable that they begin to challenge the idealized images they have held of their parents. Most people have strong tendencies to protect and excuse their parents and to rationalize the abuses they suffered as children. As they deal with these issues on a more profound level, they start to feel the full brunt of the outrage and grief they felt in being limited by these early experiences. Their basic attitude is not one of blaming, but more one of accounting for what happened in their childhood and reacting appropriately to the discoveries.

Becoming better parents

With this therapy, parents begin to develop a new perspective on how they are raising their children. They realize that they could be different from their own mothers and fathers. Becoming sensitive to their children in ways their parents were not tends to further break into the idealization of their families and the corresponding depreciation of themselves. They develop a new point of view concerning *their* parents, perceiving them more objectively as real people with strengths and weaknesses.

In isolating the traumatic experiences that were harmful to them in their formative years, parents can formulate positive attitudes and countermeasures that serve as constructive guidelines to childrearing practices which, in turn, minimize damage to their offspring. Thus, parents can become more successful in avoiding negative or destructive interactions with their children, as well as offering experiences that would enhance their child's self-esteem.

CONCLUSION

In this chapter, I described six steps couples could take to improve their relationships based on the use of Voice Therapy procedures. Negative voices represent an internal enemy that influences much of the unnecessary pain and frustration in couple relationships. The incorporated critical and self-destructive attitudes play a significant part in both partner's maladaptive responses. When their behavior and decisions are based on the voice, they are neither rational nor in the couples' best interest. To the extent that partners maintain their defenses and illusions of connection, they relinquish their opportunity to live a better life together.

In relation to parenting problems, I found that parents must come to terms with their own problems to effectively alter their approach to childrearing. Utilizing Voice Therapy in our parenting groups allows parents to better understand themselves and their children. Facing the anguish in their own upbringing and understanding the defenses based on the trauma allows parents to challenge and overcome limitations in their present-day parenting.

Notes

1. Zeitner (2012) explained the dynamics of projective identification in terms of the loss of each partner's self that occurs within numerous marriages and close relationships. Zeitner's descriptive accounts portray many examples of couple relationships characterized by the formation of a fantasy bond or imagined connection between the partners. Also see Carol Middelberg's (2001) comprehensive discussion in "Projective Identification in Common Couple Dances."

2. Voice Therapy, when applied to relationship or marital therapy, has some similarities with Emotion Focused Therapy: see Greenberg and Johnson (1988). A particularly interesting description of EFT involving an individual case, including sessions in couples therapy, can be found in Pos and Greenberg (2012).

3. Re: primary prevention through parenting groups and parent education: see Circle of Security International—Early Intervention Program for Parents & Children, an attachment-theory based program that has proven effective. For

research into the effectiveness of parent education programs in reducing the incidence of child maltreatment, see Geeraert, Van, Noortgate, Grietens, & Onghena (2004).

Sources: *"Combating Destructive Thought Processes: Voice Therapy and Separation Theory.* (1997), *Conquer Your Critical Inner Voice* (2002), and Chapter 14 "Parenting Groups Based on Voice Therapy" in *Compassionate Child-Rearing* (1990).

Chapter 14

RESISTANCE

> Given both the pervasiveness and scope of the death-related
> threats with which humans must deal and the dysfunctional de-
> sign features of the emotion-processing mind, we can appreciate
> why virtually every human walking this earth experiences a meas-
> ure of emotional dysfunction and why every patient who has en-
> tered a psychotherapy situation shows some form of resistance—
> much as every therapist who offers this treatment must deal with
> his or her own symptoms and counter-resistances as well. Such is
> human nature—and life itself.
>
> ~ Langs (2004, p. 112)

Resistance occurs in all forms of therapy and is indicative of an underlying fear and aversion to change (Newman, 2002). Resistant behavior ranges
along a continuum from the intense, at times aggressive, reactions and regressions manifested by psychotic patients, to the more common forms of
resistance exhibited by clients in psychotherapy, and finally to the fundamental resistance toward making significant character changes in "normal"
individuals. Indeed, everyone has resistance to reaching certain levels of
differentiation. Although most people who seek professional help are dis-
satisfied with their present-day lives and want to feel better, they are also
heavily invested in a defended lifestyle, which precludes a better life.
Movement toward fulfillment, independence, freedom, and happiness is
threatening and arouses considerable guilt and anxiety.

PART I. THE ULTIMATE RESISTANCE

My theoretical approach elucidates the primary source of resistance in psychotherapy, as well as the fundamental resistance to leading a more fulfilling life. The ultimate resistance to change in both cases originates in the anticipatory fear of arousing separation anxiety and existential angst. As described earlier, most individuals, to varying degrees, retreat from life and cling to their defense mechanisms in an attempt to avoid reawakening the fear and anxiety of early childhood separation experiences and, in particular, the terror and dread they felt when they first learned about death.

As clients dismantle their defenses during therapy and move toward increased individuation and self-fulfillment, resistances to these suppressed emotions come into play. Certain events and circumstances, both positive and negative, arouse or intensify these primal feelings, whereas other circumstances or defenses relieve them. Previous chapters have discussed the numerous defenses that help ameliorate the client's core anxiety, including the fantasy bond, addictions, micro-suicidal behavior, and literal and symbolic methods of denying one's eventual demise.

There is always the danger of the suppressed anxiety and dread being aroused. Certain attitudes, defensive actions, and beliefs that support illusions of connection and safety help "cool down," in a manner of speaking, unconscious fears, whereas other events and circumstances exacerbate them, causing these emotions to "heat up." The problem is that defensive reactions to death anxiety are usually put into motion before people become conscious that such anxiety has been aroused (Pyszczynski, Greenberg, & Solomon, 1999). Thus, it is often difficult for clinicians to identify the crucial situations that foster resistance and regression.

RESISTANCE SPECIFIC TO PSYCHOTHERAPY

The author agrees with Giovacchini's (1997) statements regarding clients' resistance in formal psychotherapy:

. . . conflicted and frightening feelings about death are contained in the deep unconscious. It is interesting to see how these feelings are elaborated in the therapeutic process and how they create resistance and complications for both the therapist and the patient (pp. ix-xii, para. 9).

Clients' resistance in psychotherapy can take two different forms: overt and covert. The more overt behaviors may include arriving late for appointments, manifesting unusual hostility toward the therapist, becoming delinquent in paying for sessions, or acting out self-nourishing or self-destructive behaviors outside the session.

There are other, more covert or unconscious forms of resistance. Generally, clients unconsciously resist becoming aware of painful repressed material, making basic changes in identity and relationships, and altering addictive behaviors. In addition, they feel guilty about breaking with or surpassing parents, particularly the parent of the same sex. Further, there is also resistance with respect to the therapist's personality involving relational issues—his/her real negative characteristics and defenses.

In psychoanalysis and depth psychotherapy, clients may become antagonistic, refuse to free-associate, or remain unwilling to explore and work through transference phenomena. They may be reluctant to reveal family secrets or to express feelings with respect to the material they uncover or the insights they achieve.

In Voice Therapy, clients may become resistant to following Voice Therapy procedures that separate out discordant elements of the personality. They may find it difficult to state their self-attacks in the second person as outside attacks and they may hold back significant feelings.

In general, there is a tendency for clients who have made significant progress and feel "out on a limb" to regress and lose ground. When this occurs, they tend to project their own desire for change onto the therapist, become oppositional, and strengthen their resistance. When this form of resistance takes place, it must become the central issue in the therapy process in order for clients to continue to progress.

Resistance as Defined in Separation Theory

In addition to the specific resistances to psychotherapy noted above, Separation Theory focuses on resistances concerned with maintaining and protecting the fantasy bond. This core defense is preserved by certain defensive maneuvers. While these overlap each other and are not discrete entities, they can be delineated as follows: (1) the idealization of parents and family; (2) the preservation of a corresponding negative self-image (i.e., a basic conception of oneself as unworthy, unlovable or bad); (3) the displacement of negative parental traits onto others; (4) a tendency to retreat from, and subsequent loss of, feeling; (5) the development of an inward, self-protective posture; (6) the withholding of positive emotional responses and adaptive behaviors; (7) a reliance on self-nourishing habits and routines.

For the most part, the therapist can determine when and which aspect of thought or feeling is being resisted at the time. Becoming aware of the particular defensive process being challenged is necessary in assuring continued therapeutic progress. A struggle can be expected at those points where core defenses are being exposed by the therapy procedures. The therapist who understands the components of the fantasy bond can be alert for signs of resistance and negativity as the client's progress encroaches on his/her defenses (Note 1). Negative reactions can also be anticipated whenever there is any change in the client's life that threatens either self-nurturing behavior or object dependency.

The Problem of Anger in Psychotherapy

In general, the problem of voicing anger and aggression in relation to parents or negative parental introjects in sessions is a serious issue in any therapeutic endeavor. When clients become aware of the damage they sustained in their early development, they experience a good deal of pain and sadness. These memories and emotions give rise to primitive feelings of anger and outrage. Experiencing murderous rage toward one's parents is symbolically equivalent to actually killing, or expressing death wishes toward, the parents. Therefore, clients often experience intense guilt reactions and anxiety when they mobilize these emotions. To compound matters, the symbolic destruction of parental figures leaves the client fearful of object loss. This combination of guilt and fear often precipitates regressive trends.

This is evident in Voice Therapy, where regression often occurs following sessions where clients directly challenge the voice. In attempting to counteract the effect of the voices on their lives, behavior, and emotional states, they may elect to answer the voice dramatically with strong anger. "Yelling back" at symbolic parental figures unleashes feelings of hatred. Many clients, after responding angrily to voice attacks and differentiating themselves from their parents, for example, "I'm not like you, you bastard," or even simply "I'm different," subsequently revert to the very behaviors they were challenging.

In psychoanalysis, intense negative transference reactions usually indicate the presence of strong death wishes toward parental figures. Often there will be a breakdown in the therapeutic alliance at this stage. Similar problems may be encountered where clients progress steadily until they uncover intense rage reactions about the abuses they suffered. Because of their guilt and fear, they often turn the anger against themselves, in effect siding with their parent and generally regress to a more childlike mode of interaction.

In many cases, clients never fully work through their aggression, and the therapeutic process from then on may lack the energy manifested in earlier sessions. Much attention must be paid to the possibility of negative trends in psychotherapy directly following the client's expressions of intense angry affect toward either parents or parent symbols.

PART II. EXPERIENCES THAT TRIGGER UNCONSCIOUS DEATH ANXIETY

Most people continue to exist in the state of psychological equilibrium that they established when they first learned about death. Illusions of fusion and patterns of self-parenting instituted at that time continue to function as a defensive solution, helping to cool down the original terror surrounding death. As noted in Chapter 8, most people are not aware that they fear death, yet they unconsciously guide their lives and personal interactions so as to avoid stirring up suppressed death anxiety. However, if their equilibrium is disturbed by an especially painful negative event or, paradoxically, by an unusually positive one, they are likely to experience varying degrees of conscious death anxiety.

Positive events and circumstances trigger death anxiety

In the psychological community, my associates and I have been able to observe situations that have unconsciously triggered anxiety, resistance, and regression. As noted, many people manifested negative, defensive reactions to positive circumstances that conflicted with their past experiences. This was particularly evident when they reached a high point in their personal development. At these times, they often suffered from long-term regressions characterized by a retreat from their closest relationships and a lack of energy in their pursuit of personal interests and career goals.

As previously mentioned, a special achievement or recognition, such as falling in love or making a commitment in a relationship, or even having a meaningful dialogue with a friend or a sensitive exchange with a child, makes a person cognizant that life is precious but must eventually be surrendered. Unusual successes and advances in personal development, progress in psychotherapy, and significant movement toward independence and individuation throughout the life span also make people aware of their aloneness and vulnerability to death. For this reason, resistance in the form of regression and negative therapeutic reactions can be anticipated when people make notable improvement, develop more self-awareness, and expand their boundaries.

In addition, living unconventionally, achieving personal freedom, and differentiating from parental and societal mores can contribute to a fear of standing out and being different, and to the anticipation of being ostracized from the "tribe" or group, which in evolutionary history was equated with certain death (Case & Williams, 2004). Ernest Becker (1997) and other theorists (Maslow, 1968; 1971; Rank, 1972) are in accordance with my view that the process of individuation precipitates and/or intensifies the fear of death.

Negative events precipitate increased death anxiety

Negative events, such as failure, rejection, accidents, signs of aging, ill health, and actual exposure to death tend to disrupt one's sense of safety and security and often precipitate death fears and the unconscious feelings of terror that were repressed when one originally learned about death. The subsequent adverse reactions are similar to those following positive experiences: regressing or retreating to a more childlike state, creating distance in close relationships, and increasing reliance on illusions of connection. For example, at these times people often renew or intensify their contact with parents or other family members, thereby strengthening fantasy bonds that symbolize safety and a sense of immortality.

As individuals grow older, they tend to unnecessarily constrict their lives in response to death anxiety. For example, they often prematurely reduce or give up their participation in sports and physical activities, decrease or lose interest in sex, and limit contact with friends. At the same time, they exhibit a tendency to increase sedentary or self-nurturing preoccupations. This process of gradual self-denial or micro-suicide is supported by society's stereo-typic attitudes of ageism (Martens, Greenberg, Schimel, & Landau, 2004).

DEFENSES THAT RELIEVE DEATH ANXIETY

Individual Defenses

As described in Chapter 8, there are a number of psychological defenses that function to ameliorate or cool down death anxiety, including:

The Fantasy Bond: This develops originally as a core defense against the pain of separation anxiety and eventually death anxiety. As noted, this imaginary fusion or illusion of connection with one's family, ethnic group, nation, and/or religious and ideological cause imbues one with a sense of immortality (R. Firestone, 1994b).

Denial: This major defense against death anxiety is manifested in two forms: literal immortality and symbolic immortality. Literal immortality re-fers to the attempt to negate death by solace or comfort in religious beliefs such as the survival of the soul in an afterlife or the perpetuation of one's spirit through reincarnation. Symbolic immortality refers to the attempt to live on through one's creative projects, or a cause, or through one's off-spring.

Vanity: This defense functions as a survival mechanism on an uncon-scious level. The image of exaggerated self-importance or of being special renders one impervious to death, unlike other less fortunate, ordinary peo-ple who possess no such immunity.

Preoccupation with Pseudo-problems: This defense serves as a dis-traction from existential realities. Many people are diverted by everyday events to which they overreact with intense primal feelings or inappropriate emotions of rage, fear, and panic. When preoccupied in this way, they shut off feeling for real issues and are unnecessarily tortured by innocuous situa-tions, leaving them less vulnerable to death anxiety.

Inwardness: This defense involves a restricting of life's experience to avoid feeling the painful reality of death. Many people retreat from life by turning inward, cutting off feeling for themselves and other people. An in-ward orientation to life involves a gradual withdrawal from the exchange of emotional products in the interpersonal world, a preference for isolation, and a reliance on addictive habit patterns. Inwardness also encompasses other micro-suicidal behaviors, such as progressive self-denial.

Withholding: This defense involves a holding back of positive responses, talents, and capabilities that are a natural expression of self, primarily for the purpose of controlling both the giving and receiving of gratification and love. These patterns restrict productivity in the workplace and profoundly limit personal fulfillment in life. Many people attempt to avoid especially close interactions or satisfying sexual experiences that could potentially arouse unconscious death anxiety. At other times, when people are less defended and *do* allow personal intimacy to occur, they often react negatively as unconscious feelings of death anxiety come to the surface. At this point, they tend to become more distant and withholding with little or no awareness of the process.

Societal Defenses

Socially validated mores, rituals, and institutions continually reinforce the defenses each person employs to protect against the fear of death. As noted earlier, people tend to transfer the primitive feelings that initially characterized the imagined connection with their parents onto new figures and ideologies.

For many millennia, organized religion also served as a major defense against the fear of death and dying (Vail et al., 2010). Whenever there is an increase in fear, there is a corresponding increase in religious ritual, "psychological polarization," the elevation of one point of view to the utter exclusion of competing points of view (Schneider, 2013, Loc. 127), and other defensive behaviors as well as aggression toward those with different beliefs or rituals (Pyszczynski et al., 1999).

In summary, unconscious separation and death anxiety constitute the ultimate resistance to therapeutic progress and to a better life in general. In that sense, resistance and subsequent defenses act to prevent suppressed death fears from surfacing. Positive or especially fortunate circumstances can disrupt defensive adaptations and fantasy bonds, making one acutely aware both of valuing life and of death's eventuality. On the other hand, negative events—reminders of death, illness, rejection, or financial setbacks—can also precipitate the fear of death. People utilize various defenses and methods to deny the reality of death, both literally and symbolically. Even though these may provide a sense of safety and security and imbue individuals with a sense of immortality, they adversely affect a person's overall psychological adjustment.

The decision to enter psychotherapy usually occurs when defenses, such as a fantasy bond or an addiction, are threatened. Effective psychotherapy helps clients express and work through the feelings aroused by the dismantling of these defenses. Clients deal with resistance first by recognizing and facing up to their tendency to retreat to a defensive posture. In challenging and overcoming their resistance, they then become more vulnerable and open. Later, they are encouraged to talk about and express the full range of emotions related to their personal mortality. In coping directly with existential issues, many people place greater value on their lives and find them to be more meaningful. In addition, these people tend to be more authentic and compassionate towards others.

Stolorow (2011) envisioned the potential benefits of actively coping with this core resistance:

> In such a world, human beings would be much more capable of living in their existential anxiety, rather than having to revert to the defensive, destructive, de-individualizing evasions of it that have been so characteristic of human history.... If we can help one another bear the darkness rather than evade it, perhaps one day we will be able to see the light—as individualized, finite human beings, finitely bonded to one another (Chapter 8, para.21).

PART III. CULTURAL RESISTANCE TO PSYCHOTHERAPY

> The very existence of the therapist as a humanist, as a social activist, as a systemic thinker is under attack. We must challenge the institutions that oppress our field in order to preserve not only the right to freely practice therapy, but also the right of clients to freely choose therapy without medication and even the right to freedom of thought.
>
> ~ Cloe Madanes (1999, p. 57)

From the 1950s to the 1970s, psychoanalysis and depth psychotherapy were flourishing and had a prominent place in the foreground of a cultural revolution. At that time, the majority of clinical psychologists considered it a virtual necessity to undergo their own in-depth analysis in order to better understand the experience of the clients they would be treating. There was a spirit of optimism and idealism that permeated the mental health profession and a deep investment in the psychological approach to emotional maladies.

During this era, millions of young people were fighting for their ideals in an attempt to find a better way of living. The youth movement was characterized by sentiments that opposed the Vietnam war, challenged the materialism of the American scene, favored self-development, self-expression, and sexual freedom, exposed the weaknesses and hypocrisy in the traditional family, and put a high price on individuality and human decency. This movement and its aspirations were thwarted by the fact that its positive thrust was accompanied by an extraordinary guilt and fear reaction that contributed to the ever-increasing utilization of drugs and alcohol.

In my view, many of these young men and women simply could not cope with their personal demons, reflections of their childhood trauma. It is my belief that their misguided attempt to quiet the emotional pain and anxiety of breaking symbolic dependency bonds and seeking autonomy weakened them and eventually led to the demise of their movement.

During this period of experimentation and upheaval, people were more concerned with their personal psychological development than ever before. In *The Repression of Psychoanalysis*, Jacoby (1983) observed that, "There was an obvious affinity between youthful rebellion and psychoanalysis" (p. 39). At that time, many psychologists were involved in sensitivity training groups, marathons, workshops, and encounter groups—procedures that broke out of the narrow confines of the psychotherapy office setting and extended into the business arena, education, and even international relations. People were challenging the status quo in every aspect of their lives and were willing to look at painful issues.

In the course of these events, many important but disturbing truths were being revealed. The hidden aspects of family life and of the bedroom were brought into sharp focus, and people's most cherished defenses were threatening to be uncovered. Nothing was considered too sacred to be exposed to scrutiny.

The Death of Psychoanalysis

Although the truth may eventually promote healing, when it first manifests itself, it generally inspires terror. The psychoanalytic movement caused a general sense of unrest throughout society as a whole. Something had to be done about the discomfort. This same story has echoed throughout time. There was the expected cultural counterattack, and it affected both the youth movement and the practice of psychotherapy.

Since then, I have been concerned with the decline in the use of methodologies such as free association, dream analysis, feeling-release therapies, and group encounters. These approaches represent unique psychological processes that bring into daylight the previously hidden content of our most intimate thoughts and memories. They are valuable resources, windows into the unconscious mind and an illumination of previously unavailable psychological phenomena. The discoveries made possible by these methods revealed deep-seated secrets of family dynamics. By their essential nature, the resulting insights were threatening to the social milieu, and were met with considerable resistance. The findings also aroused unconscious death anxiety because they disrupted fantasies of fusion with the family. The backlash of society was predictable and eventually the "menace" was, for the most part, effectively extinguished (Note 2). According to psychoanalyst John Gedo (2000):

> Today it has become evident that American social conditions do not favor the acceptance of psychoanalytic ideas (p. 39). In North America the *resistance* to its message has penetrated the psychoanalytic community itself, so that depth psychology has been watered down and replaced by mythic variants. . . . This is, indeed, the twilight of our profession in the New World (p. 52). [Italics added]

I believe that the demise of psychoanalysis and depth psychotherapy is closely related to a cultural phenomenon determined to deny the truth of human experience. This is an extremely dangerous trend for members of society, for how can we hope to develop a better family life if we do not honestly scrutinize the dynamics of present-day family interactions? We must effectively account for adolescent suicide, violence in our schools, the widespread use of drugs, and the many other symptoms of emotional disturbance evident in our young people today.

Increased Medicalization of Psychology

Over the past thirty-five years the biomedical approach to psycho-pathology, although partially valid in its own right, has become the dominant treatment modality, effectively overshadowing the psychological approach. The medical model conceptualizes the patient as ill, or as possibly suffering from a disease or biochemical imbalance. As such, it dehumanizes and compartmentalizes the individual by emphasizing physical indicators rather than the whole person. Anthropologist Luhrmann (2000) has described the increasing medicalization of psychiatry and psychology in her book, *Of Two Minds: The Growing Conflict in American Psychiatry*, and deplored its potential consequences: "We are so tempted to see ourselves as fixable, perfectible brains. But the loss of our souls is a high price to pay" (p. 293).

In conjunction with the ascendance of the biomedical approach, the use of antidepressants and stimulants has also had a significant increase. According to Conrad and Bergeley (2014) the increased use of drug interventions for diverse problems in living have contributed to increased medicalization in the field of psychology.

Ritalin, Adderall and other stimulants are often prescribed to patients without the benefit or justification of empirical research. Moreover, "misuse of stimulants by ADHD and non-affected individuals has dramatically increased over recent years. . . . As ADHD medications are prescribed for long-term treatment, there is a need for long-term safety studies and education on the health risks associated with misuse is imperative" (Lakhan & Kirchgessner, 2012, p. 661).

In fairness, concern has been registered about this practice in the recent literature (Chodoff 2002; Conrad & Bergeley, 2014). For example, Chodoff (2002) has cautioned that, ". . . in pursuing the Holy Grail of remedicalization, psychiatry has corrected an error in one direction but has gone too far in the other. The result has been not only the excessive emphasis on medical-model diagnosis but also a related 'furor psychopharmacologus' that seeks a specific drug for every aberrant feeling or behavior as if we were in quest of a society tranquilized by "Soma" as in the dystopia described in Aldous Huxley's *Brave New World*" (p. 1).

A number of other clinicians have called attention to psychiatrists' excessive reliance on drugs in the treatment of mental illness and have criticized their general refusal to utilize even those psychotherapy techniques whose effectiveness has been empirically validated (Breggin, 1991; 2007; Clarke 2003; Conrad & Bergeley, 2014).

In condemning the DSM's reductionist, dehumanizing categorization of patients, psychologist Paula Caplan (1995) challenged another damaging element associated with the increased medicalization of psychology. She noted that in contrast to the relatively generous remuneration the insurance companies allow consumers for the cost of drugs prescribed by psychiatrists, health care providers allow for only limited compensation for psychotherapy.

Even now, insurance providers allow for only limited compensation for psychotherapy, often covering no more than four to six sessions. Few people are able to afford additional sessions. Current practice is, therefore, limited to brief treatment programs and/or medications that cannot appropriately cope with myriad emotional problems that are debilitating for so many individuals. In this restricted time allotted for mental health care, the attempt to find shortcuts is inevitable but these efforts are, by their very nature, insufficient.

To summarize, destructive societal forces have almost completely suppressed significant knowledge concerning the widespread incidence of emotional, physical, and sexual child abuse and other destructive practices in "normal" families, as well as information about their long-term harmful effects on adult individuals. Currently, the cultural attitudes of indifference, denial, and stigmatization along with the medicalization of mental health problems, continue to impact the field of psychotherapy. These combined forces have, in large part, transformed it from a creative, compassionate enterprise to a weak and frightened community of mental health professionals dispensing drugs and quick fixes that support the status quo.

THE FUTURE OF DEPTH PSYCHOTHERAPY

It is possible for depth psychotherapy to survive and find a resurgence if courageous individuals in and outside the field of psychotherapy are willing to expose and challenge the cultural attitudes and illusions that cause so much personal damage. Energy must be directed toward understanding and improving emotional interactions within the family system. Education is crucial for achieving this goal: people must expand their awareness of the pernicious forces in society that function to stifle information, develop a more objective view of present-day family life, and critically evaluate dehumanizing childrearing practices. As Luhrmann (2000) asserted:

> The idea of the unconscious carries with it the implication that life is harder than we realize, because we act not only in accord with visible circumstances but against fears and angers we find so alarming that we refuse even to acknowledge them. And so psychoanalysis also admires the courage to look with unflinching curiosity at oneself, to attempt not to be a turtle with its head pulled in (p. 290).

Contributions from Neuropsychiatry and Attachment Theory

For psychoanalysis and depth psychotherapy to remain vital, clinicians need to become familiar with new information and scientific data, especially the new findings relevant to child development. Recently research from neuropsychiatry and attachment theory is suggestive of an empirical basis for psychoanalytic formulations, and these findings need to be integrated into current-day psychoanalysis and object relations systems. According to Hobson and Leonard (2001),

> Science has learned a lot about the brain. This knowledge has shed a powerful light on mental ills that, besides pushing back the darkness, has revealed much about how to combine medication, therapy, monitoring, and other features of sound treatment (pp. 266-267).

Research conducted by Perry and Marcellus (1997), Schore (2001) and Siegel (1999; 2001), has added to our knowledge of the development of the brain during the first three years of life. Their studies of trauma utilizing brain-imaging techniques tend to support the hypotheses that early experiences are crucial in determining an individual's personality, mental health, and ways of coping with stress throughout the life span.

In addition, therapists should be cognizant of research conducted by attachment theorists and researchers such as Main and Hesse (1990), as well as Solomon and George (1999). The seminal work of Fraiberg et al. (1980), Lieberman and Pawl (1988; 1990), and more recently Lieberman, Padron, Van Horn, & Harris (2005), who demonstrate that early attachment sets the stage for a life-long pattern of personal relationships. Their clinical investigations and follow-up have led to positive interventions that access the client's emotions and that have proved effective in averting negative outcomes in high-risk infants and toddlers.

LeDoux (1995) has suggested that "the role of therapy may be to allow the cortex to establish more effective and efficient synaptic links with the amygdala" (p. 225) which research has shown is "an important part of an aversive emotional memory system" (p. 227). Thus, it appears that these forms of treatment—that is, those therapies that involve accessing emotions associated with early trauma—could have a potentially positive effect on the future of psychoanalysis and depth therapy (Note 3). Although clinical work and psychotherapy designed to help people express these affects are time-consuming and require a good deal of emotional investment on the part of clients, the fact is that only in depth psychotherapy, or in a comprehensive treatment program that utilizes experiential as well as cognitive-behavioral methodologies, can these affects be accessed and worked through.

Discussion

The disciplines described above offer hope for a better understanding of primal pain and favor psychotherapeutic interventions that involve accessing the emotions associated with the client's trauma. As such, they could potentially have a positive effect on the future of psychoanalysis and depth therapy. Without this resurgence, much meaning in life will be sacrificed, a uniquely valuable therapeutic tool will be lost and the future will be bleak for those individuals suffering from emotional distress. A powerful methodology to help mankind move toward a truly compassionate and moral approach to life shall have been abandoned.

From this perspective, it becomes a moral imperative to revive the disciplined study and practice of depth psychotherapy and integrate the important data of human experience derived from this source (Doherty, 2017) (Note 4). We must rise to the challenge despite the threat to our most precious illusions and defenses. I am convinced that the multitudes of individuals who have benefitted in life from depth psychotherapy share this concern.

CONCLUSION

Part I of this chapter discussed the general resistance to change and explained the resistance encountered in all forms of psychotherapy. Basically, there is a core resistance to any aspect of the fantasy bond being challenged: in particular, the idealization of the family, the incorporation of a negative self-image, and the projection of parents' negative qualities onto the world at large, which predisposes distortion, fear, and distrust in interpersonal relations. Also, there is strong opposition to changing addictive self-nurturing, self-parenting practices as well as self-punishing attitudes and behaviors connected with the fantasy bond.

Part II described how there is an ultimate resistance to growth and personal development that originates in the anticipatory fear of arousing powerful latent thoughts of separation anxiety and death anxiety. When clients free themselves from defenses, move toward increased individuation and greater satisfaction, these unconscious fears threaten to emerge into consciousness and core resistances come into play. Often there is a retreat and tendency to regress following the anticipatory anxiety that has to be worked through to achieve therapeutic success.

The final section, Part III, discussed society's resistance to psychotherapy and psychoanalysis and the cultural movement away from open exposure. Indeed, there has been a denial of basic truths related to a fear of revealing negative elements in family life and society. Despite this regression, there are renewed, positive signs of advancement and a hope of integrating brain research and other forms of neuropsychiatry. I share the hope that depth therapy will survive and, once again, flourish.

Notes

1. In his book *Effective Psychotherapy, The Contribution of Hellmuth Kaiser*, Fierman (1965) called attention to this form of resistance in describing Kaiser's concept of the universal psychopathology. "Whenever the patient comes close to having it driven home to him that it is *he himself* who is going to make a decision; or that the conviction in his mind is really his, originated by his own thinking; or that it is he, and he alone, who is wanting something, a piece of delusional ideology rolls like a fog over the mental scenery" (pp. 133-134).

2. See Murray Bowen's (1978) discussion of the analogy between resistance and regression in psychotherapy and cyclical societal regressions that occur when people experience anxiety about disruptions in the status quo, in "Societal Regression as Viewed Through Family Systems Theory," in *Family Therapy in Clin-*

ical Practice. Bowen proposed that "[In society], it is possible to identify some of the manifestations of regression. Togetherness forces begin to override individuality, there is an increase in decisions designed to allay the anxiety of the moment, an increase in cause-and-effect thinking, a focus on'rights' to the exclusion of 'responsibility,' and a decrease in the overall level of responsibility…there is another paradox in the focus on togetherness. The more man anxiously strives for togetherness, the more he loses what he strives for. Man needs human closeness but he is allergic to too much of it" (pp. 279-280).

3. Leslie Greenberg (2004) has emphasized the transformative power of emotion in psychotherapy: "Emotion is foundational in the construction of the self and a key determinant of self-organization… emotion also is a primary signaling system that communicates intentions and regulates interaction (Sroufe, 1996). Emotion thus regulates self and other, and gives life much of its meaning" (p. 3).

4. For a compelling review of the history of American psychoanalysis and psychotherapy, see William Doherty's (2017) essay "Psychotherapy's Pilgrimage: Shaping the Consciousness of our Time" in Psychotherapy Networker Jan/Feb. (pp. 19-37, 67).

Sources: "The Ultimate Resistance" in *Journal of Humanistic Psychology,* (2014) and "The Death of Psychoanalysis and Depth Therapy" in *Psychotherapy,* (2002), *Creating a Life of Meaning and Compassion: The Wisdom of Psychotherapy, (2003).* Inclusive pages: pp. 347-364.

Note on Sources: Reproduced with permission © 2003 of American Psychological Association from *Creating a Life of Meaning and Compassion: The Wisdom of Psychotherapy* by Robert W. Firestone, Lisa A. Firestone, and Joyce Catlett.

Chapter 15

ETHICS AND HUMAN RIGHTS ISSUES

In essence, science without ideology, if such can be envisioned, lacks a moral compass, yet, morality without science is dangerously disconnected from the empirical world.

~ Spitzberg and Cupach (1998, p. *xvii*)

Without a proper understanding of the reasons for people's inhumanity in relation to one another and the development of a compassionate worldview, it is likely that human beings may eventually destroy themselves and life on the planet. Despite all of the advances in science and technology, if one takes a proper look at the world situation today, one must consider it to be utter madness. Millions go hungry, genocide has reached epic proportions, ethnic strife and prejudice are omnipresent, there is mass killing in the name of religion, and warfare remains a widely accepted solution to humankind's differences. With better, more efficient weapons and less reason, and with technology outrunning rationality, there can only be dire consequences.

My thesis is that people's immorality in relation to others derives from the defensive manner in which they deal with interpersonal and existential pain. There is no way to be personally defended without hurting others, particularly those people closest to us, especially our children. This conclusion reflects a clinical accounting rather than a moralistic condemnation.

Damage to one's psyche during one's developmental years bends a person out of shape and leaves one demoralized. It not only fosters aggressive responses, but also leads to toxic character traits that injure other people's self-esteem: dishonesty, intrusiveness, superiority, narcissism, tightness, domineering behavior, a martyred or victimized orientation, paranoid or suspicious attitudes, and outright hostility are destructive manifestations that take a toll on other people. I view these as human rights violations in the interpersonal sphere.

The values and ethical principles described in this chapter are based on an understanding of human nature and an awareness of the destructive forces that impinge on a healthy psychological development. Identifying these negative influences and faulty programming in family life and society, developing insight into the relationship between defenses and aggressive responses, and offering methods for counteracting negative trends constitute a challenge to what some people consider to be humankind's basically unethical nature.

AN INNOVATIVE PSYCHOLOGICAL PERSPECTIVE ON ETHICS

> I believe in the independence of moral values, whether from God or not, and I believe that moral values come from human beings alone, whether or not God exists.
>
> ~ E. O. Wilson (1998, para. 4)

Most people believe that ethics is inextricably tied to religion or spiritual considerations. Many feel that a society or social process without religion would lead to immorality, chaos, and destruction. Yet throughout history, religion and religious practices have led to antisocial, discriminatory behavior or even violence and bloodshed toward non-believers or different-believers. I believe that ethics and an ethical society can evolve separate from organized religious practices and belief systems about immortality or conceptions of an afterlife (Note 1).

My approach to the subject of ethics is from a psychological perspective: I am not prescribing, setting standards, or listing moral principles to be lived up to. This "morality" is based on sound mental health principles. My hope is that by understanding the underlying dynamics in unethical ways of living and by implementing methods for altering them, people can transform themselves and develop better, more successful modes of relating. Living a life characterized by honesty, generosity, and love for those closest to us, and then extending those feelings outward beyond the family constellation, has an optimal effect on one's sense of well-being and ultimately, on society as a whole. It is selfish in the best sense of the word.

DEFINING ETHICS IN OPERATIONAL TERMS

What criteria should be used to distinguish between ethical and unethical actions, particularly when the effects of unethical actions, in terms of destructiveness, are sometimes subtle, difficult to identify, or successfully hidden?

One may consider a specific action or communication as *ethical* when it respects, supports, and nurtures the basic human potentialities of another person. For example, at any given moment, personal exchanges can be appraised as being either supportive of the "real self" of both parties or as antagonistic to each person's ongoing, optimal sense of self and personal development. *Unethical* actions would be those behaviors that limit or damage inherent human qualities, or that interfere with personal fulfillment. Although human rights issues in relationships are rarely considered, they are as relevant to a person's well-being as food, medical care, and shelter.

Ethical principles were derived originally from man's deep reverence for life (Note 2); therefore, the ethics of a specific behavior can be evaluated in terms of whether it enhances or diminishes life, both qualitatively and materially. Ethical behavior supports the rights of children and adults, including the right to develop as an autonomous individual and the right to personal freedom and equality. At the societal level, actions can be considered as ethical when they help create the conditions necessary for the evolution of a humanistic society with concern for the well-being and fulfillment for all people, whereas attitudes and communications that interfere with or prevent the evolution of this type of society must be considered unethical.

The attempt to live according to one's ideals and principles is a difficult, yet noble endeavor. As Michael Josephson (2004) succinctly put it:

Ethics is not for wimps. It's not easy to be honest when it might be costly. It's not easy to stand up for our beliefs and still respect different viewpoints. It's not easy to stop feeling like a victim, to resist cynicism. It's not easy to be consistently kind, to think of others first, to give the benefit of the doubt. It's not easy to be grateful or to give without concern for reward or gratitude. That's why it's such a lofty goal (pp. 1-2).

Living a principled life involves a critical choice between striving to lead an honest life of feeling, meaningful activity and compassion for oneself and others or settling for a lifestyle characterized by maintaining illusions, defenses, and deadening habit patterns.

Characteristics of the Ideal Individual from an Ethical Perspective

What behaviors and personality traits would characterize the "ideal" or truly ethical individual? Obviously, there is no such person; no one is perfect, yet everyone can improve and develop themselves. Many of the personal qualities described below represent fundamental human virtues that have been elucidated by ancient as well as modern philosophers, spiritual leaders, ethicists, and psychologists (Note 3).

Integrity and Honesty: People who have personal integrity are honest and trustworthy; they represent themselves accurately to others as well as to themselves (Note 4). To achieve this level of integrity requires considerable self-knowledge, which implies a willingness to recognize aspects of one's personality that are unpleasant or destructive as well as accepting one's positive traits. Being true to oneself and one's values contributes to an inner state or feeling of being unified, whole, and integrated. Being in touch with one's self on a feeling level is fundamental to this sense of being integrated. Integrity also implies congruence between an individual's words and actions. Individuals who live with integrity are not duplicitous; they place a high value on making their behaviors correspond to their stated goals and priorities.

Consistency and Reliability: These traits are manifested by an evenness in temperament, non-melodramatic responses to events in one's life, and the lack of erratic swings in one's mood or state of mind. Men and women who live with integrity feel at harmony within themselves, and this inner peace of mind enables them to maintain consistency and regularity in their mood and responses to others.

Directness and Willingness to Self-disclose: People who have the courage to directly state their thoughts, opinions, feelings, and beliefs are more trustworthy than those who are indirect, inward, or secretive about their inner experience or perceptions. This does not refer to unnecessarily punitive frankness that serves no purpose but to injure other people's feelings. There must be as high a value placed on practicing kindness and compassion as there is on expressing oneself honesty and forthrightly.

Non-defensiveness: Non-defensiveness is a personality trait that is essential to maintaining an ethical lifestyle. It implies an objective, balanced perspective in relation to oneself and others. The appropriate response to criticism is, after careful scrutiny, to either reject the information if it proves to be inaccurate, or to acknowledge one's faults or inadequacies if the criticism is valid.

Love: As described in Chapter 9, love implies internal feelings of affection and concern as well as external manifestations of kindness, sensitivity, thoughtfulness, physical affection, and respect. Genuine love or regard includes responsible and ethical behavior toward spouses, family, and friends and extends to people beyond one's immediate surroundings.

Compassion: has been defined as concern with the distress of others as well as a desire to alleviate it. In expressing compassion, an individual would be warm, affectionate, and sensitive in his/her relationships, particularly toward those people who are closest to him/her. In addition, there would be a deep concern with the suffering of all people and an attempt made to alter their unfavorable circumstances.

Empathy: Empathy involves being sensitively attuned to another person. It is based on an awareness of the commonality between ourselves and other people as well as an acknowledgment of the differences. In an ideal relationship, mutually empathic individuals would communicate in a sensitive manner that would prevent either partner from feeling unnecessarily hurt, demoralized, or pained (Note 5).

Generosity: Altruism and generosity are the behavioral components of compassion and empathy. In the context of ethical living, an ideal exchange between people involves the capacity to both give and receive love. I have formulated three steps involved in an appropriate response to a generous act. The first is being open to accepting help and permitting someone else to meet one's needs; the second involves expressing genuine appreciation verbally; and the third entails finding ways to respond or give back with thoughtful or loving actions.

Independence: Independence is a virtue because it is an energy source, offering vitality rather than draining energy from others and the society at large. Only when people have a sense of their own identity and are truly individualistic are they able to sustain healthy give-and-take relationships. Ethically speaking, those who take power over their own lives, whose value systems are inner rather than outer directed, and who function more or less autonomously generally have a positive effect on the interpersonal world around them.

Vulnerability: Sociologist and author Brené Brown (2012) writes, "Vulnerability is the core of all emotions and feelings. To feel is to be vulnerable. To believe vulnerability is weakness is to believe that feelings are weakness" (p. 33). Remaining vulnerable to feeling is actually an adaptive and powerful position to take in life because it entails self-acceptance, inner strength, and the capacity to deal with frustration.

Tolerance and Inclusiveness: Being tolerant implies open-mindedness, understanding, benevolence, and goodwill toward one's fellows. People who are accepting of themselves tend to be more accepting of others. They are more inclusive and likely to be free of prejudice, biases, and sexual stereotyping. Living ethically requires taking a strong position against sexist, racist, and otherwise prejudiced attitudes as these lead to discrimination and cause emotional and physical suffering to large numbers of innocent people.

Those individuals who adopt the ethical principles delineated above exhibit a depth of compassion for and a basic trust in others that have beneficial effects on all of their relationships. They manifest a minimum of negative, intrusive behaviors in their personal interactions and thus have a positive influence on their mates, friends, and families, rather than having a deleterious effect.

HUMAN RIGHTS ISSUES IN
INTERPERSONAL RELATIONSHIPS

Human dignity cannot be achieved in the field of technology, in which human beings are so expert. It can be achieved only in the field of ethics, and ethical achievement is measured by the degree in which our actions are governed by compassion and love, not by greed and aggressiveness.

~ Arnold Toynbee (in Gage, 1976, p. 368)

To develop a better understanding of relationships, it is worthwhile to examine the parallels between the psychodynamics in couples and families and those operating in larger groups. An important analogy can be drawn between political systems, family systems, and interpersonal relationships. Human rights issues apply to all of these social phenomena. From an ethical standpoint, one can compare the functions of a state or political system with those served by the couple or the family in terms of the extent to which they either support or violate the rights of the individual.

Social Systems

The key consideration when analyzing the functions of a social system is what the state is offering its citizens—that is, to what extent does it provide for the welfare of its constituents? The ideal state would be concerned with economic security for its members as well as the protection of their personal freedom and basic human rights. Philosophically, this type of government would place value on the life of each person over the survival of the system itself. People would be considered as an "end in themselves" and never the means to an end providing benefit to the system (Kant, 1959/1781). Granting preeminence to the individual rather than the state or any of its institutions is logical as well as ethical; as noted previously, systems are merely abstractions, whereas people are real, living entities.

In contrast, when protection of the state or a political system takes precedence over the individual, the needs of most citizens are not served; instead they generally suffer economically, politically, and personally. Governments operating on this premise perceive issues of human rights as a low priority, thereby setting the stage for oppression and tyranny. The concept of the ideal system as described in Plato's *Republic* (trans. 1955), and Sir Thomas More's *Utopia* (1949/1551) can be contrasted with the nightmarish illustrations of Huxley's (1932) *Brave New World*, and Orwell's (1954) *Nineteen Eighty-Four*.

All social systems involve a certain amount of compromise in relation to the rights of the individual (Rawls, 1999). It is obvious that there is some sacrifice of individual freedom to live in a social order; however, it is a matter of degree. Totalitarian or authoritarian states impose numerous rules and restrictions on their citizens, while a democratic state permits more personal freedom, mobility, and possibility for members to improve their economic status.

The totalitarian state best represents a viewpoint that values the system over the individual. Totalitarian governments are tyrannical in nature in that they demand conformity and submission. The efforts of their political leaders are often directed toward categorizing and grouping persons as a means of control and manipulation (Marcuse, 1966; Turner, 1978). Havel (1990) described the "self-momentum" of impersonal power manifested in authoritarian systems as "the blind, unconscious, irresponsible, uncontrollable, and unchecked momentum that is no longer the work of people, but which drags people along with it and therefore manipulates them" (p. 166).

Unfortunately, most citizens living under this type of regimen are all too willing to submit and avoid the frightening responsibility of freedom. In that sense, they are in collusion with the social system. In describing society in 19th century Russia, Dostoyevsky (2002/1880) observed, "Man has no more agonizing anxiety than to find someone to whom he can hand over with all speed the gift of freedom with which the unhappy creature is born" (p. 298).

However, corruption, manipulation, and other iniquities exist even in a democratic society. All societies establish conventional means and mores that are effective in controlling the membership and, in many instances, these conventional attitudes and stereotypic views restrict people's thinking, increase their hostility, and negatively influence their behavior toward one another. Social conventions become ritualized activities that reinforce a collective conscience and form the foundation of social relationships in society. These rituals permeate every nuance of our daily life, and are frequently inhibiting and repressive (Alexander, Giesen, & Mast, 2006) (Note 6).

In addition to posing a threat to individual freedom, social institutions and conventions often have other negative influences on social behavior. For example, the rights of each child are largely dictated by the legal system. The court, as a social institution, presumably maintains the safety of children by establishing and enforcing definitions of maltreatment, neglect, and abuse. Child welfare agencies are bureaucratic extensions of the social system that supposedly support children, yet these institutions have often overlooked the welfare of kids in support of the primacy of the biological family in the child-care role (Baldwin, 2002, Biehal, 2007; Taussig, Clyman, & Landsverk, 2001) (Note 7). The idealization of the family, regardless of the degree of its dysfunctionality, often allows its members to avoid critical issues that are vital to mental health.

Instead of challenging destructive family practices, our society tends to reinforce and support the formation of fantasy bonds within the couple and family. The emphasis is on preserving the form of the relationship or family constellation, while disguising the fact that the substance or quality is lacking. According to Foucault (1972), we have, in a sense, normalized the discourse so that the once perceived dysfunction becomes the accepted norm, the "produced truth." Sadly, it is often the production of these "truths" that shapes human experience rather than human experience that shapes the production of truth (Note 8). Marcuse (1966) expressed similar sentiments about the collusive relationship between individuals who fear freedom and the society that oppresses them: "The struggle against freedom reproduces itself in the psyche of man . . . his self-repression in turn sustains his masters and their institutions" (p. 16).

Restrictive and irresponsible practices of the social system, as well as their idealization, have significant detrimental effects on every person. The resultant loss of meaning can be seen in the high rates of homicide and suicide, drug addiction, depression, and random acts of violence among adolescents. Many young people, once the most serious critics of the status quo, currently manifest attitudes of apathy and hopelessness. In general, contemporary social practices have a powerful delimiting effect on people's personal freedom, healthy sexuality, personal integrity, and natural drive for affiliation with others. These practices tend to become the expected norm rather than the exception. They become institutionalized routines that are unchallenged by the individuals they affect. In effect, they constitute self-fulfilling prophecies.

Family Systems

An examination of the ethics of family life is vital for us as a society because children carry our human heritage, the legacy our generation leaves behind, and our hope for the future. The ideal family would attempt to gratify the physical, economic, and emotional needs of each individual and enhance the personal development of children. There would be a minimum number of rules and restrictions, allowing for optimal freedom and autonomy.

In contrast, the less-than-ideal family tends to function in a manner that exerts excessive control over each person through rules and rituals that favor obligation over choice, image over self, and façade over authenticity. Unnecessary restrictions, manipulations, and power plays, as well as the mystification needed to deny the fact that such controls exist, cause considerable harm. It is absurd to serve an abstraction, that is, to place primary value on any social institution, whether it is the couple or family, without considering the well-being of the individual men, women, and children.

A number of clinicians and theorists have written about family systems that are similar in many respects to the totalitarian state and have described their suppressive and cult-like practices. For example, Tedeschi and Felson (1994) noted that, "People who rarely if ever use coercion with others make an exception in the case of their children" (p. 287). They called attention to the "high levels of coercive behavior, including bodily force, verbal and physical punishment, physical isolation, and deprivation of resources" (p. 290-291) in American families.

Other theorists have described couple and family systems that demand loyalty, whether it is deserved or not. In these relationships, control through guilt and a sense of obligation characterizes the interactions between members and supports the perpetuation of destructive family ties. In their classic work, *Invisible Loyalties,* Boszormenyi-Nagy and Spark (1984) emphasized that, "In families, as well as in other groups, the most fundamental loyalty commitment pertains to maintenance of the group itself" (p. 40). These theorists noted that the meaning of words like "loyalty" and "justice" eventually becomes corrupted within the context of most traditional families. Family systems theorist Murray Bowen (Kerr & Bowen, 1988) asserted that in most families whenever there is an increase in anxiety, "each person feels pressured to act in ways to preserve the attachment" (p. 84). According to Bowen, this pressure or "the force toward togetherness" leads to increased emotional enmeshment between family members, limiting self-differentiation and development of autonomy in the children.

Destructive Behaviors in Couple Relationships

As mentioned in Chapter 9, some of the most destructive behaviors, commonplace in relationships, are those that individuals act out in an attempt to ward off loving responses from their partner. Defended individuals tend to maintain the negative identity they acquired within the family context and are resistant to being seen in a more positive light. Changing their basic self-concept would threaten their defense system and arouse considerable stress, so they unconsciously strive to alter their lover's positive responses. In trying to avoid anxiety, they often hurt the people who love them the most, without meaning to.

In his work with couples, psychologist John Gottman (Gottman & Silver, 1999) found four behaviors that were hurtful and identifiable as diagnostic predictors of eventual divorce: defensiveness, stonewalling or filibustering, criticality, and contempt. The researchers found that contempt was the most serious indicator of potential divorce and could be clearly identified after observing couples for only a few minutes. Contempt implies relating to the other so as to denigrate and judge from a superior position.

A person behaving in a contemptuous manner is smug, hypercritical, and belittling, making the recipient of his/her behavior feel small, and causing a good deal of psychological pain. He/she speaks in an authoritarian, parental tone of voice that reflects a vain attitude or higher status. Contempt, criticality, negativity and the resultant tensions in relationships are associated with poor psychological health as well as "worse physiological outcomes, such as increased cardiovascular reactivity and depressed immune functioning" (Kiecolt-Glaser et al., 1993).

There are many insensitive behaviors acted out in the course of the average couple's day. They occur routinely in unpleasant exchanges about finances and childrearing, in hurtful interactions in the privacy of the bedroom, in depreciating comments made publicly in front of family, friends, and strangers, and in harsh arguments that disrupt the harmony of a shared activity. Even when blatant, these aversive behaviors often remain on the periphery of the offending partner's consciousness while he/she maintains a fantasy of being loving and responsive.

Many couple relationships are characterized by disrespectful reactions, including those that effectively intimidate or control the other person through defensive maneuvers or manipulations. Power plays, and other strategies of control are manifested in various ways: through domination, bullying, and the use of force; through self-destructive threats that cause fear reactions; and through manipulations that trigger guilt feelings in the other person.

In many relationships, people lie about money issues, addictive patterns, and, in particular, about extramarital affairs. Within some couples, a form of social terrorism is practiced in which one partner is held accountable or responsible for the unhappiness of the other. The tyranny of weakness, helplessness, and self-hatred exerted by self-denying or self-destructive individuals has a profoundly manipulative effect. Microsuicidal and self-harming behaviors are effective means of controlling because they are capable of eliciting fear, anger, guilt, or alarm in other people. There is a fear of losing the self-destructive person as well as the guilt inherent in feeling that one is responsible for another person's life or death.

People who regress to childish modes of relating and withhold adult responses are able to coerce their partner into taking care of them. In this way, they preserve the imagined security of the original fantasy bond with their parents. When the childish, victimized behaviors of a passive-aggressive person provoke an aggressive response or abusive treatment from the more dominant, assertive individual, both parties are damaged psychologically in the exchange. It is just as unethical to continue to accept abuse from a loved one, as it is to act it out. This statement does not imply that one should blame the victim or excuse the perpetrator. It merely illustrates that both people collude in this dynamic interaction, and it is in the interest of both to stop this type of relating.

In summary, to a certain extent, social systems and institutions ignore important issues of human rights. Similarly, many relationship partners and family members intrude on and violate each other's human rights, that is, their right to live freely and develop as individuals. This abuse of personal freedom can eventually evolve into an issue of human rights violations within the person; for example, the child who is intruded upon and mistreated goes on to mistreat him/herself in much the same manner.

We must conclude that human rights issues, values, and ethics are unavoidable in an analysis of couples, family relationships, and social structures. However, the conventional approaches to interpersonal and societal ills often ignore these issues and indeed, they are de-emphasized or completely overlooked by many practitioners in the mental health profession.

COPING WITH UNETHICAL WAYS OF LIVING

Mastering Anger

> A man that does not know how to be angry does not know how to be good.

~ Henry Ward Beecher (1887), Proverbs from Plymouth Pulpit

Ethically speaking, the ability to cope with angry emotions is of major significance. The inability to do so plays a central role in people's inhumanity toward one another. Specific ethical considerations are associated with the consequences of mishandling anger. For instance, the failure to effectively communicate angry feelings in an intimate relationship leads to an increase in hostility and cynicism that damages both parties and creates distance.

For these reasons, it is important to understand the initial frustration or primal feelings that trigger anger, and the voices that determine its mode of expression. As noted in Chapter 7, there are countless maladaptive ways that people react to anger: it can be externalized and manifested in violent acts against other people; it can be internalized, that is, turned against the self in the form of psychosomatic illness, depression, or suicide; or it can be used unconsciously to avoid closeness in an intimate relationship. To avert these and other serious consequences, it is necessary for people to learn to accept and manage their angry emotions.

Dealing Effectively with the Primal Aspects of Anger: Becoming sensitive to the types of situations that arouse intense reactions of anger is valuable in making a distinction between *primal* and present-day emotions. Whereas the anger in the current situation may be fitting, when the intensity that accompanies it is not appropriate to the reality of the event, it probably has more to do with painful or frustrating experiences in one's childhood. People can learn to recognize when their feelings are primal or highly-charged emotionally and spare themselves a good deal of suffering. An awareness of the primal components of one's anger not only helps defuse the intensity of the feeling, but also allows time for rational self-reflection and a more thoughtful consideration of the consequences of one's actions.

In therapy, clients are encouraged to freely express their angry emotions. The therapist and client then evaluate the meaning or cause, explore the primal elements, and discuss ways of dealing with anger in the real-life situation. If one is able to experience angry feelings and is comfortable with them, one becomes a much stronger person. People who are not afraid of their anger possess an inner strength because they can feel their anger fully without losing control. They are able to choose when and where to express their anger and can amplify its expression if necessary.

Identifying Voices that Fuel Angry Feelings: In Voice Therapy, expressing destructive thoughts in the second person format often reveals the specific aggression toward oneself and other people underlying the voices. It is valuable to be able to identify the specific hostile, cynical thoughts and voices that intensify anger and lead to the acting out of aggression.

People who learn to distinguish between projections based on their voices and realistic perceptions of another's traits are better able to communicate their angry feelings honestly and appropriately, and maintain harmonious relations. One can recognize when the shift in one's attitude (from positive to negative) takes place and understand the underlying meaning behind this change in perspective. This awareness provides an element of control over the acting out of maladaptive, aggressive behaviors.

Education and Prevention: Teaching children about anger is a vital part of helping them to adapt to life. In general, children need to learn about emotions as much as they need to learn about academic subject matter and the practical aspects of life. Every child should be taught about adaptive and maladaptive forms of aggression and become skilled at handling angry feelings.

To avoid raising children who become unethical, undesirable adults, parents need to teach young children not to whine, pout, sulk, or act out abusive responses. As noted in Chapter 11, children should know that it is helpful to cry when they are sad, but they need to learn that using tears in an attempt to control through weakness is counterproductive.

Lastly, anger can be a source of energy and vitality when people understand its nature, accept angry feelings as an inherent part of their emotional makeup, and learn how to utilize aggression constructively. Mastering angry feelings is vital for good mental health, enhances personal power, and facilitates the pursuit of goals and priorities. Taking a broader perspective, people developing healthy attitudes about feeling anger and controlling aggression could play a part in preventing much of the trouble in today's world.

Addressing Toxic Personality Traits

> There are indeed people who are hazardous to others' mental, emotional, and physical health.
>
> ~ Lillian Glass (1995, p. 12)

Toxic personality traits are characteristic ways of being and behaving that hurt other people. They are deeply ingrained and relatively enduring patterns of thought, feeling, and behavior that cause considerable damage in interpersonal relationships and in the workplace. For example, Lubit (2004) observed that "Toxic managers divert people's energy from the real work of the organization, destroy morale, impair retention, and interfere with cooperation and information sharing" (p. 1). In this sense, individuals who possess a preponderance of objectionable or "toxic" traits could be conceptualized as being psychologically corrosive or poisonous to others in a wide range of situations and settings.

Toxicity in the personalities of national and political leaders is a critical issue with respect to international relations. Historically speaking, many destructive leaders have been narcissistic, dishonest, hypocritical, and quite a few have acted out sociopathic tendencies (Kellerman, 2004; Post, 2004).

A number of research studies have attempted to determine the relative toxicity of diverse traits that are considered detrimental to people in both work and home environments (Babiak & Hare, 2006; Kowalski, 2001a; Spitzberg, & Cupach, 1998). For example, some studies identify hostility and anger as being the most toxic traits of personality in terms of the potential psychological and/or physical damage that people who possess these qualities can inflict on others.

Other researchers investigating the effects of these pernicious traits on marital relationships stressed the fact that hostility, in the form of criticism and intrusiveness, leads to tension and stress within the couple (Betchen, 2005; Ruszczynski & Fisher, 1995). Research also shows that the aversive effect of a "toxic" person on the quality of an interaction is generally stronger than the constructive effect of a person who has more positive characteristics.

Toxic personality traits can be difficult to identify because they are often ego-syntonic in that they resonate well with the individual who possesses them, causing little or no distress (Meissner, 1995). For example, people who are stingy may see themselves as being frugal or thrifty. Similarly, people may be proud of their self-denial when it may, in fact, be an indication of pathology.

Individuals who are submissive and subservient can be as damaging to relationships as those who are domineering or imperious. An acquiescent style of deferring is irritating and serves the function of pushing others away. People who are defended in this manner often provoke anger and hostility in others. Other traits, including insensitivity, dependency, childishness, phoniness, indifference, aloofness, coldness, and the tendency to respond impersonally, also cause others emotional pain.

The degree of emotional impairment caused by a "toxic" person varies and is affected by many factors. These are not necessarily consistent and may manifest themselves in some situations and not in others. For example, some people can be extremely unpleasant in interactions with coworkers and employees, yet easy-going and friendly in relating to family members (Cavaiola & Lavender, 2000). Others may be relatively congenial and flexible at work, yet rigid and authoritarian at home.

However, the general trend is for people to manifest the same offensive or disagreeable traits in a wide variety of situations and in the majority of their personal interactions (Forward, 1989). The degree of destructiveness associated with a specific toxic trait is affected by the frequency and intensity with which it is manifest in one's social interactions. Some negative traits are so noxious that even when they occur infrequently, they can have long-lasting adverse effects (Kowalski, 2001b).

Invalidation is a common toxic behavior and has been defined as any act that puts "other people down to bring yourself up" (Leiter, 2003, p. xi).

Invalidators tend to possess a number of other distasteful personality traits, including hostility, vanity, intrusiveness, insensitivity, contemptuousness, coldness, and a lack of feeling that seriously undermine the self-esteem and mental health of the people close to them. This type of individual uses many methods to contradict or dismiss other people's feelings and thoughts, such as projection, overgeneralization, judgment, manipulation, double messages, and the double bind wherein the "the invalidator puts you in a position where you are wrong if you do and wrong if you don't" (p. 17).

In general, in any interaction, the specific positive and negative traits of the participants have a powerful impact, both on the outcome of their exchanges and on each party's emotional state. When positive traits are dominant, the exchange is beneficial and conducive to good feeling, whereas when noxious traits prevail in one (or both) parties, the exchange is inevitably harmful to both people. In *The Politics of Experience*, R. D. Laing (1967) described how both kinds of traits are manifested in personal interactions:

> Personal action can either open out possibilities of enriched experience or it can shut off possibilities. Personal action is either predominantly validating, confirming, encouraging, supportive, enhancing, or it is invalidating, denying, discouraging, undermining and constricting. It can be creative or destructive. In a world where the normal condition is one of alienation, most personal action must be destructive both of one's own experience and of that of the other (p. 34).

POWER AND THE CORRUPTION OF POWER

> If it is not only power and coercion that enslave man, then there must be something in his nature that contributes to his downfall; since this is so, the state is not man's first and only enemy, but he himself harbors an "enemy within."
>
> ~ Ernest Becker (1975, pp. 39-40)

For centuries, philosophers, social scientists, and psychologists have struggled to answer ethical questions regarding the use and misuse of power. They have described both the beneficial and harmful effects that powerful, influential figures have had on historical events, current world affairs, religious movements, politics and government, the business world, and individual members of society as a whole. According to R. Martin (1971), "Power is one of the most central and yet problematic concepts in sociological theory" (p. 240). The sociologist Talbot Parsons (quoted in Martin, 1971) asserted that individuals working together to achieve a collective goal require "the acceptance of the [power] relation by both sides because of its function in achieving social system goals" (p. 244).

Historically, power has often been viewed with suspicion or given a negative, even evil, connotation. Pejorative terms such as "harsh", "exploitive", "fascist", "sadistic", and "Machiavellian" have been used to describe the ways in which power and influence have been exercised. However, power *per se*, like leadership, is neither positive nor negative; it is neutral or amoral. It is the specific types of power that people tend to develop over time and the methods whereby they utilize the power they have accumulated—to either inspire or to dominate other people—that can be evaluated from an ethical point of view.

Sources of Power

Strength of character, integrity, charisma, athletic ability, and positive physical attributes such as beauty or good looks are all potential sources of power. People accrue power though wealth, popularity, being competent and knowledgeable in a given field, and by living according to a certain belief system or set of ethical principles. They can also accumulate power by being dominating, intimidating, coercive, aggressive, or violent.

The sources of power available to individuals vary across cultures, subcultures, and interest groups. Every society or mini-culture places high value on specific personality traits or achievements of its members; thus, individuals with these traits have considerable influence or power within that group. For example, in the political arena, the orator who is charismatic and convincing or the former general who succeeded in battle can rise to a prominent position; in a motorcycle gang, the most daring and fastest rider becomes the leader; in the business world, the executive whose company generates high earnings possesses considerable prestige; in sports, the athlete who is named "most valuable player" will be more popular than his teammates.

Types of Power

There is a clear distinction between the accumulation of power as part of one's self-development, self-assertion, and a natural, healthy striving for love, satisfaction, and meaning in one's interpersonal world, and the amassing of power as part of a defensive process. There are three basic types of power: (1) *personal power,* which is based on strength of character, confidence, and competence that individuals gradually acquire in the course of their development; (2) *covert negative power,* which is based on passive-aggression and is manifested in behaviors indicating weakness, incompetence and self-destructive tendencies which manipulate others in the interpersonal world by arousing their feelings of fear, guilt, and anger; and (3) *overt negative power,* which is characterized by aggressive tendencies and is exercised through the use of force and/or coercion to control others.

Personal Power represents a positive, natural striving for satisfaction and meaning in life that is exercised in the honest attempt to realize one's unique potentialities. In a previous work, I defined personal power as "direct, goal-oriented behavior using all of one's resources. It is persuasive and logical rather than manipulative in relation to other people. It is strong rather than oppressive or hostile" in relation to upholding one's values (R. Firestone & Catlett, 1989, pp.184-185).

The process of seeking to fully develop one's potential while being sensitive to others who are pursuing their goals is a worthwhile, mentally healthy, and ethical endeavor. People who have a great deal of personal power tend to be competent and knowledgeable, and possess many of the qualities that are prerequisites for becoming an outstanding leader. Personal power is more an attitude or state of mind than an attempt to maneuver or control others. When externalized, it is likely to be more service-oriented and humane than other forms of power. People who possess personal power are independent rather than pseudo-independent or overly dependent on others. They are more likely to be ethical and direct in their interactions, have standards that make them unwilling to accept abuse, and are not afraid to compete for what they want.

From a developmental perspective, the processes of separation, individuation, and personal growth can be seen as providing opportunities for accumulating personal power. As children move from a position of dependence to one of independence and develop increased assertiveness, autonomy, and confidence in their abilities, they accrue more personal power and can exert a more positive influence on others. Those who continue to develop themselves throughout the life span tend to be creative, nonconformist, and autonomous.

There are three major reasons why people who possess personal power are rare in our culture. First, many people retreat from pursuing personal power because of a learned social stigma, which regards power as exploitive, corrupt, and selfish. Second, some people relinquish power because, on an unconscious level, they do not really want to be responsible adults. They anticipate the anxiety that would be aroused if they were to become fully individuated and autonomous. They prefer to depend on more familiar, indirect, or manipulative forms of power—similar to those they utilized as children to get what they wanted without risking self-assertion. Third, some people fear retaliation for competing. In this regard, many people are afraid of competition, particularly with members of the same sex. The anxiety regarding competition results from inappropriate and, at times, punitive reactions to competition experienced within the family of origin.

I believe that each person has the right to pursue personal power—to choose a specific direction in life and to engage in actions directed toward fulfilling his/her particular goals. One has the right to challenge conventions, social mores, and systems of conformity and to work toward changing attitudes, prejudices, or laws that are unjust.

Personal power is essentially strength of character and integrity. Strong individuals are neither defiant nor submissive because these dysfunctional traits are reactions to outside influences rather than being motivated from within. Neither position is independent and autonomous. Contrary to conventional thinking, the pursuit of personal power is essentially respectful and need not intrude on the rights of others.

Covert Negative Power is any behavior that controls or elicits a response from others through the manipulation of their feelings of fear, guilt, anger, pity, sympathy, or remorse. In contrast to personal power, this form of power is based on maintaining an immature or childish orientation toward life. Whereas personal power is a significant indication of being an adult, covert negative power is indicative of remaining a child. By definition, the two positions or ego-states are mutually exclusive because a person has to sacrifice personal power to manipulate or control another through weakness.

People who exercise this form of destructive power are passive rather than action-oriented, have difficulty dealing with direct anger, feel victimized and self-righteous, and, to varying degrees, are suspicious or paranoid. They act weak, powerless, and have a complaining attitude. They are fearful of competitive situations and tend to retreat from goal-directed behavior when there are indications of opposition, contention, or rivalry. Instead of recognizing competitive feelings, they censor these emotions, turn on themselves, and become demoralized, thereby giving up personal power. When they back away from competing for what they want, they lack integrity and are unable to honestly communicate their wants and desires.

While the exercise of covert negative power or control through weakness might not appear to be immoral or unethical, this subtle type of power contributes to distress in relationships and instability in organizations. For example, the worker who acts more incompetent than he/she really is exerts a strong social pressure that drains others of energy and vitality. Cavaiola and Lavender (2000) have underscored the fact that employees with passive-aggressive personalities "are quite difficult to work with, given their negativity and resentful moods and attitudes" (p. 126). The passive-aggressive personality "can be insidious, wiping out your hard drive "by mistake" or losing the twenty-page proposal that you've been spending months working on" (p. 128).

Even though covert negative power may bring about the desired results or attention, the cost to the perpetrator is immense. Therapists often point out to clients that this mode of seeking power is never worth the trouble or the limitations it necessitates. Adults who persist in using this childish form of control not only damage others but harm their own development as well. This type of unconscious manipulation necessarily leaves one in an unhappy, miserable state.

Overt Negative Power. When people exercise overt negative power through force, military might, or coercion, they necessarily inflict harm on other people or infringe on their human rights. This is clearly unethical. Leaders who use force or threats of punishment to accomplish their goals eventually upset the stability of the larger society, depress its economy, and oppress its citizens. Totalitarian leaders and dictators tend to play on the fears of their constituents in order to establish, maintain, and increase their sphere of influence.

Most people lack the desire to change the world or to influence the masses. McClelland (1975) and his associates reported that most people have a strong need for achievement, which is different than the need for power itself. They desire only to have some element of control over their personal lives, families, finances, and economic situation, and their health and work environment. Yet, there are certain types of people who actively and persistently seek out and obtain power and supremacy through corrupt means. In many cases, the personality structure of these individuals reflects underlying psychological disturbance, including problems with anger, narcissism, vanity, and sociopathic tendencies (Kellerman, 2004).

People who utilize overt negative power are generally compensating for inferiority feelings and for real or perceived inadequacies (Lowen, 1985). They tend to be cut off from feeling for themselves and others. In terms of the parent-child dichotomy described earlier, they lean toward the parental side, acting superior and judgmental. They try to deny their feelings of helplessness and powerlessness in relation to death by controlling other people (Lipman-Blumen, 2005). Their vanity offers them a sense of being special and, as such, exempt from natural forces. This fantasy operates along with their success in dominating others to defend against death anxiety. Because this process never succeeds in completely eliminating the fear of death, the need for power becomes increasingly compelling, often leading to disastrous outcomes in a business enterprise or to serious crimes against humanity in the political scene.

Research has shown that individuals who become authoritative political figures tend to be intensely ambitious, somewhat paranoid, and driven to seize ever more authority and influence (Robins & Post, 1997). The exhilaration of having complete control over others can become addictive in that it produces feelings of elation and diminishes feelings of insecurity and inferiority, albeit temporarily.

The Corruption of Power on the Societal Level

On a societal level, when power is corrupted—when it is utilized to control others, to intimidate or oppress others—there is a corresponding increase in the incidence of social violence and other forms of "social evil." In the business world and in politics, the abuse of power is facilitated when individuals become "morally disengaged" from their values and their concern for others (Bandura, 1999) (Note 9).

Nowhere is "evil" more apparent than in the manifestation of prejudice, racism, ethnic strife, and in the horror of ethnic cleansing and unjust warfare (Note 10). It is my opinion that people's hostility and violence are responses to painful issues of childhood compounded by the frightening specter of death. Psychological defenses that minimize or shut out psychological pain tend to be collectively expressed in restrictive, dehumanizing cultural patterns.

Group Identification

A number of theorists assert that group identification is a major causative factor in religious, racial, and international conflict. Freud's (1955/1921) work on the subject, which stressed the "mindlessness of the group mind" supports my thesis that group membership offers a false sense of superiority, specialness, and omnipotence to individuals who feel helpless and powerless in an uncertain world. Freud noted that "a group is extraordinarily credulous and open to influence, it has no critical faculty, and the improbable does not exist for it. . . . A group knows neither doubt nor uncertainty" (p. 78). In his work, Erich Fromm (1941; 1950) traced the social and psychological elements of the Nazi movement to their sources in the Age of Reformation. He explained that existential fears of aloneness compel people to take actions as a group that would be unthinkable to them as individuals:

> There is nothing inhuman, evil, or irrational which does not give some comfort provided it is shared by a group. . . . Once a doctrine, however irrational, has gained power in a society, millions of people will believe in it rather than feel ostracized and isolated (1950, p. 33).

As I emphasized in Chapter 8, identification with a particular ethnic or religious group is at once a powerful defense against death anxiety and a system of thought and belief that can set the stage for hatred and bloodshed. Group identification provides individuals with an illusion of immortality through imagined fusion with the membership. Conformity to the belief system of the group, that is, to its collective symbols of immortality, protects one against the horror of facing the objective loss of self.

In *Escape from Evil* Ernest Becker (1975) explored the relationship between the fear of death and the social evil, which finds its primary expression in warfare. My viewpoint is congenial to Becker's in arguing that existential dread is the foremost predisposing influence at the core of man's inhumanity to man. He wrote:

> No wonder the divine kings repeatedly staged their compulsive campaigns and inscribed the mountainous toll of their butchery for all time . . . their pride was holy; they had offered the gods an immense sacrifice and a direct challenge, and the gods had confirmed that their destiny was indeed divinely favored, since the victories went to them (p. 106).

In summary, people tend to disown traits they dislike in themselves and project them onto other people and perceive them as inferior, impure, or dirty. These defensive mechanisms are the dynamic forces underlying racism and genocide. I propose that the terror of death, the feeling of utter helplessness in contemplating the cessation of existence as one knows it, provides the impetus driving members of a group or citizens of a nation to build up grandiose images of power at the expense of others. It propels them to act on their projections and distortions, and to attempt to eliminate impure and despised enemies from the face of the earth. As Wirth (2004) correctly observed, "The tragedy is that the struggle against evil engenders further evil" (p. 178) (Note 11).

The explanations set forth here provide a clear perspective concerning the underlying meaning of ethnic warfare and terrorism, and offer a positive, pragmatic, and action-oriented outlook. It offers hope for the future, whereas the deterministic conception of man's essential savagery may well provide a self-fulfilling prophecy. Indeed, pessimistic forecasting generally precludes constructive action and people tend to feel progressively more demoralized and helpless.

FUNCTIONS OF AN IDEAL (ETHICAL) SOCIETY

> The roots of social order are in our heads, where we possess the instinctive capacities for creating not a perfectly harmonious and virtuous society, but a better one than we have at present (Note 12).

> ~ Matt Ridley (1996, p. 264)

The functions of an ethical or 'virtuous' society described here are based in part on Becker's four criteria, regarding the functions of the good society. The "ideal society" (1) provides for the physical needs of its people within limits of its technology and resources; (2) provides opportunities for as many people as possible to feel good about themselves; (3) fulfills the first two functions without damaging others, either inside the culture or outside; and (4) teaches its people how to die well—or more precisely, it teaches people how to live well—despite their limitation in time. It also provides people with meaningful answers to cosmological questions.

Becker contended that a good culture provides stories about the origins of life—creation myths—and stories about what happens after death (Becker, 1964, 1997). In this regard, religion and, to some extent, new age spiritualities provide people with literal immortality—beliefs about actual life after death in some form or another. Similarly, the prospect of living on through a group, a cause, one's business, one's children, a creative work or accomplishment all offer some form of symbolic immortality. As noted, I disagree with Becker's idea of the good culture being one in which it is necessary to provide myths about spiritual existence or life after death.

Becker also considered a scientific study of societies to be of value because it would "make public a continuing assessment of the costs of mankind's impossible aims and paradoxes. . . . Then men might struggle, even in anguish, to come to terms with themselves and their world" (p. 68). In concluding *The Denial of Death* (1997), he argued that it is impossible for individuals to find any viable solution to the pain and anguish of the human condition, not through the 'heroic' roles prescribed by society, nor through religion or psychotherapy: "Whatever is achieved must be achieved from within the subjective energies of creatures, without deadening, with the full exercise of passion, of vision, of pain, of fear, and of sorrow" (pp. 283-284).

From my point of view, the ideal society or culture would face the existential realities of aloneness and death, allow for them to be a topic for open communication, and accept the full range of feelings associated with the subject. People could develop a humanistic, inclusive worldview rather than a sectarian view; an approach that respects and reveres life, despite the limitation in time.

CONCLUSION

I believe in humankind's capacity to alter negative personality characteristics and unethical practices. Just as the individual can create a more positive identity and new destiny for him/herself, a similar result can be achieved in society and culture. In spite of the present state of affairs and the complexity of the battleground—the demonstrable selfishness, narcissism, and hatred, the powerful force of resistance and the psychopathic predilection of those individuals who attempt to become leaders—one must not fail to maintain hope. Without cautious optimism, without giving significant value to life and experience, all that is precious about civilization will be lost.

By taking an approach that is compassionate and humane rather than moralistic or prescriptive, we can gradually learn to overcome defenses that act as barriers to ethical living. Focusing on psychological ideas could also enable people everywhere to contend with difficult subjects that arise among social groups, such as competition, sexual rivalry, and jealousy.

In every society, there should be a particular emphasis on each member's independence, on his/her feelings of being a separate individual. We can develop our own values and principles and seek our own solutions to life and living. We can cultivate a concern for human rights issues in our personal relationships and learn to value self-fulfillment, freedom, and independence for all people. Living by these ethical principles is necessary for insuring the survival of humankind. Transforming an ideal, ethical vision into a reality depends on the unique combination of understanding of our psychological makeup, compassionate, dedicated and courageous leadership, desire by the populace for authenticity and personal freedom, and incredible resolve.

Notes

1. My approach to ethics is similar in many respects to that of the philosopher Peter Singer (1994), who pointed out that, "Ethics has no necessary connection with any particular religion, nor with religion in general" (p. 5).

2. Hauser (2006) proposed that rational thinking or conscious deliberation alone does not determine human beings' sense of right and wrong: "When we judge an action as morally right or wrong, we do so instinctively, tapping a system of unconsciously operative and inaccessible moral knowledge" (pp. 418-419). Ev-

idence for an innate human potential for moral judgments and behaviors can be found in the attachment literature (Gillath, Shaver, & Mikulincer, 2005).

3. See Aquino and Reed's (2004) concept of *moral identity*. In a related article, Hardy, Bhattacharjee, Reed, & Aquino (2010) observed that "authoritative" parenting characterized by all three dimensions: responsiveness, autonomy-granting, and demandingness seems to facilitate moral identity development (Hart, Atkins, & Ford, 1999; Pratt, Skoe, & Arnold 2004).

4. Most philosophers assert that honesty is not a universal or absolute moral duty. Moreover, being dishonest can be a virtue in unusual circumstances. With respect to this ethic, the philosopher Comte-Sponville (2001) contended that truthfulness "is less important than justice, compassion, and generosity and certainly less important than love; to put it another way, truthfulness, as love of truth, is less important than love of one's fellowman, or charity" (p. 204).

5. Decety and Jackson (2006) have delineated three primary components of empathy: "(a) An affective response to another person, which often, but not always, entails sharing that person's emotional state; (b) a cognitive capacity to take the perspective of the other person; and (c) emotional regulation. . . . Self-regulatory processes are at play to prevent confusion between self- and other feelings" (p. 54).

6. However, in certain situations, ritual has served a constructive purpose. See Tanya Goodman's (2006) chapter, "Performing a 'New Nation': the Role of the TRC in South Africa", which shows that emotionally charged, broadly inclusive rituals remain potent forms of social performance even at the turn of the twenty-first century.

7. See "Children Who Return Home from Foster Care: A 6-Year Prospective Study of Behavioral Health Outcomes in Adolescence" by Taussig et al. (2001). Also see "Reuniting Children with their Families: Reconsidering the Evidence on Timing, Contact and Outcomes" by Nina Biehal (2007); "50,000 Children Are Waiting: Permanency, Planning, and Termination of Parental Rights under the Adoption Assistance and Child Welfare Act of 1980" by Jill Sheldon; "Termination of Parental Rights: Statistical Study and Proposed Solutions; Legislative Reform," by Hillary Baldwin (2002).

8. However, see Taylor's (1984) critique of Foucault in "Foucault on Freedom and Truth." Taylor notes that according to Foucault, "The idea of a liberating truth is a profound illusion. There is no truth that can be espoused, defended, or rescued against systems of power. On the contrary, each such system defines its own variant of truth" (pp. 152-153). Taylor argues that, "Foucault's analyses are terribly one-sided. Their strength is their insightfulness and originality in bringing usually neglected aspects to light. The weakness is that the other aspects seem denied altogether (p.164).

9. There is an extensive literature regarding the concept of "moral disengagement." For example, see "Moral Disengagement in the Perpetuation of Inhu-

manities" by Albert Bandura (1999). According to Moore (2008), "Two cognitive mechanisms (displacement of responsibility and diffusion of responsibility) *minimize the role of the individual* in the harm that is caused by an individual's actions"" ("Moral disengagement" section, para. 5). I suggest that these cognitive mechanisms, including thoughts that attribute blame to others, are part of the destructive voice process described throughout this book.

10. My concerns regarding racism and ethnic warfare are similar in many respects to the cautionary statements written by Hannah Arendt (1976) in *The Origins of Totalitarianism*:

> Racism may indeed carry out the doom of the Western world and, for that matter, of the whole of human civilization. When Russians have become Slavs, when Frenchmen have assumed the role of commanders of a *force noire,* when Englishmen have turned into 'white men', as already for a disastrous spell all Germans became Aryans, then this change will itself signify the end of Western man. For no matter what learned scientists may say, race is, politically speaking, not the beginning of humanity but its end, not the origins of peoples but their decay, not the natural birth of man but his unnatural death (Loc. 3714).

11. Wirth (2004) quotes Freud's statements from "Thoughts for the Times on War and Death": "Evil cannot be 'eradicated'. Psychological—or, to be exact, psychoanalytic—investigations demonstrates instead that . . . a human being is rarely completely good or evil, but mostly, 'good' in one relationship, 'evil' in another, or 'good' under certain external circumstances and under others, decidedly 'evil'"(p. 176).

12. In "Rights, Capabilities, and the Good Society," West (2001) asserted, "A liberal society defined in part by its recognition of *rights to care,* and a liberal culture that took the care to embellish its assumptions, would enrich, not undermine the egalitarianism and individualism of citizens that the liberal rights tradition, to its credit, has always sought to foster" (pp. 1930-1931). Also see Schneider's (2009) description of "The Experimental Democracy Project" in *Awakening to Awe: Personal Stories of Profound Transformation.*

Sources: *Fear of Intimacy* (1999) Chapter 3, "An Ethical Perspective: Human Rights Issues in Personal Relationships" and *The Ethics of Interpersonal Relationships* (2009).

Note on Sources: Portions of this chapter were originally published in *The Ethics of Interpersonal Relationships* by Robert W. Firestone and Joyce Catlett (Published by Karnac Books in 2009), and are reprinted with the kind permission of Karnac Books.

Chapter 16

THE SEARCH FOR A MEANINGFUL LIFE: A LIVING EXPERIMENT

> The story we live by is more important than the actual chronology of our life history. The ideals we pursue are more important than our past achievements. . . . After all, it is meaning that gives life clarity, direction, and passion. It is meaning that endows life with a sense of significance and fulfillment.
>
> ~ Paul Wong (2012, p. 636)

A person's search for meaning and purpose is as fundamental as his/her physical drive for self-preservation. Without this core pursuit, we function on a less than fully human level, lack a center, and suffer from a kind of emotional poverty.

Existentialists have long asserted that meaning and meaninglessness are fundamental elements of the human condition that exert a powerful influence on people's thoughts, feelings, and actions (Note 1). Psychoanalysts and clinical psychologists have written extensively about both concepts and have described potentially measurable variables associated with the search for meaning. In addition to assuming a personal attitude or stance toward existential issues of aloneness, meaninglessness, freedom, responsibility, and death, one must take concerted action in order to achieve a meaningful life. This process requires dedication and commitment because most people rely heavily on psychological defenses that are limiting of this type of endeavor.

THE SEARCH FOR PERSONAL MEANING

Human beings have an innate sense that there is "something more" to life than creature comforts and material success. As Viktor Frankl (1963) observed, people cannot pursue happiness in and of itself. Rather, they need to seek authentic personal meaning in their lives—through their relationships, children, work, and creativity. By doing so, they will experience happiness as an outgrowth of their journey (Note 2).

Life itself may have no hidden meaning or intrinsic significance. People find meaning for themselves when they invest their own feeling and personal energy in activities that express their unique wants and priorities. The painter, musician, or novelist finds meaning in artistic self-expression. Some people experience it primarily through interaction with friends and family. Others do so by contributing to a humanitarian cause or improving the lot of future generations.

The search for meaning is a basic component of achieving a more fulfilling life. In seeking meaning, people go beyond their gratification of basic needs to engage in activities that they regard as having significant value for themselves and/or society. As Becker (1997) wrote: "The most that any one of us can seem to do is to fashion something—an object or ourselves—and drop it into the confusion, make an offering of it, so to speak, to the life force" (p. 285).

When I think about finding meaning in life, I am reminded of a client in psychotherapy, an engineer and scientist who suffered from an obsessive-compulsive disorder with paranoid ideology. This man found himself in a great deal of psychological pain and was nearly overcome by depression, yet his consuming interest in working on a NASA project at Cape Canaveral in those early, glamorous days of rocket science virtually saved his life. Working closely with others on a common goal that transcended a narrow view of his personal life had a profoundly positive effect on his psyche.

WHAT CONSTITUTES A MEANINGFUL LIFE?

There is no particular formula for what constitutes a meaningful life for a given individual, nor could there be. However, it is possible to ground one's goals for a better life in sound mental health principles that include an understanding of what it truly means to be human. (Maslow, 1971; Ryan & Deci, 2008). These include those capacities and personal qualities that enhance life for one's self and others, both qualitatively and quantitatively. This endeavor involves having a desire for self-knowledge and self-understanding as well as a vision of one's future. The process of developing these attributes is unique to each person's ability and circumstances.

If a meaningful life is fundamentally one in which we seek to fully develop our life-affirming human potentialities, describing them is essential. They include: the ability to love and feel compassion for oneself and others; the capacity for abstract reasoning and creativity; the capability to set goals and develop strategies to accomplish them; the desire for social affiliation and an awareness of existential concerns.

PRE-REQUISITES FOR THE SEARCH FOR MEANING

The essential preconditions for embarking on this lifelong enterprise are 1) a commitment to life—that is wholeheartedly embracing one's existence regardless of the circumstances and 2) learning to value one's self. This is an ennobling project that lifts a person out of the mundane everyday routine to a higher level of existence. However, learning to value one's self is a difficult task because the ability to see one's self and one's life as having worth is often damaged early on. Therefore, it becomes an ongoing endeavor to liberate ourselves from the residuals of childhood programming and to learn to exchange restrictive, conventional modes of thinking for a kinder and less judgmental perception of ourselves and the world. The attempt to achieve a more meaningful life revolves around certain core issues:

An Openness to Experience

A crucial step toward achieving your personal, career, and transcendent goals involves moving away from inward, self-parenting habit patterns.

Instead, it requires reaching out while remaining open and vulnerable to experiencing your emotions, thoughts, fantasies, and dreams.

Autonomy and Social Affiliation

To be fully alive, you need to seek and develop both autonomy and social affiliation. In order to preserve feeling for yourself, you must confront the internalized voices that accuse you of being inadequate, destructive, or bad. Facing the enemy within is liberating. As you become more autonomous, you tend to experience a changing, rather than a fixed, identity and are constantly open to growth and evolution, both in the moment and over time.

Human beings have the need and the desire for social affiliation. Individuals who are truly centered in themselves naturally develop empathy, a sense of compassion toward other people, and a desire to work for the good of the larger society. People cannot achieve societal goals such as these through guilt, rules, and prescriptions. A harmonious society becomes a possibility only when its constituents are authentic and develop their own set of values. It is particularly worthwhile to create an environment with others who share one's values, ideals, and desire to search for meaning. Developing a congenial, close friendship with another person or persons represents a meaningful goal for most people.

Generosity

Each dimension of a life-affirming existence challenges the methods that individuals use to impose unnecessary limitations, restrictions, and suffering on themselves. Nowhere is this more evident than when people have the opportunity to extend themselves to others through sensitive acts of kindness and generosity. Giving freely of oneself and of one's time and energy counteracts self-protective defenses, increases feelings of self-esteem, and makes one feel worthwhile.

The process is circular: as people give themselves more value and come to cherish their own experience, they naturally feel motivated to extend this same valuing and appreciation to others through altruistic acts. The ability to contribute to the well-being of others brings one pleasure and imbues life with meaning (Note 3).

Love and Transcendent Goals

As noted, loving others and being loved helps to compensate for the anguish and torment inherent in the human condition. In pursuing a richer emotional life, a person gradually develops the capacity to offer and accept love. Love requires outward expressions of affection, kindness, and consideration, as well as internal feelings of tenderness, love, and warmth. Finally, to be fully alive to all of life's experiences means to live in a manner that attempts to satisfy basic transcendent goals—to love, to feel, to create, to help others, and to ponder the mystery of existence (Note 4).

OVERCOMING BARRIERS TO SEEKING A MEANINGFUL LIFE

To achieve an authentic existence, one must make a passionate commitment to realize the possibilities and the potentials. One must also make choices and act on them. In other words, in order to create meaning in life by means of constructing an authentic existence, individuals have to recognize that they are free to make choices, decisions, and to act on them.

~ Israel Orbach (2008, p. 284)

The crucial elements involved in fulfilling one's potentialities as a human being lie in becoming aware of the defenses that one developed as a protection against the pain of childhood—deprivation, rejection, and the fear of death—and in identifying how they limit one's present-day life. As defenses break down, an individual begins to experience deep feeling toward self and others. It *is* possible to live a relatively undefended, open, and free life in this world. People can fulfill their potential for finding transcendent meaning in their lives if they are willing to question and alter rigid views and negative programming from the past.

Overcoming Defenses Against Feeling

In exploring obstacles to living a more meaningful life, it is worthwhile to consider factors that diminish one of our most important human capacities: the ability to feel a wide range of our emotions. Much of human behavior is directed toward the avoidance of feeling, both the painful primal feelings from childhood as well as the sad and hurtful feelings in the present (Fosha, 2000; Janov, 1970).

It is useful for people to become aware of the habit patterns and routines that they may be using as painkillers to avoid experiencing emotional distress. Identifying these specific defenses against feeling places them more under one's conscious control. For example, exploring the origins of an addictive habit pattern is a critical step in disrupting the defense and regaining feeling.

People who remain connected to their emotions retain their vitality and excitement in living. The capacity for feeling contributes to their spontaneity and creativity and adds dimensions to their personality. Psychologically healthy individuals have a strong emotional investment in living and respond with appropriate affect to both positive and negative experiences in life. Nevertheless, basing one's emotional reactions on real events and circumstances rather than maintaining a self-protective stance does leave one wide open to painful existential anxieties.

Challenging Voice Attacks

As described earlier, anxiety and strong voice attacks are often aroused when people take steps toward pursuing independent goals and priorities in life. For this reason, it is beneficial to identify the critical voices that emerge as individuals move forward and to break withholding patterns and other defenses that interfere with their progress (Note 5). If they challenge the voices that are activated, they will continue to grow and develop. Indeed, people report that their self-attacks gradually diminish if they sweat through the anxiety and persist in maintaining the new behavior over an extended period of time.

Some people have difficulty conceptualizing their goals because they have been hurt early on in their basic feeling about themselves and have turned against their own wants and desires—a fundamental part of their identity. In addition, as noted previously, many who have suffered rejection and deprivation come to rely excessively on fantasy to gratify their wants and needs rather than seeking satisfaction in goal-directed behavior. This is manifested in a resistance to taking the practical steps necessary to succeed.

Still others exercise what existential philosophers and psychologists Rank (1972), Nietzsche (1966/1886), and Yalom (1980) refer to as "negative will" or "counter-will" in relation to fulfilling their aspirations or accomplishing their personal life goals. For example, in a lecture "Neurosis as a Failure in Creativity," Rank (1935, quoted in Kramer, 1996) asserted:

Instead of affirming or asserting his will, the neurotic has to find an excuse to prove to himself as well as to others his inability or incapability. *Instead of saying, "I don't want to do that," he says, "I cannot do it, because I am afraid or feel guilty."* This formulation contains the whole problem of neurosis in a nutshell. . . . To the neurotic, the attainment of any definite goal means the end, in the sense of death (pp. 254-256).

Later in the same lecture, Rank further elucidated his concept of *negative will*, which I see as similar, in some respects, to the anti-self system:

The neurotic type starts by saying no to life itself, and furthermore he manifests his rebellion against it by further noes, that is by setting his negative will against the laws of nature, or practically against his own *being* (p. 257).

Rank (1935, quoted in Kramer, 1996) suggested a solution to this impasse: the patient needs to use "creative imagination—instead of negative will—in order to change the world according to his own ideals" (p. 258). In describing the creative impulse in *Art and Artist* (1932), Rank further asserted,

In short, the patient must find the courage to *choose* that which is absolutely determined: his/her own life . . . deliberately saying "Yes!" to the "Must." We have no choice other than to choose freely that which is *already* given to us: life. . . .

More precisely stated, I conceive of the creative drive as the life-impulse (including sexuality) put at the service of the individual will (pp. 63-65).

CREATING A LIFE OF MEANING AND COMPASSION

Numerous books are published each year offering ideas and theories about how to live a fuller life, achieve better relationships, raise happier children, succeed in business, and realize personal and spiritual goals. In the following pages, I relate the experiences of the more than 100 individuals in the psychological community described earlier who formulated similar ideologies and put these concepts into practice. The members, who range in age from infancy to those in their 80s, are long-time friends and associates of mine.

This friendship circle functions in an urban setting, has been unusually successful in its endeavors and has withstood the test of time. The people involved are committed to compassion and feeling, lead honest, open lives, and are not afraid to challenge the status quo when it seems appropriate.

As I have mentioned, I have lived and worked closely with these individuals and have observed first hand as they have transformed their lives in ways that have allowed them to more fully develop their human potential. In attempting to bring their idea of a meaningful life to fruition, they conceptualize it not as a specific outcome, but rather as an ongoing psychological journey. Their purpose was never to arrive at a particular destination in their personal development; instead, it was to embark on a lifetime venture that challenges defenses and addictive, routine habit patterns. This process has enabled these individuals to feel increasingly alive, helped them to overcome obstacles to their truthful communication and loving experiences, and empowered them to accomplish high-level practical goals in the real world.

These people have found that living an authentic life involves a complex process of acculturation. In striving to live without their customary defenses, they have developed a warmer, more growth-enhancing manner of relating and have gradually adapted to the vast difference between this new environment and the world they knew as children. However, their positive growth and development have not been achieved without substantial growing pains. In their discussions over the years, these men and women confronted their own personal demons and struggled with those of their friends. In their commitment to change, they have had to suffer through states of anxiety and take the risks necessary for self-actualization. In the name of truth, they have had to relinquish some of their most precious illusions. In striving to lead more fulfilling lives with a minimum of defenses and a close involvement with other persons, they have developed an increased sense of vulnerability.

Background and History

Historically, the group originated with a few families who enjoyed sharing life's experiences in close friendship. They never set out to form an extended group or create a new society. As these people led a life of adventure and enterprise, they met others who were compatible and the group of friends gradually increased in numbers. This growth was spontaneous; there was no sense of an "in" or "out" group differentiation, nor was there an element of exclusivity. There never was any attempt to proselytize or increase the "membership." People gradually formed close ties that have endured for more than fifty years.

As noted, these women and men are strongly individualistic and came from various backgrounds, but they share a common interest in psychology and philosophical issues. In their discussions together, they have challenged themselves and revealed their thoughts and feelings in a manner that has created a unique psychological laboratory.

I have been fortunate in having had the opportunity to participate in this friendship circle from the beginning. In writing about these people, I have described their past and present experiences as a love story, not the narrow definition of what one usually thinks of as romantic or sexual love, although certainly not exclusive of that connotation. Nor was I writing about an ethereal, spiritual meaning of the word love, although when love is omnipresent it reaches a level of spirituality. I was describing a love of people, places, and natural surroundings—in particular, the sea—a love of sharing projects, both material and ideological, with others in close personal interaction, a love of feeling and adventure, and ultimately a love of life itself.

A Vision of a Meaningful Life

The story of this extended friendship circle has diverse roots. Its beginnings may be traced to a fantasy that is probably common to most people—that is, a dream to share a better world with close friends. This fantasy was particularly strong in the individuals who formed this environment, though they never fancied themselves as pioneers of a new order. They saw themselves as ordinary people with a natural desire to find an atmosphere where they could be themselves, and be generous and caring toward others. In their pursuit of this vision, they have created an extraordinary life and unique set of circumstances (R. Firestone, L. Firestone, & Catlett, 2003).

Their experience now spans four generations of family life, shedding light on typical childrearing patterns that are either nurturing or potentially toxic to child development. From this understanding, they have developed an implicit morality based on an acute awareness of the kind of destructive "toxic" personality characteristics that cause emotional pain and suffering.. They had a strong desire to break the chain of passing this destructive style of relating from one generation to the next. In addition, the process of working together in close harmony and friendship in an accepting and warm environment led to unusual successes, both vocationally and in personal fulfillment.

Stuart Boyd, psychologist and former professor at St. John's College in Santa Fe, New Mexico, visited the community and observed the interactions and activities of its population for a three-month period in 1982 (R. Firestone, 1985). He summarized his findings in an essay about this society and its participants:

> This is a community of some 90 persons—women, men, children—who seem to have achieved the better life together with a minimum of dogma, political authority, withdrawal, mysticism, insulation, isolation, dispossession of the goods and comforts of modern technology. There is no golden lie, no coercion, no constitution, no turning out at the expense of in, no turning in at the expense of out. It is not, nor claims to be, Utopia.

Basic Psychological Principles

Given the unprecedented power human beings have to destroy life, it is significant that they also have a wide variety of positive qualities that make each person potentially admirable. If unnecessary frustration and interpersonal suffering in children's lives was minimized, human beings might well achieve a sense of compassion both as individuals and in society. If the majority of individuals chose to develop their potential for love and decency, they might collectively alter the course of history.

My belief in the possibility of a benign social movement or society is an outgrowth of studying the development of ethical principles of human behavior within this circle of friends. Extrapolated from these were several psychological principles that we found particularly valuable. One basic premise is that people need to differentiate from negative influences in their lives, both internally and externally, in order to develop their personal autonomy, sense of self and value system. When individuals formulate values and ethics from within themselves rather than from without, they can chart the course of their lives in a manner that is harmonious and well integrated.

Lastly, they must become more aware of their personal power. If they are dedicated, they have the capacity to change any of their negative behaviors and personality traits as well as influencing others to do the same.

Some additional principles are important to adhere to for optimal mental health, including the following: there is no room for prejudice, status, stereotyping, or the superiority of one group over another; it is inadvisable to think in terms of absolutes; men and women have more commonalities than differences; friendship cannot exist in a vacuum, therefore there is value in working together on mutual projects and sharing endeavors with other people to achieve common goals.

Communication in the Friendship Circle

This friendship circle was shaped by a key value from which everything else flowed: the freedom for people to speak their minds, including the seemingly unspeakable. This right was protected for each person in this milieu in a manner that differentiated the internal dynamics of this group from family and societal practices that are generally more restrictive.

In the process of talking together, these individuals have gradually created a new way of living based on an implicit code of ethical principles that focuses on avoiding behaviors that hurt other people—behaviors that are hurtful to personal development, especially to that of children.

The subjects that people discuss in these talks are varied; they might choose to talk about their dreams, their fantasies, their anger, or their fears. They may have positive or negative perceptions about another person that they feel would be relevant to the other's development. They may have negative reactions that they want communicate to clear the air so there will be no unresolved issues with anyone. In the talks, people actively solicit realistic perceptions about themselves from others. They have confidence in the process of change and feel that they can effectively alter their lives to become the kind of people they want to be. Therefore, if they hear critical feedback, it can be even more favorable to their development than being told something positive because they can use the constructive criticism to further develop themselves.

In addition, sharing everyday life, including living together, working together, traveling and sailing the oceans together, provided a crucible in which people's negative traits were incidentally modified by their proximity to one another. Many of the rough edges in their personalities were smoothed out and behaviors that were abrasive at close quarters gradually diminished as they co-existed and cooperated to achieve their goals.

After years of talking in this style, most people have become remarkably open; for instance, they tend to not be embarrassed about revealing their innermost secrets. Because they have developed deep, personal feelings toward each other, even the larger talks can take on the feeling of a close, intimate group. In his *Analysis,* Stuart Boyd (1982) described the atmosphere of these talks:

> The talk is disciplined in the sense that it is not the chatter you hear when a large group of people come into a room together, which swiftly escalates to a roar as everyone talks at once and no one hears. These meetings are a blend of the informal, some announcements, some joking of a personal nature, relevant and good-natured. Then often the emergence, spontaneously, of a problem of pain someone is having with the self or others, in the most intimate of relationships, or in work or some aspect of the community.
>
> The communication of circumstance and the open expression of feeling, negative and positive, the deep impression of community relationship, the respectful listening and participation by others than those directly involved is a moving experience.

As I mentioned in Chapter 1, over the course of the evolution of this circle of friends, my colleagues and I assembled and documented information gleaned from these discussions regarding the emotional damage that people sustained as children and how specific defenses perpetuated their suffering throughout their lives. Our investigations led to conclusions about both the type and quality of experiences that are conducive to the well-being of individuals, as well as those that are limiting and destructive. Thus, the implicit ethical code that has gradually evolved is based on solid mental health precepts, not on rules, authoritarian codes, or parental prescriptions. I have shared much of what we learned in a number of books, journal articles, and videos.

Values of the Friendship Circle

> How the community lives raises some very interesting issues for moral and ethical philosophy, but as far as "conventional" morali-

ty is concerned it's no contest—truth versus hypocrisy; manifest improvement in happiness and stability versus anxiety and broken, hating relationships.

~ Stuart Boyd (1982)

The values and ideals endorsed by the individuals in this group are derived from an understanding of much of what is essentially human: mankind's deep need for social affiliation, the desire for affection and attention, the need to be seen as one really is, and the importance of not being intruded on. These ideals involved an active search for a meaningful life and the development of a living philosophy of compassion based on love and respect for humanity. This extended to a general reverence for life.

One core belief in the friendship circle is that any group function, social more or commitment that intrudes on or compromises the essential individuality of its members is a negative or destructive institution and is considered generally distasteful. These people are particularly concerned about human rights issues. This concern reaches its highest level in relation to the respect for children and their well-being, but it applies to adult interactions as well. All people are worthy of a basic respect, regardless of their individual strengths or weaknesses. There is a minimum of racial, religious or gender prejudice, class-consciousness, or other stereotyping. This group of people supports a positive worldview over nationalistic interests and is strongly opposed to guns and violence. There is a love of people at far reaches and close quarters.

Overall, the group is constantly monitoring itself, reviewing its practices and scrutinizing itself to detect any inequities or unfairness. Criticism without malice is always welcome and there are discussions about any dissatisfaction with the systems politic. There is an ongoing effort to improve everyone's living circumstances in the deepest and broadest sense, both material and psychological.

Generosity—A Core Value: There are frequent acts of kindness and generosity among the individuals of the friendship circle. If there is something that someone really wants or needs that is not entirely beyond our means, we take joy in buying it for them. This type of generosity has become a happy tradition. At one time or another, sensitive and thoughtful presents have been given to every one of my friends. For us, giving is a year-round proposition, not restricted to birthdays or holidays. Gifts are given from the heart rather than out of form or obligation.

There are innumerable examples of generosity and small kindnesses manifested daily by this circle of friends. The sweet concern for each other, the helping hand that is extended, the casual sharing of money, cars, or food, the immediate positive response when asked a favor, and the spontaneous affection between friends and acquaintances are the rule rather than the exception.

One of the few rules for our group is that each person must have health insurance. Because we care so deeply for one another, if any one required medical help, we would respond without hesitation. We realized that this could prove costly. Many years ago, a friend of ours became seriously ill and needed a liver transplant. The expensive operation had to be performed before we knew if her insurance would cover it. The cost was far beyond our means, but we all pooled our credit cards to cover the medical fees.

Each of us is grateful for the chance to participate in any act of kindness inside or outside of our group. We are not looking to be charitable in the grand sense, nor are we looking for approval as do-gooders. We simply respond to the personal adversity or ongoing need of individuals whom we encounter in the course of our lives. This brings us a great deal of satisfaction.

These types of charitable acts are always offered on an individual basis and nothing is formalized or institutionalized. People casually go about sharing domestic and other practical tasks of everyday living without much, if any, status differential. Everyone pitches into the activities and offers their specific skills and expertise.

As noted in Chapter 1, consideration and kindnesses extended to others without an expectation of reciprocal treatment not only feels good, but it counters inward attitudes of tightness and habitual patterns of withholding. When giving to others, people tend to feel liberated in terms of having more energy for productive work, and feel both more vulnerable and more satisfied in their relationships.

Power and Leadership: In a humane social system such as the friendship circle, power is invested for the "good," with "good" being what nurtures people in general and what supports the unique traits of the individual. Our small society is based on the ideal of democracy combined with a thriving emotional Bill of Rights.

Within this framework, individuals who are most highly regarded become popular as leaders. This is for a number of reasons. First, they most ardently represent the group values and initiative. Next, they are the most empathic, honest and generous, and devote themselves to the well-being of both the individual participants and the overall group enterprise on a daily basis. Lastly, they contribute a great deal to the cheerful, uplifting atmosphere of friendliness and good humor.

Some became prominent because of seamanship and boat handling skills, others for their competence in business affairs and, more importantly, still others for their knowledge and innate psychological sensitivity. These men and women are significantly valued for their mastery in particular areas, but they are also respected because of their positive attitude and concern for people in general. Without the humanitarian aspect, their skills alone would not have garnered the respect they have earned.

A person's power is naturally limited to the functions of the tasks for which he/she is valued and does not extend beyond those parameters. Those in leadership positions function primarily in a service or advisory capacity; they have no desire to impose rules or require action from the membership. There are no hidden agendas or politicking, and the leaders are afforded no protection from public scrutiny. Their behavior and decisions are talked about openly and freely evaluated. If someone abuses power in any way, it leads to immediate censorship in the talks. And although these leaders are widely respected, they would never expect or ask for special privileges or advantages.

Politics: This group's political ideology could be considered to be capitalism with a social conscience. My friends and I believe that people should be rewarded according to their contribution, but also that everyone should share in the successes of the enterprises and live the lifestyle afforded by these successes. In this community, the main advantage to being wealthy is that you are able to give more to others, and this is considered a lucky thing.

We share a strong belief in free enterprise and a respect for the democratic political system of the larger culture that has allowed us to succeed financially. We are grateful for the opportunities we have been afforded. In a real sense, we have achieved the American Dream, starting with very little and building large companies that have raised everyone's standard of living considerably.

The Committee: Even though my friends and I dislike surplus rules or organization, at some point, it became apparent that we needed a way to oversee and manage the ever-growing array of practical matters. We decided to elect a committee of fifteen people who would look after the practical and personal aspects of living together and who would address any problems that might arise. This committee would meet periodically. There would be no closed or restricted meeting; anyone who wanted to could attend and enter into the discussion.

Committee elections would be held every year. On a practical level, the committee would handle finances and maintain and improve our physical surroundings. On an emotional level, members of the committee would arbitrate any disputes and offer suggestions to anyone seeking help in a problem area. In fact, there are rarely personal disputes to settle and the committee is principally concerned with three major functions: financial issues, the childcare program and overall people concerns.

Finances: The monetary success of this community was amassed through shared business ventures, and those who were most instrumental benefitted accordingly. These same entrepreneurs shared their wealth in various ways. They made considerable gifts of company stock to their friends, in particular to the children. These children, who are now adults, have continued this custom of passing on to their own children the benefits of their success.

The members of the community have adopted what can be described as a policy of "enlightened capitalism." Of course, each member controls his/her own finances. The committee assesses the financial needs of the community and recommends how much each person will contribute to the shared functions based on a sliding scale according to each one's financial condition. By this standard, the wealthiest individuals contribute by far the most, but each person finds it important to contribute what he/she is able. The money collected pays for rent, food, boats, recreational activities, and other expenses of the community. Many of the members of the community have also found it important to provide support to The Glendon Association, a nonprofit organization established by the group of friends to disseminate psychological information to both mental health professionals and the general public. Aside from paying for these shared resources, all other financial affairs are a private matter.

This practice of enlightened capitalism has enabled every member of the community to share in the business successes. Because of the general concern for the financial well-being of each individual, there is a financial subcommittee for those who want help with their personal finances; it also marshals resources to provide financial aid to those in need. It has become a yearly tradition that every child within our group of friends receives a sizeable financial contribution from the community so that they are financially secure by the time they are 21. Conversely, we make sure that our elderly members are solvent and well looked after by family and friends, treated with sensitivity and kindness, chauffeured, accompanied to doctors and other appointments. They have no practical reason to worry about retirement. They are spared the feelings of insecurity and anxious concern that pose a serious problem for so many older people in contemporary society.

Voluntary financial gifts are common in order to express appreciation to people who have made special contributions to the community. These gifts often are made at the end of the year and include a gathering where each person is thanked for his/her contribution. It is an emotional experience for many and happy smiles are often mixed with tears of gratitude.

The Children

It was good to see young ones present during the discussion. There seem to be no inhibitions or taboos of content or language among them, and they are learning the tales and anecdotes. The process of transmission through generations is preserved. The young ones are respected as children but are not encouraged to be falsely childish—and of course there is a considerable difference in the two conditions, a difference that the community is sensitively aware of. They are never given token recognition of their presence, and then ignored. They have their rights for recognition and audience and serious attention respected too, and they are never brushed aside or cut off in what they are saying, or trying to say. The youngsters are such fun to be with and are the bright hope of the community.

~ Stuart Boyd (1982)

As these individuals became more sophisticated psychologically and developed more compassion, they gradually focused more attention on the physical and emotional health and security of each child. Pre-school children have a nursery school available daily, operated by men and women who have chosen to be seriously involved with childcare functions. The children learn to be independent, develop peer relationships early on and feel remarkably comfortable with adults other than their parents.

In addition, the overall well-being of the children is an ongoing subject in our talks. Any issues that a specific child faces are discussed and solutions are sought. This pattern of helping and sharing in the functions of childrearing has had a constructive impact on many children. Friends are always willing to offer what they can in the service of helping to care for youngsters. In this close community, very little goes unnoticed and the children are spared much of the emotional, as well as physical abuse, which is commonplace in the culture at large.

Older members, who had raised their children in the conventional family unit, have noted the positive differences in this milieu. Parents are freed from much of the everyday childcare tasks and are able to spend more quality time with their children. Sharing the responsibilities of parenthood with close friends has made for more loving and endearing relationships with the youngsters. The majority of the children have done well and have grown into respectful, decent adults with a feeling for other people.

SPIRITUALITY, MYSTERY, AND THE SEARCH FOR MEANING

Another critical component in pursuing a meaningful life involves developing one's sense of the sacred, enhancing the spiritual dimensions of our experience and exploring the mystery of existence. Each person must reach his/her own conclusions, that is, to develop one's own beliefs and speculations about the vital questions in life based on one's own personal experiences, rather than on ideas and beliefs mediated through diverse religious or secular systems.

All people possess the ability to have spiritual experiences and to sense mysteries that elude human understanding. At many points on the journey through life, they encounter events that bring out an appreciation of nature and the unknown and that generate spiritual experiences, which evoke deep emotional responses. Tomer and Eliason (2008) wrote of these peak experiences, which are associated with "feelings of wonder, surprise, awe, and so on" (p. 9) and posed questions about existence unanswerable by Aristotelian logic. William James (2004/1902) argued that "these peak experiences should not be conceptualized, however, as including only 'mystical states of consciousness', either of Eastern or Western tradition" (cited in Tomer & Eliason, 2008, p. 10).

Indeed, many people of no particular religious persuasion have reported having experiences that inspire awe and that, at times, have been life-transforming (Schneider, 2004; 2009). When this search for meaning and spiritual awareness takes people to the edge of human understanding, where they accept the ultimate mystery of their lives and the limitations of science and rationality, they know, at the most profound level, what it means to be fully human.

As my friends and I have learned to accept the uncertainty and ambiguity of life, we have come to believe that there are no absolute truths to be discovered. We have determined that wherever there is an absence of fact, we have the right to choose and embrace our own beliefs regarding the origins and nature of life. Without knowledge, there is room for faith, and faith can take many forms. Some people embrace traditional beliefs, while others seek the sacred in nature, others in music and the arts, and many find it in love.

Even after considering the impact on belief systems caused by scientific advances in the understanding of the origin of Homo sapiens and the development of life on the planet earth, one cannot rule out faith, for much is still unknown. Aristotelian logic and modern science not only fail to explain existence, they preclude its possibility. All that we know in the scientific sense points to the fact that something cannot come from nothing; even if one postulates a God, one is burdened by the question of where that essence could have come from.

Faced with this preposterous logical contradiction, we are left with a hypothetical conundrum that goes beyond human intelligence and intellect. In the current vernacular, we are faced with a mind-blowing problem. We are forced to accept the assault on our vanity and face the painful truth of our intellectual limitations. But there is a consolation. We are left with the fact of mystery, free to contemplate the awesome spectacle of existence of all varieties, and we are left open to form our own conclusions about life and meaning.

Spirituality in the Friendship Circle

> They share a set of beliefs and consequent behaviors that have embraced all of their ventures in a web of feeling and motivation that has led to adventurous courage on the high seas, to spectacular business success, and to a remarkable complex of living and loving relationships where it would seem that energy and laughter and good feeling significantly outweigh their opposites.
>
> ~ Stuart Boyd (1982)

Most individuals in the friendship circle are non-denominational and do not participate in organized religious practices as such. Few attend church or involve themselves in other forms of ritualized worship. They personally hold a wide range of beliefs about creation and the existence or concept of God or a superior being. Some believe in prayer while others are agnostics or atheists. In spite of their lack of participation in organized religion, it would be a gross misconception to consider these people as lacking in spirituality. Indeed, their mode of existence is imbued with a deep spiritual quality, a reverence for life and humanity that pervades every aspect of their being.

This is not an isolated phenomenon relegated to designated occasions; instead, it is lived out each day. These people are actively concerned with moral principles and with human rights issues that transcend conventional morality. They exhibit an abiding regard for people's feelings, their well-being and personal freedom and, as described above, these sentiments are expressed through everyday acts of kindness, sensitivity, and compassion.

CONCLUSION

To varying degrees, each participant in this community has contributed and lived according to the values described above. Although ours is not a perfect world, I think it is worthwhile to consider the basic ideals and aspirations of this community. In revealing the experiences of the people in the friendship circle and their efforts to overcome defensive barriers to fully embracing emotionally richer, more satisfying lives, I am not suggesting that others need to imitate this particular social milieu or pursue the same pathway in their struggle to find a life of meaning.

Lastly, I share the belief of many philosophers that the pursuit of a meaningful life requires consideration and conscious reflection about existential issues. However, I do not agree with those who believe that this requires a prescribed adherence to a particular religious code or to any leader or philosopher accorded near-divine status. On the contrary, I recognize that to pursue and find personal meaning in life, one must seek to develop one's potentialities and values in one's own unique manner.

For me personally, my life has been enhanced by my efforts to support clients, friends, family, and loved ones as they each strive to fulfill their own vision of a better life. It has always been my belief that the good life involves a concern for other people, starting with your own family, giving value and respect to other human beings, serving others, wanting to better the world that you live in—to heal, to help, to share—making your life the best story possible (Note 6). However long this friendship circle may last, I am deeply grateful to have lived among so many people who share life in harmony, with a high level of honesty and deep feeling.

Notes

1. Re: meaning: see *Man's Search for Meaning* Frankl (1963), Maslow (1967), Wong (2008), and Orbach (2008), among many others. Orbach's discussion of high order and low order meanings in Chapter 12, "Existentialism and Suicide" is particularly relevant.

    Re: meaninglessness: see Kierkegaard (1954), Nietzsche (1966/1886), and Camus (1991). Yalom (1980) attributed a sense of meaninglessness to "a failure to find sufficient answers to existential concerns. . . . Existential freedom bestows the responsibility of independently creating life-structures; a task that some individuals may find overwhelming" (cited by Orbach, 2008, p. 291). Orbach went on to propose an alternative hypothesis to explain the dynamics of meaninglessness: "lack of meaning does not cause suffering, rather suffering is the cause for lack of meaning. Suffering causes an interruption in the natural flow of the creation of meaning" (p. 298).

2. In his critique of pursuing happiness for its own sake as a part of one's "self-actualization," Frankl (1963) argued, "What is called self-actualization is not an attainable aim at all, for the simple reason that the more one would strive for it, the more he would miss it. In other words, self-actualization is possible only as a side-effect of self-transcendence" (Loc. 1146).

3. Generosity and altruism are also conducive to physical and mental health. See "Altruism, Happiness, and Health: It's Good to Be Good" by Stephen G. Post (2005). Research has also shown that death salience often increases people's acts of altruism and generosity, with certain qualifications (Jonas, Schimel, Greenberg & Pyszczynski, 2002).

4. With respect to love in the context of a meaningful life, Frankl (1963) wrote, "Love is the only way to grasp another human being in the innermost core of his personality. . . . Furthermore, by his love, the loving person enables the be-loved person to actualize these [his or her] potentialities" (Loc. 1151-1154).

5. A potentially helpful exercise for overcoming resistance to taking action in relation to one's goals consists of listing one's wants, interests, and goals on the left-hand side of a page. In the middle column, one lists any destructive voices that might prevent one from pursuing these wants and goals. On the right-hand side of the page, one writes down a realistic point of view about one's wants and goals (See R. Firestone, L. Firestone, & Catlett, 2002, Figure 6.4 "Going After What You Want").

6. Robert W. Firestone's statements from the conclusion of "Friendship: A Life of Meaning and Compassion" Documentary Film, (Parr, 2002—finalist in the 2003 New York International Film and Video Competition.)

Sources: *Creating a Life of Meaning and Compassion: The Wisdom of Psychotherapy* (2003) Inclusive pages: pp. 3-34, and *Evolution of a Psychotherapist* (2010) unpublished autobiography.

Note on Sources: Reproduced with permission © (2003) of American Psychological Association from *Creating a Life of Meaning and Compassion: The Wisdom of Psychotherapy* by Robert W. Firestone, Lisa A. Firestone, and Joyce Catlett.

EPILOGUE

LIFE-AFFIRMING
DEATH AWARENESS

Man lives on amid the senseless nihilism of the universe . . . he has endured all the hard and purposeless suffering, and still he wants to live. . . . Thus, it is impossible to scorn this creature. For out of his strong belief in life, this puny man made love. At his best, he *is* love. Without him there can be no love . . .

Why, then, should any living man ally himself with death, and, in his grief and blindness, batten on his brother's blood?

~ Thomas Wolfe (1934, p. 411)

As long as man is an ambiguous creature he can never banish anxiety; what he can do instead is to use anxiety as an eternal spring for growth into new dimensions of thought and trust.

~ Ernest Becker (1997, p. 92)

Although most people, when contemplating death or its reminders, tend to regress and become more inward and defended, one could use the same set of circumstances to give greater value to life. In this sense, acknowledging death could enhance our experience and lead to a sense of freedom rather than to cynicism or despair. Realizing life's finitude in an undefended state of mind can heighten one's awareness, give more value to each moment, and increase the likelihood of investing more of oneself in one's unique personal goals and relationships. It can inspire greater creativity, support the desire to separate from destructive vestiges of our past, add to our sense of wholeness and integrity, and lead to a more compassionate view toward humankind. We all share the same fate.

As the poet Joy Grisham (in *Shadowlands*, 1993) put it when she confronted her husband, C.S. Lewis, about his despair at her impending death, "The pain of the ending is part of the happiness now. That's the deal." People everywhere encounter the same essential problems and struggle for survival. Therefore, we are all brothers and sisters, and there is no room for indifference to suffering, starvation, poverty, prejudice, exclusionary nationalism, ethnic strife, or warfare.

In thinking about and developing a philosophy that enhances life in the face of death and emphasizes personal freedom and living in the moment, I began to consider some basic guidelines that might prove to be of value. In order to achieve a freer existence, there are certain principles derived from the wisdom of psychotherapy that people could apply to their lives. Some of these ideas have been mentioned briefly before, but they are especially relevant here.

* Approach yourself with kindness, much as a compassionate therapist or trusted friend would. It is never acceptable to attack or punish yourself, even when you have made a mistake or done something bad or wrong; it's more important to explore the origins of your actions, to understand and to change, rather than judge yourself. In addition, you can apologize or try to make amends for hurtful actions.

* All feelings are acceptable, whereas your actions are subject to both reality concerns and moral considerations. Thoughts and feelings arise spontaneously and are therefore essentially innocent.

* Anger is an automatic reaction to frustration; it is not related to rationality or logic. Rather, it is proportional to the degree of frustration. When anger is suppressed, it leads to projection or is turned inward against the self; both solutions are dysfunctional. Angry or vicious thoughts hurt no one, whereas even a mildly sarcastic remark may cause pain. It is important to fully feel your anger and to decide how, when and where to express it. According to the writer Saul Bel-

low (2003), "One thought- murder a day keeps the psychiatrist away" (Loc. 1785).

* It is dysfunctional to play the victim; it's more adaptive to feel one's anger directly in relation to the source of frustration and express it appropriately. Feeling victimized leads to passive inward brooding and obsessing, rather than to a healthy release and/or an opportunity to take appropriate action to address the situation.

* Being vulnerable is not a weakness; it is a strength. Being open and sensitive to your feelings and your wants leads to more goal-directed action and you are more likely to succeed in your endeavors. Being vulnerable also leaves you less duplicitous in your communications and other people are more likely to give you what you want. Being controlling is the opposite of being vulnerable.

* You have the right to ask for what you want; however, you are not entitled to get what you want. Feeling entitled generally leads to a sense of victimization and paranoid thoughts.

* You have no proprietary rights over another person. You cannot possess or "belong" to anyone else; a romantic partner, husband, or wife. Children do not belong to their parents; they belong only to themselves. Each person is unique, separate, and genetically different from everyone else, and cannot be owned. This recognition does not deny the possibility of long-standing genuine intimacy, love, and closeness.

* Love is not just a feeling; it must include action as well. Many people believe that they love each other, but their actions are disrespectful and unkind. Real love includes such behaviors as affection, kindness, respect for each other's personal freedom and boundaries, equality, and support for each other's goals and priorities. If these characteristics are not present, it would be inappropriate to consider the relationship loving.

* You can learn to love. You are best served by developing your capacity to love; it is the only antidote to the despair inherent in the human condition. As you free yourself from traumatic feelings from your early years, develop insight and work through deep-seated per-

sonal problems, you can expand your capacity for sensitivity, respect and compassion.

* You have the right to choose your relationship partner and an equal right to reject him/her in the course of your development. This does not imply casual abuses or inconsideration of another person's feelings.

* A person has the right to win in a competition, even if it means another person loses. Feeling competitive is not a moral issue; it's a normal feeling reaction to wanting and is directed toward the person or persons who are competing for the same thing. Many people feel guilty about their competitive feelings and shy away from competing, to their own detriment.

* Generosity is not merely an act of kindness; it is a sound mental health principle. It is its own reward because it contributes heavily to a sense of well-being and good feeling.

Everyone has the personal power to change, but they are up against deeply engrained defense mechanisms and habit patterns. For this reason, it is challenging to apply the above ideas in everyday life. However, with energy and dedication, you can develop to the point where these precepts become a more automatic and integrated part of your personality and approach to life.

Working in the field of psychology for more than sixty years, I am impressed with the vision of human beings as a frightened species terrified of its eventual demise. Looking at present day civilization as if coming from another planet, I have observed people moving about frantically, racing their vehicles, hurtling through the air at high speed while at the same time building monuments to their existence and tearing them down. But where is humanity going, and how far have we strayed from our true nature? What has become of a worldview of true friendship, loyalty, love, and compassion for others?

Life can be symbolized as movement toward a multitude of choices, whereas death can be symbolized by the absence of choice. Faced with death's certainty, we can choose to identify with life or, on a symbolic level, align ourselves with death. We can move toward our individual goals and basic humanity, or in some fashion retreat from, or actually give up, our aspirations. Every decision is either in the interest of pursuing one's life and personal freedom or sacrificing it for some form of illusion or false safety. We are either feeling our emotions or deadening them. We are either expanding the range of our choices or narrowing our focus in a manner that limits and circumscribes our lives.

The defense of denial, giving up, and gradually relinquishing life on an individual level is also characteristic of the larger society and can be observed worldwide. From primitive cultures to modern societies, people have created countless methods, rituals, and myths in their attempt to soothe the fear of death. James Baldwin (1963) put it this way, "Perhaps the whole root of our trouble, the human trouble, is that we will sacrifice all the beauty of our lives, will imprison ourselves in totems, taboos, crosses, blood sacrifices, steeples, mosques, races, armies, flags, nations, in order to deny the fact of death" (Loc. 872).

Tortured by the reality that each person faces a death sentence, we strive to defend ourselves from the associated emotional pain and sadness. However, we cannot deny existential realities and cut off emotional pain without losing real feeling for ourselves and others. As I've said, we cannot be innocently defended; our defenses hurt others, especially those closest to us, our mates and our children.

Expressing the deep feelings of sadness and sorrow about existential realities has an ameliorative, rather than disturbing, effect on those who are open to this emotional experience. Living a less defended life allows us to experience all of our emotions and we are better able to tolerate intimacy.

At every stage in life the choice of whether to invest or to retreat, presents itself. When faced with conflict, it is often wise to take the path that makes the best, most interesting, most uplifting story. How often, though, are we relieved to give up, remain passive and let things go? We wake up on a rainy day and feel a sense of relief to not be able to take the planned excursion, roll over in bed and resume our repose. In a similar way, we may feel better or experience a sense of relaxation when we are rejected—often, we are proud that our cynicism has been confirmed by reality. However, as I have illustrated in this book, we *can* take control of our lives and, in that sense, create ourselves, but it requires complete honesty, deep self-reflection, courage, persistence and the willingness to take chances. In this way, we can take full advantage of the unique life we have been offered.

In conclusion, it *is* possible to be aware of the inevitability of death, deal with the painful emotions and fear openly and, at the same time, give greater value to our lives. We can take a position philosophically that our uniqueness, our separateness, and our creativity are essential human qualities that must be protected at all costs. I believe that the ideal approach to existential concerns is to commit oneself to a life of integrity, truth, and love.

REFERENCES

Ackerman, S. J., & Hilsenroth, M. J. (2003). A review of therapist characteristics and techniques positively impacting the therapeutic alliance. *Clinical Psychology Review, 23*(1), 1-33. doi: 10.1016/S0272-7358(02)00146-0AS

Alexander, J. C., Giesen, B., & Mast, J. L. (Eds.). (2006). *Social performance: Symbolic action, cultural pragmatics, and ritual.* Cambridge University Press.

American Psychiatric Association. (2013). *Diagnostic and statistical manual of mental disorders* (DSM-5). Washington, DC: Author.

Angus, L., & Kagan, F. (2007). Empathic relational bonds and personal agency in psychotherapy: Implications for psychotherapy supervision, practice, and research. *Psychotherapy: Theory, Research, Practice, Training, 44*(4), 371. doi: 10.1037/0033-3204.44.4.371

Anthony, E. J. (1987). Children at high risk for psychosis growing up successfully. In E. J. Anthony & B. J. Cohler (Eds.), *The invulnerable child* (pp. 147-184). New York: Guilford Press.

Anthony, S. (1973). *The discovery of death in childhood and after.* Harmondsworth, UK: Penguin Education. (Original work published 1971).

Attenborough, R. (Producer, Director), Eastman, B. (Producer). (1993). *Shadowlands* [Motion Picture]. United States: Savoy Pictures.

Aquino, K., & Reed II, A. (2002). The self-importance of moral identity. *Journal of Personality and Social Psychology, 83*(6), 1423-1440. doi: 10.1037/0022-3514.83.6.1423

Arendt, H. (1976). *The origins of totalitarianism.* New York: Houghton Mifflin Harcourt.

Arndt, J., Greenberg, J., Pyszczynski, T., & Solomon, S. (1997). Subliminal exposure to death-related stimuli increases defense of the cultural worldview. *Psychological Science, 8*, 379-385.

Arnett, J. J. (2000). Emerging adulthood: A theory of development from the late teens through the twenties. *American Psychologist, 55,* 469-480. doi: 10.1037/0003-066X.55.5.469

Auerbach, J. S., & Blatt, S. J. (2001). Self-reflexivity, intersubjectivity, and therapeutic change. *Psychoanalytic Psychology, 18*(3), 427-450. doi:10.1037//0736-9735.18.3.427

Babiak, P., & Hare, R. D. (2006). *Snakes in suits: When psychopaths go to work.* New York: HarperCollins.

Badenoch, B. (2008). *Being a brain-wise therapist: A practical guide to interpersonal neurobiology.* New York: W. W. Norton.

Bader, E., & Pearson, P. T. (with J. D. Schwartz). (2000*). Tell me no lies: How to face the truth and build a loving marriag*e. New York: St. Martin's Press.

Badinter, E. (1981). *Mother love: Myth and reality: Motherhood in modern history.* New York: Macmillan. (Originally published, 1980).

Baglivio, M. T., Wolff, K. T., Piquero, A. R., & Epps, N. (2015). The relationship between adverse childhood experiences (ACE) and juvenile offending trajectories in a juvenile offender sample. *Journal of Criminal Justice, 43*(3), 229-241. doi:10.1016/j.jcrimjus.2015.04.012

Baldwin, H. (2002). Termination of parental rights: Statistical study and proposed solutions; Legislative reform. *Journal of Legislation 28*(2), 238-323.

Baldwin, J. (1963). *The fire next time.* New York: Dial Press.

Bandura, A. (1986*). Social foundations of thought and action: A social cognitive theory.* Englewood Cliffs, NJ: Prentice-Hall.

Bandura, A. (1999). Moral disengagement in the perpetration of inhumanities. *Personality and Social Psychology Review*, 3, 193-209. doi: 10.1207/s15327957pspr0303_3

Bandura, A., & Walters, R. H. (1963). *Social learning and personality development.* New York: Holt, Rinehart & Winston.

Bartholomew, K. (1990). Avoidance of intimacy: An attachment perspective. *Journal of Social and Personal Relationships, 7,* 147-178. doi: 10.1177/0265407590072001

Bassett, J. F. (2007). Psychological defenses against death anxiety: Integrating terror management theory and Firestone's separation theory. *Death Studies, 31(*8), 727-750. doi:10.1080/07481180701490628

Bateson, G., Jackson., D. D., Haley, J., & Weakland, J. (1956). Toward a theory of schizophrenia. *Behavioral Science 1*(4), 251-254. doi: 10.1002/bs.3830010402

Baumeister, R. F., Bratslavsky, E., Finkenauer, C., & Vohs, K. D. (2001). Bad is stronger than good. *Review of General Psychology, 5*, 323-70. doi: 10.1037/1089-2680.5.4.323

Baumeister, R. F., Smart, L., & Boden, J. M. (1996). Relation of threatened egotism to violence and aggression: The dark side of high self-esteem. *Psychological Review, 103*(1), 5-33. doi/10.1037/0033-295X.103.1.5

Beavers, W R., & Hampson, R. B. (1990). *Successful families: Assessment and intervention.* New York: W. W. Norton.

Beck, A. T. (1976). *Cognitive therapy and the emotional disorders.* New York: International Universities Press.

Beck, A. T. (1978a). *Beck Depression Inventory.* San Antonio, TX: Psychological Corporation.

Beck, A. T. (1978b). *Beck Hopelessness Scale.* San Antonio, TX: Psychological Corporation.

Beck, A. T. (1991). *Beck Suicide Inventory*. San Antonio, TX: Psychological Corporation.

Beck, A. T., Rush, A. J., Shaw, B. F., & Emery, G. (1979). *Cognitive therapy of depression*. New York: Guilford Press.

Beck, A. T., Steer, R. A., Beck, J. S., & Newman, C. W. (1993). Hopelessness, depression, suicidal ideation, and clinical diagnosis of depression. *Suicide and Life-Threatening Behavior, 23*, 139-145. doi: 10.1111/j.1943-278X.1993.tb00378.x

Beck, A. T., Steer, R. A., Kovacs, M., & Garrison, B. (1985). Hopelessness and eventual suicide: A 10-year prospective study of patients hospitalized with suicidal ideation. *American Journal of Psychiatry, 142*, 559-563.

Becker, E. (1964). *The revolution in psychiatry: The new understanding of man*. New York: Free Press.

Becker, E. (1971). *The birth and death of meaning: A perspective in psychiatry and anthropology* (2nd ed.). New York: Free Press.

Becker, E. (1975). *Escape from evil*. New York: Free Press.

Becker, E. (1997). *The denial of death*. New York: Free Press. (Original work published 1973).

Bedrosian, R. C., & Beck, A. T. (1979). Cognitive aspects of suicidal behaviors. *Suicide and Life-Threatening Behavior, 9*, 87-96.

Bellow, S. (2003). *Herzog*. New York: Penguin Classics. (Original work published 1964).

Belsky, J., & de Haan, M. (2011). Annual research review: Parenting and children's brain development: The end of the beginning. *Journal of Child Psychology and Psychiatry 52*(4), 409-428. doi: 10.1111/j.1469-7610.2010.02281.x

Berke, J. H. (1988). *The tyranny of malice: Exploring the dark side of character and culture*. New York: Summit Books.

Berkowitz, L. (1993). Pain and aggression: Some findings and implications. *Motivation and Emotion, 17*, 277-293. doi: 10.1007/BF00992223

Bernstein, R. J. (2013). *Violence*. Cambridge, UK: Polity Press.

Bertin E., & Striano, T. (2006). The still-face response in newborn, 1.5, and 3-month-old infants. *Infant Behavior & Development, 29*, 294-297. doi: 10.1016/j.infbeh.2005.12.003

Betchen, S. J. (2005). *Intrusive partners, elusive mates: The pursuer-distancer dynamic in couples*. New York: Routledge.

Bettelheim, B. (1971). *Dialogues with mothers*. New York: Avon Books. (Original work published 1962).

Beutler, L., & Harwood, M. (2000). *Prescriptive psychotherapy: A practical guild to systematic treatment selection*. New York: Oxford University Press.

Beutler, L. (1977a). Foreword *Combating destructive thought processes: Separation theory and voice therapy*. Santa Barbara: The Glendon Association

Biehal, N. (2007). Reuniting children with their families: Reconsidering the evidence on timing, contact and outcomes. *British Journal of Social Work, 37*(5), 807-823. doi:10.1093/bjsw/bcl051

Blatt, S. J. (1995). The destructiveness of perfectionism: Implications for the treatment of depression. *American Psychologist, 50*(12), 1003-1020. doi:10.1037//0003-066x.50.12.1003

Borges, G., Nock M. K., Abad, J. M. H., Hwang, I., Sampson, N. A., Alonso, J.,...Kessler, R. C. (2010). Twelve month prevalence of and risk factors for suicide attempts in the WHO World Mental Health Surveys. *Journal of Clinical Psychiatry, 71,* 1617–1628. doi: 10.4088/JCP.08m04967

Boszormenyi-Nagy, I., & Spark, G. M. (1984). *Invisible loyalties: Reciprocity in intergenerational family therapy.* New York: Brunner/Mazel. (Originally published, 1973.)

Bowen, M. (1978). *Family therapy in clinical practice.* New York: Jason Aronson.

Bowins, B. (2004). Psychological defense mechanisms: A new perspective. *American Journal of Psychoanalysis 64*(1), 1-26. doi: 10.1023/B:TAJP.0000017989.72521.26

Bowlby, J. (1973). *Attachment and loss, Vol. 2, Separation: Anxiety and anger.* New York: Basic Books.

Bowlby, J. (1980). *Attachment and loss, Vol. 3, Loss: Sadness and depression.* New York: Basic Books.

Boyd, S. (1982). Analysis of the psychotherapeutic community. Unpublished manuscript.

Bramley, W. (2008). *Bewitched, bothered, and bewildered: How couples really work.* London: Karnac.

Brazelton, T. B., & Sparrow, J. D. (2001). *Touchpoints 3 to 6: Your child's emotional and behavioral development.* New York: Perseus Book Group.

Breggin, P. R. (1991). *Toxic psychiatry.* New York: St. Martin's Press.

Breggin, P. R. (2007). *Brain-disabling treatments in psychiatry: Drugs, electroshock, and the psychopharmaceutical complex.* New York: Springer.

Brescoll, V. L., & Uhlmann, E. L. (2008). Can an angry woman get ahead? *Psychological Science, 19*(3), 268-275. doi:10.1111/j.1467-9280.2008.02079.x

Bretherton, I. (1996). Internal working models of attachment relationships as related to resilient coping. In G. G. Noam & K. W. Fischer (Eds.), *Development and vulnerability in close relationships* (pp. 3-27). Mahwah, NJ: Lawrence Erlbaum.

Bretherton, I., & Munholland, K.A., (2016). The internal working model construct in light of contemporary neuroimaging research. In J. Cassidy & P.R. Shave, (ds/). *Handbook of attachment: Theory, research, and clinical applications (Loc. 2726-3697). New York: Guilford Press.*

Briere, J. N. (1992). *Child abuse trauma: Theory and treatment of the lasting effects.* Newbury Park, CA: Sage.

BrilliantMaps. (2015). [Infographic]. Where Americans are killed by guns: US homicide & suicide death rates. Retrieved 8/13/2017 from http://brilliantmaps.com/us-gun-deaths

Bronfenbrenner, U., & Morris, P. (2006). The bioecological model of human development. In W. Damon & R. M. Lerner (Eds.), *Handbook of child psychology. Vol. 1, Theoretical models of human development.* Wiley Online Library. doi: 10.1002/9780470147658.chpsy0114

Brown, B. (2012). *Daring greatly: How the courage to be vulnerable transforms the way we live, love, parent, and lead.* New York: Gotham Books.

Bugental, D. E., Love, L. R., Kaswan, J. W., & April, C. (1971). Verbal-nonverbal conflict in parental messages to normal and disturbed children. *Journal of Abnormal Psychology, 77*(1), 6-10. doi: 10.1037/h0030497

Buscaglia, L. F. (1987, November 22). Living & loving: Out of the mouths of 10-year-olds. *Los Angeles Times*, Part VI, p. 10.

Calderone, M. S., & Johnson, E. W. (1989). *The family book about sexuality* (rev. ed.). New York: Harper & Row.

Camus, A. (1991). *The Myth of Sisyphus and Other Essays* (J. O'Brien, Trans.). New York: Vintage. (Original work published 1955).

Caplan, P. J. (1995). *They say you're crazy: How the world's most powerful psychiatrists decide who's normal.* Reading MA: Perseus Books.

Case, T. I., & Williams, K. D. (2004). Ostracism: A metaphor for death. In J. Greenberg, S. L. Koole, & T. Pyszczynski (Eds.), *Handbook of experimental existential psychology* (pp. 336-351). New York, NY: Guilford Press.

Cassidy, J. & Mohr, J. J. (2001). Unresolvable fear, trauma, and psychopathology: Theory, research, and clinical considerations related to disorganized attachment across the life span. *Clinical Psychology: Science and Practice, 8*, 275-298. doi: 10.1093/clipsy.8.3.275

Cavaiola, A. A., & Lavender, N. J. (2000). *Toxic coworkers: How to deal with dysfunctional people on the job.* Oakland, CA: New Harbinger Publications.

Centers for Disease Control and Prevention. (2015a). *Suicide and self-inflicted injury. National Center for Health Statistics,* Retrieved from https://www.cdc.gov/nchs/fastats/suicide.htm

Centers for Disease Control and Prevention. (2015b). *Assault or homicide. National Center for Health Statistics,* Retrieved from https://www.cdc.gov/nchs/fastats/homicide.htm

Chadwick, P., Birchwood, M. J., & Trower, P. (1996). *Cognitive therapy for delusions, voices, and paranoia.* Chichester, UK: Wiley.

Chambless, D. L. & Ollendick, T. H. (2001). Empirically supported psychological interventions: Controversies and evidence. *Annual Review of Psychology, 52,* 685-716. doi: 10.1146/annurev.psych.52.1.685

Chodoff, P. (2002). The medicalization of the human condition. *Psychiatric Services, 53*, 627-628. doi.org/10.1176/appi.ps.53.5.627

Chu, J. Y. (2014). *When boys become boys: Development, relationships, and masculinity.* New York: New York University Press.

Clarke, L. (2003). *Challenging ideas in psychiatric nursing.* London: Routledge.

Coelho, P. (2004). *Eleven minutes* (M. J. Costa, Trans.). New York: HarperCollins.

Cohen, F., Ogilvie, D. M., Solomon, S., Greenberg, J., & Pyszczynski, T. (2005). American roulette: The effect of reminders of death on support for George W. Bush in the 2004 presidential election. *Analysis of Social Issues and Public Policy, 5*(1), 177-187. doi: 10.1111/j.1530-2415.2005.00063.x

Colt, G. H. (1991). *The enigma of suicide.* New York: Summit Books.

Comte-Sponville, A. (2001). *A small treatise on the great virtues: The uses of philosophy in everyday life* (C. Temerson, Trans.). New York: Metropolitan Books. (Original work published 1996).

Conrad, P., & Bergey, M. R. (2014). The impending globalization of ADHD: Notes on the expansion and growth of a medicalized disorder. *Social Science & Medicine, 122,* 31-43. doi: 10.1016/jsocscmed.2014.10.019

Copen, C. E., Daniels, K., Vespa, J., & Mosher, W. D. (2012, March 22). First marriages in the United States: Data from *the 2006–2010 National Survey of Family Growth. National Health Statistics Reports, 49.* Washington, DC. Centers for Disease Control.

Courtois, C. A. (1999). *Recollections of sexual abuse: Treatment principles and in guidelines.* New York: W. W. Norton.

Courtois, C. A. (2000). The aftermath of child sexual abuse: The treatment of complex posttraumatic stress reactions. In L. T. Szuchman & F. Muscarella (Eds.), *Psychological perspectives on human sexuality* (pp. 549-572). New York: John Wiley.

Cozolino, L. (2006). *The neuroscience of psychotherapy: Healing the social brain* (2nd ed.) New York: W.W. Norton.

Cozolino. L. (2015). *Why therapy works: Using our minds to change our brains.* New York: W.W. Norton.

Curtin, S. C., Warner, M., & Hedegaard, H. (2016, April). *Increase in suicide in the United States, 1999-2014* (NCHS Data Brief No. 241). Washington, DC: Centers for Disease Control. Retrieved from http://www.cdc.gov/nchs/data/databriefs/db241.

Davies, P. T., & Cummings, E. M. (1995). Children's emotions as organizers of their reactions to interadult anger: A functionalist perspective. *Developmental Psychology, 31*(4), 677-684. doi:10.1037//0012-1649.31.4.677

Davies, P. T., & Cummings, E. M. (1998). Exploring children's emotional security as a mediator of the link between marital relations and child adjustment. *Child Development, 69*(1), 124. doi:10.2307/1132075.

Debbane, M., Salaminios, G., Luyten, P., Badoud, D., Armando, M., Tossi, A. S., Brent, B. K. (2016). Attachment, neurobiology, and mentalizing along the psychosis continuum. *Frontiers of Human Neurology, 10,* 406. doi: 10.3389/fnhum.2016.00406

Decety, J., & Jackson, P. L. (2006). A social-neuroscience perspective on empathy. *Current Directions in Psychological Science, 15,* 54-58. doi: 10.1111/j.0963-7214.2006.00406.x

DeRogatis, L. R., & Burnett, A. L. (2008). The epidemiology of sexual dysfunctions. *Journal of Sexual Medicine, 5(*2), 289-300. doi:10.1111/j.1743-6109.2007.00668.x

De Ruiter, C., & Van Ijzendoorn, M. H. (1992). Agoraphobia and anxious-ambivalent attachment: An integrative review. *Journal of Anxiety Disorders, 6*(4), 365-381.

Doherty, W. (2017, January-February). Psychotherapy's pilgrimage: Shaping the consciousness of our time. *Psychotherapy Networker,* (18-31, 67).

Dostoyevski, F. (2002). *The brothers Karamazov.* New York: Farrar, Straus and Giroux. (Original work published 1880).

Doucette-Gates, A., Firestone, R. W., & Firestone, L. A. (1999). Assessing violent thoughts: The relationship between thought processes and violent behavior. *Psychologica Belgica, 39,* 113-134.

Downing, C. (1977). Jealousy: A depth-psychological perspective. In G. Clanton & L. G. Smith (Eds.), *Jealousy* (pp. 72-79). New York: Lanham.

Dugal, C., Bigras, N., Godbout, N., & Belanger, C. (2016). Childhood interpersonal trauma and its repercussions in adulthood: An analysis of psychological and interpersonal sequelae. In *A multidimensional approach to post-traumatic stress disorder: From theory to practice,* (pp. 71-107). Montreal, Canada: CRIPCAS. doi:10.5772/64476

Dutton, D. G. (with Golant, S. K.). (1995). *The batterer: A psychological profile.* New York: Basic Books.

Edwards, V. J., Holden, G. W., Felitti, V. J., & Anda, R. F. (2003). Relationship between multiple forms of childhood maltreatment and adult mental health in community respondents: Results from the adverse childhood experiences study. *American Journal of Psychiatry, 160*(8), 1453-1460. doi:10.1176/appi.ajp.160.8.1453

Ellis, A., & Grieger, R. M. (Eds.). (1986). *Handbook of rational-emotive therapy, Vol. 2.* New York: Springer.

Ellis, A., & Harper, R. A. (1975). *A new guide to rational living.* North Hollywood, CA: Wilshire Book.

Epstein, S. (2003). Cognitive-experiential self-theory of personality. In I. B. Weiner (Ed.), *Handbook of psychology* (pp. 159-184). Wiley Online. doi:10.1002/0471264385.wei0507

Erikson, E. H. (1963). *Childhood and society* (2nd ed.). New York: W. W. Norton.

Erlich, H. J. (1973). The social psychology of prejudice: A systematic theoretical review and propositional inventory of the American social psychological study of prejudice. Oxford, UK: John Wiley.

Fairbairn, W. R. D. (1952). *Psychoanalytic studies of the personality*. London: Routledge & Kegan Paul.

Falk, A. (2004). *Fratricide in the Holy Land: A psychoanalytic view of the Arab-Israeli conflict*. Madison, WI: University of Wisconsin Press.

Farberow, N. L. (I 980). Introduction. In N. L. Farberow (Ed.), *The many faces of suicide: Indirect self-destructive behavior* (pp. 1-12). New York: McGraw-Hill.

Feeney, J. A. (2016). Adult romantic attachment: Developments in the study of couple relationships. In J. Cassidy & P. R. Shaver (Eds.), *Handbook of attachment: Theory, research, and clinical applications* (3rd ed.), (pp. 435-463). New York: Guilford Press.

Fehr, B. (1996). *Friendship processes*. Thousand Oaks, CA: Sage.

Felson, R. B. (2002). *Violence and gender reexamined*. Washington, DC: American Psychological Association.

Fenchel, G. H. (1998). Introduction. In G. H. Fenchel (Ed.), *The mother-daughter relationship: Echoes through time* (pp. xv-xviii). Northvale, NJ: Jason Aronson.

Fierman, L. B. (Ed.). (1965). *Effective psychotherapy: The contribution of Hellmuth Kaiser*. New York: Free Press.

Firestone, R.W. (1957). *A concept of the schizophrenic process*. Unpublished doctoral dissertation, University of Denver.

Firestone, R. W. (1984). A concept of the primary fantasy bond: A developmental perspective. *Psychotherapy, 21,* 218-225. doi: 10.1037/h0085976

Firestone, R. W. (1985). *The fantasy bond: Structure of psychological defenses*. Santa Barbara, CA: Glendon Association.

Firestone, R. W. (1986). The "inner voice" and suicide. Psychotherapy, 23, 439-447. doi: 10.1037/h0085976

Firestone, R. W. (1987). The "voice": The dual nature of guilt reactions. *American Journal of Psychoanalysis, 47,* 210-229.

Firestone, R. W. (1988*). Voice therapy: A psychotherapeutic approach to self-destructive behavior*. Santa Barbara, CA: Glendon Association.

Firestone, R. W. (1990a). *Compassionate child-rearing: An in-depth approach to optimal parenting*. Santa Barbara, CA: Glendon Association

Firestone, R. W. (1990b). Prescription for psychotherapy. *Psychotherapy: Theory, Research, Practice, Training, 27*(4), 627. doi: 10.1037/0033-3204.27.4.627

Firestone, R. W. (1990c). Voice therapy. In J. Zeig & W. Munion (Eds.), *What is psychotherapy? Contemporary perspectives* (pp. 68-74). San Francisco, CA: Jossey – Bass.

Firestone, R. W. (1990d). Voices during sex: Application of Voice Therapy to sexuality. *Journal of Sex & Marital Therapy, 16,* 258-274. doi: 10.1080/00926239008405462

Firestone, R. W. (1994a). A new perspective on the Oedipal complex: A voice therapy session. *Psychotherapy: Theory, Research, Practice, Training, 31*(2), 342-351. doi: 10.1037/h0090217

Firestone, R. W. (1994b). Psychological defenses against death Anxiety. In R. A. Neimeyer (Ed.), *Death anxiety handbook: Research, instrumentation, and application* (pp. 217-241) Washington, DC: Taylor & Francis.

Firestone, R. W. (1996). The origins of ethnic strife. *Human Mind and Interaction, 7,* 217-241. doi:10.15417/1881

Firestone, R. W. (1997a). *Combating destructive thought processes: Voice therapy and separation theory.* Sage Publications.

Firestone, R. W. (1997b). *Suicide and the inner voice: Risk assessment, treatment, and case management.* Thousand Oaks, CA: Sage Publications.

Firestone, R.W. (2002). The death of psychoanalysis and depth psychotherapy. *Psychotherapy: Theory, Research, Practice, Training, 39*(3), 223-232. doi.org/10.1037/0033-3204.39.3.223

Firestone, R. W. (2015). The ultimate resistance. *Journal of Humanistic Psychology, 55*(1), 77-101. doi: 10.1177/0022167814527166

Firestone, R. W., & Catlett, J. (1989). *Psychological defenses in everyday life.* Santa Barbara, CA: Glendon Association.

Firestone, R. W., & Catlett, J. (1999*). Fear of intimacy.* Washington, DC: American Psychological Association.

Firestone, R. W., & Catlett, J. (2009a). *Beyond death anxiety: Achieving life-affirming death awareness.* New York: Springer.

Firestone, R. W., & Catlett, J. (2009b). *The ethics of interpersonal relationships.* London: Karnac Books.

Firestone, R. W., & Firestone, L. (2006). *Firestone Assessment of Self-Destructive Thoughts (FAST) manual.* Lutz, FL: Psychological Assessment Resources.

Firestone, R. W., & Firestone, L. (2008a). *Firestone Assessment of Violent Thoughts (FAVT) manual.* Lutz, FL: Psychological Assessment Resources.

Firestone, R. W., & Firestone, L. (2008b). *Firestone Assessment of Violent Thoughts— Adolescent (FAVT-A) manual.* Lutz, FL: Psychological Assessment Resources.

Firestone, R. W., Firestone, L., & Catlett, J. (2002*). Conquer your critical inner voice: A revolutionary program to counter negative thoughts and life free from imagined limitation*s. Oakland, CA: New Harbinger.

Firestone, R. W., Firestone, L. A., & Catlett, J. (2003). *Creating a life of meaning and compassion: The wisdom of psychotherapy.* Washington, DC: American Psychological Association.

Firestone, R. W., Firestone, L. A., & Catlett, J. (2006). *Sex and love in intimate relationships.* Washington, DC: American Psychological Association.

Firestone, R. W., Firestone, L. A., & Catlett, J. (2012). *The self under siege: A therapeutic model for differentiation.* New York: Routledge.

Firestone, R. W., & Seiden, R. H. (1987). Microsuicide and suicidal threats of everyday life. *Psychotherapy, 24,* 31-39. doi: 10.1037/h0085688

Firestone, R. W., & Seiden, R. H. (1990). Suicide and the continuum of self-destructive behavior. *Journal of American College Health, 38*(5), 207-213. doi: 10.1080/07448481.1990.9936189

Fisher, S., & Fisher, R. L. (1986). *What we really know about child-rearing: Science in support of effective parenting.* Northvale, NJ: Jason Aronson.

Fitzgerald, F. S. (1960). *Six tales of the Jazz Age.* New York: Scribner. (Original work published 1920).

Fletcher, P.C. & Firth, C.D. (2009). Perceiving is believing: A Bayesian approach to explaining the positive symptoms of schizophrenia. *Nature Reviews, Neuroscience, 10,*48-58.

Florian, V., & Mikulincer, M. (2004). A multifaceted perspective on the existential meanings, manifestations, and consequences of the fear of personal death. In J. Greenberg, S. L. Koole, & T. Pyszczynski (Eds.), *Handbook of experimental existential psychology* (pp. 54-70). New York: Guilford Press.

Fonagy, P. (2004). The developmental roots of violence in the failure of mentalization. In F. Pfäfflin & G. Adshead (Eds.), *A matter of security: The application of attachment theory to forensic psychiatry and psychotherapy* (pp.13-56). London: Jessica Kingsley.

Fonagy, P. (2008). A genuinely developmental theory of sexual enjoyment and its implications for psychoanalytic technique. *Journal of the American Psychoanalytic Association, 56*(1), 11-36. doi:10.1177/0003065107313025

Fonagy, P., & Bateman, A. W. (2007). Mentalizing and borderline personality disorder. *Journal of Mental Health, 16*(1), 83-101.

Fonagy, P., & Higgitt, A. (2007). The development of prejudice: An attachment theory hypothesis explaining its ubiquity. In H. Parens, A. Mahfouz, S. W. Twemlow, & D. E. Scharff (Eds.), *The future of prejudice: Psychoanalysis and the prevention of prejudice* (pp. 63-79). Lanham, MD: Rowman & Littlefield.

Fonagy, P., Luyten, P., Allison, A., & Campbell, C. (2016). Reconciling psychoanalytic ideas with attachment theory. In J. Cassidy & P. R. Shaver (Eds.), *Handbook of attachment* (3rd ed.), (pp. 780-804). New York: Guilford Press,

Fonagy, P., & Target, M. (2005). Commentary: Bridging the transmission gap: An end to an important mystery of attachment research? *Attachment and Human Development, 7,* 333-343. doi: 10.1080/14616730500269278

Forward, S. (with C. Buck). (1989). *Toxic parents: Overcoming their hurtful legacy and reclaiming your life.* New York: Bantam Books.

Fosha, D. (2000). *The transforming power of affect: A model for accelerated change*, New York: Basic Books.

Foucault, M. (1972). *Power/knowledge*. New York: Pantheon Books.

Fowles, D. C., & Kochanska, G. (2000). Temperament as a moderator of pathways to conscience in children: The contribution of electrodermal activity. *Psychophysiology, 37,* 788-795. doi: 10.1111/1469-8986.3760788

Fox, B. H., Perez, N., Cass, E., Baglivio, M. T., & Epps, N. (2015). Trauma changes everything: Examining the relationship between adverse childhood experiences and serious, violent and chronic juvenile offenders. *Child Abuse & Neglect, 46,* 163-173.

Fraiberg, S. Adelson, E., & Shapiro, V. (1980). *Ghosts in the nursery: A psychoanalytic approach to the problems of impaired infant-mother relationships.* In S. Fraiberg (Ed.). *Clinical studies in infant mental health: The first year of life* (pp. 164-196) New York: Basic Books.

Frankl, V. (1963). *Man's search for meaning.* Boston: Beacon Press. [Kindle Edition].

Freud, S. (1961). The ego and the id. In J. Strachey (Ed. and trans.*), The standard edition of the complete psychological works of Sigmund Freud (Vol. 19*, pp. 3-66). London: Hogarth Press. (Originally published, 1923).

Freud, A. (1966). *The ego and the mechanisms of defense* (Rev. ed.). Madison, CT: International Universities Press. (Original work published 1936).

Freud, H. C. (2011). *Electra vs Oedipus: The drama of the mother-daughter relationship* (M. de Jager, Trans.). London: Routledge. (Original work published 1997).

Freud, S. (1955). Three essays on the theory of sexuality. In J. Strachey (Ed. and Trans.), *The standard edition of the complete psychological works of Sigmund Freud (Vol. 7*, pp. 123-246). London: Hogarth Press. (Original work published 1905).

Freud, S. (1955). Group psychology and the analysis of the ego. In J. Strachey (Ed. and Trans.), *The standard edition of the complete psychological works of Sigmund Freud (Vol. 18*, pp. 63-143). London: Hogarth. (Original work published 1921).

Freud, S. (1957). On the universal tendency to debasement in the sphere in love: Contributions to the psychology of love II. In J. Strachey (Ed. & Trans.), *The standard edition of the complete psychological works of Sigmund Freud (Vol. 11,* pp. 179-190). London: Hogarth Press, (Original work published 1912).

Freud, S. (1957). On narcissism: An introduction. In J. Strachey (Ed. & Trans.), *The standard edition of the complete psychological works of Sigmund Freud (Vol. 14*, pp. 73-102). London: Hogarth Press, (Original work published 1914).

Freud, S. (1957). Our attitude toward death. In J. Strachey (Ed. And Trans.), *The standard edition of the complete psychological works of Sigmund Freud (Vol. 14*, pp. 289-300). London: Hogarth Press. (Original work published 1915).

Freud, S. (1959). An autobiographical study. In J. Strachey (Ed. And Trans.), *The standard edition of the complete psychological works of Sigmund Freud (Vol. 20*, pp. 7-75). London: Hogarth Press. (Original work published 1925).

Freud, S. (1961). The ego and the id. In J. Strachey (Ed. and Trans.), *The standard edition of the complete psychological works of Sigmund Freud (Vol. 19*, pp. 12-67). London: Hogarth Press. (Original work published 1923).

Freud, S. (1962). Further remarks on the neuro-psychoses of defense. In J. Strachey (Ed. and Trans.), *The standard edition of the complete psychological works of Sigmund Freud (Vol. 3*, pp. 159-221). London: Hogarth. (Original work published 1896).

Freud, S. (1977). *Introductory lectures on psychoanalysis.* New York: W.W. Norton. (originally published, 1920)

Friedman, M. S., Marshall, M. P., Guadamuz, T. E., Wei, C., Wong, C. F., Wong, E. M., & Stall, R. (2011). A meta-analysis of disparities in childhood sexual abuse, parental physical abuse, and peer victimization among sexual minority and sexual nonminority individuals. *American Journal of Public Health, 101,* 1481-1494. doi: 10.2105/AJPH.2009.190009

Fromm, E. (1941). *Escape from freedom.* New York: Avon Books.

Fromm, E. (1947). *Man for himself.* New York: Fawcett Books.

Fromm, E. (1950*). Psychoanalysis and religion.* New Haven: Yale University Press.

Fromm, E. (1956a). *The art of loving.* New York: Harper.

Fromm, E. (1956b). *The sane society.* New York: Routledge.

Furer, P., & Walker, J. R. (2008). Death anxiety: A cognitive-behavioral approach. *Journal of Cognitive Psychotherapy, 22*(2), 167-182. doi:10.1891/0889-8391.22.2.167

Gage, R. L. (Ed.). (1976). *Choose life: A dialogue:* Arnold Toynbee and Daisaku Ikeda. Oxford, UK: Oxford University Press.

Garbarino, J. (2015). *Listening to killers: Lessons learned from my twenty years as a psychological expert witness in murder cases.* Berkeley, CA: University of California Press.

Garbarino, J., Guttmann, E., & Seeley, J. W. (1986). *The psychologically battered child.* San Francisco: Jossey-Bass.

Gedo, J. B. (2000). A time of discontent: Contemporary psychoanalysis in America. In S. de Schill, *Crucial choices-crucial changes: The resurrection of psychotherapy* (pp. 39-54). Amherst. NY: Prometheus Books.

Geen, R. G. (1998). Processes and personal variables in affective aggression. In R. G. Geen & E. Donnerstein (Eds*.) Human aggression: Theories, research, and implications for social policy* (pp. 1-21). Philadelphia: Elsevier. doi:10.1016/b978-012278805-5/50002-x

Geeraert, L., Van den Noortgate, W., Grietens, H., & Onghena, P. (2004). The effects of early prevention programs for families with young children at risk for physical child abuse and neglect: A meta-analysis. *Child Maltreatment, 9*(3), 277-291. doi: 10.1177/1077559504264265

Geis, F. L. (1993). Self-fulfilling prophecies: A social psychological view of gender. In A. E. Beall & R. J. Sternberg (Eds*.), The psychology of gender* (pp. 9-54). New York: Guilford Press.

George, C., Kaplan, N., & Main, M. (1984). *Adult Attachment Interview*. Unpublished manuscript, University of California.

George, C., & Solomon, J. (1996). Representational models of relationships: Links between caregiving and attachment. *Infant Mental Health Journal, 17*, 198-216. doi: 10.1002/(SICI)1097-0355(199623)17:3<198::AID-IMHJ2>3.0.CO;2-L

Giddens, A. (1991). *Modernity and self-identity: Self and society in the late modern age*. Stanford, CA: Stanford University Press.

Giddens, A. (2013). *The transformation of intimacy: Sexuality, love and eroticism in modern societies*. New York: John Wiley,

Gilbert, P. (1989). *Human nature and suffering*. Hillsdale, NJ: Erlbaum.

Gillath, O., Shaver, P. R., & Mikulincer, M. (2005). An attachment-theoretical approach to compassion and altruism. In P. Gilbert (Ed.), *Compassion: Conceptualisations, research and use in psychotherapy* (pp. 121-147). London: Routledge.

Gilligan, C. (1982). *In a different voice: Psychological theory and women's development*. Cambridge, MA: Harvard University Press.

Gilligan, C., Rogers, A.G. & Tolman D. L. (Eds.). (1991). *Women, girls & psychotherapy: Reframing resistance*. Binghamton, NY: Hayworth Press.

Gilligan, J. (2001). *Preventing violence*. New York: Thames & Hudson

Gilligan, J. (2007). Terrorism, fundamentalism, and nihilism: Analyzing the dilemmas of modernity. In H. Parens, A. Mahfouz, S. W. Twemlow, & D. E. Scharff (Eds.), *The future of prejudice: Psychoanalysis and the prevention of prejudice* (pp. 37-59). Lanham, MD: Rowman & Littlefield.

Gilligan, J. (2011). *Why some politicians are more dangerous than others*. Cambridge, UK: Polity Press.

Gilligan, J., & Lee, B. (2004). Beyond the prison paradigm: From provoking violence to preventing it by creating "anti- prisons" (residential colleges and therapeutic communities). *Annals of the New York Academy of Sciences, 1036*(1), 300-324. doi:10.1196/annals.1330.030

Ginot, E. (1997). The analyst's use of self, self-disclosure, and enhanced integration. *Psychoanalytic Psychology, 14*, 365-381. doi: 10.1002/(SICI)1097-0355(199623)17:3<198::AID-IMHJ2>3.0.CO;2-L

Ginot, E. (2009). The empathic power of enactments: The link between neuropsychological processes and an expanded definition of empathy. *Psychoanalytic Psychology, 26*(3), 290-309. doi: 10.1037/a0016449

Giovacchini, P. L. (1997). Foreword. In R. Langs, *Death anxiety and clinical practice* (pp. ix-xiii). London: Karnac Books.

Glass, I. (1995). *Toxic people: 10 ways of dealing with people who make your life miserable*. New York: St. Martin's Griffin.

Glass, S. P. (with J. C. Staeheli). (2003). *Not 'just friends': Protect your relationship from infidelity and heal the trauma of betrayal*. New York: Free Press.

Glass, S. P., & Wright, T. L. (1988). Clinical implications of research on extramarital involvement. In R. A. Brown & J. R. Field (Eds.), *Treatment of sexual problems in individual and couples therapy* (pp. 301-346). Costa Mesa, CA: PMA Publishing.

Glass, S. P., & Wright, T. L. (1997). Reconstructing marriages after the trauma of infidelity. In W. K. Halford & H. J. Markman (Eds.*), Clinical handbook of marriage and couples interventions* (pp. 471-507). New York: John Wiley.

Goldbrunner, J. (1964). *Teaching the sacraments: Penance, eucharist, confirmation.* New York: Herder and Herder.

Goodman, T. (2006). Performing a "new nation:" The role of the TRC in South Africa. In J. C. Alexander, B. Giesen, & J. L. Mast (Eds.), *Social performance: Symbolic action, cultural pragmatics, and ritual* (pp. 169-192). New York: Cambridge University Press.

Gottman, J. M., & Silver, N. (1999). *The seven principles for making marriage work.* New York: Three Rivers Press.

Greenberg, J., Koole, S. L., & Pyszczynski, T. A. (2004). *Handbook of experimental existential psychology.* New York: Guilford Press.

Greenberg, L. S. (2004) Emotion-focused therapy. *Clinical Psychology and Psychotherapy, 11,* 3-16. doi: 10.1002/cpp.388

Greenberg, L. S., & Johnson, S. (1988*). Emotion focused therapy for couples.* New York: Guilford.

Greenberg, L. S., Rice, L. N., & Elliott, R. (1993*). Facilitating emotional change: The moment-by-moment process.* New York: Guilford Press.

Greenberg, L. S., & Safran, J. D. (1987). *Emotion in psychotherapy: Affect, cognition, and the process of change.* New York: Guilford Press.

Grencavage, L. M., & Norcross, J. C. (1990). Where are the commonalities among the therapeutic common factors? *Professional Psychology: Research and Practice, 21*(5), 372-378. doi: 10.1037/0735-7028.21.5.372

Grinshteyn, E., & Hemenway, D. (2016). Violent death rates: The US compared with other high-income OECD countries. *American Journal of Medicine, 129*(3), 266-273. doi.org/10.1016/j.amjmed.2015.10.025

Groen, M., & Lawick, J. V. (2009). *Intimate warfare: Regarding the fragility of family relations* London: Karnac Books.

Gunderson, M. P., & McCary, J. L. (1979). Sexual guilt and religion. *Family Coordinator, 28,* 353-357. doi: 10.2307/581948

Guntrip, H. (1961). *Personality structure and human interaction.* New York: International Universities Press.

Guntrip, H. (1969). *Schizoid phenomena object-relations and the self.* New York: International Universities Press.

Hansen, N. B., Lambert, M. J. & Forman, E. M. (2002). The psychotherapy dose-response effect and its implications for treatment delivery services. *Clinical Psychological Science and Practice 6,* 329-343. doi: 10.1093/clipsy.9.3.329

Harding, C. (2001). Introduction. In C. Harding (Ed.), *Sexuality: Psychoanalytic perspectives* (pp. 1-17). East Sussex, UK: Brunner-Routledge.

Hardy, S. A., Bhattacharjee, A., Reed, A., & Aquino, K. (2010). Moral identity and psychological distance: The case of adolescent parental socialization. *Journal of Adolescence, 33,* 111-123. doi: 10.1016/j.adolescence.2009.04.008

Hare, R. D. (1991). *The Hare Psychopathy Checklist–Revised: Technical manual.* Toronto, Canada: Multi-Health Systems.

Hare, R. D. (1998). The Hare PCL- R: Some issues concerning its use and misuse. *Legal and Criminological Psychology, 3*(1), 99-119.

Harper, R. A. (1981). Limitations of marriage and family therapy. *Rational Living, 16*(2), 3-6.

Hart, D., Atkins, R., & Ford, D. (1999). Family influences on the formation of moral identity in adolescence: Longitudinal analyses. *Journal of Moral Education, 28*(3), 375-386.

Hart, J., & Goldenberg, J. L. (2008). A terror management perspective on spirituality and the problem of the body. In A. Tomer, G. T. Eliason, & P. T. P. Wong (Eds.), *Existential and spiritual issues in death attitudes* (pp. 91—113). New York: Lawrence Erlbaum.

Hauser, M. D. (2006). *Moral minds: How nature designed our universal sense of right and wrong.* New York: HarperCollins.

Havel, V. (1990). *Disturbing the peace: A conversation with Karel Hvizdala* (P. Wilson, Trans.). New York: Alfred A. Knopf.

Hayes, J., Schimel, J., Arndt, J., and Faucher, E. H. (2010). A theoretical and empirical review of the death-thought accessibility concept in terror management research. *Psychological Bulletin, 136*(5), 699-739. doi: 10.1037/a0020524

Hazan, C., & Shaver, P. (1987). Romantic love conceptualized as an attachment process. *Journal of Personality and Social Psychology, 52*(3), 511-524. doi: 10.1037/0022-3514.52.3.511

Heckler, R. A. (1994). *Waking up, alive: The descent, the suicide attempt, and the return to life.* New York: Ballantine Books.

Herman, J. (1992). *Trauma and recovery.* New York: Basic Books.

Herzog, J. M. (2001). *Father hunger: Explorations with adults and children.* Hillsdale, NJ: Analytic Press.

Hobson, J. A. & Leonard, J. A. (2001). *Out of its mind: Psychiatry in crisis: A call for reform.* Cambridge, MA: Perseus Books.

Hoffer, E. (n.d.). Quotation retrieved from http://www.azquotes.com/quote/134279.

Hoffman, S. I., & Strauss, S. (1985). The development of children's concepts of death. *Death Studies, 9,* 469-482. doi: 10.1080/07481188508252538

Hogg, M. A., Adelman, J. R., & Blagg, R. D. (2010). Religion in the face of uncertainty: An uncertainty-identity theory account of religiousness. *Personality and Social Psychology Review, 14*(1), 72-83. doi: 10.1177/1088868309349692

Hrdy, S. B. (2009). *Mothers and others: The evolutionary origins of mutual understanding.* Cambridge, MA: Harvard University Press.

Hughes, T., & McCullough, F. (Eds.). (1982). *The journals of Sylvia Plath.* New York: Ballantine.

Iacoboni, M. (2009). Imitation, empathy, and mirror neurons. *Annual Review of Psychology, 60,* 653-670. doi: 10.1146/annurev.psych.60.110707.163604

Ivancovich, D. A., & Wong, P. T. P. (2008). The role of existential and spiritual coping in anticipatory grief. In A. Tomer, G. T. Eliason, & P. T. P. Wong (Eds.), *Existential and spiritual issues in death attitudes* (pp. 209—233). New York: Lawrence Erlbaum.

Jacobson, K. (2009, April). Considering interactions between genes, environments, biology, and social context. *American Psychological Association Science Briefs.* Retrieved 9/8/2010 from www.apa.org/science/about/psa/2009/04/sci-brief.aspx

Jacoby, R. (1983). *The repression of psychoanalysis: Otto Fenichel and the political Freudians.* Chicago: University of Chicago Press.

James, W. (2017). The consciousness of self. In W. James, *The principles of psychology* (Chapter X) [Kindle edition]. (Original work published 1890).

James, W. (2004). *The varieties of religious experience.* New York: Touchstone. (Original work published 1902).

Janov, A. (1970). *The primal scream.* New York: G.P. Putman.

Jobes, D. A. (2012). The collaborative assessment and management of suicidality (CAMS): An evolving evidence-based clinical approach to suicidal risk. *Suicide and Life-Threatening Behavior, 42*(6), 640-653. doi: 10.1111/j.1943-278X.2012.00119.x

Jobes, D. A., & Berman, A. L. (1993). Suicide and malpractice liability: Assessing and revising policies, procedures, and practice in outpatient settings. *Professional Psychology: Research and Practice, 24,* 91-99.

Jonas, E., Schimel J., Greenberg, J. & Pyszczynski, T. (2002). The scrooge effect: Evidence that mortality salience increases prosocial attitudes and behavior. *Personality and Social Psychology 28,* 1342-1353. doi: 10.1177/014616702236834

Jones, D. & Shuker, R (2004). Concluding comments: A humane approach to working with dangerous people. In D. Jones (Ed.), *Working with dangerous people: The psychotherapy of violence* (pp. 191-198). Oxford, UK: Radcliffe Publishing.

Josephson, M. (2004). Weekly commentary from Michael Josephson, May 3-7, 2004. Retrieved 9/26/05 from http://www.charactercounts.org/knxwk356.htm

Kafka, F. (1969). *The trial* (Muir Trans.). New York: Vintage Books. (Original work published, 1937).

Kaiser, H. (1955). The problem of responsibility in psychotherapy. *Psychiatry, 18,* 205-211.

Kant, I. (1959). *Foundations for a metaphysics of morals.* New York: Bobbs-Merrill. (Original work published 1781).

Kannan, D., & Levitt, H. M. (2013). A review of client self-criticism in psychotherapy. *Journal of Psychotherapy Integration, 23*(2), 166-178. doi:10.1037/a0032355

Kaplan, H. S. (1995). *The sexual desire disorders: Dysfunctional regulation of sexual motivation.* Levittown, PA: Brunner/Mazel.

Karon, B. P., & VandenBos, G. R. (1981). *Psychotherapy of schizophrenia: The treatment of choice.* Lanham, MD: Rowman & Littlefield.

Kastenbaum, R. (2000). *The psychology of death* (3rd ed.). New York: Springer.

Kaufmann, G. (1993). *Shame: The power of caring* (3rd ed.). Rochester, VT: Schenkman Books.

Kellerman, B. (2004). *Bad leadership: What it is, how it happens, why it matters.* Boston: Harvard Business School Press.

Kernberg, O. F. (1980). *Internal world and external reality: Object relations theory applied.* Northvale, NJ: Jason Aronson.

Kernberg, O. F. (1995). *Love relations: Normality and pathology.* New Haven, CT: Yale University Press.

Kerr, M. E., & Bowen, M. (1988). *Family evaluation: An approach based on Bowen theory.* New York: W. W. Norton.

Keys, A., Brozek, J. Henschel, A., Mickelsen, O., & Taylor, H. L. (1950). *The biology of human starvation, (Vol. 2).* Minneapolis: University of Minnesota Press.

Kiecolt-Glaser, J. K., Malarkey, W. B., Chee, M., Newton, T., Cacioppo, J. T., Mao, H. Y., & Glaser, R. (1993). Negative behavior during marital conflict is associated with immunological down-regulation. *Psychosomatic Medicine, 55*(5), 395-409. doi: 10.1097/00006842-199309000-00001

Kierkegaard, S. (1954). *The sickness unto death* (W. Lowrie, Trans.). New York: Anchor. (Original work published 1849).

Kipnis, L. (2003). *Against love: A polemic.* New York: Pantheon Books.

Kipnis, L. (2009). *The female thing: Dirt, envy, sex, vulnerability.* New York: Vintage Books.

Kobak, R., Zajac, K., & Madsen S. D. (2016). Attachment disruptions, reparative processes, and psychopathology: Theoretical and clinical implications. In J. Cassidy & P. R. Shaver (Eds.), *Handbook of attachment: Theory, research, and clinical implications* (pp. 25-39). New York: Guilford Press.

Kowalski, R. M. (2001a). Aversive interpersonal behaviors: On being annoying, thoughtless, and mean. In R. M. Kowalski (Ed.), *Behaving badly: Aversive behaviors in interpersonal relationships* (pp. 3-25). Washington, DC: American Psychological Association.

Kowalski, R. M. (2001b). The aversive side of social interaction revisited. In R. M. Kowalski (Ed.), *Behaving badly: Aversive behaviors in interpersonal relationships* (pp. 297-309). Washington, DC: American Psychological Association.

Kramer, R. (Ed.) (1996). *Otto Rank: A Psychology of Difference: The American Lectures.* Princeton, NJ: Princeton University Press.

Lachmann, F. M., & Beebe, B. (1989). Oneness fantasies revisited. *Psychoanalytic Psychology, 6*(2), 137-149. doi:10.1037//0736-9735.6.2.137

LaFreniere, P., & MacDonald, K. (2013). A post-genomic view of behavioral development and adaptation to the environment. *Developmental Review, 33*(2), 89-109. doi:10.1016/j.dr.2013.01.002

Laing, R.D. (1971*). Self and others.* Harmondsworth, UK: Penguin Books. (Original work published 1961).

Laing, R. D. (1969). *The divided self.* London: Penguin Books. (Original work published 1960).

Laing, R. D. (1967). *The politics of experience.* New York: Ballantine.

Laing, R. D. (1976). *The facts of life: An essay in feelings, facts, and fantasy.* New York: Pantheon.

Laing, R. D. (1985a). *Existential therapy* [Videotape]. Phoenix, AZ: Milton H. Erickson Foundation.

Laing, R. D. (1985b). Foreword. In R. W. Firestone, *The fantasy bond: Structure of psychological defense* (pp. 17-20). Santa Barbara, CA: Glendon Association.

Laing, R. D. & Esterson. (1970). *Sanity, madness and the family: Families of schizophrenics.* London: Penguin Books. (Original work published 1964).

Lakhan, S. E. & Kirchgessner, A. (2012). Prescription stimulants in individuals with and without attention deficit hyperactivity disorder: Misuse, cognitive impact, and adverse effects. *Brain and Behavior, 2*(5), 661-677. doi: 10.1002/brb3.78

Langs, R. (1982). *Psychotherapy: A basic text.* New York: Jason-Aroson.

Langs, R. (2004). *Fundamentals of adaptive psychotherapy and counseling: An introduction to theory and practice.* Palgrave Macmillan.

Lasch, C. (1979). *The culture of narcissism: American life in an age of diminishing expectations.* New York: W. W. Norton.

Laumann, E. O., Gagnon, J. H., Michael, R. T., & Michaels, S. (1994). *The social organization of sexuality: Sexual practices in the United States.* Chicago: University of Chicago Press.

Laumann, E. O., Paik, A., & Rosen, R. C. (1999). Sexual dysfunction in the United States: Prevalence and predictors. *Journal of the American Medical Association, 281,* 537-544. doi: 10.1001/jama.281.6.537

Lazarus, A. (1994). How certain boundaries and ethics diminish therapeutic effectiveness. *Ethics and Behavior, 4*(3), 255-261. doi: 10.1207/s15327019eb0403_10

LeDoux, J. E. (1995). Emotion: Clues from the brain. *Annual Review of Psychology, 46,* 209-227. doi: 10.1146/annurev.ps.46.020195.001233

Lehto, R. H., & Stein, K. F. (2009). Death anxiety: An analysis of an evolving concept. *Research and Theory for Nursing Practice, 23*(1), 23-41. doi: 10.1891/1541-6577.23.1.23

Leiter, L. D. (2003). From a student. In J. Carter, *Nasty people: How to stop being hurt by them without stooping to their level* (rev. ed.) (pp. xi-xii). New York: McGraw-Hill.

Leonard, R. C., Knott, L. E., Lee, E. B., Singh, S., Smith, A. H., Kanter, J., Wetterneck, C. T. (2014). The development of the functional analytic psychotherapy intimacy scale. *Psychological Record, 64,* 647-657. doi: 10.1007/s40732-014-0089-9.

Lester, D., & Tartaro, C. (2002). Suicide on death row. *Journal of Forensic Science, 47*(5), 1-4.

Lewis, H. B. (1971). Shame and guilt in neurosis. *Psychoanalytic Review, 58*(3), 419.

Lewis, M. D., & Todd, R. (2004). Toward a neuropsychological model of internal dialogue: Implications for theory and clinical practice. In H. J. M. Hermans & G. Dimaggio (Eds.), *The dialogical self in psychotherapy* (pp. 43-59). Hove, UK: Brunner-Routledge.

Lieberman, A. F., Padron, E., Van Horn, P., & Harris W. W. (2005). Angels in the nursery: The intergenerational transmission of benevolent parental influences. *Infant Mental Health Journal, 26*(6), 504-520. doi: 10.1002/imhj.20071

Lieberman, A. F. & Pawl, J. H. (1988). Clinical applications of attachment theory. In J. Belsky & T. Nezworski (Eds.). *Clinical implications of attachment.* (pp. 327-351), Hillsdale, NJ: Erlbaum.

Lieberman, A.F. & Pawl, J. H. (1990). Disorders of attachment and secure base behavior in the second year of life. In M. Greenberg, D. Ciechetti, & E. M. Cummings (Eds.). *Attachment in the preschool years. Theory, research, and intervention,* (pp 375-397). Chicago: University of Chicago Press.

Lieberman, A. F., Van Horn, P., & Ippen, C. G. (2005). Toward evidence-based treatment: Child-parent psychotherapy with preschoolers exposed to marital violence. *Journal of the American Academy of Child & Adolescent Psychiatry, 44*(12), 1241-1248. doi: 10.1097/01.chi.0000181047.59702.58

Lieberman, A. F., & Zeanah, C. H. (1999). Contributions of attachment theory to infant-parent psychotherapy and other interventions with infants and young children. In J. Cassidy & P. R. Shaver (Eds.), *Handbook of attachment: Theory, research, and clinical applications,* (2nd ed.) (pp. 555-574). New York: Guilford Press.

Lifton, R. J. (1979). *The broken connection.* New York: Simon & Schuster.

Lifton, R. J. and Olson, E. (1976). The human meaning of total disaster: The Buffalo Creek experience. *Psychiatry, 39*, 1-18. doi: 10.1080/00332747.1976.11023872

Linehan, M. M. (1993). *Cognitive behavioral treatment of borderline personality disorder.* New York: Guilford Press.

Linehan, M. M., Goodstein, J. L., Nielsen, S. L., & Chiles, J. A. (1983). Reasons for staying alive when you are thinking of killing yourself: The Reasons for Living Inventory. *Journal of Consulting and Clinical Psychology, 51*, 276-286.

Lipman-Blumen, J. (2005). *The allure of toxic leaders: Why we follow destructive bosses and corrupt politicians—and how we can survive them.* New York: Oxford University Press.

Lowen, A. (1985). *Narcissism: Denial of the true self.* New York: Simon & Schuster.

Lubit, R. (2004, March/April). The tyranny of toxic managers: Applying emotional intelligence to deal with difficult personalities. *Ivey Business Journal*, 1-7.

Luhrmann, T.M. (2000). *Of two minds: The growing disorder in American psychiatry.* New York: Alfred A. Knopf.

Lykins, E. L., Segerstrom, S. C., Averill, A. J., Evans, D. R., & Kemeny, M. E. (2007). Goal shifts following reminders of mortality: Reconciling posttraumatic growth and terror management theory. *Personality and Social Psychology Bulletin, 33*(8), 1088-1099. doi:10.1177/0146167207303015.

MacNeil-Lehrer Productions, WNET, WETA. (1987, March 12*). Open door policy? Teen suicide: Fall from grace* (Transcript 2989 of the MacNeil/Lehrer NewsHour). New York: Author.

Madanes, C. (1999, July/August). Rebels with a cause. Honoring the subversive power of psychotherapy. *Family Therapy Networker,* (44-49, 57).

Main, M. & Hesse, E. (1990). Parents' unresolved traumatic experiences are related to infant disorganized attachment status: Is frightened and/or frightening parental behavior the linking mechanism? In M. T. Greenberg, D. Cicchetti, & E. M. Cummings (Eds.), *Attachment in the preschool years: Theory, research and interventions* (pp. 161-182). Chicago: University of Chicago Press.

Malone, T. P. (1981). Psychopathology as non-experience. *Voices,* 17(2), 83-91.

Maltsberger, J. T., & Buie, D. H. (1989). Common errors in the management of suicidal patients. In D. Jacobs & H. N. Brown (Eds.*), Suicide: Understanding and responding* (pp. 285-294). Madison, CT: International Universities Press.

Marcuse, H. (1966). *Eros and civilization: A philosophical inquiry into Freud.* Boston: Beacon Press. (Original work published 1955).

Martens, A., Greenberg, J., Schimel, J., & Landau, M. J. (2004). Ageism and death: Effects of mortality salience and perceived similarity to elders on reactions to elderly people. *Personality and Social Psychology Bulletin, 30*, 1524- 1536. doi:10.1177/0146167204271185

Martin, R. (1971). The concept of power: A critical defence. British Journal of Sociology, 22, 240-256. doi: 10.2307/588888

Maslow. A. H. (1967). A theory of metamotivation: The biological rooting of the value-life. *Journal of Humanistic Psychology, 7*(2), 93-127. doi: 10.1177/002216786700700201

Maslow, A. H. (1968). *Toward a psychology of being* (2nd ed.). New York: Van Nostrand Reinhold.

Maslow, A. H. (1971). *The farther reaches of human nature.* New York, NY: Penguin.

May, D. S., & Solomon, M. (Producers). (1984). *Theoretical aspects of attachment* [Video]. Los Angeles: UCLA Neuropsychiatric Institute and Hospital.

McCarthy, B. W. (1997). Strategies and techniques for revitalizing a nonsexual marriage. *Journal of Sex & Marital Therapy, 23*, 231-240. doi: 10.1080/00926239708403928

McClelland, D. C. (1975). *Power: The inner experience.* New York: John Wiley.

McCoy, S. K., Pyszczynski, T., Solomon, S., & Greenberg, J. (2000). Transcending the self: A terror management perspective. In A. Tomer (Ed.), *Death attitudes and the older adult: Theories, concepts, and applications* (pp. 37-63). Philadelphia: Brunner-Routledge.

Mead, G. H. (1934). *Mind, self, and society.* Chicago: University of Chicago Press.

Meaney, M. J. (2010). Epigenetics and the biological definition of gene-environment interactions. *Child Development, 81*, 41-79. doi: 10.1111/j.1467-8624.2009.01381.x.

Meissner, W. W. (1995). *Treatment of patients in the borderline spectrum.* Northvale, NJ: Jason Aronson.

Menninger, K. A. (1938). *Man against himself.* New York: Harcourt, Brace & World.

Metzinger, T. (2003). *Being no one: The self-model theory of subjectivity.* Cambridge, MA: MIT Press.

Middelberg, C.V. (2001). Projective identification in common couple dances. *Journal of Marital and Family Therapy, 27*(3), 341-352. doi: 10.1111/j.1752-0606.2001.tb00329.x

Mikulincer, M., & Florian, V. (2000). Exploring individual differences in reactions to mortality salience: Does attachment style regulate terror management mechanisms? *Journal of Personality and Social Psychology, 79*, 260-273. doi: 10.1037/0022-3514.79.2.260

Mikulincer, M., & Florian, V. (2008). The complex and multifaceted nature of the fear of personal death: The multidimensional model of Victor Florian. In A. Tomer, G. T. Eliason, & P. T. P. Wong (Eds.), *Existential and spiritual issues in death attitudes* (pp. 39-64). New York: Lawrence Erlbaum.

Mikulincer, M., & Shaver, P. R. (2016). *Attachment in adulthood* (2nd ed.). New York: Guilford Press.

Miller, H. (1947). *Remember to remember.* New York: New Directions.

Minuchin, S. (1984). *Family kaleidoscope.* Harvard University Press: Cambridge, MA.

Moor, A. (2002). Awareness of death: A controllable process or a traumatic experience? *Folklore, 22,* 92—114.

Moore, C. (2008). Moral disengagement in processes of organizational corruption. *Journal of Business Ethics, 80*(1), 129-139. doi: 10.1007/s10551-007-9447-8

Morrison, A. P. (1989). *Shame, the underside of narcissism.* Hillsdale, NJ: Analytic Press.

Nagy, M. H. (1959). The child's view of death. In H. Feifel (Ed.), *The meaning of death* (pp. 79-98). New York: McGraw-Hill. (Original work published 1948).

Nansel, T. R., Overpeck, M., Pilla, R. S., Ruan, W. J., SimonsMorton, B., & Scheidt, P. (2001) Bulling behaviors among U.S. youth: Prevalence and association with psychosocial adjustment. *Journal of the American Medical Association, 285,* 2094-2100. doi: 10.1001/jama.285.16.2094

Newman, C.F. (2002). A cognitive perspective on resistance in psychotherapy. *Journal of Clinical Psychology, 58*(2), 165-174. doi: 10.1002/jclp.1140

Newman, L. S., Duff, K. J., & Baumeister, R. F. (1997). A new look at defensive projection: Thought suppression, accessibility, and biased personal perception. *Journal of Personality and Social Psychology, 72*(5), 980-1001. doi: 10.1037/0022-3514.72.5.980

Nietzsche, F. (1966). *Beyond good and evil: Prelude to a philosophy of the future* (W. Kaufmann, Trans.). New York: Random House. (Original work published 1886).

Oaklander, V. (1978). *Windows to our children: A gestalt therapy approach to children and adolescents.* Moab, UT: Real People Press.

Oaklander, V. (2006). *Hidden treasure: A map of the child's inner self.* London: Karnac Books.

Ochs, E., & Capps, L. (1996). Narrating the self. *Annual Review of Anthropology, 25,* 19-43. doi: 10.1146/annurev.anthro.25.1.19

Oquendo, M. A., Currier, D., & Mann, J. J. (2006). Prospective studies of suicidal behavior in major depressive and bipolar disorders: What is the evidence for predictive risk factors? *Acta Psychiatrica Scandinavica, 114*(3), 151-158. doi:10.1111/j.1600-0447.2006.00829.x

Orbach, I. (1988). *Children who don't want to live.* San Francisco: Jossey-Bass.

Orbach, I. (2008). Existentialism and suicide. In A. Tomer, G. T. Eliason, & P. T. P. Wong (Eds.), *Existential and spiritual issues in death attitudes* (pp. 281-316). New York: Lawrence Erlbaum.

Parker, G. (1983). *Parental overprotection: A risk factor in psychosocial development.* New York: Grune & Stratton.

Parker, M., & Morris, M. (2004). Finding a secure base: Attachment in Grendon Prison. *Forensic Focus, 25,* 193-210.

Parr, G. (2002). (Producer and Director) *Creating a life of meaning and compassion* Documentary Film. Santa Barbara, CA: The Glendon Association. .

Parr, G. (Producer and Director). (2008). *The roots of violence, Part I, Voices of violence.* Documentary Film. Santa Barbara, CA: The Glendon Association.

Parr, G. (Producer and Director). (2009). *Effective treatments for violent individuals, Part II, Voices of violence.* Documentary Film. Santa Barbara, CA: The Glendon Association.

Parr, G. (Producer and Director). (2012a). *Advances in the treatment of suicidal clients: An interview with Dr. David Jobes.* Documentary Film. Santa Barbara, CA: The Glendon Association.

Parr, G. (Producer and Director). (2012b). *Society, relationships, and pleasure: An interview with Dr. Carol Gilligan.* Documentary Film. Santa Barbara, CA: The Glendon Association.

Perry, B. D. (2002). Childhood experience and the expression of genetic potential: What childhood neglect tells us about nature and nurture. *Brain and Mind, 3,* 79-100. doi: 10.1023/A:1016557824657

Perry, B. D., & Marcellus, J. (1997). The impact of abuse and neglect on the developing brain. *Colleagues for Children, 7,* 1-4.

Perry, B. D. & Szalavotz, M. (2006). *The boy who was raised as a dog and other stories from a child psychiatrist's notebook.* New York: Basic Books.

Pines, A. M. (1998). *Romantic jealousy: Causes, symptoms, cures.* New York: Routledge.

Pines, A., & Aronson, E. (1983). Antecedents, correlates, and consequences of sexual jealousy. *Journal of Personality, 51,* 108-136. doi: 10.1111/j.1467-6494.1983.tb00857.x

Piven, J. S. (2004a). *Death and delusion: A Freudian analysis of mortal terror.* Greenwich, CT: Information Age Publishing.

Piven, J. S. (2004b). Death, neurosis, and normalcy: On the ubiquity of personal and social delusions. In J. S. Piven (Ed.), *The psychology of death in fantasy and history* (pp. 245-266). Westport, CT: Praeger.

Pos, A. E. & Greenberg, L. S. (2012). Organizing awareness and increasing emotion regulation: Revising chair work in emotion-focused therapy for borderline personality disorder. *Journal of Personality Disorders, 26*(1), 84–107. doi: 10.1521/pedi.2012.26.1.84

Post, J. M. (2004). *Leaders and their followers in a dangerous world: The psychology of political behavior.* Ithaca, NY: Cornell University Press.

Post, S. G. (2005). Altruism, happiness, and health: It's good to be good. *International Journal of Behavioral Medicine, 12*(2), 66-77. doi: 10.1207/s15327558ijbm1202_4

Pratt, M.W., Skoe, E.E., & Arnold, M.L. (2004). Care reasoning development and family socialization patterns latter adolescence: A longitudinal analysis. *International Journal of Behavioral Development, 28,* 139-147.

Prentice, D. A., & Carranza, E. (2002). What women and men should be, shouldn't be, are allowed to be, and don't have to be: The contents of prescriptive gender types. *Psychology of Women Quarterly, 26,* 261-281. doi: 10.1111/1471-6402.t01-1-00066

Prescott, J. W. (1975, November). Body pleasure and the origins of violence. From *The Bulletin of the Atomic Scientists*, pp. 10-20. Retrieved 2/27/04, from http://www.violence.de/prescott/bulletin/article.html.

Prescott, J. W. (1996). The origins of human love and violence *Pre- and Peri-natal Psychology Journal, 10*(3), 143.

Pyszczynski, T., Greenberg, J., & Solomon, S. (1999). A dual-process model of defense against conscious and unconscious death-related thoughts: An extension of terror management theory. *Psychological Review, 106,* 835-845. doi: 10.1111/1471-6402.t01-1-00066

Quinsey, V. L., Harris, G. T., Rice, M. E., & Cormier, C. A. (1998). *Violent offenders: Appraising and managing risk.* Washington, DC: American Psychological Association.

Rank, O. (1932). *Art and artist: Creative urge and personality development* (C. F. Atkinson, Trans.). Oxford, UK: Knopf.

Rank, O. (1972). *Will therapy and truth and reality* (J. Taft, Trans.). New York: Alfred A. Knopf. (Original work published 1936).

Rawls, J. (1999). *A theory of justice* (rev. ed.). Cambridge, MA: Harvard University Press.

Reik, T. (1941). *Masochism in modern man.* (M. H. Beigel & G. M. Kurth, trans.). New York: Farrar-Straus.

Reinherz, H. Z., Tanner, J. L., Berger, S. R., Beardslee, W. R., & Fitzmaurice, G. M. (2006). Adolescent suicidal ideation as predictive of psychopathology, suicidal behavior, and compromised functioning at age 30. *American Journal of Psychiatry, 163*(7), 1226-1232.

Reis, H. T., & Shaver P. (1988). Intimacy as an interpersonal process. In S. W. Duck (Ed.), *Handbook of personal relationships.*(pp. 367-389). New York: John Wiley. & Sons, Ltd

Rheingold, J. C. (1967). *The mother, anxiety, and death: The catastrophic death complex.* Boston: Little, Brown.

Rice, W. R., Friberg, U., & Gavrilets, S. (2012). Homosexuality as a consequence of epigenetically canalized sexual development. *Quarterly Review of Biology, 87*(4), 343-368. doi: 10.1086/668167

Ridley, M. (1996). *The origins of virtue: Human instincts and the evolution of cooperation.* New York: Penguin.

Ritter, K. Y., & Terndrup, A. I. (2002). *Handbook of affirmative psychotherapy with lesbians and gay men.* New York: Guilford Press.

Robins, R. S., & Post, J. M. (1997). *Political paranoia: The psychopolitics of hatred.* New Haven, CT: Yale University Press.

Rochlin, G. (1967). How younger children view death and themselves. In E. A. Grollman (Ed.), *Explaining death to children* (pp. 51-85). Boston: Beacon Press.

Roderick, R. (1993). Nietzsche and the postmodern condition. In *Introduction to the Guide to The self under siege: Philosophy in the twentieth century* [Audio Cassette]. Chantilly, VA: The Teaching Company (TTC).

Rohner, R. P. (1986). *The warmth dimension: Foundations of parental acceptance-rejection theory*. Beverly Hills, CA: Sage Publications.

Rohner, R. P. (1991). *Handbook for the study of parental acceptance and rejection*. Storrs, CT: University of Connecticut.

Roizen, J. (2002). Epidemiological issues in alcohol-related violence. In M. Galanter (Eds.), *Recent developments in alcoholism, Vol. 13* (pp. 7-40). New York: Plenum Press.

Rosen, J. H. (1953). *Direct analysis: Selected papers*. New York: Grune & Stratton.

Roth, S., Newman, E., Pelcovitz, D., van der Kolk, B., & Mandel, F.S. (1997). Complex PTSD in victims exposed to sexual and physical abuse: Results from the DSM-IV field trial for posttraumatic stress disorder. *Journal of Traumatic Stress, 10(4)*, 539-555. doi: 10.1002/jts.2490100403

Routledge, C., & Juhl, J. (2010). When death thoughts lead to death fears: Mortality salience increases death anxiety for individuals who lack meaning in life. *Cognition & Emotion, 24*(5), 848-854. doi:10.1080/02699930902847144

Rubin, T. I. (1975). *Compassion and self-hate*. New York: David McKay.

Ruszczynski, S., & Fisher, J. (Eds.). (1995). *Intrusiveness and intimacy in the couple*. London: Karnac Books.

Ryan, R. M. & Deci, E. L. (2008). Self-determination theory and the role of basic psychological needs in personality and the organization of behavior. In O. P. John, R. W. Robins, & L. A. Pervin (Eds.), *Handbook of personality: Theory and research* (3rd ed.), (pp. 654-678). New York: Guilford Press.

Schachner, D. A., & Shaver, P. R. (2004). Attachment dimensions and sexual motives. *Personal Relationships, 11,* 179-195. doi:10.1111/j.1475-6811.2004.00077.x

Scharff, D. E., & Scharff, J. S. (1991). *Object relations couple therapy*. Northvale, NJ: Jason Aronson.

Schimel, J., Hayes, J., Williams, T., & Jahrig, J. (2007). Is death really the worm at the core? Converging evidence that worldview threat increases death-thought accessibility. *Journal of Personality and Social Psychology, 92*(5), 789-803. doi:10.1037/0022-3514.92.5.789

Schnarch, D. M. (1991). *Constructing the sexual crucible: An integration of sexual and marital therapy*. New York: Norton.

Schneider, K. J. (2004). *Rediscovery of awe: Splendor, mystery, and the fluid center of life*. St. Paul, MN: Paragon House.

Schneider, K. J. (2007). The fluid centre: An awe-based challenge to culture. In P. T. P. Wong, L. C. J. Wong, M. J. McDonald, & D. W. Klaassen (Eds.), *The positive psychology of meaning & spirituality* (pp. 372-378). Abbotsford, Canada: INPM Press.

Schneider, K. J. (2009). *Awakening to awe: Personal stories of profound transformation.* Lanham, MD: Jason Aronson.

Schneider, K. J. (2013). *The polarized mind: Why it is killing us and what we can do about it.* Colorado Springs, CO: University Professors Press.

Schoenewolf, G. (1989). *Sexual animosity between men and women.* Northvale, NJ: Jason Aronson.

Schore, A. N. (2000). Attachment and the regulation of the right brain. *Attachment & Human Development, 2,* 23-47. doi:10.1080/146167300361309

Schore, A. N. (2001). The effects of early relational trauma on right brain development, affect regulation, and infant mental health. *Infant Mental Health Journal, 22(*1-2), 201-269. doi:10.1002/1097-0355(200101/04)22:1<201::aid-imhj8>3.0.co;2-9

Schore, A. N. (2003a). *Affect regulation and disorders of the self.* New York: W. W. Norton.

Schore, A. N. (2003b). *Affect dysregulation and the repair of the self.* New York: W. W. Norton.

Schore, A. N. (2012). *The science of the art of psychotherapy* (Norton Series on Interpersonal Neurobiology). New York: W. W. Norton.

Schwartz, S. J., Zamboanga, B. L., & Weisskirch, R. S. (2008). Broadening the study of the self: Integrating the study of personal identity and cultural identity. *Social and Personality Psychology Compass, 2*(2), 635-651. doi:10.1111/j.1751-9004.2008.00077.x

Searles, H. F. (1961). Schizophrenia and the inevitability of death. *Psychiatric Quarterly, 35,* 631-665. doi:10.1007/BF01563716

Searles, H. F. (1979*). Countertransference and related subjects: Selected papers.* Madison, CT: International Universities Press.

Shapiro, D. (2000). *Dynamics of character: Self-regulation in psychopathology.* New York: Basic Books.

Shaver, P. R. (2013). Foreword. In R. W. Firestone, L. Firestone, & J. Catlett, *The self under siege: A therapeutic model for differentiation* (pp. ix-xvii). New York: Routledge.

Shaver, P. R., & Clark, C. L. (1994). The psychodynamics of adult romantic attachment. In J. M. Masling & R. F. Bornstein (Eds.), *Empirical perspectives on object relations theory* (pp. 105-156). Washington, DC: American Psychological Association.

Sheldon, J. (1997). 50,000 children are waiting: Permanency, planning and termination of parental rights under the Adoption Assistance and Child Welfare Act of 1980. *BC Third World LJ*, 17, 73.

Shengold, L. (1989). *Soul murder: The effects of childhood abuse and deprivation*. New Haven, CT: Yale University Press.

Shengold, L. (2000). *Soul murder revisited: Thoughts about therapy, hate, love, and memory*. New Haven, CT: Yale University Press.

Shengold, L. (2007). *Haunted by parents*. New Haven, CT: Yale University Press.

Shneidman, E. S. (1966). Orientations toward death: A vital aspect of the study of lives. *International Journal of Psychiatry*, 2, 167-200.

Shneidman, E. S. (1985). *Definition of suicide*. New York: John Wiley.

Shneidman, E. S. (1993). *Suicide as psychache: A clinical approach to self-destructive behavior*. Northvale, NJ: Jason Aronson.

Shneidman, E. S. (1996). *The suicidal mind*. New York: Oxford University Press.

Siegel, D. (1999). *The developing mind*. New York: Guilford Press.

Siegel, D. (2001). Toward an interpersonal neurobiology of the developing mind: Attachment relationships, "mindsight," and neural integration. *Infant Mental Health Journal*, 22, 67-94. doi:10.1002/1097-0355(200101/04)22:1<67::AID-IMHJ3>3.0.CO;2-G

Siegel, D. J. (2007). *The mindful brain: Reflection and attunement in the cultivation of well-being*. New York: W. W. Norton.

Siegel, D. J., & Bryson, T. P. (2014*). No-drama discipline: The whole-brain way to calm the chaos and nurture your child's developing mind*. New York: Bantam Books.

Siegel, D. J., & Hartzell, M. (2003). *Parenting from the inside out: How a deeper self-understanding can help you raise children who thrive*. New York: J. P. Tarcher/Putnam.

Siegel, P., & Weinberger, J. (1998). Capturing the" mommy and I are one" merger fantasy: The oneness motive. In R. F. Bornstein & J. M. Masling (Eds.), *Empirical studies of psychoanalytic theories, Vol. 7. Empirical perspectives on the psychoanalytic unconscious* (pp. 71-97).

Silverman, L. H., Lachmann, F. M., & Milich, R. H. (1982). *The search for oneness*. New York: International Universities Press.

Simons, J. S., & Carey, M. P. (2001). Prevalence of sexual dysfunctions: Results from a decade of research. *Archives of Sexual Behavior*, 30(2), 177-219. doi:10.1023/A:1002729318254

Singer, P. (1994). Introduction. In P. Singer (Ed.*), Ethics* (pp. 3-13). Oxford, UK: Oxford University Press. (Original work published 1986).

Skeem, J. L., Monahan, J., & Mulvey, E. P. (2002). Psychopathy, treatment involvement, and subsequent violence among civil psychiatric patients. *Law and Human Behavior*, 26(6), 577. doi.org/10.1023/A:1020993916404

Smith, A. (2007). Not "waiving" but drowning: The anatomy of death row syndrome and volunteering for execution. *Boston University Public Interest Law Journal, 17,* 237 – HeinOnline.

Snyder, D. K., Castellani, A. M., & Whisman, M. A. (2006). Current status and future directions in couple therapy. *Annual Review of Psychology, 57,* 317-344. doi:10.1146/annurev.psych.56.091103.070154

Sohlberg, S., Birgegard, A., Czartoryski, W., Ovefelt, K., & Strömbom, Y. (2000). Symbiotic oneness and defensive autonomy: Yet another experiment demystifying Silverman's findings using "mommy and I are one." *Journal of Research in Personality, 34*(1), 108-126. doi:10.1006/jrpe.1999.2264

Sohlberg, S., & Jansson, B. (2002). Unconscious responses to" mommy and I are one": Does gender matter? In R. F. Bornstein & J. M. Masling (Eds.), *The Psychodynamics of Gender and Gender Role: Empirical Studies in Psychoanalytic Theories, Vol. 10* (pp. 165-201). Washington, DC American Psychological Association.

Solomon, J. & George, C. (1999). The place of disorganization in attachment theory: Linking classic observations with contemporary findings. In J. Solomon & C. George (Eds*), Attachment disorganization* (pp. 3-32). New York: Guilford Press.

Solomon, J., & George, C. (2011). The disorganized attachment-caregiving system: Dysregulation of adaptive processes at multiple levels. In J. Solomon & C. George (Eds.), *Disorganized attachment and caregiving* (pp. 3-24). New York: Guilford Press.

Solomon, S., Greenberg, J., & Pyszczynski, T. (2004). The cultural animal: Twenty years of terror management theory and research. In J. Greenberg, S. L. Koole, & T. Pyszczynski (Eds.), *Handbook of experimental existential psychology* (pp. 13-34). New York: Guilford Press.

Solomon, S., Greenberg, J., & Pyszczynski, T. A. (2015). *The worm at the core: On the role of death in life.* New York: Random House.

Speece, M. W., & Brent, S. B. (1984). Children's understanding of death: A review of three components of a death concept. *Child Development, 55,* 1671-1686. doi: 0.2307/1129915

Spitzberg, B. H., & Cupach, W. R. (1998). *The dark side of close relationships.* Mahwah, NJ: Lawrence Erlbaum.

Steele, B. F. (1990). Some sequelae for the sexual maltreatment of children. In H. B. Levine (Ed.), *Adult analysis and childhood sexual abuse* (pp. 21-34). Hillsdale, NJ: Analytic Press.

Stern, D. N. (1985). *The interpersonal world of the infant: A view from psychoanalysis and developmental psychology.* New York: Basic Books.

Stern, M. M. (1972). Trauma, mortal fear and fear of death in psychoanalytic theory and practice. *Psyche, 26*(12), 901-928.

Stolorow, R. (2011). Individuality in context: The relationality of finitude. In R. Frie & W. J. Coburn (Eds.), *Persons in context: The challenge of individuality in theory and practice* (pp. 59-68). New York, NY: Taylor & Francis.

Strupp, H. H. (1989). Can the practitioner learn from the researcher? *American Psychologist 44,* 717-724. doi: 10.1037/0003-066X.44.4.717

Styron, W. (1979). *Sophie's choice.* New York: Random House.

Tangney, J. P., & Dearing, R. L. (2002). *Shame and guilt.* New York: Guilford Press.

Tartaro, C., & Lester, D. (2005). An application of Durkheim's theory of suicide to prison suicide rates in the United States. *Death studies, 29*(5), 413-422.

Taussig, H. N., Clyman, R. B., & Landsverk, J. (2001). Children who return home from foster care: A 6-year prospective study of behavioral health outcomes in adolescence. *Pediatrics, 108*(1), e10. doi:10.1542/peds.108.1.e10

Taylor, C. (1984). Foucault on freedom and truth. *Political Theory 12*(2), 152-183. doi: 10.1177/0090591784012002002

Taylor, R. (2000). *A seven-year reconviction study of HMP Grendon therapeutic community.* London: Great Britain Home Office.

Tedeschi, J. T., & Felson, R. B. (1994). *Violence, aggression, and coercive actions.* Washington, DC: American Psychological Association.

Timberlake, D., Meyer, D., Hitchings, S., Oakley, A., Stoltzfus, L., Aguirre, S., & Plumb, A. (2016). Sexually compulsive behaviors: Implications for attachment, early life stressors, and religiosity. *Sexual Addiction & Compulsivity, 23*(4), 361-373. doi: 10.1080/10720162.2016.1189862

Tomer, A., & Eliason, G. T. (2008). Existentialism and death attitudes. In A. Tomer, G. T. Eliason, & P. T. P. Wong (Eds.), *Existential and spiritual issues in death attitudes* (pp. 7-37). New York: Lawrence Erlbaum.

Tremblay, R. E., & Szyf, M. (2010). Developmental origins of chronic physical aggression and epigenetics. *Epigenomics, 2,* 495-499. doi: 10.2217/epi.10.40

Tronick, E. Z., Cohn, J., & Shea, E. (1986). The transfer of affect between mothers and infants. In T. B. Brazelton & M. W. Yogman (Eds.), *Affective development in infancy* (pp. 11-25). Norwood, NJ: Ablex Publishing.

Turner, J. (1978). Social categorization and social discrimination in the minimal group paradigm. In H. Tajfel (Ed.), *Differentiation between social groups: Studies in the social psychology of intergroup relations* (pp. 101-140). London: Academic Press.

University of Illinois, Board of Trustees. (2004). *Healthy sexuality.* Retrieved from http://mckinley.uiuc.edu/health-info/sexual/intro/healthse.html.

Vail, K. E., Rothschild, Z. K., Weise, D. R., Solomon, S., Pyszczynski, T., & Greenberg, J. (2010). A terror management analysis of the psychological functions of religion. *Personality and Social Psychology Review, 14*(1), 84-94. doi:10.1177/1088868309351165

Vail III, K. E., Juhl, J., Arndt, J., Vess, M., Routledge, C., & Rutjens, B. T. (2012). When death is good for life: Considering the positive trajectories of terror management. *Personality and Social Psychology Review, 16*(4), 303-329.

Vailliant, G. (1977). *Adaptation to life.* Cambridge, MA: Harvard University Press.

Vailliant, G. (2011). Involuntary coping mechanisms: A psychodynamic perspective Dialogues in Clinical Neuroscience, 13(3), 366–370.

van Praag, H. M., Plutchik, R., & Apter, A. (Eds.). (1990). *Violence and suicidality: Perspective in clinical and psychobiological research.* New York: Brunner/Mazel.

Varese, F., Smeets, F., Drukker, M., Lieverse, R., Lataster, T., Viechtbauer, W., ... & Bentall, R. P. (2012). Childhood adversities increase the risk of psychosis: A meta-analysis of patient-control, prospective-and cross-sectional cohort studies. *Schizophrenia Bulletin, 38*(4), 661-671. doi: 10.1093/schbul/sbs050

Vergote, A. (1988*). Guilt and desire: Religious attitudes and their pathological derivatives* (M. H. Wood, Trans.). New Haven, CT: Yale University Press. (Originally published, 1978).

Verona, E., Patrick, C. J., & Joiner, T. E., (2001). Psychcopathy, antisocial personality, and suicide risk. *Journal of Abnormal Psychology 110*(3) 462-470. doi: 10.1037//0021-843X.110.3.462

Verrocchio, M. C., Carrozzino, D., Marchetti, D., Andreasson, K., Fulcheri, M., & Bech, P. (2016). Mental pain and suicide: A systematic review of the literature. *Frontiers in Psychiatry, 7,* 661-671. doi:10.3389/fpsyt.2016.00108

Wachtel, P. (2008). *Relational theory and the practice of psychotherapy.* New York: Guilford Press.

Wallerstein, J. S., & Blakeslee, S. (1995). *The good marriage: How and why love lasts.* Boston: Houghton Mifflin.

Walsh, M. R. (Ed.). (1997). *Women, men, and gender: Ongoing debates.* New Haven, CT Yale University Press.

Wampold, B. E. (2001). *The great psychotherapy debate: Models, methods, and findings.* Mahwah, NJ: Lawrence Erlbaum.

Webster, C. D. (1997). *HCR-20: Assessing risk for violence.* Burnaby, Canada: Simon Fraser University.

Welldon, E. V. (1988). *Mother, madonna, whore: The idealization and denigration of motherhood.* London: Free Association Books.

Welldon, E. V. (2011). *Playing with dynamite: A personal approach to the psychoanalytic understanding of perversions, violence, and criminality.* London: Karnac Books.

Welling, H. (2000). On the therapeutic potency of Kaiser's techniques: Some misunderstandings? *Psychotherapy: Theory, Research, Practice, Training, 37*(1), 57-63. doi:10.1037/h0087665

West, R. (2001). *Rights, capabilities, and the good society.* Georgetown Public Law and Legal Theory Research Paper No. 11-54.

Whitaker, C. A., & Malone, T. P. (1953). *The roots of psychotherapy*. New York: Brunner/Mazel.

Whittle, S., Yap, M. B. H., Yucel, M., Sheeber, L., Simmons J. G., Pantelis, C., & Allen, N. B. (2009). Maternal responses to adolescent positive affect are associated with adolescents' reward neuroanatomy. *Social Cognitive and Affective Neuroscience, 4*(3), 247-256. doi: 10.1093/scan/nsp012

Willi, J. (1982). *Couples in collusion: The unconscious dimension in partner relationships* (W. Inayat-Khan & M. Tchorek, Trans.). Claremont, CA: Hunter House. (Original work published 1975).

Wilson, E. O. (1998). The biological basis of morality. *Atlantic Monthly, 281*(4), 53-70.

Winnicott, D.W. (1958). *Collected papers: Through paediatrics to psycho-analysis*. London: Tavistock Publications.

Winnicott, D. W. (1971). *Playing and reality*. London: Tavistock Publications.

Wirth, H. J. (2004). Thoughts for the times on terrorism, war, and death. In J. Piven (Ed.) *The Psychology of Death in Fantasy and History, 177*. Westport, CT: Praeger.

Wolfe, T. (1998). *You can't go home again*. New York: Harper & Row. (Original work published 1934).

Wong, P. T. P. (2008). Meaning management theory and death acceptance. In A. Tomer, G. T. Eliason, & P. T. P. Wong (Eds.), *Existential and spiritual issues in death attitudes* (pp. 65-87). New York: Lawrence Erlbaum.

Wong, P. T. (2012). From logotherapy to meaning-centered counseling and therapy. *The human quest for meaning: Theories, research, and applications, 2*, 619-647.

World Health Organization. (2002). *World report on violence and health: summary*. Geneva: Author.

Yalom, I. D. (1980). *Existential psychotherapy*. New York: Basic Books.

Yehuda, R., Cai, G., Golier, J. A., Sarapas, C., Galea, S., Ising, M.,…Buxbaum, J. D. (2009). Gene expression patterns associated with posttraumatic stress disorder following exposure to the World Trade Center attacks. *Biological Psychiatry, 66*(7), 708-711, doi: 10.1016/j.biopsych.2009.02.03

Yehuda, R., Engel, S. M., Brand, S. R., Seckl, J., Marcus, S. M., & Berkowitz, G. S. (2005). Transgenerational effects of posttraumatic stress disorder in babies of mothers exposed to the World Trade Center attacks during pregnancy. *Journal of Clinical Endocrinology & Metabolism, 90*, 4115-4118. doi: 10.1210/jc.2005-0550

Zeitner, R. M. (2012). *Self within marriage: The foundation for lasting relationships*. New York: Routledge.

Zillman, D. (1998). *Connections between sexuality and aggression* (2nd ed.). Mahwah, NJ: Lawrence Erlbaum.

Zinner, J. (1976). The implications of projective identification for marital interaction. In H. Grunebaum & J. Christ (Eds.), *Contemporary marriage: Structure, dynamics, and therapy* (pp. 293-308). Boston, MA: Little, Brown.

INDEX